The Spirit and
Its Letter

The Spirit and Its Letter

Traces of Rhetoric in Hegel's Philosophy of *Bildung*

*

John H. Smith

CORNELL UNIVERSITY PRESS

Ithaca and London

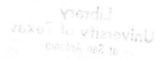

CORNELL UNIVERSITY PRESS GRATEFULLY ACKNOWLEDGES
A GRANT FROM THE ANDREW W. MELLON FOUNDATION
THAT AIDED IN BRINGING THIS BOOK TO PUBLICATION.

First published 1988 by Cornell University Press.

International Standard Book Number 0-8014-2048-2
Library of Congress Catalog Card Number 87-47960

Printed in the United States of America

*Librarians: Library of Congress cataloging information
appears on the last page of the book.*

*The paper in this book is acid-free and meets the guidelines for
permanence and durability of the Committee on Production Guidelines
for Book Longevity of the Council on Library Resources.*

For Jane and Julian

Contents

Contents

Preface

This book began several years ago as a rhetorical analysis of Hegel's early philosophy. My goal at that time was to trace the development of Hegel's philosophical style from his earliest school writings, through his theological manuscripts and Jena essays, to the *Phenomenology of Spirit*. Since Hegel's style is infamous, I set out to explore its origins and influences. The question I posed was simple: How did his style develop, that is, how did his philosophy gradually take on the form that it did?

This examination of the "gradual taking on of form" of a philosophy led to a consideration of Hegel's education in the broadest sense of the term, since, in German, development, education, and taking-on-form are contained in one word, *Bildung*. To explore the role of Hegel's own *Bildung*, of the pedagogical theories and practices that influenced the way he gave form to his ideas and the way his very ideas took shape, I had to go beyond the original textual scope of stylistic analysis and introduce the disciplinary or institutional history of rhetoric, especially as it came into conflict with philosophy in the modern period. Thus the more strictly rhetorico-philological thrust was augmented by an effort to situate Hegel's writing within a wider historical development of the disciplines responsible for principles of education and representation in Western culture.

Finally, I turned to the significance of the *concept* of *Bildung* in Hegel's philosophy. The multifaceted meanings of *Bildung* in Hegel's early writings show not only that its analysis in Hegel is central to a history (*Begriffsgeschichte*) of this master concept of Western thought but also that the wider history of this concept, especially its anchoring in rhetorical pedagogy, illuminates a central category of Hegel's philosophy. The philosophical concept of coming-to-form is informed by Hegel's individual appropriation of a rhetorical tradition that itself focused on processes of acquiring and producing forms. Hegel paradoxically transforms a traditional concept of rhetorical *Bildung* into a philosophical concept according to the rules of that very rhetorical tradition, and this transformation helps explain the implicit self-reflexive structure of his early philosophy.

Based on textual, institutional, and conceptual analyses, this book strives to make a contribution to contemporary discussions of fundamental philosophical issues. Hegel, as both Hegelians and anti-Hegelians argue, has offered the greatest solution to, or at least formulation of, the problem of representation. According to Hegel's unification of logic and ontology, the "world," "reality," "the absolute," can be represented truthfully because the representation and the thing represented are not separate entities linked arbitrarily by a philosopher's subjectivity; rather, things and thought are engaged in a common movement toward self-representation. Whereas Hegelians would view this movement as an unfolding dialectical logic of the concept, and anti-Hegelians would skeptically (problematically) argue for the difference between representation and the thing represented, I would claim that Hegel's approach to representation is powerful, and limited, precisely because it is the first to think through "reality" in terms of the categories and conditions that underlie Western theories and practices of representation. The power of the argument lies in its circular self-reflexivity: Hegel has justified his philosophy by attributing the conditions of its representation to the object of representation. Indeed, the object of representation attains its highest form of existence in the very representation that is the fulfillment of its conditions. The limits of this argument emerge from the historicity of the concepts involved: If we give the name "rhetoric" to the principles of representation which have guided expression in Western culture since the Greeks, we can say that Hegel is the philosopher who thought through ontology in terms of rhetoric, a circumscribable, albeit widely embracing, "language game."

The thesis of this book, therefore, is that Hegel's own *Bildung*, his formative education as a writer of philosophy, led to an internalization of the traditional rhetorical system, that his concept of *Bildung* reflects differing facets of rhetoric with different degrees of emphasis at different times, and that the continued existence of a rhetorical *Bildung* in this antirhetorical philosopher of *Bildung* is responsible for essential paradoxes that form the motor of his philosophy. My argument rests on the parallelism drawn between the development of Hegel's writings and the formation of his concept of *Bildung*, both of which took place under the sign of rhetoric. I offer a kind of biography of his writings that traces at different stages of development the connections between their "formative education" and an emerging notion of philosophical representation.

In a prefatory discussion, "On Prefacing," I offer a reading of Hegel's Preface (*Vorrede*) to the *Phenomenology of Spirit*. Written in the spirit of Hegel's own Preface, which demonstrates both the necessity and impossibility of a "prediscourse" of philosophy, it presents my methodology not so much in advance as at work. It shows the tensions and paradoxes present in an exemplary Hegelian text and argues for the need to introduce rhetorical categories in order to understand them. The Introduction then provides a more abstract elucidation of the book's central concepts: representation, rhetoric, and *Bildung*.

Chapter 1 lays out in greater detail the aspects of the rhetorical system to which Hegel was introduced through his schooling. The conservative and traditional rhetorical pedagogy in Stuttgart formed the foundation for the development of the form and key strategies of his philosophy. Chapter 5, on Hegel's experience as a teacher and director of the *gymnasium* in Nuremberg some thirty years later, forms a kind of closing and confirming parenthesis of rhetorical pedagogy around the formation of his first systems. The theological manuscripts discussed in Chapter 2 reveal both the transition of formal, pedagogical, and rhetorical practices of writing into philosophical discussion, and the crucial way in which the universalizing system of rhetoric contains structures to engender an individual writer. Hegel's concern with the development and representation of Christianity was modeled on the prescribed concerns he had with overcoming imitativeness and dependence on tradition.

Only with his entry into the public sphere in the Jena essays (Chapter 3), however, did Hegel confront the need to justify his principles and practice of philosophical representation. He came to develop a paradoxical, dialectical method that translates (though not fully) the categories of rhetorical argumentation he had to use (criticism, ad hominem differentiation) into needs of "philosophy itself." The concrete preconditions of his writing became abstracted into the self-developments of a subject-object, although the praxis leaves its unrecuperated marks on his theory. Here we see that a practice of *Kritik* rooted in rhetoric was necessary for the development of his system, although that necessity cannot be argued for on philosophical grounds.

Preface

The *Phenomenology of Spirit* (Chapter 4) can be seen as the fullest formulation of a philosophy that depends on, brilliantly transforms, yet cannot account for its own rhetorical traces. The tensions within Hegel's system between a truth-as-self-presence and truth-as-representation, between philosophy and its written form of argumentation, between the spirit and its letter, are thus traced back to rhetorical *Bildung*, to the formation and education of Hegel into a writer of philosophy.

When work on this book was largely complete, Donald Phillip Verene's *Hegel's Recollection: A Study of Images in the Phenomenology of Spirit* appeared (Albany: State University of New York Press, 1985). Verene's insightful work and his support of my own were invaluable in the final, doubt-filled stages. The independently reached analyses of his book and my fourth chapter—the point of greatest overlap—show that the concept of *Zeitgeist* is not without merit. I think we both agree that the sisters of the trivium—at least *Rhetorica* and *Dialectica*—are more powerful when they work in unison. My historical research on the rhetorical tradition and my treatment of Hegel's works surrounding the *Phenomenology* provide additional support for almost all aspects of Verene's discussion.

My research would not have been possible without financial assistance from the German Academic Exchange Service (DAAD) and the School of Humanities, University of California, Irvine. Professors Stanley Corngold and Walter Hinderer of Princeton University, Wilfried Barner and Rüdiger Bubner of the University of Tübingen, and Wolfgang Iser and Hans Robert Jauß of the University of Constance all provided encouragement and fruitful criticisms at different points along the way. The critical and bibliographical talents of Gary Campbell, my research assistant, provided more than mere assistance throughout the final stages of manuscript preparation. My gratitude to Professor Jane O. Newman of the University of California, Irvine— Jane—cannot be expressed in the rhetoric of such acknowledgments.

JOHN H. SMITH

Irvine, California

The Spirit and
Its Letter

On Prefacing:
The Prediscourse (*Vorrede*)
of the *Phenomenology*

An explanation, as it customarily precedes a book in a preface—
about the purpose the author had in mind in writing it, or about
the motivations and the relationships that the author sees his work
entertaining to earlier or contemporary treatments of the same
topic—such an explanation seems not only superfluous for a philosophical text but by the very nature of the matter even inappropriate and counterpurposeful. For the manner and content of what
could be conveniently said about philosophy in a preface—like a
historical *indication* of the tendency, standpoint, the general argument and results, or like a connection between the conflicting
claims and assurances about the truth—, these things cannot be
valid given the way philosophical truth is to be depicted.

Eine Erklärung, wie sie einer Schrift in einer Vorrede nach der
Gewohnheit vorausgeschickt wird— über den Zweck, den der Ver-
fasser sich in ihr vorgesetzt, sowie über die Veranlassungen und
das Verhältnis, worin er sie zu anderen früheren oder
gleichzeitigen Behandlungen desselben Gegenstandes zu stehen
glaubt—, scheint bei einer philosophischen Schrift nicht nur
überflüssig, sondern um der Natur der Sache willen sogar unpas-
send und zweckwidrig zu sein. Denn wie und was von Philosophie
in einer Vorrede zu sagen schicklich wäre—etwa eine historische
Angabe der Tendenz und des Standpunkts, des allgemeinen Inhalts
und der Resultate, eine Verbindung von hin und her sprechenden
Behauptungen und Versicherungen über das Wahre—, kann nicht
für die Art und Weise gelten, in der die philosophische Wahrheit
darzustellen sei.

[*Phenomenology of Spirit*, p. 11]

Hegel's first formulation of his philosophical system, the *Phenomenology of Spirit* (1807), begins with a paradox. In the opening paragraphs

of the Preface (*Vorrede*), Hegel defines the function of a preface to philosophical works in a manner that his Preface then seems to contradict. He lists a number of topics that ought not be the subject of a philosophical preface, but then proceeds to deal with precisely these kinds of topics. In the initial sentences (cited above)[1] he states, for example, that a preface should not contain a summary of the work, or a formulation of its goals and purpose; it should not present a historical discussion of the background of the work, or the personal position of the writer vis-à-vis other works and writers in the same field. It seems an inexplicable contradiction, then, that these very subjects make up the content of Hegel's Preface. As Walter Kaufmann points out: "What is so odd is merely that the preface itself—as Hegel admits with some embarrassment—is an example of the kind of writing that Hegel tries in the preface to banish from philosophy."[2]

This paradox of the Preface—namely, that Hegel writes in a form and about topics that he explicitly criticizes—becomes more than a curious anomaly or oversight on Hegel's part if one considers both the origins of the banned themes and the central concept of the Preface, philosophical *Bildung*, as the "pre-discourse" of his *Wissenschaft*, that is, as underlying conditions of his writing. My own writing here, "On Prefacing," which likewise does not have the form and function one might customarily expect, will analyze central arguments and strategies of the Preface to the *Phenomenology of Spirit* in order to show how, through the key concept and process of *Bildung*, rhetoric enters into and prestructures Hegel's writing in such a way as to engender such paradoxes. I shall offer a paradigmatic reading, then, of one of Hegel's best-known and richest texts, paradigmatic since my reading of the Preface demonstrates both my approach here and tensions found in many of Hegel's early philosophical writings. The paradoxes that arise out of the tension between rhetoric and philosophy, because Hegel tries to negate the structures of representation he had inherited from his rhetorical *Bildung* even as they influence his writing, are indicative of basic aporias encountered in all antirhetorical speculative philosophy.

1. All references to the *Phenomenology of Spirit* are taken from the *Theorie-Werkausgabe* (Frankfurt am Main: Suhrkamp, 1970). In this Preface page numbers within parentheses refer to this edition. All translations throughout the following study are my own unless otherwise indicated.

2. Walter Kaufmann, *Hegel: Reinterpretation, Texts and Commentary* (New York: Doubleday, 1965), p. 120. He also makes a similar statement in his commentary on the first paragraphs of the *Vorrede* (p. 371, n. 4): "The oddity here noted is indeed a striking characteristic of the preface that follows."

We can note, to begin with, that the topics Hegel rejects in the opening to the Preface reformulate categories belonging to the *ars rhetorica* as developed in antiquity and handed down in humanist, baroque, and Enlightenment handbooks. For example, the idea that a work should attain a specific goal and serve the author's predetermined purpose (*Zweck*) had characterized rhetoric—the *technē* of purposeful writing and speaking—since the Greeks and became in the eighteenth century the specific means of differentiating rhetoric from other activities, especially poetry and philosophy.[3] Similarly, the cataloging of the causes and reasons (*Veranlassungen*) of a work, the way an author arrived at the topic and formed the appropriate arguments, corresponds to the rhetorical doctrine of *inventio*, since Aristotle one of the five tasks (*officia*) of the orator.[4] Also, the requirement that the author establish the work's relationship to earlier or contemporary treatments of the subject at hand, belonged to rhetoric as the *ars disputandi*, the technique—closely related to the sister discipline of dialectic—of engaging in critical and argumentative dialogue before a public forum.[5] Likewise, the notion of making in advance general statements about the content and direction of the argumentation, as well as the reliance on claims and

3. Walter Jens, in the article on *Rhetorik* in the *Reallexikon der deutschen Literaturgeschichte* (vol. 2, ed. Werner Kohlschmidt and Wolfgang Mohr [Berlin: Walter de Gruyter, 1958]), gives a brief overview of this negative approach to the purpose-oriented and persuasive nature of rhetoric (p. 433): "The attacks against rhetoric made under the auspices of idealism confirm *ex negativo* that far into the nineteenth century rhetoric was clearly understood to be an intentional discipline that aimed at a real effect and not at the promotion of beauty. Hence the invectives directed against its 'technique of disguise' (*Verstellungs-Technik*—Goethe), against the 'machinery of persuasion' (*Maschinen der Überredung*) which the rhetorician might make use of, against its 'deceptive cunning' (*Überlisten*) and 'trickery' (Kant); hence especially the playing off of 'pure poetry,' which 'never has any purpose outside of the poem itself' (Schelling), against the 'purely purposeful context,' which determines the orator's work (Hegel)." As is clear from these citations, the criticisms of purposeful speech from the perspective of "pure poetry" paralleled those from the perspective of "pure philosophy." See also Heinrich Lausberg, *Handbuch der literarischen Rhetorik* (Munich: Max Hueber, 1960), par. 256 on the concept of *persuadere*.

4. On *inventio*, see Lausberg, *Handbuch*, par. 260ff. (esp. p. 146). Aristotle essentially defines rhetoric as *inventio*, namely, the ability to seek out arguments for a particular cause. He defines rhetoric as a science as follows: "that its function is not so much to persuade, as to find out in each case the existing means of persuasion" (*Rhetoric*, 1355b; bk. 99 I, I, 14). Or even more explicitly: "Rhetoric then may be defined as the faculty of discovering the possible means of persuasion in reference to any subject whatsoever" (bk. I, II, 1).

5. Rhetoric as an *ars disputandi* thrived throughout the Middle Ages, especially in the universities. See, e.g., James Murphy, *Rhetoric in the Middle Ages: A History of Rhetorical Theory from St. Augustine to the Renaissance* (Berkeley: University of California Press, 1974). The last remnant of this tradition, the *disputatio*, was still significant throughout the eighteenth century and lives on in such vestiges as dissertation defenses.

assurances to the audience which serve to convince it of the truth, both recall features of the rhetorical system, namely, the task of *dispositio*, by which the author orders the discourse, and the "proof" unique to rhetoric, the *enthymeme*, which, according to Aristotle, depends on the common opinions and assumptions of the audience.[6]

Having rejected this long list of rhetorical categories as superfluous for a philosophical preface, Hegel goes on, however, to indicate that rhetoric, that is, the question of representation and depiction, will be a topic of concern after all. For, he writes, the central concern of his Preface is the manner in which philosophical truth is to be depicted (*darzustellen sei*), and thus he must concern himself with the issues of philosophical rhetoric and *elocutio* before dealing with "philosophy itself." The paradox of the Preface, which has been mentioned but not yet analyzed in Hegel research, revolves around the uneasy though necessary position of rhetorical issues in philosophy. This paradox leads us to the heart of issues concerning representation.

Ironically, then, Hegel employs and discusses rhetorical categories in the course of the Preface even though he denies their role in a philosophical text. In fact, in rejecting specific categories because they seem to him "not only superfluous . . . but by the very nature of the matter inappropriate and counterpurposeful" (p. 11), he appeals to rhetorical criteria of aptness, purpose, and agreement between the *res* and *verba*, the matter and verbal expression.[7] Hegel's interest in a proper mode of depicting truth "philosophically" cannot avoid rhetorical criteria for dealing with the question of expression. Thus, given its argumentative strategy of employing rhetorical categories even as it rejects them, the Preface to the *Phenomenology* provides a classic example of *rhetorica contra rhetoricam*.[8] The parameters preestablished for all discourse by the *ars rhetorica* still hold in a philosophical discourse that would dispense with them.

---

6. On *dispositio*, see Lausberg, *Handbuch*, par. 443. Aristotle introduced the distinction between syllogism and enthymeme in his *Rhetoric*. Formally, the enthymeme is an abreviated syllogism (*breviter*). This implies that one of the premises or the conclusion is left out so that the audience must fill in the missing assertion on the basis of its own opinions. Aristotle writes: "that rhetorical demonstration is an enthymeme which, generally speaking, is the strongest of rhetorical proofs" (bk. I, I, 11); and further: "our proofs and arguments must rest on generally accepted principles . . . when speaking of converse with the multitudes." See also Lausberg, *Handbuch*, pars. 371, 875.

7. *Aptum* (or *decorum*) was one of the major "virtues" of classical rhetoric. See Lausberg, *Handbuch*, par. 460. Hegel also speaks below against discussions of "purpose and such generalities" (*Zweck und dergleichen Allgemeinheiten;* p. 11).

8. I take the phrase from Walter Jens's study of Hugo von Hoffmannsthal in *Von deutscher Rede* (Munich: Fink, 1969). Also see Gerd Ueding, *Einführung in die Rhetorik: Geschichte, Technik, Methode* (Stuttgart: Metzler, 1976), for a discussion of this phenomenon in eighteenth-century arts and letters.

In order to discover how this paradoxical relationship between rhetoric and philosophy developed and came to take the unique form it has in Hegel's writing, we must inevitably confront questions concerning *Bildung*, a key concept that unites problems of development, education, and form. If one of Hegel's great contributions to the history of ideas was his convincing demonstration that our understanding of any thing's, person's, or concept's significance must be grounded in its *Bildung*, then, in a Hegelian spirit, we can analyze the case of his own discourse in terms of his development, education, and cultivation to a specific form of philosophizing.

✳

In the Preface Hegel defines the *Phenomenology*: "This becoming [development, *Werden*] of *scientific knowledge as such* (*Wissenschaft überhaupt*) or of *knowledge* (*Wissen*) is what this *phenomenology* of Spirit depicts" (p. 31). Hegel's first formulation of a philosophical system represents, gives form and expression to, an earlier act of becoming or coming-to-knowledge. Both the act of attaining knowledge and the act of depicting that development—the two fundamental features or tasks of Hegel's philosophy—define the concept of *Bildung*: "The task of leading the individual from his uneducated and unformed (*ungebildeten*) standpoint to knowledge was to be grasped in its universal sense and the universal individual, the self-conscious Spirit, was to be considered in its education and formation (*Bildung*)" (p. 31). In other words, the *Phenomenology* depicts for the reader the *Bildung* of the Spirit. This definition, with its powerful equivocation between the individual and the universal—in the first edition, "the self-conscious spirit" (*der selbstbewußte Geist*) read "the World Spirit" (*der Weltgeist*)—has led one strand of Hegel criticism to interpret the *Phenomenology* as a kind of *Bildungsroman*.

Josiah Royce was the first to approach the *Phenomenology* in such literary terms. Although he did not use the term *Bildungsroman* in describing it, he did compare its structure to that of traditional novels of education or cultivation, including Goethe's *Wilhelm Meisters Lehrjahre*, Carlyle's *Sartor Resartus*, Novalis's *Heinrich von Ofterdingen*, and Tieck's *William Lovell*. "Now under the influence of the literary habits of the time, it unquestionably occurred to Hegel to make his portrayal of what he calls the experience of the *Geist*, or typical mind of the race, something that could be narrated in a story, or in a connected series of stories in which typical developments are set forth. . . . The world spirit, then, is the self viewed metaphorically as the wanderer through the course of history, the incarnate god to whom the events of human life

5

may be supposed to happen."[9] Walter Kaufmann reiterates this view: "The *Phenomenology* is the *Bildungsroman* of the *Weltgeist*, the story of its development and education."[10] And M. H. Abrams in *Natural Supernaturalism* analyzes the structure of the *Phenomenology* more extensively in terms of novelistic forms: "Hegel's book, taken as a literary form, is thus one of the earliest, yet at the same time the most intricate and extreme, of modern involuted works of the imagination. It is a self-contained, self-sustained, and self-implicative puzzle-book, which is enigmatic in the whole and deliberately equivocal in all its parts and passing allusions. . . . [It] is the representative autobiography of spiritual education, told explicitly in the mode of two consciousnesses."[11]

Both Royce and Abrams assume that the process of *Bildung* depicted in the *Phenomenology* and in the *Bildungsroman* unfolds in metaphorical, enigmatic, equivocal, double, allusive, and disguised formal structures. Perceptively, even if unconsciously, they thereby characterize Hegel's major text on *Bildung* in terms taken from a rhetorical tradition predating that of the *Bildungsroman*. Yet they do not pursue the historical and formal links between rhetoric and *Bildung*, either for Western culture in general or for Hegel's development in particular. A close reading of the Preface shows, however, that *Bildung*, or "the forming, educating, cultivating movement" (*bildende Bewegung*; p. 33), whose presentation and depiction is the enterprise of Hegel's *Wissenschaft*, contains within itself traces of the classical and humanist rhetorical systems which can be summarized in three points: (1) *elocutio*, or the ability to find and employ the appropriate expression for any matter; (2) imitative and emulative *exercitatio*, or the young writer-orator's hermeneutical struggle with traditions; and (3) dialectical *inventio* and *disputatio*, or the discovery and application of arguments against a partner in public dialogue. The Preface of the *Phenomenology*, in which Hegel explicitly and extensively equates his philosophy with a process of *Bildung*, is a prime example of the palimpsest-structure of both *Bildung* and his philosophical writing—a philosophical discourse written over, containing, and prestructured by traces of a rhetorical prediscourse. The contours of the prediscourse are formed by these three fundamental features of *Bildung* in the classical and humanistic *ars rhetorica*.

9. Josiah Royce, *Lectures on Modern Idealism* (New Haven, Conn.: Yale University Press, 1919 [1964]), pp. 149–50.

10. Kaufmann, *Hegel*, p. 158. This statement is repeated in his commentary to the Preface (p. 381). It is important, given what I will propose, that Kaufmann's discussion of *Bildung* and the *Phenomenology* as a *Bildungsroman* is preceded by a brief mention of problems of translating the word *Bildung*. See also Ivan Soll, "Bildung, Geschichte und Notwendigkeit bei Hegel," *Hegel-Jahrbuch* (1972):292–96.

11. M. H. Abrams, *Natural Supernaturalism: Tradition and Revolution in Romantic Literature* (New York: Norton, 1973), pp. 225–37 (this quote, p. 236).

6

Elocutio. The main theme of the Preface is philosophical *elocutio*, the depiction or repiesentation of philosophical ideas by the appropriate linguistic expressions. Hegel returns time and again to issues of presentation, depiction (*Darstellung*), representation, idea or image (*Vorstellung*), formation or formulation (*Gestaltung*), form, execution, composition, or argumentation (*Ausführung*), and method. The entire Preface can be considered a defense of the significance of form for the writing of philosophy, although this defense follows the paradoxical lines of a self-reflexive oratory that strives to overcome itself. Hegel writes near the beginning of the Preface, for example: "For the matter (*Sache*) is exhausted not in its purpose alone, but in its execution [composition, *Ausführung*] and the result is not the real [effective, *wirkliche*] whole unless considered with its becoming" (p 13). Viewed from the perspective of rhetorical theory and practice, this sentence becomes a dizzying *mise-en-abîme* in which a position continually reflects the negative image of itself. The identification of the "matter" (*Sache*) with the execution or composition recalls a fundamental position that underlies all rhetorical *elocutio*, namely, the intricate relationship between *res* and *verbum*.[12] All rationally grounded systems of rhetoric from Aristotle through the eighteenth century justify the clothing of ideas by words—the defining function of *elocutio*—with the argument that the former (*res*) would be incomprehensible and incomplete without verbal expression. Although Hegel seems to support this rhetorical principle, he apparently does so by denying the relevance of "purpose" and hence by negating perhaps the second most significant characteristic of rhetorical discourse. The purposeful, that is, rhetorical and persuasive use of language, however, reenters Hegel's argument when he emphasizes the "real [effective] whole." His criterion of *das wirkliche Ganze*, the whole against which he measures the execution of the *res*, still implies that the speech act of philosophy must fulfill a purpose, since the word *wirklich* in Hegel's system echoes its etymological origin in *werken* and *wirken*, "to work, to have an effect." The "real," according to Hegel, is always implicated in some effective totality, what contemporary philosophical hermeneutics would call *Wirkungsgeschichte*.[13] Indeed, if we recall that the *Werden* that contributes to the totality of philosophy refers not to an arbitrary act of

---

12. The relationship between *res* and *verbum*, that is, the question of the proper representation of the *res* by *verba*, is certainly the underlying issue of rhetoric. See Lausberg, *Handbuch*, par. 45. For a discussion of this concept in Hegel, see Rüdiger Bubner, "Die 'Sache selbst' in Hegels System," in *Zur Sache der Dialektik* (Stuttgart: Reclam, 1980).

13. For example, Hans-Georg Gadamer, *Wahrheit und Methode: Grundzüge einer philosophischen Hermeneutik* (Tübingen: Mohr [Paul Siebeck], 1960): "The true, historical object (*Gegenstand*) is not an object but, rather, the unity of this one and the Other, a

becoming but to the process of *Bildung* which gives form and expression to knowledge as *Wissenschaft*, we recognize that this abstract statement strives to account for a mode of persuasive philosophical expression by appealing to apparently nonrhetorical concepts. Though Hegel occasionally seems to reject categories from traditional rhetoric ("purpose," "result"), his choice of terms to justify his philosophical *elocutio*—*Werden, das wirkliche Ganze, Ausführung*—in fact reformulates traditional categories.

Thus we can identify *Bildung* in Hegel's philosophy with his emphasis on the "extended formulation or expression of form" (*Ausbildung der Form*; p. 19), the necessity of which he defends with versions of arguments that had been used in the rhetorical tradition to explain and support *elocutio*. He writes: "Without this extended formulation (*Ausführung*) scientific knowledge lacks general comprehensibility (*Verständlichkeit*) and appears to be the esoteric possession of a select few" (pp. 21–22). The subtle reference to the public indicates that Hegel is appealing to a conception of truth, or more precisely of the expression of knowledge, which relies on audience consensus. Rather than arguing for a status of the "matter" independent of form and public reception (along the lines of: What does truth care if it is understood?), he emphasizes that the "matter" cannot be known if both it and the audience are not "well formed, educated in form" (*ausgebildet*). Hegel's appeal here to the comprehensibility that derives from the proper formal *Bildung* or *Ausbildung* reformulates a fundamental concept of rationally grounded *elocutio*, namely, *perspicuitas*, the connection between *res* and *verba* which allows for the latter to be comprehended. The doctrine of *perspicuitas* says not so much that ideas should be expressed clearly as that the author must seek the appropriate means of expressing any given ideas, whereby the expression becomes an inherent feature of the ideas and not just a secondary supplement. Indeed, without their verbal representation (*Ausbildung*) the ideas would be meaningless, irrelevant, without effect, less than real (*mere* imaginings or *Einbildungen*).

Hegel's reformulation of *perspicuitas*, or the necessity of the extended formulation (*Ausbildung*) of ideas, into philosophical terminology, has

---

relation in which the effective reality (*Wirklichkeit*) of history as well as the effective reality of historical understanding exists. A hermeneutics adequate to its object of study (*eine sachangemessene Hermeneutik*) would have to make manifest in understanding itself the effective reality of history. That which is demanded I call an effective history (*Wirkungsgeschichte*)" (p. 283). Gadamer later identifies himself with Hegel by agreeing that the active force of historical understanding is appropriately called *Substanz* (pp. 285f.).

major consequences for the point of beginning of his (indeed any) philosophical system:

> If form is asserted to be identical with essence, then it is therefore a misunderstanding to believe that knowledge could spare itself form and be satisfied with essence or that which is in and of itself. It would be a misunderstanding to believe that some absolute principle or absolute intuition would render the extended execution (*Ausführung*) of essence or the formal development (*Entwicklung*) of form unnecessary. Precisely because the form is as essential to essence as essence itself, essence cannot be grasped or expressed merely as essence, that is as unmediated substance or as pure self-intuition of the divine, but must also involve *form* and the complete richness of developed form; only in that way can essence be grasped and expressed as something real [effective, *Wirkliches*]. [P. 24]

Hegel expresses this same idea in a manner closer to that of traditional handbooks on *elocutio* when he writes that there are no such things as "naked truths" (p. 42), since the matter (*Sache*) or Spirit must always appear, take form, be clothed (*eingehüllt*; p. 19) or covered (*verhüllt* p. 19) in some formulation (*Gestalt* or *Gestaltung*).[14] Moreover, the "richness" of the formation that encases the *Sache* echoes the *copia verborum et rerum*, the copiousness that was the goal of Roman and especially humanist oratory.[15] Ironically, the philosophy of Spirit requires cultivation of the letter to express, indeed to grasp and become, truth, for becoming, as *Bildung*, is a process of adopting form. Thus, no principle can serve as a foundation for philosophy that does not always already contain a movement toward form and expression. Hegel rejects for this reason any philosophy that does not presume the primacy of formal mediation.

The "misunderstanding" that Hegel refers to concerning the relationship between form and essence, *verba* and *res*, such that one might falsely posit the independence and insignificance of the former, has in fact arisen in various interpretations of the *Phenomenology* and its Preface. One of the first such misunderstandings occurred between two friends and intellectual companions, Schelling and Hegel. As is well known, the break between Schelling and Hegel occurred after Schell-

---

14. We shall see in chap. 1, below, that rhetorical handbooks from Melanchthon on often define *elocutio* as the "clothing" of thoughts in language.

15. On the concept of *copia*, see Lausberg, *Handbuch*, pars. 442,4; 1102; 1151. See also Terence Cave, *The Cornucopian Text: Problems of Writing in the French Renaissance* (Oxford: Clarendon Press, 1979), for a discussion of *copia* in humanism.

ing read the Preface and felt personally attacked by Hegel's critique of abstract formalism in philosophy. The misunderstanding may very well have been sparked by the paradoxical structure of Hegel's remarks: His defense of "extended formation or cultivation of form" is accompanied by an attack against particular forms and formalisms found in his contemporaries' works. These attacks could easily foster an antiformalist, antirhetorical reading of Hegel if one does not take into account the underlying thrust of his argument. For example, he rejects the "the forms [formations or figures, *Gebilde*], which are neither fish nor animal, neither poetry nor philosophy" (p. 64), that is, the creations of the Romantic poet-philosophers like numerous Novalis, Schlegel, and Schelling epigones. Similarly, he rebukes philosophers of religious feeling for wrapping base sentiments in deceptive "cover" or "garb" (*Einhüllung*; p. 18), or "in a high priest's cloak" (*im hohenpriesterlichen Gewande*; p. 65). Moreover, in his extensive passages on method and formalism (pp. 47–50, 55–59), he rejects earlier forms of philosophical methodology as belonging to "a lost culture, education, form" (*einer verschollenen Bildung*; p. 47) and attacks virtually all other philosophies (especially those based on the mathematical approach) for imposing an arbitrary form on the material. He proposes instead his own "speculative philosophy" as the "proper or literal depiction" (*eigentliche Darstellung*; p. 55). Such antiformalist statements could, and did, lead to the misunderstanding that Hegel had abandoned all traditional belief in the importance of form and rhetorical *elocutio* for the writing of philosophy.

And yet Hegel's conception of true or proper philosophy as the story of *Bildung* can also be interpreted in a radically different way, one that sees the act of figuration as central to the philosophical activity. Hegel writes succinctly and ambiguously early in the Preface: "The power of the Spirit is only as great as its expression" (*Äußerung*; p. 18). Since Hegel is certainly aware of the specifically linguistic connotation of "expression," we may read this statement as a reformulation of the key principle of *elocutio*: Force of mind can be attained only by re-presenting, re-creating, doubling itself as forceful expression. Such expression, which in traditional rhetoric falls under the heading of figurative language, is attained, according to Hegel, through a process of "re-formulation" (*Umgestaltung*) and "in ever progressing movement" (p. 18), a process he summarizes in the concept *Bildung*, the result of which is the creation of "the figure [form, *Gebilde*] of the new world" (p. 19). Rather than an antiformalist attack, we encounter in Hegel's philosophy of *Bildung* a hidden theory of tropological representation. The very definition of *Wissenschaft*—"Scientific knowledge depicts this for-

ming and educating (*bildende*) movement" (p. 33)—contains within itself a self-reflexive structure of doubling which provides both a philosophical foundation for his rhetoric and a rhetorical foundation for his
philosophy. Scientific knowledge is itself already a depiction, a re-presentation, that is, it presents again an original presentation or formation. The "movement" of and in philosophy—a metaphorical image
that requires explication—consists in the very process that lies at the
heart of rhetorical *elocutio*, namely, the act of giving figurative expression and form to ideas in language. The ideas themselves, or the *Sache
selbst*, are in fact never merely "in themselves," for it is the nature of the
Sache, if it is to become real, *effective* "scientific knowledge" (*Wissenschaft*), to double itself in some form.

In explaining this crucial principle in which his philosophy intersects
with a central doctrine of rhetoric, Hegel again expresses himself paradoxically. He begins his critique of contemporary views of methodological formalism with some hesitation (p. 47), but he then clearly and
harshly rejects their mere ideas, images, representations (*Vorstellungen*)
for the sake of the "proper or literal depiction" (*eigentliche Darstellung*)
of his "speculative philosophy" by means of the construction he calls
the "speculative sentence."[16] This emphasis on "proper or literal
(*eigentliche*) depiction" would seem to entail a rejection of the entire
realm of *elocutio* and its concern with figurative (*uneigentliche*) speech.
When he actually explains this "proper depiction," however, it turns
out to be not "literal" at all but, rather, copiously figurative. In fact, he
even introduces his analysis of the "speculative sentence" (pp. 58–62)
with phrases including terms he apparently rejected earlier; for example, "in order to imagine it" (*[um] es so vorzustellen*; p. 58), and "formally,
the above mentioned can be expressed as follows" (*formell kann das
Gesagte so ausgedrückt werden*; p. 59), thereby showing that there is place,
indeed the most central position, for images, form, and figurative expressions in his philosophy.

Indeed, the speculative sentence, whose "dialectical movement" (p.
61) is the means of depicting *Bildung* and hence the "becoming of
scientific knowledge" (which, it will be recalled, Hegel characterized as
a *bildende Bewegung*), contains an inherently double, and therefore figurative and in the widest sense metaphorical, structure. Whereas in a
normal sentence or judgment the predicate is attached unambiguously

16. For the most detailed and revealing discussion of the "speculative sentence," see
Günter Wohlfahrt, *Der spekulative Satz: Bemerkungen zum Begriff der Spekulation bei Hegel*
(Berlin: Walter de Gruyter, 1981). Although Wohlfahrt analyzes the philosophical significance and background of Hegel's concept of the "speculative sentence," he never
considers it in terms of its rhetorical tradition, form, function, or effect.

to the stable subject that forms its ground (for example, "The grass is green"), in the speculative sentence the subject and predicate are mutually dependent on each other, and only by a comparison between them can some meaning be found outside the actual assertion. Hegel gives two examples: "God is Being" (*Gott ist das Sein*; p. 59) and "The effectively real is the universal" (*Das Wirkliche ist das Allgemeine*; p. 60). These sentences are neither tautological identities, nor situations of entailment or attribution, nor matters of shared properties. Rather, according to Hegel, a transference takes place from the subject to predicate (as in a normal sentence) which then forces us to reflect back on the nature of the subject which threatens to lose itself in the predicate. Hegel writes: "Thought, instead of moving forward in a transition from subject to predicate, feels itself hindered because the subject has been lost; hence, thought is thrown back onto the subject that it had missed" (p. 59). The sentence expresses a simultaneous similarity and difference, thereby compelling thought to abandon the secure position of objective and concrete understanding: "Thought thus loses its firm, objective ground, which it had in the subject, to the extent that it is thrown back onto the predicate and then does not remain there but returns to the subject of the content" (p. 60). The sentence is called "speculative" because its double structure, the reflexive interaction between subject and predicate, acts like a mirror (*speculum*) which makes an otherwise hidden truth visible by engendering a nonlinear and nonliteral thought process. Its "movement" is actually that of the reader or listener who follows the figurative transitions of the sentence in order to repeat a process of *Bildung* which gives knowledge its graspable form. Hegel's abstract descriptions of dialectical structures gain precision, then, when considered from the perspective of a process of writing and reading, forming and interpreting, rhetorical figures. The speculative sentence conforms to standard definitions of tropes, which form the core of all *elocutio*, as a tension maintained between literal and figurative levels of meaning.

The result of a philosophy in the form of speculative sentences is, according to Hegel, not "the insufficiency of common sense but formed and educated (*gebildete*) and complete knowledge" (p. 65). This statement recalls Aristotle's statement in the *Poetics* that from metaphor—a "happy" expression that is neither tautology nor a positing of difference (Hegel's dialectical "unity as harmony"; p. 59)—arises genuine knowledge.[17] Hegel points out that such sentences are the reason why (his) philosophy is often considered incomprehensible by those

17. "We learn above all from metaphors." Aristotle, *Rhetoric*, 1410b.

who otherwise possess "the necessary conditions of education (*Bildung*) to understand it" (p. 60), thereby implying that other conditions of formative education besides the strictly philosophical will be necessary to comprehend his discourse. By arguing against the imposition of form from without and for the inherent, doubling drive to form, Hegel paradoxically but eloquently justifies both the "perspicuity" and the "copiousness" of his philosophical *elocutio* (*Durchsichtigkeit* and *Reichtum*; pp. 19, 67). The internal movement of thought and language, *res* and *verba*, leads to transformative figuration (*Umbildung*; p. 34) and more precisely to what Hegel calls "system." It follows, he writes, "that knowledge (*Wissen*) is only real [effective, *wirklich*], and can only be depicted, as scientific knowledge (*Wissenschaft*) or *system*" (p. 27). That is, Hegel's concept of science as system follows from his concept of the internal doubling and self-reflexive drive of *Bildung* in the same way as the goal of traditional *elocutio* consists in both the appropriate and richest formulation of ideas in language.

In this initial analysis of the Preface we see that *Bildung* is identified with form, with the mode of depicting the development of knowledge. It therefore corresponds to that part of classical and humanistic rhetorical systems, *elocutio*, which supplies the form and expression for ideas. In both traditional rhetoric and in Hegel's discussion of philosophical representation an apparent paradox arises from the rejection of form, in favor of the true *res* or *Sache,* even as linguistic form and expression is considered indispensable to all knowledge. In Hegel the paradox is exacerbated since he does not thematize the issue of rhetorical *elocutio*, indeed even might seem to mask it in his reformulation of its categories. Thus, where *elocutio* deals with the doubling involved in *res* versus *verbum, perspicuitas, figura, copia verborum, tropus,* and so on, Hegel writes of the reflexive and speculative nature of *Sache* versus "form," "proper (*eigentliche*) depiction," "richness (*Reichtum*) of Spirit," "formations" (*Gestaltungen, Gebilde*), "transformations" (*Umbildung*), and more. And yet by emphasizing the inherently representative force and movement in all thought and language (*die bildende Bewegung*) and by equating scientific knowledge with *Bildung* and the production of an appropriate and copious *Bild* or *Gebilde*, Hegel places the concerns of *elocutio* at the heart of his philosophical endeavor.

Exercitatio. Because *elocutio* must be learned, rhetorical *Bildung* also involves the strenuous educative process of acquiring, practicing, and varying modes of expression. This hermeneutical core of the classical rhetorical system, namely, an individual's appropriation and reinterpretation of past models on the way to a unique style, forms the second aspect of the prediscourse to Hegelian *Wissenschaft*. In a passage cited in the previous section, "*Elocutio,*" Hegel defined the force of the Spirit as being only as great as its expression. He goes on to say of the Spirit: "its depth [is] only as deep as it allows itself to expand and lose itself in its interpretation or exegesis (*Auslegung*)" (p. 18). This statement implies that part of the Spirit's power of expression, part of its *Bildung*, arises from a power of interpretation, explication, application, and self-loss in its object. It implies further an underlying logic by which self-loss in some Other can lead to better self-expression. It implies, finally, that the Spirit's drive to double, figure, represent itself in linguistic form is directly related to, even dependent on, its ability to lose itself in its interpretation. Depth in expression relies on a prior act of expansive interpretive gestures. The unfolding of the Spirit involves not only a force of figuration, but also a hermeneutical impulse to interpret, an impulse that presumes and philosophically reformulates a temporal-historical component of rhetorical *Bildung*.

In the discussion of Hegel's notion of *Bildung* in terms of *elocutio* and figurative representation, we considered the acts of giving form without introducing either a subject who performs and undergoes the process of formation or a concept of temporality which must accompany the formative becoming. Yet the doubling whereby the *Sache* gives itself a form and whereby the form comes to contain a meaning can be fully understood only within a larger process of a subject's history. The very self-reflexive formulations "gives itself" or "doubles itself" imply both a subject and a temporal difference. Hegel, in keeping with most rationally grounded systems of rhetoric, attempts to explain not only the intricate self-reflexive, speculative relationship between *res* and *verba*, but also the way in which the doubling within the "idea"—which is, as we saw, essentially both idea and form—developed. Between an "original" and a "mirror image" or imitator there exists not only spatial but also temporal distance. According to Hegel, then, the *Sache* or Spirit, which is never single but always double, is always already the product of some effective process. Even the beginning is in some sense always an end or product:

> The beginning of the new Spirit is the product of a wide-ranging upheaval of multifarious forms of educative development (*Bildungs-formen*), the price of an extremely tortuous path and likewise extreme strain and effort. This beginning is the totality that has returned to itself out of succession and expansion, the *simple concept* of totality which has come to be. The effective reality of this simple totality, however, consists of a process in which those formations that have become past moments develop once again and give themselves form, though in their new element, in their developed meaning. [p. 19]

Since, according to Hegel, this secondary "concept" determines the form of philosophical exposition—"Scientific knowledge must be organized around the proper (*eigene*) life of the concept" (p. 51)—philosophy repeats in its *Bildung* the history of *Bildungsformen*. This self-reflexive structure is actually the same as that of the "speculative sentence"; here, however, we have to do with a developmental process of a quasi- or really living subject that learns to adopt and give up forms. We can see this shift to a subjective temporal structure in the shift in focus from the earlier paradoxically figurative "proper or literal depiction" to the equally paradoxical and catachrestical, even personifying "proper life" of the concept. *Bildung* applies now not just to a figuration or metaphoricity inherent in the use of language for expressing ideas but to the manner in which the transsubjective Spirit comes to take on forms and figures historically and in which an individual comes to master those historical forms. Although Hegel is clearly interested in the development of the "universal" Spirit, the equivocation of general *Bildungsformen* and an individual's *Bildung* allows Hegel to model the phenomenological becoming of Spirit on the education of an individual to language. The model for that individual's *Bildung*, we shall see, was the course of strenuous training offered by rhetorical *exercitatio*.

In the Preface, Hegel initially defines the individual on which he will model the *Bildung* of philosophy (and hence his entire enterprise) in abstract terms. An individual is characterized by the domination of one particular shaping moment, although the individual being does contain within itself other moments as well. As a temporal structure, then, the present form of the individual contains past forms—both of its own development and of the surrounding culture. Hegel writes:

> The particular individual is the incomplete Spirit, a concrete form (*Gestalt*), in whose total existence one particularity is dominant and in which the others are present only in vague outlines (*verwischten Zügen*). In the Spirit that stands higher than another, the lower concrete existence has sunk to an inapparent moment (*zu einem unscheinbaren Momente herabgesunken*); what was earlier the matter itself is now only a trace (*Spur*); its form (*Gestalt*) is enwrapped (*eingehüllt*) and has become a simple shadow. The individual, whose substance is the higher standing Spirit, proceeds through this past. [p. 32]

If earlier we were concerned with the apparently timeless force within the *Sache* and Spirit that drives them to double themselves into a form of expression, here we see that *over time* the *Sache* becomes a form or figure by "sinking" to the status of a recorded trace.

Hegel then offers a concrete image to explain this abstract process, or rather (and this is the key to my approach) he offers the concrete experience *from which* he abstracted his philosophical analysis. The example describes how an individual subject passes through the traces of the past, which for Hegel have the form of established cultural phenomena. I quote at length to make clear the pedagogical emphasis in the original. The individual Spirit, Hegel writes, proceeds through historical forms of expression,

> . . . like he, who in taking up a higher science, proceeds through the preparatory information that he has long since mastered in order to make its content present to himself; he calls back its memory, without lingering or finding there his main interest. The individual must also pass through the content of the pedagogical stages of the universal Spirit, but as forms already laid aside by the Spirit, as stages of a path that is already worked out and leveled; in this way, when we think of knowledge, we see things that in earlier times had occupied mature spirits now reduced to information, exercises, even games for youth, and we recognize in pedagogical progression the history of the world's *Bildung* as if traced out in a silhouette. This past existence is already acquired property of the universal Spirit that makes up the substance of the individual and thus appears external to him.—*Bildung*, so considered and viewed from the side of the individual, consists in the individual's acquiring that which is already present beforehand, consuming and digesting its inorganic nature, and taking full possession of it.

> . . . wie der, welcher eine höhere Wissenschaft vornimmt, die Vorbereitungskenntnisse, die er längst inne hat, um sich ihren Inhalt gegenwärtig zu machen, durchgeht; er ruft die Erinnerung derselben zurück, ohne darin sein Interesse und Verweilen zu haben. Der Einzelne muß auch dem Inhalte nach die Bildungsstufen des allgemeinen Geistes durchlaufen, aber als vom Geiste schon abgelegte Gestalten, als Stufen eines Weges, der ausgearbeitet und geebnet ist; so sehen wir in Ansehung der Kenntnisse das, was in früheren Zeitaltern den reifen Geist der Männer beschäftigte, zu Kenntnissen, Übungen und selbst Spielen des Knabenalters herabgesunken, und werden in dem pädagogischen Fortschreiten die wie im Schattenrisse nachgezeichnete Geschichte der Bildung der Welt erkennen. Dies vergangene Dasein ist bereits erworbenes Eigentum des allgemeinen Geistes, der die Substanz des Individuums und so ihm äußerlich erscheinend seine unorganische Natur ausmacht. — Die Bildung in dieser Rücksicht besteht von der Seite des Individuums aus betrachtet darin, daß es dieses Vorhandene erwerbe, seine unorganische Natur in sich zehre und für sich in Besitz nehme. [Pp. 32–33]

The temporal process of *Bildung* is, therefore, an individual's recapitulation, in an activity of formative education, of cultural formations. One must not allow oneself to be deceived by the organic image that appears in the final sentences. Although Hegel seems to stress the organic over the cultural, he does so in the spirit of the paradoxical strategy dominating the entire Preface which rhetorically masks traces of rhetoric. Hence, one should emphasize and take quite literally the *pedagogical* model that Hegel proposes, by which a pupil takes possession of external forms and contents of past cultures, imprints them onto his or her spirit by means of preparatory exercises, and then, by means of a strong memory, makes this inorganic material present time and again.[18] The (individual and universal) Spirit that has passed through this process of formative education resembles a repository of dead matter which it has mastered and can make accessible to itself by the powers of well-trained recollection. The individual's acts of identifying with and transforming preexisting fixed forms (*das Vorhandene*) correspond to the paradoxical rhetorico-hermeneutic process, prescribed by traditional pedagogical programs based on the *institutio oratoria*, which involves grappling with written traditions in order to attain facility in self-expression.

To see why the process of *Bildung* as described by Hegel is best conceived not in vague organic terms but as taking place in language and leading to a proper form of linguistic expression, one can consider two processes that Hegel opposes to *Bildung*. In the one, "natural consciousness" remains trapped in its habitual behavior and does not rise above its inner imaginings or representations (*Vorstellungen*) or recognize itself as a rational agent in an external world. In the other, a consciousness insists on its freedom to act in the world and to impose itself forcefully on external objects with the power of its willful reasoning (*Räsonnieren*). In both cases subjectivity dominates, either by lacking abstract knowledge of that which is other than itself or by dominating that Other which it views as its opposite. In the ideal *Bildung* of consciousness, however, the differentiation between the thinking subject and the thought object disappears.[19] The opposing negative moment

18. In another connection (p. 42) Hegel uses the pun on *Inwendig-lernen* and *Auswendig-lernen* in order to convey the interplay of internal and external forms. *Bildung* begins with *auswendig-lernen*, the mere memorization and "turning outward" of external knowledge, but then proceeds to an internal reworking (the neologism *inwendig-lernen*) of the internalized material.

19. These distinctions in Hegel have remarkable parallels to Schiller's discussions of the drives toward "matter," "form," and "play" (*Stofftrieb, Formtrieb*, and *Spieltrieb*) in the *Briefe über die ästhetische Erziehung des Menschen*. The rhetorical background of Schiller's texts has been uncovered by Hermann Meyer, "Schillers philosophische Rhetorik," in *Zarte Empirie* (Stuttgart: Metzler, 1963); and Elizabeth M. Wilkinson, "Zur Sprache und Struktur der Ästhetischen Briefe," *Akzente* 6 (1959), 398–418. That Schiller speaks of *Erziehung* and *Bildung(strieb)* supports the working hypothesis of my study: that rhetorical concepts and categories provided structures as well as content to arguments within late eighteenth-century idealism.

of objectification is internalized as a constitutive part of consciousness itself. The individual consciousness learns to treat external forms as part of itself as well as to treat itself as consisting of incorporated external forms. The formative acts of appropriating preexisting external forms to the self in a process of creative transformation (literally a spiritual "digestion") provides the necessary educative and historical precondition for the essential identification of essence and form which we saw in the internal doubling of the speculative sentence. External existence (*Dasein*), that which we confront as Other, is actually the same "substance" as our reason since both undergo the same self-differentiation and reappropriation that makes them already a "determined universal" (*bestimmte Allgemeinheit*) or qualified "type" (*Art*). Hegel writes:

> In its simpleness or self-identity, substance appears firm and constant. But this self-identity is just as much negativity; thereby its firm existence passes over into its dissolution. The determined particularity appears at first to be such only insofar as it relates to an *Other*, and its movement [seems] to be imposed on it by a foreign external force; but the fact that its otherness is a part of itself and that it is self-movement, this is contained in that *simpleness* [oneness] of thought itself; for this simpleness is the self-moving and self-differentiating thought and proper interiority, the pure *concept*. [P. 54]

The movement and *Bildung* of both thinking and being take place, for Hegel, within a "substance" that is at the same time subjective and objective, that is, objective, yet capable of subjective internalization and transformed reobjectification. That substance, which Hegel calls the concept (*Begriff*) is not just a subjective representation in the mind (*Vorstellung*) but the tradition that each individual repeats in his or her development, in Hegel's terms, the "product of an extensive transformation of multifarious forms of educative development (*Bildungsformen*)" (p. 19).

Hegel describes in the Preface two modes of transforming these past forms of *Bildung*, modes of transformation which result in the language of *Wissenschaft*. These two modes indicate that he is modeling his philosophy of the "pure concept" on a concrete pedagogical process, the prediscourse of rhetorical training. He divides the modes along the lines of the topos of the *querelle des anciens et des modernes*. In the first, *Bildung* is understood as a literal education and cultivation to a higher, more universal and well-defined standpoint, the process by which an individual learns the principles of formulating and arguing in general terms. Hegel explains that one's *Bildung* and the process of working one's way free of the immediacy of life must always begin "by acquiring knowledge of *general* [universal] principles and perspectives, by working one's way up to the very thought of the matter (*Sache überhaupt*), by supporting or rejecting it with reasons, by grasping the concrete and rich fullness according to particulars, and by knowing how to pass a serious judgment on them" (p. 14). *Bildung* so conceived is thus the power to abstract from, transform, and order previously acquired concrete knowledge. It is a kind of education that leads the individual to internalize a variety of specific experiences in order to overcome their specificity by schematizing and then expressing them again as general precepts. The individual develops critical judgment not by striving for "originality" but by imitating, memorizing, and practicing well-established principles. This generalizing power of *Bildung* through which the individual takes in preformed knowledge in order to work through the tradition like a lifeless structure Hegel calls the task and "manner of study [effort, *Studium*] of the ancients" (p. 36), that is, the classical rhetorical pedagogical practice.

The other side of *Bildung* Hegel explicates by proposing it as a complement to the first the way the moderns complement the accomplishments of the ancients. Once the precepts of the classical systems of thought have become fully organized and internalized by the particular mind (for example, the school child) or the general understanding of an age (for example, post-Enlightenment Western culture), the task becomes to add one's individual spirit to the appropriated letter. In the second, modern stage of *Bildung* "the labor consists not so much in purifying the individual of its immediate sensual manner and making it a thought and thinking substance, as rather in the opposite, in realizing [making effective, *verwirklichen*] and inspiring (*begeisten*) the universal by dissolving (*Aufheben*) the firm particular determinations of thought" (p. 37). This description of the loosening and putting-into-motion of hardened categories is but the wider context around the process of figuration and specular doubling achieved by the speculative sentence. Seen from this perspective, *Bildung* means not just the ability of *elocutio* to make knowledge vivid (*bildlich*) through images (*Bilder, Gebilde*) but the making of abstract past forms present to a temporally different understanding. Once the modern mind has acquired the precepts and traditional forms of the ancients through the "knowledge, exercises, and even games of youth . . . in pedagogical progression" (p. 32), it must learn to fill them with its own meaningful content.

Both of these aspects of *Bildung*—as acquisition of past abstract forms and as their reformulation in the individual's concrete contemporary terms—require, according to Hegel, effort and hard work. He emphasizes the rigors of *Bildung*: "Therefore, the studious acquisition of scientific knowledge (*Studium der Wissenschaft*) depends on the individual's taking the effort of the concept (*Anstrengung des Begriffs*) upon himself" (p. 56). Translated into Hegel's other formulations, this means that the individual must work through the preformed content of the past by "consuming," "digesting," and "reinterpreting" the fullness of already existing formulations. More precisely, the very images of digestion and economic appropriation themselves refer back to a tradition of rhetorico-hermeneutic pedagogical praxis according to which the student, after having mastered the *praecepta* of the *ars rhetorica*, "consumes" the great texts of the pasts by *lectio*, "digests" them by *selectio* and *imitatio*, and transforms them creatively by a program leading from literal translation (*interpretatio*) to independent production (*aemulatio*).[20] For Hegel, as well as for the rhetorico-hermeneutic tradition, this process of *exercitatio* involves the risk of self-loss since the individual must dare to be taken over by the forms and voice of the Other in order, paradoxically, to attain an independent style. If we recall that *Wissenschaft* for Hegel means the re-presentation of *Bildung*, and that *Bildung* means the process by which the individual develops a language through an act of temporary self-loss in the language of tradition, the following definition becomes a paradigm of a philosophical reformulation of a process of rhetorical praxis:

> Scientific knowledge demands, however, that one give oneself over to the life of the object, or, what is the same thing, to have before onself, and to express, its inner necessity. Thus losing oneself in one's object, the individual forgets about that overview that is only the reflection of knowledge out of content back onto itself. But sunken in matter and flowing with its movement, the individual does come back to itself, but not until the fulfillment or content takes itself back into itself, simplifies itself as a particularity, reduces itself to *one* aspect of existence, and passes over to a higher truth. Through this process the simple totality with an overview over itself emerges out of the richness in which its reflection seemed lost. [p. 52–53]

This central dialectical movement, which guarantees that the formations (*elocutio*) of both the individual and universal Spirit are appropriate to the *Sache* (*res*), thus has its foundation in a theory of rhetorico-hermeneutic pedagogy. The reflexive structure of the Spirit's movement first out of and then back to itself in a higher form can become a model of representation since it derives from a practice of reading, imitating, translating, and writing which every writer or orator must—and which Hegel did in fact—pass through in order to

20. See Quintilian, *Institutio Oratoria*, x, 1, 19, for his discussion of reading and writing in terms of digestion.

develop a historically grounded sense of self-expression. The self recognizes itself in the Other of representation thanks to the hermeneutics of *Bildung*, which involves both self and Other, qua representations, in the same "substance": the language of an ongoing tradition. Hegel's philosophy thus describes the development of an individual parallel to the way the *ars rhetorica* accounts for the development of an individual style paradoxically out of a confrontation with, and self-loss in, preexisting forms.

Inventio and *Disputatio*. In the first two analyses of *Bildung* we have considered the implicit negativity that gives rise to doubling—either the inherent differentiation of the *Sache* as idea into expressed form, or the self's loss into and gradual appropriation of the Other of tradition—so to speak in a positive light, since this negativity was seen to be a creative force for the self, driving it to self-expression. Hegel defines negativity itself, however, as follows: "The inequality that takes place in consciousness between the I and the substance that is its object, is its difference, the *negative* itself" (p.39). If Hegel's philosophy consists in the movement (*bildende Bewegung*) of scientific knowledge, if that movement arises out of negativity, if negativity results from the self's recognition of the difference between itself and its "substance," and if the substance mediating self and Other is written tradition—then Hegel's philosophy of *Bildung* will contain traces of the self's critical self-differentiation from others' writings. In this third sense, *Bildung* implies not just figurative doubling or the self's gradual appropriation of the Other of tradition, but the polemical struggle between the self and its dialogic double in the public sphere of representation. As in the first two senses, we would expect to encounter a paradox concerning this aspect of rhetorical-philosophical *Bildung* since Hegel's argumentation masks its rhetoric in antirhetoric. And in fact, in the Preface Hegel employs rhetorical differentiation from contemporaries as an indispensable prediscourse of philosophical *Bildung* even as he explicitly denies, as we saw in the opening passages, the role of polemics. We must therefore look for hidden and paradoxical traces of confrontations between formal logic and modes of critical, even polemical, argumentation; between philosophical dialectic and rhetorical dialogue (*disputatio*); between conceptions of absolute truth and consensus theories of convincing an audience of the truth. For at these points of intersection negativity and differentiation from others, as key moments of a philosopher's and philosophy's *Bildung*, are recorded in Hegel's system.

Hegel's use of the concept *Bildung* in this third sense appears in a context that makes it easy to overlook. After talking about the expansive and developed form (*Ausbildung*) of his philosophy, its *elocutio*, he generalizes the term to apply not just to his own but to his contemporaries' philosophies as well. Referring to two contradictory trends of his day he declares: "This opposition seems to be the principal knot on which philosophical (*wissenschaftliche*) *Bildung* is at present working itself weary and about which it has not yet gained appropriate self-understanding" (p. 20). The two distinct, insufficient developments or formations (*Ausbildungen*) which characterize contemporary *Bildung* could be summarized under the headings "Empiricism," which Hegel criticizes for merely cataloging facts, and "Subjective Idealism," which he attacks for proposing unmediated first principles and then imposing them on all phenomena. Implicit in his criticism, which becomes extremely harsh and even ad hominem without mentioning names—for example, charges of "boredom" (*Langeweile*) and "indifference" (*Gleichgültigkeit*)—is the formal rhetorical criterion to which they can never measure up, namely, his ideal end of *Bildung* as *elocutio*, the ideal of a philosophy consisting of the extended image (*Bild*) or "world formation" (*Gebilde einer Welt*). But he also introduces a different approach to philosophical argumentation and representation of truth by defining the *Bildung* of scientific knowledge indirectly as the conflict of philosophical opinion of his day. *Wissenschaftliche Bildung* consists not just of one but of many representations struggling against one another. Given the significance he places on *Bildung* for his own *Wissenschaft*, he thus implicates himself within a dialectic of, or dialogue among, accepted interpretations, each striving for public consensus.

Hegel's implication in the *Bildung* of critical dialogue and differentiation leads to a series of complex and paradoxical arguments. Precisely these strategic moves around and through rhetorical, even polemical, positions lead to formulations of some of his major dialectical stances. In particular, his dialectic of finitude—which will come to play an even greater role in the *Logic*—becomes formulated in terms of the "limit" (*Grenze*) and "difference" between matters, issues, causes (*Sachen*), whereby the underlying process involves the differentiation and evaluation of conflicting polemical positions. Here the *Sache* clearly echoes the *res* of a forensic controversy. Hegel's rejection of, yet implication in, this process leads to a dialectical, indeed paradoxical structure of his arguments.[21] Early in the Preface, for example, we find him criticizing critics and differentiating himself from those who focus on differences:

> Likewise *differentiation* is rather the *limit* of the matter; it is there where the matter stops, or it is what the matter is not. Such efforts . . . [dealing]

21. Bubner, in "Die 'Sache selbst' in Hegels System," says, e.g.: "There arises the paradox that the matter itself (*Sache selbst*) in principle first appears before one's eyes as it is referred to from an external viewpoint (*Standpunkt*)" (p. 41).

with the differences and judgments of the one or the other are thus an easier labor than they perhaps appear to be. For instead of grasping the matter itself (*Sache selbst*), such activity always reaches beyond it; instead of lingering in the matter and forgetting itself in it, such knowledge always grabs for an Other; and it remains self-absorbed rather than giving itself over and being absorbed by the matter at hand. (P. 13)[22]

By appealing to the *Sache,* Hegel hopes to avoid the dilemma he would face at the level of conflicting opinions within the public sphere, the sphere of rhetoric and *doxa,* namely, he would always be in the position of "either confirming or contradicting an existing philosophical system" (p. 12). Yet he makes this appeal to the *Sache* or *Begriff* in order to place himself in contradiction to the "conviction (*doxa, Überzeugung*) of the age" a contradiction that he then dwells on as central to the Preface, without explaining why he feels the need to explain his stated difference from others. That is, he says that "an explanation of this contradiction [or opposition to others] thus does not seem superfluous" (p. 15), but gives no indication why it *isn't* superfluous. He even implies the opposite opinion in the similar words elsewhere (p. 11). He is caught in the paradox of both emphasizing his differences from others and of not being able to justify this emphasis.

One of the most famous organic images in all of Hegel's oeuvre attempts to mediate the paradox of *Bildung* conceived as polemical differentiation: The progressive development through various forms of philosophical argumentation is compared to the transformation of a plant; though each form seems to contradict or annihilate earlier conflicting forms in its unfolding, in fact all forms prove to be necessary for the growth of an "organic unity" (p. 12). But as we saw earlier, such organic images are often deceptive, especially those that apply to the concept of *Bildung.* Indeed, this powerful image serves as a powerful mask for a different concept of philosophical *Bildung* which proceeds according to complex rhetorical mechanisms of polemics.[23]

22. In the *Wissenschaft der Logik* (1812) Hegel develops a full dialectic of the limit (*Grenze*) which strives to overcome the apparent paradox in his present stance. That dialectic declares that all finitude (*Endliches* or *Endlichkeit*) is determined by its limit. Hence, to understand or comprehend something finite is to understand its borders. Such understanding implies a concept of the infinite beyond such limitations. Applied to the present issue, we could say that Hegel strives to subsume rhetorical polemic, and bring it to its end, under a broader system of dialectical argumentation.

23. It is interesting that Goethe seems to have sensed something else at work behind this image—either as it appears here in the *Phenomenology* or as it reappears in a similar form in the Preface to the *Logic*—since he sees in it not gradual organic progression but, rather, a process of development at the cost of other, earlier forms. Goethe even calls Hegel's mode of arguing here "sophistical." See Günther Nicolin, ed., *Hegel in Berichten seiner Zeitgenossen* (Hamburg: Felix Meiner, 1970), no. 159.

The Spirit and Its Letter

At stake in Hegel's intricate and apparently contradictory discussion of differentiation in philosophical *Bildung* is a reformulation of the essential principles of rhetorical *inventio*, namely, the discovery and judgment of arguments derived systematically from the *res* and used in a critical dialogue (*disputatio*) with others to establish a general consensus in an audience. This *officia* of rhetoric, which traditionally paralleled *elocutio* in significance, offers an essential precondition for any speech. It strives to systematize the process of constructing arguments and thus, though not opposed to the belief in natural talent, nonetheless emphasizes the aspect of *ars* or *technē* in rational argumentation and cannot be reduced to "organic development." In the context of this task of rhetoric Hegel's harsh critique against the "genius" (ingenuity, *Genialität*; p. 63) of contemporary romantic philosophers becomes clearer. With sharp sarcasm he relates the task of developing philosophical argumentation to crafts. The brilliantly and subtly biting tone contrasts with the coolness of the *Sache selbst*:

> Of all sciences, arts, skills, and crafts, the general conviction is true that a considerable effort of learning and training is necessary to master them. Concerning philosophy, on the contrary, the prejudice seems to hold sway that even though anyone with hands and eyes, who got hold of leather and tools, would not be capable of making shoes, nonetheless anyone knows how to philosophize and judge philosophy simply because he possesses with his natural faculty of reason the appropriate measure stick—as if he did not likewise possess the measure of a shoe on his own feet.

> Von allen Wissenschaften, Künsten, Geschicklichkeiten, Handwerken gilt die Überzeugung, daß, um sie zu besitzen, eine vielfache Bemühung des Erlernens und Übens derselben nötig ist. In Ansehung der Philosophie dagegen scheint jetzt das Vorurteil zu herrschen, daß, wenn zwar jeder Augen und Finger hat, und wenn er Leder und Werkzeug bekommt, er darum nicht imstande sei, Schuhe zu machen, jeder doch unmittelbar zu philosophieren und die Philosophie zu beurteilen verstehe, weil er den Maßstab an seiner natürlichen Vernunft dazu besitze,—als ob er den Maßstab eines Schuhes nicht an seinem Fuße ebenfalls besäße. [Pp. 62–63]

Although he does not mention the *ars rhetorica* or *ars inveniendi* in this critique, he goes on to associate the "considerable effort of learning and training" with the "long path of *Bildung*" as a confrontation "with other knowledge" (*mit anderem Wissen*; p. 64). If one avoids this *Bildung* one produces merely a "rhetoric of trivial truths" (*Rhetorik trivialer Wahrheiten*; p. 65). Once again Hegel uses a formulation that apparently rejects rhetoric although in fact the process of argumentative interaction he calls for is derived from the tasks of educating an orator to the *ars bene et sapiente dicendi*. Hegel takes on Ciceronian ideas about *Bildung* which he acquired in his own *Bildung*, in particular, the kind of dialectical rhetoric which guides the formation of dialogues. He thus criticizes that type of philosopher who would rely totally on "feeling" and "his internal oracle" (*sein inwendiges Orakel*) for trodding on the very root of humanity: "In other words, he stamps on the roots of humanity. For the nature of humanity is to insist on the consensus with others, and the existence of humanity is only in the commonality of consciousness[es] thus brought about" (p. 65). The philosophical concept of "humanity" used here has its origins in the pedagogical and rhetorical tradition of "humanism." And so, based on this tradition, we can define the third perspective of the long path of *Bildung* which is depicted in Hegel's philosophy as the effort to develop arguments and criteria of criticism, to deal with the Other in a dialogue, and to strive for a consensus with the audience.

The last pages of the Preface play through the paradoxes of Hegel's antipolemical reformulation of polemical prediscourse once again, this time in terms of the relationship between scientific knowledge and audience, concept and dialogue. He repeats his definition of *Wissenschaft* as the "self-movement of the concept" (p. 65), seemingly removed from issues of rhetoric, representation, and polemical argumentation. He then follows this emphasis on the apparent self-sufficiency of philosophy—as if the concept were outside and independent of thinking humans—with a reference to the "representative ideas (*Vorstellungen*) of our time" which run counter to his own and therefore "offer no promise of a positive reception (*keine günstige Aufnahme*)" of his philosophy (p. 66). First, it is odd that Hegel should feel the need to mention the reception of his work after defining its main principle as "self-movement of the concept," for it is not immediately obvious that the concept should care about its reception. And second, it is somewhat unclear why Hegel then proceeds to discuss Plato, especially his *Parmenides*, as "probably the greatest masterpiece of ancient *dialectic*" (p. 66), in terms of different receptions throughout history.

The mention and juxtaposition of these matters are not as arbitrary, even contradictory, as they seem, however, if one considers the "self-movement of the concept" as an act of *Bildung* which, like Plato's philosophy, lives in a dialogue both among partners and between the author and public through the medium of the partners. This dialogic discovery, working out, and conflict of arguments leading to a consensus on the truth constitutes the very movement of the concept.[24] Thus

24. My investigation of the role of the "dialogic" within Hegel's dialectic would be impossible were it not for the work of Mikhail Bakhtin, especially the essays in *The*

Hegel concludes: "We must be persuaded that the truth, by nature, breaks through when its time has come and that it only appears when its time has come, and thus neither appears too early nor finds an unripe audience; moreover, the individual requires this effect in order to confirm thereby that which is but his isolated matter and to experience as something universal that which initially belongs to him peculiarly" (p. 66). The "movement" or *Bildung* of the *Sache* can and must take the reception of the public into account, because a key feature of *Bildung* is the development and application of arguments in dialogue with an Other. The "appearance" of philosophy—in the double sense of its form and its entrance on the stage—takes place in the re-presentation of the "dialectic of experience," that is, in the dialogic unfolding of formal and critical arguments.[25]

As a consequence of his position Hegel must seek out ("invent") a new form of philosophical argumentation which internalizes the counterposition of the Other. In fact, this endeavor is by no means new, as his reference to Plato indicates. However, it did become a crucial issue for philosophical rhetoric at the end of the eighteenth century as a reaction against the dominance of both empirico-historical and mathematical methods of structuring arguments in philosophy. The major neohumanists called for a return to the older ideal, embodied especially in Cicero's works and their humanist reception, of the philosophical orator and well-spoken philosopher. Hegel's extensive discussions of the "historical" and "mathematical truths" (pp. 40–47), certainly a significant core of the critiques in the Preface, belong together with the general "conservative" trend among the rationalist rhetoricians of his day. In such brilliant formulations as the following Hegel gives abstract expression to a traditional practice of disputation:

> The inner origin[ating] and becoming of substance is inevitably the passing over into exteriority or into a state of being-there, being for an Other; conversely, the becoming of the state of being-there is the taking

---

Dialogic Imagination, trans. and ed. Michael Holquist (Austin: University of Texas Press, 1972). Since Bakhtin considers "dialogism" (or "heteroglossia") the dominant generic feature of novelistic discourse, we can see that the earlier references to the *Phenomenology* as a *Bildungsroman* can be made even more precise by means of a rhetorical-structural analysis of levels of discourse than was possible by the thematic analyses of Royce, Kaufmann, and Abrams.

25. These references are taken from the Introduction to the *Phenomenology*, which will be dealt with below, in chap. 4. It is significant, however, that such discussions of appearance and representation in terms of *dialektische* or *bildende Bewegung* serve as parentheses around the entire text since, as is well known, Hegel wrote the Introduction *before* and the Preface *after* the work itself.

back of the self into essence. The movement is thus the double process and becoming of the totality, such that at the same time each being posits the Other and both therefore have two perspectives.

Das innere Entstehen oder das Werden der Substanz ist ungetrennt Übergehen in das Äußere oder in das Dasein, Sein für Anderes, und umgekehrt ist das Werden des Daseins das sich Zurücknehmen ins Wesen. Die Bewegung ist so der gedoppelte Prozeß und Werden des Ganzen, daß zugleich ein jedes daß andere setzt und jedes darum auch beide als zwei Ansichten an ihm hat. [P. 43]

Hegel is tracing out here the discovery and development of arguments in a dialogue, in which each partner must take the views of the other into account in order to unfold a convincing whole. This is a process of *Bildung* not just in the objective or structural sense discussed above of giving form to the *Sache*, or in the subjective, pedagogical sense of an individual's appropriation of past forms and already developed styles, but in the more intersubjective sense of seeing in the *res* the means to enter into critical exchanges with others. One of Hegel's many terms for this process is, of course, "dialectical movement," a phrase that recalls the *Bildung* of consensus in dialogue. Another term is "reflection" (p. 25), which he divorces from the sterility of contemporary "reflection philosophy" (actually the object of his harshest critiques) and brings closer to the traditional thought figure (*figura rerum*) of rhetoric, *reflexio*, which is defined as the unfolding of arguments in an internalized dialogue.[26]

Thus, the concept of *Bildung* in the Preface contains within itself a third paradoxical structure of representation, one that forms the prediscourse of Hegel's own development of a dialectical philosophy. He must enter into a critique of critique, an argument of *rhetorica contra rhetoricam*, since his philosophy of *Bildung* must internalize and differentiate itself from contemporary "philosophical *Bildung*," which he views as caught in polemical differentiation. He must develop a form of argumentation that makes critiques of other forms a constitutive moment of consciousness and the concept or *Sache* itself. Given the devel-

---

26. Lausberg defines *reflectio* as: "The *reflectio* is a *distinctio* in the form of a dialogue. A word used by the first partner in the dialogue is taken up and given a partial and emotional (*parteisch-emphatisch*) sense. . . . The *reflectio* distinguishes itself from irony in that in irony the opposing word in the new context is presented as being nonsensical on this particular occasion; in the *reflectio*, on the other hand, the opposing meaning of the word as well as the meaning imputed to it by the new partner carry a habitual character, and the partial (*parteisch*) reinterpretation has a habitual foundation. The prejudicial reinterpretation must be deep-seated and emotional, and thus fathom the true *voluntas* of the opposite party of language itself" (pars. 663, 664).

opment of his own philosophy and his *Bildung* in classical rhetoric and critical debate, Hegel reaches back to a theory of *inventio*. Like neo-humanist or Ciceronian rhetoricians of his day, he develops a mode of argumentation that sees critical dialogue aimed at the consensus of the partner and audience as indispensable to the *Sache,* for *inventio* is the doctrine of systematically extracting arguments from the very nature of the *res.* The "dialectical" or "forming and educating movement" (*bildende Bewegung*) of his philosophy therefore internalizes "philosophical *Bildung*" as critical debate.

The *Phenomenology* is Hegel's first formulation of his system of speculative or absolute idealism. The function of the Preface is to explain how such a representation of the absolute is possible. It might seem as if no representation was possible, since truth or the absolute—from Latin *absolutum,* without relation to an Other—is defined in terms of the *Sache selbst* or "life of the concept," and thus independent of any rhetorical model of depiction. But Hegel finds a brilliant solution: He defines the *Sache* and the "concept" as the products of *Bildung,* whereby the process of *Bildung* is inseparable from an inherently rhetorical act of doubling and representation—in the three forms of figuration, hermeneutic stylistics, and polemical disputation with an Other. Thus, representation of knowledge, or *Wissenschaft,* is possible in the *Phenomenology* since it rests on, or retraces, a process of self-representation. This solution, however, introduces significant assumptions that lead to paradoxes since it relies on the very rhetorical tradition it hopes to banish from philosophy. Preinscribed into *Wissenschaft,* as the precondition of its development and representability, is the multilayered and ambiguous tradition of rhetorical *Bildung.*

Introduction: Representation, Rhetoric, *Bildung*

> Philosophy's central concern is to be a general theory of represen-
> tation . . .
>
> Richard Rorty, *Philosophy and the Mirror of Nature*

Representation

Few concepts have undergone such intensive analysis and criticism in recent decades as the notion of representation in and of philosophy. From different theoretical perspectives, philosophers and literary critics in different countries have been challenging fundamental principles of the Western tradition by reevaluating the relationship between thought (or truth) and its appearance in language. In Germany, philosophers building upon the foundation of Heidegger's analysis of Being and *Dasein* have introduced a model of the hermeneutic dialogue to replace theories of consciousness based on self-reflection and self-presentation.[1] In America, the neopragmatist, neo-Wittgenstein-

---

1. Hans-Georg Gadamer, *Wahrheit und Methode: Grundzüge einer philosophischen Hermeneutik* (Tübingen: Mohr [Paul Siebeck], 1960), established the framework for the discussion. Gadamer's students from Heidelberg have been applying, advancing, and modifying his insights in literary theory (Wolfgang Iser and Hans Robert Jauß and the Constance school of reception theory) and philosophy (Rüdiger Bubner and Manfred Frank). Iser has over the last five to ten years in fact shifted his interest somewhat from the phenomenology of reading and reception to the anthropological and sociological foundations of representation through doubling and fictionality. Gadamer has also been engaged in a dialogue with members of the Frankfurt school of critical theory, especially Jürgen Habermas, who likewise replaces reflexive representation with a model of "communicative action." In France, Paul Ricoeur has been the major representative of the hermeneutic approach, as represented in his works *Le conflit des interprétations: Essais d'herméneutique* (Paris: Editions du Seuil, 1969) and *Freud and Philosophy: An Essay on Interpretation*, trans. Denis Savage (New Haven, Conn.: Yale University Press, 1970). However, given Ricoeur's background in religious studies, he foregrounds the notion of the symbol over that of dialogue.

ian philosopher Richard Rorty has critically reinterpreted the image of philosophy as nature's commensurate representation and of the mind as its "mirror" in epistemology from Locke through contemporary analytic thought.[2] In France, poststructuralists have used developments in linguistics and semiotics to reveal how the traditional "metaphysics of presence," from Plato through Husserl, is unable to account fully for the processes of differentiation which underlie its very modes of discursive representation.[3] In the debates surrounding the concept of representation and the challenges to definitions of meaning as self-presence, Hegel is involved on both sides. He is held up as the philosopher who epitomizes or overcomes the model criticized. His theory and practice of dialectical argumentation are understood as the crowning achievement of, or the means of surpassing, metaphysics. This book contributes to contemporary discussions by investigating both Hegel's concept of representation and the development of his own system's forms of representation.

The fundamental issue of philosophical representation can be analyzed in terms of two positions, and it is not too much of an over-

---

2. Richard Rorty, *Philosophy and the Mirror of Nature* (Princeton, N.J.: Princeton University Press, 1978). In many other essays he attempts to retell the history of philosophy in a way that sees the late eighteenth century as the point at which the standard model of representation gradually recognized its contradictions and began looking for alternatives, a search culminating in some contemporary approaches. See the collection of essays he edited, *The Linguistic Turn* (Chicago: University of Chicago Press, 1968). See also "Nineteenth-Century Idealism and Twentieth-Century Textualism," *Monist* (Autumn 1981), 155–74; "Philosophy as a Kind of Writing: An Essay on Derrida," *New Literary History* 10, no. 1 (1978), 141–60; "Deconstruction and Circumvention," *Critical Inquiry* 11, no. 1 (1984), 1–23. In fact, it can be argued that much of twentieth-century analytic philosophy is a response to the same kind of "crisis" of representation after (in Rorty's terms) the "linguistic turn." Quine, Putnam, and Davidson, as well as Austin and Searle with their speech-act theory, have challenged traditional conceptions of representation no less than Nietzsche and Heidegger in continental philosophy.

3. Jacques Derrida, *De la grammatologie* (Paris: Editions de Minuit, 1967); *L'écriture et la différence* (Paris: Editions du Seuil, 1967); *Marges de la philosophie* (Paris: Editions de Minuit, 1972); *Glas* (Paris: Editions Galilée, 1974). Paul de Man, more than almost any other individual, can be credited with helping to introduce deconstruction to America, especially through his books *Blindness and Insight: Essays in the Rhetoric of Contemporary Criticism* (New York: Oxford University Press, 1971) and *Allegories of Reading: Figural Language in Rousseau, Nietzsche, Rilke, and Proust* (New Haven, Conn.: Yale University Press, 1979). Near the end of his life, de Man turned to Hegel in the essay "Hegel on the Sublime" in *Displacement: Derrida and After*, ed. Mark Krupnik (Bloomington: Indiana University Press, 1983). Werner Hamacher (like Manfred Frank) has been one of the few philosophers or comparatists to mediate between West German hermeneutics and French poststructuralism, especially through his *pleroma: Zu Genesis und Struktur einer dialektischen Hermeneutik bei Hegel*, introduction to Hegel, *Der Geist des Christentums und sein Schicksal: Schriften 1796–1800* (Frankfurt am Main: Ullstein, 1978).

simplification to see the history of philosophy as a debate between these two views. According to the first, which might be considered the "anti-representation" view of representing, the truth, or things-as-they-are, or thoughts, can be known in and of themselves in a universal, abstract, and internal "form" that is independent of observer and context. The form, which exists only in pure ideality, has shed its cloak of external appearance and presents itself reflexively. Plato's conception of anamnesis and critique of mimesis, realism during the Middle Ages and Renaissance, Locke's theory of distinct ideas, nineteenth-century scientific positivism—all these doctrines are related by the central hermeneutic principle of revelation, or clarification, which sees knowledge as a return from a state of murky mediation to an original, pure immediacy. According to the second position, which might be considered the "antipresence" view of representation, what is, or what is true, exists only in some mode of appearance or representation-for-a-mind, whereby knowledge can consist only of myriad, necessarily incomplete, particular perspectives. Proponents of this position emphasize the mediated nature of all knowledge and question the epistemological, metaphysical, and ethical value of a self-present spirit independent of its bodily letter. Aristotle's encyclopedic and empirical science, the nominalist response to the realists, Nietzsche's perspectivism and practice of "genealogy" rather than history, Wittgenstein's philosophical investigations of meaning as "rules of the game" rather than ideas—all these positions are concerned with the intermediary step of representation in its own right instead of with the supposedly prior presence, with the how and why rather than what of signification.

This polarity has recently been extended into new fields that seem to thrive on the tension. For example, literary theorists are divided over whether a poem is able to represent, reflect, or refer to an extratextual world; and philosophers of science are divided over whether theoretical models, in a way similar to metaphors, create as much as represent the scientist's empirical reality. The debate rages on since both positions seem untenable in isolation. The first position has difficulty giving a measure of commensurability which can guarantee that the process of re-presenting has in fact returned to the things as they are. Furthermore, it becomes caught in an infinite regress since any measure would also have to be represented and shown to be accurate by some measure. The second position has difficulty explaining its prioritization of representations, since at some point it either implicitly assumes or does not sufficiently account for the sense of an original presence logically or temporally prior to the re-presentations. It likewise falls into a regress by positing itself as a more adequate representation of things as they are (or philosophy as it is) even as it argues against representations of things as they are.

Hegel's philosophy, especially his early writings before the *Logic* (1815), is concerned more explicitly than most others with grounding the "fact of representation"[4] in a way that would account for the strongest claims of the two counterpositions. Although never cast in quite these terms, his contribution to the history of Western thought can be considered the most comprehensive, intricate meditation on philosophy's paradoxical task of representing truth "in and of itself" even as it acknowledges its status as representation. From his earliest school diaries, essays, and declamations exemplifying traditional modes of composition, through the theological manuscripts dealing with different appearances of Christianity and through the Jena essays criticizing all other contemporary forms of philosophizing, to the by no means merely marginal prefaces explaining and justifying his method, Hegel was preoccupied with issues of expression. He was acutely aware of both the attractions and pitfalls of the two traditional positions. The Preface to the *Phenomenology of Spirit* (1807, as we have seen, is an extended discussion and justification of his *Wissenschaft* as the "true form (*Gestalt*) of the truth" (p. 14). He rejects those philosophies that place all emphasis on "feeling," "intuition," "the divine" (pp. 15, 25), since they lack understanding of, and hence avoid the necessity of, mediation. And yet he also stresses that the "otherness" of the mediation does in fact include its self-identity, for the Other is only a reflection of the self (p. 23).

The *Phenomenology* presents Hegel's first systematic attempt to find a solution joining these opposing views, which see philosophy as either recapturing an immediate self-presence or as caught in a relativizing dependence on alterity. He grounds his theory and practice of philosophical representation with the circular argument that the to-be-represented itself—*Sache*, Spirit, "concept"—is involved in a developmental process of self-representation, a process culminating in his philosophy, the representation of which therefore demonstrates the very assumptions of a movement toward self-representation. Hence, he manages to avoid an infinite regress by appealing to the image of a cyclical process: "It is the process of its own becoming, the circle that posits its end as its purpose, has its end thus at its beginning, and only

---

4. Here I play off Rüdiger Bubner's phrase *Faktum der Reflexion*, in "Der 'Sache selbst' in Hegels System," in *Zur Sache der Dialektik* (Stuttgart: Reclam, 1980), p. 48, a fact that he sees underlying Hegel's entire (especially early) philosophizing. In fact, however, reflection and representation are united. By focusing on representation rather than reflection I feel I can introduce a wider range of historic and systematic issues.

becomes at the end what it really [effectively, *wirklich*] is" (p. 23).[5] The state of "absolute knowledge" is the state of philosophical representation which conceptually formulates the unfolding of the absolute Spirit to that very point, the point of conceptual self-formulation. The very formulation of this process by Hegel thus confirms the correctness of his representation of the Spirit's development, since the Spirit's development should lead up to this self-depiction. If the representation exists—as it does in Hegel's philosophical system—then the theory it represents must be true since the theory presumes the inner drive toward systematic representation. A teleological process of development, what Hegel calls *Bildung,* mediates between the oppositions of presence and representation by inscribing into the original presence its destiny as self-representation. The Spirit is destined to develop, to become form, to take on a letter, which is in turn destined to be appropriate to the Spririt by becoming perspicuous to itself, self-effacing.

This solution would seem to satisfy the major considerations of traditional views. It explains the need for the formation of particular, historically bound representations out of an inner need of the to-be-represented. It unites the otherwise isolated representations of particular human subjects as mere facets and reflections of the Spirit's own process. And yet tensions persist within the apparently closed circularity of Hegel's system. Hegel gives full logical and temporal priority to the Spirit, and hence to the first "antirepresentation" position. He mentions that his *Logic,* for example, "is the truth as it is, without any covering (*Hülle*), in and of itself" (p. 44). At the same time, he incorporates into the "pure" and spiritual concept, at least in the manner of a controlled detour, a *via negativa* of alienation through expression. Hegel seems to have solved the divisive paradox of philosophical representation by embracing the paradox itself. How did he come upon this

---

5. In Hegel's own terms: "The image of the progression into the infinite is the straight *line,* on both ends of which is only the infinite, and the latter only exists, where it [the line]—and it is existence—is not, and the line *proceeds out* into this nonexistence, that is, into the undetermined; as true infinity [on the other hand], turned back onto itself, its image is the *circle,* the line that has reached itself, which is closed and entirely present, without *initial point* and end ("Das Bild des Progresses ins Unendliche ist die gerade *Linie,* an deren beiden Grenzen nur das Unendliche [ist] und immer nur ist, wo sie—und sie ist Dasein—nicht ist, und die zu diesem ihrem Nichtdasein, d.i. ins Unbestimmte *hinausgeht*; als wahrhafte Unendlichkeit, in sich zurückgebogen, wird deren Bild der *Kreis,* die sich erreicht habende Linie, die geschlossen und ganz gegenwärtig ist, ohne *Anfangspunkt* und *Ende*"). *Logic,* in *Theorie-Werkausgabe* (Frankfurt am Main: Suhrkamp, 1969), p.164. Or, as put succinctly in a recent study: "Indeed, on Hegel's own view, his system forms a circle and thus has, strictly speaking, no presuppositions and no starting-point." M. J. Inwood, *Hegel* (London: Routledge and Kegan Paul, 1983), p. 3.

solution? And do elements that led to his solution remain unaccounted for or limit its horizon? As we shall see, the concept of *Bildung*, which signifies the process of the Spirit's development to philosophical form, contains a tradition and a personal history of formative education which can allow a reevaluation of Hegel's theory and practice of philosophical representation.

Contemporary responses to Hegel have explored tensions within Hegel's system but have failed to provide an account of the actual development of, and theory of development within, his philosophical discourse. Work by neo-idealists in Germany over the past twenty years has focused largely on individual concepts from Hegel's system: reflection (Düsing, Bubner, Frank), consciousness (Cramer), negation and self-differentiation (Henrich), contradiction (Stiehler, Guyer).[6] Most of these can be considered investigations of aspects of Hegel's master concept and methodological operator, dialectic. They point out that many of Hegel's key terms lack consistent definition, and without abandoning the Hegelian enterprise, they strive to supply missing steps in argumentation.[7] With the exception of Frank's turn to Schleiermacher for an alternative concept of representation which accounts for "the individual universal," the other critical approaches do not challenge the horizons of the model of representation offered by Hegel.[8] The "Critical Theory" of the Frankfurt school, although ideologically different from more traditional neo-Hegelians and richer in sociological analysis, tends to follow a parallel pattern of criticism and support.

6. For a brief overview of some of these major positions, see the essays edited by Rolf-Peter Horstmann in *Seminar: Dialektik in der Philosophie Hegels* (Frankfurt am Main: Suhrkamp, 1978). Henrich deals with different formulations of self-reflexive theories of representation in his appropriately titled essay collection *Selbstverhältnisse: Gedanken und Auslegungen zu den Grundlagen der klassischen deutschen Philosophie* (Stuttgart: Reclam, 1981).

7. See, e.g., in Horstmann, *Seminar*: Henrich, pp. 213–4; Bubner, p. 101; Cramer, p. 361.

8. Manfred Frank, *Das individuelle Allgemeine: Textstrukturierung und -interpretation nach Schleiermacher* (Frankfurt am Main: Suhrkamp, 1977); *Der unendliche Mangel an Sein: Schellings Hegelkritik und die Anfänge der Marxschen Dialektik* (Frankfurt am Main: Suhrkamp, 1975); *Was ist Neostrukturalismus?* (Frankfurt am Main: Suhrkamp, 1983); *Das Sagbare und das Unsagbare: Studien zur neuesten französischen Hermeneutik und Texttheorie* (Frankfurt am Main: Suhrkamp, 1980). In his attempt to mediate between contemporary French (post)structuralism and German hermeneutics, Frank has reinterpreted the history of idealist philosophy. His general goal has been to demonstrate the inadequacy of the "model of reflection" and theory of representation, on the one hand, and of a simplistic notion of the individual subject on the other. He offers an insightful reading of Hegel which points out the limitations of the primacy of the universal. But he also demonstrates that many a Hegel critic fails to develop a sufficient account of the interpreting subject. My interpretation builds on Frank's basic approach, but I try to analyze how Hegel's philosophy of representation, and its paradoxes, *came about* over the course of his *Bildung*.

Adorno, Horkheimer, and Bloch, for example, agree in rejecting Hegel's "identity theory" of subject and object that posits the absolute Spirit's self-representation, and yet they adopt the dialectic straightforwardly as a form of depicting reality and developing thought that corresponds to its object.[9] By crediting Hegel with a full comprehension of the dialectical nature of Being and with a dialectical method to represent it adequately, they undermine their own challenge to the structure of a self-reflexive parallel between *representandum* and *representans*.

At the same time as the Frankfurt school, and as if answering its general acceptance of Hegel's discourse and theory of dialectical form, one strand of linguistically oriented thinkers has been endeavoring to translate or update Hegel into the terminology of philosophies of language. Liebrucks, Simon, Bodammer, and Wohlfahrt argue for Hegel's relevance to contemporary notions of linguistic consciousness given Hegel's own implicit or explicit theory of language.[10] And yet none of them considers either the origins of Hegel's own discursive practice and theory in nonphilosophical areas or the effects of his origins on his basic ideas.[11]

Hermeneutics, on the other hand, following Heidegger's critique of metaphysics, has attempted to move beyond Hegel's indebtedness to dependence on traditional treatments of philosophical representation—for even an ingenious response remains within the horizon of the question—by introducing a *dialogic* structure to displace the dialectic of presence and expression. Understanding, Gadamer argues both with and against Hegel, does not take place thanks to a method, dialec-

9. Martin Jay, *The Dialectical Imagination: A History of the Frankfurt School and the Institute of Social Research, 1923–1950* (Boston: Little, Brown, 1973). Bloch, *Subjekt-Objekt* (Frankfurt am Main: Suhrkamp, 1971). Adorno, *Drei Studien zu Hegel*, in *Gesammelte Schriften*, vol. 5 (Frankfurt am Main: Suhrkamp, 1970). Adorno, in a statement parallel to ones by Bloch, refers to Hegel's expression as "film images of thought" ("Filme des Gedankens"; p. 353).

10. Theodor Bodammer, *Hegels Deutung der Sprache: Interpretationen zu Hegels Äußerungen über die Sprache* (Hamburg: Felix Meiner, 1969). Josef Simon, *Das Problem der Sprache bei Hegel* (Stuttgart: Kohlhammer, 1966). Bruno Liebrucks, *Sprache und Bewußtsein* (Frankfurt am Main: Akademische Verlagsgesellschaft, 1964–69), vols. 1, 3, and 7 concentrate on Hegel. Günter Wohlfahrt, *Der spekulative Satz: Bemerkungen zum Begriff der Spekulation bei Hegel* (Berlin: Walter de Gruyter, 1981). Wohlfahrt goes furthest in connecting Hegel's concrete practice of philosophical writing with Hegel's theories of representation; he opens his book as follows: "The problem of the speculative sentence is the problem of the linguistic representation of the speculative" (p. v).

11. In terms of their analysis of how Hegel's thought and writing developed, these works do not go beyond Theodor Haering, *Hegel: Sein Wollen und Sein Werk—Eine chronologische Entwicklungsgeschichte der Gedanken und Sprache Hegels* (Leipzig: Teubner, 1929–38), the title of which indicates the strictly unilateral relationship of thought influencing form.

tical or not, which allows the philosopher to see clearly and depict timeless truths; rather, understanding unfolds over time in the way successive performances of a play reveal, indeed produce, new significance for different generations. This hermeneutic turn, however, has in turn been criticized by means of a poststructuralist argument charging its failure to escape the dominant specular and speculative structure of Hegelian idealism by merely shifting the self-revealing, self-representing "supersubject" from the Spirit to tradition or *Wirkungsgeschichte*.[12] The hermeneutic dialogue turns out to be as monological as Hegel's dialectic since the otherness of the partner and the medium of expression is subordinated to the act of self-signification. Jacques Derrida and Werner Hamacher have thus undertaken to radicalize the hermeneutic reading of Hegel by bringing to light those places in his system of representation where general principles of linguistic signification, opposition, and alterity (even at the level of the morpheme) are employed in a way that cannot be explained by the system.[13] The deconstructive readings strive to undermine the self-revelatory aspect of the Spirit by indicating the places where the letter insists on imposing its opaqueness. But they have not yet undertaken to study the historical, rhetorical structures of representation which concretely informed the *development* of Hegel's thought and writing—that is, those structures that gave form to his philosophy but remain unassimilated by the concept of the Spirit's self-representation—in a way that relates to other studies of idealism. Deconstruction has not yet been able, in spite of its various insights into the workings of Hegel's writing, to engage in a genuine dialogue with Hegel which explores both the background and consequences of his theory and practice of representation.[14]

To appreciate Hegel's contribution to theories of representation as well as to understand the limits of his solution, we must investigate the historical origin of his argumentation and locate it within the wider

12. Frank formulates this critique most forcefully in *Das individuelle Allgemeine*: "The being of the Other as Other gets left behind (*bleibt auf der Strecke*). It is appropriated (*vereinnahmt*) as the self-appearance of the selfsame thing in a subjectless subjectivism of effective history (*Wirkungsgeschichte*). . . . However, in actuality [the self] does not give itself over as a self-reflection of effective history; rather, it simulates the 'dialogue between I and You.' Feuerbach reproached the Hegelian dialectic, saying 'it only pretends to do so, but does not really mean it; it's playing (*sie spielt*)'" (pp. 33–34).

13. *Glas* and *pleroma* have gone furthest in opening up a "double reading," what Hamacher calls a *Dialektüre* (p. 17) within Hegel; they have even attempted to express this doubleness graphically by introducing bicolumnated pages and numerous types.

14. As Frank writes in his lectures *Was ist Neostrukturalismus?*: "The dialogue with Hegel remains an *ou topos*, a u-topia of poststructuralism" (p. 345).

context of the development of his system. In order to investigate systematic and historical factors that determine Hegel's philosophical representation, we must pursue the discursive theories and practices that constitute the preconditions of his (concept of) formative development. We shall see that the principle of *Bildung*, as a central concept of his philosophy and as the process by which his philosophy in fact took shape, not only underlies his theory and practice of representation but also implicates the tradition of rhetoric in his philosophy. Hegel's thinking and writing thus contain from their conception and throughout their development a tension between philosophy and rhetoric, the self-present Spirit and the letter of its effective discursive formation.

Rhetoric

The history of philosophy's debate with itself over the two positions vis-à-vis the process of truthful representation can be told in another fashion, as a conflict between two disciplines, philosophy and rhetoric. This interdisciplinary struggle forms the general context of my reading. There was a time, it seems, before anyone made a profession of writing down ideas, when most of the oppositions connected to stances about representation, oppositions that keep us occupied today, would not have been a source of controversy. Thought versus talk, the sensible versus the intelligible, appearance versus reality—these significant binaries did not become issues of central concern until (Plato's) Socrates deemed it necessary to "divide culture up into the areas which represent reality well, those which represent it less well, and those which do not represent it at all (despite their pretense of doing so)."[15] The deep-running incision that cut through and altered the course of Western institutions was that between philosophy (dialectic) and rhetoric. Whereas the former adopted the position of "antirepresentation" in its endeavor to conceive of the nature of "things as they are," the latter took over the domain of representation, that is, the function of systematizing forms of discourse which produce an effect on individual subjects and reality. That effect, according to rhetoric, can be brought about either indirectly, by instructing individuals in the powers of expression, or directly, by bringing about a public consensus on presented issues. But once it was banished from philosophy to rhetoric, the concern with effectiveness and persuasion, as serious as it might be, lost its claim to "absolute truth."

15. Rorty, *Philosophy and the Mirror of Nature*, p. 3.

From that point on the two disciplines have struggled throughout Western intellectual history. The "purity" of philosophy allowed it to coopt for itself the categories of truth, knowledge, and goodness, whereas rhetoric, with increasing self-consciousness, became limited to purpose and interest. Pure thought came to belong to the former, action to the latter. By the first century A.D., the split had developed far enough for Cicero to tell one of the earliest versions of this story: According to him, for the early Greeks "wisdom" included both eloquence and ethical (philosophical) virtues about truth and the good life.[16] But then Pythagoras, Democritus, and Anaxagoras "abandoned the sphere of government and gave themselves entirely to study." Gradually, some, debarred from politics, "created for themselves a new interest and amusement as dialecticians . . . and sciences invented for the purpose of moulding the minds of the young on the lines of culture and virtue." With Socrates, the split became final:

> . . . whereas the persons engaged in handling and pursuing and teaching the subjects that we are now investigating were designated by a single title, the whole study and practice of the liberal sciences being entitled philosophy, Socrates robbed them of this general designation, and in his discussions separated the science of wise thinking (*sapienter sentiendi*) from that of elegant speaking (*ornate dicendi*), though in reality they are closely linked together. . . . This [Socrates] is the source from which has sprung the undoubtedly absurd and reprehensible severance between the tongue and the brain, leading to our having one set of professors to teach us to think and another to teach us to speak.[17]

From here Cicero traces the development of the liberal arts and the widening gap between rhetoric and philosophy after Plato, neo-Aristotelian thinkers, and the Greek and Latin Stoics.

Throughout the intellectual and institutional history of the West, some periods and places (the early Roman Empire, Europe in the sixteenth and seventeenth centuries) and some thinkers (Cicero, Quin-

16. All citations here and below from *De Oratore*, III, xv, 57–59 (Loeb edition, Cambridge, Mass.: Harvard University Press, 1971). For similar kinds of statements on the history of this tradition, see also Cicero's *De Inventione* and Quintilian's *Institutio Oratoria*, I, pref., 13ff.; I, pref., 18; III, I, 8ff.; and II, XXI, 13.

17. These descriptions by Cicero, and others like them by Quintilian, of the way rhetoric was banished from significant areas of intellectual life because it lost influence in the public-political sphere under dictatorial rulers parallels the situation in Germany in the late eighteenth century. We shall see how rhetoric was forced "underground" into schools and theories of writing once public decision making no longer took place through deliberative oratory.

tilian, Melanchthon, Nietzsche), used rhetorical representation explicitly as a guide to systematic thought. For these times, places, and thinkers, rhetoric maintained its widest function of *ars bene et sapiente dicendi*, a function that rests on a strict relationship of interdependence of thought and expression, *representandum* and *representans*. On the other hand, some philosophers have attempted to limit the scope of rhetoric by defining it as the technique of artificial speech in the service of "mere" convention and persuasion.[18] Expression thus becomes separate from and secondary to thought, and rhetoric, identified only with the former, loses its rationale as a theory and practice of truthful representation. German idealism in modern times, for example, like Plato among the ancients, can be credited with successfully divorcing the two disciplines and thereby clearly placing philosophical knowledge and the dialectical method over "mere" rhetorical technique.[19]

In recent years, rhetoric has increased in significance for philosophically oriented literary criticism, especially in France, Germany, and the United States, as the result of a remarkable inversion. As opposed to the tendency of the Western tradition toward a limitation of rhetoric from the general sphere of public culture first to the pulpit, then to the schools, and finally to a textbook theory of a handful of tropes and figures, some contemporary theorists have been attempting to play up rhetoric against philosophy. Their first studies in rhetorical criticism were generally historical, a rediscovery of the richness of analytical techniques in the *ars rhetorica* which had influenced so much writing from the Renaissance through the nineteenth century. Between the 1930s and 1970s, writers such as I. A. Richards and Kenneth Burke,

18. See Lawrence Manley, *Convention: 1550–1750* (Cambridge, Mass.: Harvard University Press, 1982). Manley offers one of the most insightful readings of this struggle between "topics" and "rhetoric," between the "philosophical" and "rhetorical" views of poetry's ability to depict the truth. The broader conception of rhetoric is defined in the German tradition as the "art of speaking" (*Kunst zu reden*), whereas the narrower one is the "discipline of artful speaking" (*Disziplin kunstmäßigen Redens*); Frank, *Das individuelle Allgemeine*, p. 163.

19. Recall Jens's article on *Rhetorik* in the *Reallexikon der deutschen Literaturgeschichte*, (vol. 2, ed. Werner Kohlschmidt and Wolfgang Mohr [Berlin: Walter de Gruyter, 1958]). Chaim Perelman and L. Obrechts-Tyteca, in *Rhétorique et philosophie* (Paris: Presses Universitaires de France, 1952), consider Descartes the first modern philosopher to separate philosophical certainty from rhetorical persuasion; but their descriptions apply as well, indeed even more forcefully, to German idealism. In his lectures on aesthetics, Hegel limits the sphere of rhetoric to the realm of external purposiveness. Although otherwise he rarely deals with the discipline of rhetoric outright, he almost always mentions the term in a pejorative context —e.g., "rhetoric of mere trivialities" (*Rhetorik bloßer Trivialitäten*) in the Preface to the *Phenomenology*. See Frank, *Das individuelle Allgemeine*, pp. 164–67.

Roland Barthes and Gérard Genette, and Klaus Dockhorn, Henrich Lausberg, Walter Jens, and Wilfried Barner have demonstrated the persistent survival of classical rhetoric even in modern, postromantic times.[20] Then, predominantly in France and the United States, a new form of rhetorical criticism took hold which hoped to relativize the entire Western (philosophical) tradition by systematic (rhetorical) readings against the grain. In particular, the necessary though apparently uncontrollable appearance of tropes, which displace—literally "turn"—meaning from its source or original location, has been used to question the very oppositions upon which the "metaphysics of presence" rests (literal versus figural, proper versus metaphorical).[21]

This poststructuralist or deconstructive approach, which reaches its highest and most stimulating form in essays by Jacques Derrida and Paul de Man, has successfully unsettled the firm, antirhetorical and antirepresentational ground of philosophical discourse.[22] And yet in spite of its insights, this approach has limited itself needlessly, since it takes the limited sphere of rhetoric, namely, rhetoric reduced to a catalog of tropes (just a fraction of one-fifth of the structure of the

20. I. A. Richards, *Philosophy of Rhetoric* (Oxford: Oxford University Press, 1936). Among his numerous and diverse studies I mention Kenneth Burke's *The Grammar of Motives* (Berkeley: University of California Press, 1969; 1st ed., 1949) since it discusses grammar, dialectic, and rhetoric. The entire "new critical" school would have been impossible had it not been for initial concentration on rhetoric as a self-contained, historically transmitted system of textual analysis. Barthes, "L'ancien rhétorique — Aidememoire," *Communications* 16 (1970), 172–223; Genette, "Rhétorique et enseignement" and "La rhétorique restreinte," in *Figures* II and III, respectively (Paris: Editions du Seuil, 1969, 1972); Klaus Dockhorn, *Macht und Wirkung der Rhetorik: Vier Aufsätze zur Ideengeschichte der Vormoderne* (Bad Homburg: Gehlen, 1968); Jens's article on *Rhetorik* in the *Reallexikon*, his essays in *Von deutscher Rede* (Munich: Piper, 1969), and the introduction to his edition of Adam Müller's *Reden über deutsche Beredsamkeit* (Frankfurt: Insel, 1967); Lausberg (a romanist!), *Handbuch der literarischen Rhetorik: Eine Grundlegung der Literaturwissenschaft* (Munich: Hueber, 1960); Wilfried Barner, *Barockrhetorik: Untersuchungen zu ihren geschichtlichen Grundlagen* (Tübingen: Max Niemeyer, 1970); Walter Hinderer, *Über deutsche Literatur und Rede: Historische Interpretationen* (Munich: Wilhelm Fink, 1981); Helmut Schanze, ed., *Rhetorik: Beiträge zu ihrer Geschichte in Deutschland vom 16.-20. Jahrhundert* (Frankfurt: Athenäum-Fischer, 1974); Heinrich Plett, *Rhetorik: Kritische Positionen zum Stand der Forschung* (Munich: Wilhelm Fink, 1977).

21. The antirepresentational approach mentioned above can be seen as a theory of "proper" meaning, as a theory aimed at "properly" depicting the "inherent property" of nature. Cast in these terms, it stands opposed to rhetoric conceived of as figurative speech. The opposition is clearer in German, where *eigentliche* Rede versus *uneigentliche* Rede connotes both proper versus improper and literal versus figurative.

22. Especially de Man's "Epistemology of Metaphor," *Critical Inquiry* (Autumn 1978), pp. 13–30, and Derrida's "La mythologie blanche," in *Marges*. Hayden White, *Metahistory* (Baltimore, Md.: Johns Hopkins University Press, 1973), uses a tropological analysis to discuss the rhetoric of (philosophies of) history.

original *ars*), as philosophy's foil.[23] It would be more fruitful, I shall argue, to take the wider system of rhetoric as it has existed throughout the Western tradition. Thus, although the poststructuralist approach forms one impetus for this book, I find that the systematic and the historical uses of rhetorical criticism must join forces in order to offer both an alternative to antirepresentational philosophy and a philosophical understanding of rhetoric.[24]

"Rhetoric," as I shall use the term throughout this work, refers to the systematized forms of linguistic representation that throughout the Western tradition defined the possibilities of effective expression. That is, I shall use the term in its wider definition, which includes theories of figuration, composition, instruction, and argumentative persuasion. Each of these different aspects will be used to illuminate features of Hegel's development as a writing philosopher and of his conception of philosophy as formative development. Ironically, this wider field of rhetoric, internalized by Hegel through his education, guides the structuration of his philosophy even as his dialectic strives to delimit particular aspects of rhetorical approaches to representation.

The fundamental ideas of rhetoric as a theory and practice of representation are contained in Quintilian's *Institutio Oratoria*. His formulations not only outline the most sophisticated and systematic arguments to justify the domain of rhetoric but also provide the form in which rhetoric had its concrete impact on intellectual and institutional history. A brief summary of some of his points will indicate what lies behind the term "rhetoric" as I shall employ it, what concepts and images form the parameters of theories of representation. Although these structures and *termini technici* were part of the standard vocabulary of textual production and analysis up to a century ago, and thus formed the implicit or explicit prestructures of all writing, they have lost their earlier familiarity, especially for postidealist and logic-oriented discussions of philosophy.

23. Henry Sussmann's *Hegelian Aftermath* (Baltimore, Md.: Johns Hopkins University Press, 1982), especially the chapter on Hegel, demonstrates the limitation that harms an otherwise insightful argumentation. The tropes of metaphor and metonymy are insufficient weapons for attacking the fortress of Hegel's system (even the first chapters of the *Phenomenology*, to which Sussmann restricts his argument).

24. Schanze points to an opposition between "historical and systematic" methods of rhetorical criticism which have not been successfully connected (*Rhetorik: Beiträge zu ihrer Geschichte*, pp. 8–12). Similarly, Plett concludes: "[Thus] two opposing concepts of analysis are to be found presently in the field of literary studies: one, ahistorical and systematic, which can be made operational, and one, historical and pragmatic, which still has not demonstrated that it can be. It will be one of the essential tasks of literary rhetoric to mediate between these two positions" (*Rhetorik: Kritische Positionen*, p. 12).

The Spirit and Its Letter

The *Institutio Oratoria*, written in just a few years around A.D. 94, is the most comprehensive, systematic, and lively study of classical rhetoric.[25] The aim that Quintilian sets himself "is the education of the perfect orator" (I, Preface, 9). By "perfect," Quintilian means an ideal figure who, like the "perfect sage" of ancient philosophers (he clearly and ironically has Plato in mind), does not yet exist but is a necessary goal of our aspirations (I, Preface, 19). His depiction of an orator's tasks and development thus has a telos, which he defines with deceptive simplicity as *bene dicere* (II, xxv, 38). This goal demands encyclopedic knowledge and abilities. For this reason he must "include in [the] twelve books a brief demonstration of everything which may seem likely to contribute to the education of an orator" (I, Preface, 25), a task that, were it not for the clear telos, would be endless.

Formally, the argumentation of the twelve books is divided according to two schemas that provide the terms and structures that thenceforth have near absolute validity in the theory and practice of effective representation in all fields. The first schema divides the core of the text into the five "duties"or "tasks" (*officia*) that must be fulfilled both in an orator's education and in the preparation of any individual speech act: *inventio* (Books III–V) deals with the "discovery" of arguments and culminates in the theory of "status" (or topics, *loci*), the possible positions that can be defended or refuted in a dialogue (e.g., court case or disputation); *dispositio* (Books VI–VII) deals with the various arrangements (*ordo*) that can be used in composing a speech and the techniques of a good opening (*exordium* or *prooemium*), argument (*narratio*), and persuasive closing (*peroratio*); *elocutio* (Books VIII–X) deals with style, figures of speech, and tropes, including extensive literary criticism of other orators' styles and what should be learned or avoided; *memoria* and *actio* (Book XI) deal with the means—all important for Quintilian as an active public speaker—by which an orator can deliver a speech in the most effective manner. These books on the *ars* and the *praecepta* that must be mastered are enclosed by an opening on prerhetorical training in grammar and tips on early education (Books I– II) and by a conclusion, the "most important part of the work," describing the accomplished orator at the end of these tasks (see the following section of this Introduction on these pedagogical aspects). After Quintilian, these structures undergo many minor adjustments in medieval, humanistic,

25. Quintilian, *Institutionis Oratoriae Liber Decimus*, ed. W. Peterson (Hildesheim: Georg Olms, 1967): "The *Institutio Oratoria* differs from all other previous rhetorical treatises in the comprehensiveness of its aim and method" (p. xvi). All following citations of Quintilian are taken from the Loeb edition, trans. H. E. Butler (Cambridge, Mass.: Harvard University Press, 1967).

baroque, and Enlightenment rhetoric, but otherwise they remain in place as the most powerful codification of discursive praxis. What grammar is to the mechanics of speech, these rhetorical structures were to effective representation.

Just as important as the complex and nuanced system of structural categories presented in the *Institutio Oratoria* is the conceptual dialectic that holds it together and supports its claim to an all-encompassing theory of representation. At this more abstract level, we see within rhetoric a struggle over, and paradoxical resolution of, the issue of self-presence versus expression. Quintilian's, like each great formation of the *ars rhetorica*, relies on a tension between *res* (concept, thought, subject, *Sache*) and *verba* (words, language, expression) which gives preference now to the one, now to the other, but in the end insists on their mutual interdependence. This insistence characterizes all philosophical rhetoric and rhetorical philosophy. Quintilian writes: "All speech expressive of purpose involves also a subject (*rem*) and words (*verba*)" (III, iii, 1; also III, v, 1). Invention, which according to Quintilian's structure subsumes arrangement, is the most "conceptual" or strictly speaking "philosophical" of the orator's tasks. Quintilian agrees with Cicero that "matter" (*res*) should be assigned to *inventio* (III, iii, 7). This part of rhetoric involves the techniques of thinking an issue through before speaking. It might seem, therefore, as if Quintilian would argue for a purely conceptual activity prior to actual rhetorical expression. It is significant, however, that the major discussions of *inventio* fuse two fields that came to be separated in modern times, dialectic and forensic oratory. The discovery of the "subject" or "matter" at hand—the *res ipsa*—means getting to the bottom of an issue, discovering the "basis" or "status." As such, *inventio* coincides with Aristotle's *Topics*, which provides the first codified rules for formal logical thinking.

Behind these rules is the concrete situation of two disputing parties: The "basis" is "the kind of question which arises from [the first] conflict" (III, vi, 5); and "the essence of the status," in the words of one interpreter, "is determined by the conflict (*Auseinandersetzung*) of two differing viewpoints."[26] For this reason, Quintilian supports Cicero in stressing the significance of "judgment" (*iudicium*) in invention (III,iii, 5ff.), since the thinker must always be thinking in advance of the concrete speaking situation in which opinions clash before a judging instance. Thus the most private, conceptual, and "rational" parts of rhetoric—*inventio* and *dispositio*,—are already intricately tied to the public and effective

26. Quintilian, *Institutionis Oratoriae Liber III*, ed. Joachim Adamietz (Munich: Wilhelm Fink, 1966), p. 17.

43

verbal context. In fact, for Quintilian the relationship between *res* and *verba* is like that between "rational" and "legal" questions, the only difference being that the latter are concerned with what is *written* (III, v, 4). The structures of discovery and analysis remain the same.

It should not come as a surprise that the books on *elocutio, memoria,* and *actio*, which apparently emphasize forms of expression and make up the narrowly speaking "rhetorical" side of rhetoric, likewise involve categories that fuse *verba* and *res*. The discussion of *elocutio* places it squarely in the realm of *verba*: "Style is revealed both in individual words and in groups of words" (VIII, i, 1). Similarly, "rhetorical ornament . . . may reside either in individual words or in groups of words" (VIII, iii, 15). And yet the principle that underlies good style, which includes the twin virtues of *perspicuitas* and ornament, is intentionally and explicitly equivocal in a way that allows Quintilian to bridge the gap between *res* and *verba* in a nuanced manner. The essential principle, namely, is "propriety" (*proprietas*). Quintilian points out four meanings: (1) "calling things by their right names" (VIII, ii, 1), that is, the proper logical and linguistic correspondence; (2) use of the "original term from which [all] others are derived" (VIII, ii, 7), again a concern for objectively determined priorities; (3) awareness of a term's use in "some one particular context" (VIII, ii, 8); and (4) the form that deserves highest praise, "the employment of words with the maximum of significance" (VIII, ii, 9), especially in the sense of effect on the audience. The collection of these four meanings makes clear that propriety, and hence style in general, since "without propriety ornament is impossible" (VIII, iii, 15), seems to balance delicately on the line connecting knowledge, either of things or of words, and social tact. Quintilian's *Institutio Oratoria* and the codification of discourse it propagated through the centuries—what I mean by the term "rhetoric"—thus strive to overcome a merely unilateral dependence of *res* on *verba* or *verba* on *res*. Precisely this play of interdependence allows rhetoric to function as a comprehensive theory and practice of representation with significant implications for philosophy.

Hence, to point out "rhetorical traces" in Hegel's philosophy is not to "deconstruct" him in the sense of relativizing or reducing his achievements by circumscribing them within a *limited* field of rhetorical figuration. Rather, it is to open up the debate within his philosophy between conflicting conceptions of representation, a debate traditionally waged between disciplines that have been too narrowly defined. The analysis of such traces demonstrates that the theories and practices of rhetorical expression which seem to have been displaced by philosophy live on in masked and unaccounted for form within philosophy.[27] To the extent that Hegel's philosophy relies, at least in its explicit pronouncements, on an antirhetorical and antirepresentational stance, any rhetorical approach points out its limitations. To the extent that it can be shown that Hegel successfully and necessarily employs arguments and structures from the rhetorical tradition, even as he rejects them, his solution to the problem of representation is shown to be richer, not poorer. I perform what Hegel might call a negation of a negation, a criticism of the limited views of philosophy as antirhetorical and rhetoric as antiphilosophical. Only by continuing this dialogue can we hope to have a solution to the problem of representation which does not self-contradictorily exclude some all too literal rhetorical forms in the name of a self-presenting spirit.

Bildung

In his chapter "Philosophy without Mirrors," Richard Rorty holds up Gadamer's hermeneutics as one of the most viable alternatives to our epistemologically based philosophical tradition.[28] Gadamer, according to Rorty, shifts the focus of philosophical concerns from principles claiming, and methods testing, the commensurability of representations to the phenomenon of human consciousness engaged in a process of understanding and continual self-formation. The task of "philosophy"—or better, the "human sciences" (*Geisteswissenschaften*), since like Heidegger Rorty sees no point in the discipline of philosophy—shifts correspondingly from a search for universal foundations to a discovery of forms of intersubjective effectiveness, an understanding of *Wirkungsgeschichte*. It is a shift from the antirepresentational to the antipresence mode of philosophizing, from a conception of philosophy as superior to, that is, more fundamental than, rhetoric, to one of philosophy as one more way of creating one's world by depicting it for others. Gadamer accomplishes this shift, Rorty writes, "by substituting

---

27. Gerd Ueding, et al., *Einführung in die Rhetorik—Geschichte, Technik, Methode* (Stuttgart: Metzler, 1976): "Thus rhetoric often continues to live on in the work of those who despise it: The most prominent example is still Friedrich Schiller, but Hegel is also one of these, and a thorough analysis would bring to light not only the rhetorical structure of his prose, but equally the many rhetorical motives of his philosophy and aesthetics, from his 'genre theory of poetics' to his theory of the philosophical introduction, which was already formulated precisely in the *Phenomenology of Spirit*" (p. 4).

28. Rorty, *Philosophy and the Mirror of Nature*, pp. 357–94.

the notion of *Bildung* (education, self-formation) for that of 'knowledge' as the goal of thinking."[29]

Although Rorty mentions Gadamer's discussion of *Bildung* as a "guiding concept" of the *Geisteswissenschaften*, and although Rorty mentions that the use of *Bildung* by philosophical hermeneutics attempts to divorce an idealist concept from its tie to the philosophy of absolute Spirit, he never analyzes the relation between Hegel, Gadamer, and the "humanistic tradition" on this clearly central point.[30] Reading Rorty, one could get the impression that Gadamer employed the concept of *Bildung* in order to dislodge absolute idealism, the ultimate form of self-presencing foundationalism, without much problem or tension. In fact, however, Gadamer's debt to Hegel concerning precisely this concept is very great. Gadamer is emphatic about Hegel's position as *the* philosopher of *Bildung*: "Hegel worked out the notion of *Bildung* more distinctly than anyone else."[31] Indeed, although many of Hegel's concepts may be criticized, that of *Bildung* remains an "ideal" even for the "historical human sciences."[32] Concerning the concept of *Bildung*, which opens upon the general issues of representation, self-development, and the means of conceiving a new mode of philosophizing, Gadamer's relation to Hegel is ambivalent: On the one hand, Gadamer wishes to reject the end of Hegelian *Bildung*—the dissolution of otherness in the Spirit's self-understanding; on the other, he appeals to notions of idealist form and speculative structures in explaining the "truth" of (represented by) an artwork and language.[33] In Hegel, Gadamer, and Rorty *Bildung* functions as the means of overcoming the basic oppositions—either within philosophical debates concerning rep-

29. Ibid., p. 359.

30. Rorty does not consider that Gadamer uses terms "in any sense which could be given an idealistic interpretation" (p. 358), and he quotes Gadamer's point of differentiation from Hegel: "But we may recognize that *Bildung* is an element of spirit without being tied to Hegel's philosophy of absolute spirit, just as the insight into the historicity of consciousness is not tied to his philosophy of world history" (p. 358, n. 3). It is, however, not so easy to cut the ties, especially concerning the concept of *Bildung*, which is tied to so many traditions.

31. Gadamer, *Wahrheit und Methode*, p. 9. Despite this position of Hegel in the development of the concept of *Bildung*, little work has been done on Hegel's contribution. Two early and outdated works try to show the usefulness of Hegel's philosophy for developing a theory of pedagogy: William Bryant, *Hegel's Educational Ideas* (Chicago: Scholarly Press, 1896); and Millicent MacKenzie, *Hegel's Educational Theory and Practice* (Westport, Conn.: Greenwood Library, 1909). A more recent study provides an excellent overview of Hegel's contact with the sphere of pedagogy without tracing *Bildung* in terms of classical or humanist approaches; see Otto Pöggeler, "Hegels Bildungskonzeption in geschichtlichem Zusammenhang," *Hegel-Studien* 15 (1980):241–69.

32. Gadamer, *Wahrheit und Methode*, p. 12.

33. Ibid., esp. pt. III, sec. 3, pp. 460–62.

resentation or between humanistic disciplines—but in all three philosophers the dependence of *Bildung* on idealist or anti-idealist traditions remains vague.[34]

Paradoxically, then, this concept comes to be viewed as both Hegel's great achievement and the means of defining an alternative to the idealist enterprise; it is both the key to Hegel's solution of the dilemma of representation in favor of absolute presence and the means of displacing presence by relativized intersubjective representations. To understand this paradox, we must explore the background of this concept and its relation to rhetoric. We will see how Hegel's concept of *Bildung* includes two conflicting traditional conceptions, one organic-teleological and the other humanist-representational. By stressing the coexistence of these two directions we can develop a broader, self-consciously dialogical conception of *Bildung* which reveals the tensions within Hegel's paradigm of the "model of representation."

The understanding of the concept *Bildung* which is most widely known to modern readers, largely thanks to the reception of the *Bildungsroman*, fuses various traditions into a subjectivist and organic strand. Writers such as Herder, Goethe, Humboldt, and Schleiermacher, each in his own way, combined pietistic, philanthropical, mystical, or Neoplatonist notions of an inner form determining the human spirit with the pictorial, scientific, or teleological associations of *Bild* and *Bildung*. Etymologically, this conception of *Bildung* goes back to translations of the Latin *imago* (as *Bild, Abbild,* or *Ebenbild,* image, reflection, likeness), *imitatio* (*Nachbildung*), *forma* (*Gestalt*) and *formatio* (*Gestaltung*). The term thus refers to a complex of ideas: the specular relationship between God, humans, and world; the process of their interaction (especially the human itinerary back to God); and the end product of that process.[35] The individual probably most responsible

34. In fact, Rorty's relationship to the idealist tradition is even more ambivalent than he lets on. He translates *Bildung,* taken from Gadamer and Hegel, for example, as "edification," but the German word that means "edification" is *Erbauung,* concerning which Hegel says in the Preface to the *Phenomenology*: "Philosophy must prevent itself (*sich hüten*) from the desire to be edifying" (p. 17).

35. Rolf Selbmann, *Der deutsche Bildungsroman* (Stuttgart: Metzler, 1984), p. 1 (also for other bibliographical references). See also *Religion in Geschichte und Gegenwart,* ed. Kurt Galling (Tübingen: Mohr, 1957–65, article on *Bildung*). Gadamer reviews the standard definitions largely on the basis of I. Schaarschmidt, "Der Bedeutungswandel der Worte 'bilden' und 'Bildung' in der Literaturepoche von Gottsched bis Herder" (Ph.D. diss., Erlangen, 1931). Two of the most significant, though unfortunately little known, recent works on the concept of *Bildung* are by Günther Buck: *Hermeneutik und Bildung—Elemente einer verstehenden Bildungslehre* (Munich: Fink, 1981) and *Rückwege aus der Entfremdung—Studien zur Entwicklung der deutschen humanistischen Bildungsphilosophie* (Munich: Fink, 1984).

for converting these different notions (without yet using the term *Bildung*) into a coherent philosophical position was Leibniz, whose "monadology" envisioned a soullike entity that proceeded, thanks to its independent, internal power, through the process of self-realization to an approximation of its inherent likeness to the divine (or the universe as a whole).[36]

The secularization of these ideas, which took place in Germany at the end of the eighteenth century, gave *Bildung* its modern contours. Johann Gottfried Herder can be considered the greatest influence in this development. He introduced if not the linguistic then at least the conceptual possibility of understanding *bilden* as a reflexive verb, *sich bilden*. From his early *Journal meiner Reise* (Journal of My Travels; 1769), through the essay "Auch eine Philosophie der Geschichte zur Bildung der Menschheit" (A Philosophy of History on the Development of Mankind; 1776), to his major *Ideen zur Philosophie der Geschichte der Menschheit* (Ideas on a Philosophy of History of Mankind; 1784–91), the term *Bildung* accrues in meaning and scope to include: (1) the development of an individual thing's form; (2) education, especially that of advanced nations; (3) the process and product of the formation of human cultures; (4) the historical unfolding of "humanity" (*Humanität*); and (5) the scientific view that all of nature is unified by a principle (force, *Kraft*) according to which each being strives for its ideal organic form.[37] These views are summarized in what Charles Taylor calls the "expressivist anthropological theory" that "human life is both fact and meaningful expression; . . . man comes to know himself by expressing and hence clarifying what he is and recognizing himself in this expression."[38] Significantly, this theory of expression is transmitted and interpreted largely in organic and subjectivist terms throughout the nineteenth century. Goethe and Schleiermacher contributed considerably to this tendency, Goethe by means of his general theory of morphology

36. See Clemens Menze, "Grundzüge der Bildungsphilosophie Wilhelm von Humboldts," in *Bildung und Gesellschaft: Zum Bildungsbegriff von Humboldt bis zur Gegenwart*, ed. Hans Steffen (Göttingen: Vandenhoeck und Ruprecht, 1972), pp. 6–7. Charles Taylor, *Hegel* (Cambridge: Cambridge University Press, 1975), esp. pp. 11–29. Ernst Lichtenstein, "Die Entwicklung des Bildungsbegriffs," in *Die Bildung des Bürgers: Die Formierung der bürgerlichen Gesellschaft und die Gebildeten im 18. Jahrhundert*, ed. Ulrich Hermann (Weinheim: Beltz, 1982): "But the problem of self-education and self-formation (*Selbstbildung*) was first thought through in metaphysical terms by Leibniz" (pp. 165–66).

37. Irmgard Taylor, *Kultur, Aufklärung, Bildung, Humanität und verwandte Begriffe bei Herder* (Gießen: Swets und Zeitlinger, 1968), esp. pp. 22–25. F. M. Barnard, *Herder's Social and Political Thought: From Enlightenment to Nationalism* (Oxford: Clarendon, 1965), stresses the elements of organicity, continuity, and unity (esp. pp .31–54).

38. Taylor, *Hegel*, p. 17.

and Schleiermacher by means of his belief in the "predisposition" (*Anlage*) to religiosity.[39] They paved the way for aesthetic and anthropological theories that conceived of the human being as both an artist and an artwork with the task of "self-formation" (*unmittelbar sich bilden*).[40]

This tradition, with its introspective, organic, and teleological overtones, has come to predominate, to the extent to which *Bildung* is a meaningful concept at all. Ironically, the very predominance of this view in the nineteenth century as part of the ideology of developing capitalism can be seen as one of the reasons for an avoidance of the term *Bildung* in contemporary thought.[41] The tradition of the *Bildungsroman* or, more important, the reception of the *Bildungsroman* in literary criticism over the course of the nineteenth and twentieth cen-

39. Goethe's concept of *Bildung* has been widely investigated from diverse perspectives. See Heide Kalmbach, *Bildung und Dramenform in Goethes 'Faust'* (Göppingen: Alfred Kümmerle, 1974), which pursues the "natural laws of *Bildung*" through dramatic forms. Margaret Scholl, *The Bildungsdrama of the Age of Goethe* (Bern: Lang, 1976), extends the concern with the fusion of drama and *Bildung* onto a larger number of texts without ever really analyzing the background and textual complications connected with *Bildung*. Klaus-Dieter Sorg, *Gebrochene Teleologie: Studien zum Bildungsroman von Goethe bis Thomas Mann* (Heidelberg: Carl Winter, 1983), analyzes the *Bildungsroman* from the perspective of the breakdown of established teleological socialization structures, a crisis to which this literary form is an open-ended response. Claus Günzler, *Bildung und Erziehung im Denken Goethes* (Köln: Böhlau, 1981), is one of the few recent efforts to combine the pedagogical, scientific, and aesthetic components of *Bildung*, but he is more interested in developing a meaningful pedagogical theory for today out of Goethe's own theory than with a historical investigation of the sources and transformations of Goethe's ideas. See Friedrich Schleiermacher, *Reden über die Religion an die Gebildeten unter ihren Verächtern* (1799; Hamburg: Felix Meiner, 1958), pp. 63, 75–97 ("Über die Bildung zur Religion"), in which he argues that man possesses an inner drive (*Anlage, Bildungstrieb*) for the infinite which must develop in its own unique way. For Schleiermacher, it is a question of developing the religious "feeling" (*Gefühl*) for the divine. This subjectivist tendency, or at least the subjectivist interpretation of the concept of "divination," led Gadamer to reject Schleiermacher as a possible foundation for his philosophical hermeneutics (*Wahrheit und Methode*, pp. 172–185). Manfred Frank, however, has attempted to resuscitate Schleiermacher, and part of his argument has involved interrelating hermeneutics, rhetoric, grammar, and dialectic (*Das individuelle Allgemeine*, pp. 160–85).

40. Schleiermacher, *Reden*: "The mere outward appearance has disappeared and the essence is reached; firm is his gaze and bright is his perspective that recognizes beneath all disguises the same thing everywhere, and which comes to rest nowhere except in the infinite and the One. . . . The greatest work of art is that of which mankind forms the raw material and which directly forms (*unmittelbar bildet*) the universal." (p. 96).

41. The subjectivist conception of *Bildung* allowed the term to mean anything and everything that had to do with the individual's sense of self-development as opposed to the outside world. It seems to have lost its significance: "The concept of *Bildung* has, essentially (*sachlich*) as well as linguistically, rather lost its contours . . . and many pedagogues avoid the word completely because it no longer has any unambiguous meaning" (article on *Bildung* in *Religion in Geschichte und Gegenwart*, p. 1277).

turies tended toward the subjective, naturalistic, and inner-visionary. A brief review of this tradition reveals that although the problem of representation and its solution in terms of *Bildung* have been dealt with in literary form, this literary treatment remains but one approach that affects but does not cover Hegel's solution. The comparison between the standard view of *Bildung* from the perspective of the history of the *Bildungsroman* and a rhetorically oriented view should indicate the former's limitations.

Blanckenburg, the first general theorist of the novel genre in Germany, stressed the psychological aspect in his 1774 *Versuch über den Roman* (Essay on the Novel). Although he never used the term *Bildungsroman*, his general definition of the novel as the "inner history" of the "education [and] formation of the hero's character" (*Ausbildung [und] Formung des Charakters*) is based on an interpretation of Christian Martin Wieland's *Agathon*, which is widely accepted as the first *Bildungsroman* for the very reasons given by Blanckenburg.[42] Morgenstern, who is credited with coining the term, sees the *Bildungsroman* as a "philosophical novel," by which he means that it depicts the development of the author.[43] Although this autobiographical and personal element is a standard part of the generic definition, this conception of *Bildung* and the *Bildungsroman* has a difficult time accounting for the strong emphasis on the self-reflective nature of this genre to depict an individual's formative education to socially proper modes of self-representation (commonly artistic writing) since it lacks a historical and systematic understanding of learning as objectivation. Swales points to the tendency in many theorists of the *Bildungsroman* to concentrate almost exclusively on the "personal growth," "inwardness," and "self-understanding" of the hero.[44] It culminates in Thomas Mann's characterization of German culture, *Bildung*, as one of introspection.[45] It is no

42. Selbmann, *Der deutsche Bildungsroman*, p. 9. Martin Swales, *The German Bildungsroman from Wieland to Hesse* (Princeton, N.J.: Princeton University Press, 1978), begins his historical treatment of this genre with Wieland's *Agathon*, as opposed to Goethe's *Wilhelm Meister*.

43. Selbmann (*Der deutsche Bildungsroman*, p. 12) quotes Morgenstern: "With the thesis 'the genuine poet is an absurdity (*Unding*) without the genuine man' (p. 183), Morgenstern shifted the attention from the work to the author. The author as 'the mirror of the entire man' (p. 183) transmits in the novel 'the (hi)story of his own formative education (*Bildung*) and perfection (*Vollendung*)' (p. 193). In his novel one should and can observe the 'cultivating, further development and transformation (*Bearbeitung, Fortbildung, Umbildung*) of the author himself as writer' (p. 183) and see this process reflected in the figure of the hero."

44. Swales, *The German Bildungsroman*, pp. 4, 17.

45. Quoted from a lecture held in 1923; in Walter H. Bruford, *The German Tradition of Self-Cultivation: 'Bildung' from Humboldt to Thomas Mann* (Cambridge: Cambridge Univer-

wonder, then, that *Bildung* has been criticized and has now become largely devalued as a mere product of the Enlightenment and the educated bourgeoisie, the *Bildungsbürger*, as the ideological superstructure of capitalism and its mythology of the individual.

And yet there is another side to *Bildung* which stretches back far beyond the Enlightenment, capitalist origins of the individualistic strand, a conception that opens up broader issues of objective or intersubjective form, education, and representation. *Bildung* has as its primary meaning "education." The large majority of compound words beginning with *Bildung* refer to the sphere of schooling.[46] Although basically synonymous, especially in modern German, with *Erziehung* (a literal translation of "education"), the history and etymology of the concept *Bildung* gives it a different connotation. Its root, *bilden* (to form, give form to, to make), connects *Bildung* to a very special kind of educational process, in fact a discipline, which is not usually mentioned in discussions of the term even though it can be considered the backbone of the Western pedagogical tradition.[47] The discipline that has been responsible for educating a person *to* form by educating him (for this has been an exclusively male sphere) *through* form is rhetoric. For this reason, Quintilian is of such central importance in the development of Western culture and serves as the model in the following discussions of rhetorical *Bildung*. This connection involves not so much the history of the word *Bildung* (although the *Institutio Oratoria* is generally translated into German as the *Ausbildung des Redners*) but, rather, broader conceptual developments in intellectual and pedagogical history.

Quintilian's conception of the "education of the ideal orator" was the most influential structure in European, and even Anglo-American,

---

sity Press, 1975): "The inwardness, the culture ('Bildung') of a German implies introspectiveness; and individualistic cultural conscience; consideration for the careful tending, the shaping, deepening and perfecting of one's own personality or, in religious terms, for the salvation and justification of one's own life; subjectivism in the things of the mind, therefore, a type of culture that might be called pietistic, given to autobiographical confession and deeply personal" (p. viii).

46. In contemporary German, the word most often appears in such pedagogical compounds as *Bildungswesen, Bildungsanstalt, Bildungsministerium*. Rorty opts for the translation "edification," as he writes in *Philosophy and the Mirror of Nature*, "since 'education' sounds a bit flat and *Bildung* a bit too foreign" (p. 360).

47. Swales differentiates *Erziehungsroman* from *Bildungsroman*: "The word *Bildung* implies the generality of culture, the clustering of values by which a man lives, rather than a specifically *educational* attainment" (*The German Bildungsroman*, p. 14). Note that the first part of his definition demonstrates his desire, like mine, to go beyond the subjectivist interpretation of *Bildung*, although the second part goes too far in separating education and *Bildung*.

pedagogy, at least into the nineteenth century, since it made appropriate representation and self-expression both the goal and the means for acquiring and demonstrating knowledge. Oratory, as defined by Quintilian, is essentially linked to *Bildung* since oratory is an "instrument"— "that without which the material cannot be brought into the shape necessary for the effecting of our object" (II, xxi, 24). It is an instrument applied not just to the object of our thought (for that would strictly prioritize the *res*) but also to the orator himself, who must be granted a shape and ability to shape. Even in those periods, places, and thinkers that are characterized by an antirhetorical stance, the interplay between idea and expression, *res* and *verba*, which Quintilian so powerfully codified guided the major institutions of instruction.[48]

If, as we have seen, the principal features, parts, and tasks of the *ars* are outlined in the middle books of the *Institutio Oratoria*, Book x summarizes specifically the pedagogical means of developing the skills of expression. Rhetorical *Bildung*, and after Quintilian all other forms of education, consist in a basic three-step process: rote memorization and application of the rules and *praecepta* (internalization); mastery of the rules and the best *exempla* from the tradition through reading and imitative *exercitium stili* (reworking and "digestion"); independent composition and public declamations in the form of *disputationes* and *controversiae* that lead to dialogues with and emulation of the models (externalization). Only at the end of this process, which requires both hard work and mechanical self-alienation, not simple "originality," could the young orator begin "meditations" on new ideas and solutions to issues. The ideal orator described in Book XII, what in German would be called a *gebildeter Mensch* (a cultivated, well-educated person), is the product of a process of self-formation by means of the acquisition of well-established forms that allow the individual to participate in the public sphere. The individual proves his well-formed *Bildung* by being able to master the art of formulation.

These two strands of *Bildung*—the self-reflexive versus the intersubjective, the introspective versus the formative, the organic versus the mechanical—like the two positions on representation within philoso-

---

48. Genette, "Rhétorique et enseignement," and Barthes, "L'ancien rhétorique," both point to the lasting influence of rhetoric on Western thought through the medium of the school system. Jens, especially in his article for the *Real-Lexikon*, stresses (like Klaus Dockhorn before him) the continued existence of the classical model. Barner traces the impact of Quintilian and the basic tripartite structure of *praecepta*, *exercitatio*, and *imitatio* through the German baroque. Hinderer shows how rhetoric, once it was banned from the political arena in absolutism, took refuge on the pulpit and in the classroom ("Kurze Geschichte der deutschen Rede," in *Über deutsche Literatur und Rede* [Munich: Fink, 1981]).

phy and the two disciplines, philosophy versus rhetoric, underwent numerous conflicts and peculiar combinations in the Western tradition since the seventeenth century, especially in pedagogical theory and practice. Strict oppositions developed, for example, between the philanthropic, pragmatic, and pietistic doctrines on the one hand, with their emphasis on practical studies or religious contemplation, and neohumanists, on the other, with their emphasis on the "conservative," prestructured methods of the Greco-Latin rhetorical tradition. In contrast, major theorists of *Bildung* in the late eighteenth century often strove for uneasy fusions. It has been convincingly argued, for example, that Friedrich Schiller wrote the *Briefe über die ästhetische Erziehung des Menschen* (Letters on the Aesthetic Education of Man), one of the most significant treatises on the inner, aesthetic, subjective *Bildungstrieb*, while he was simultaneously grappling with Quintilian.[49] This other side of Schiller's work grants it intersubjective and political effectiveness. Similarly, Wilhelm von Humboldt, whose pedagogical reforms laid the foundations for the university and, to a large extent, the humanistic *gymnasium* in Germany, brought together the ideals of introspection and civic responsibility, the models of modern romanticism and classical antiquity. Humboldt's theory and practice of *Bildung*, however, largely suffered the same fate as the *Bildungsroman*, since it has been interpreted mostly according to the ahistorical and individualistic tradition, and so his ideas have fallen into disrepute.[50]

These strands are interwoven in Hegel, creating a powerful tension between the rhetorical tradition and the "spirit" of organicity, between a rigorous training handed down from antiquity and a mystifying teleological "force." It is necessary to bring out the mechanistic, liter-

49. Hermann Meyer, "Schillers philosophische Rhetorik," in *Zarte Empirie: Studien zur Literaturgeschichte* (Stuttgart: Metzler, 1963). Elizabeth Wilkinson, "Zur Sprache und Struktur der Ästhetischen Briefe," *Akzente* 6 (1959), 398–418, shows the impact of Schiller's rhetorical training in Quintilian on the argumentative form and tropological formulations of the essay. One could conceive of my study as a combination of Meyer's historical and Wilkinson's analytical treatments, applied to Hegel.

50. Thus, the fascination with Greece, which could be read as a public (rhetorical) response to the dangers of over-subjectivization of *Bildung*, became over the course of the nineteenth century just one more ahistorical adornment of the bourgeoisie. Clemens Menze, in *Bildung und Gesellschaft*, tries to resuscitate Humboldt's ideas by emphasizing the element of "objectification" in the supposedly subjectivist and individualist concept of *Bildung*. Udo Müllges, "Das Verhältnis von Selbst und Sache in der Erziehung, problematisch aufgewiesen bei Basedow, Humboldt, Herbart und Hegel" (Ph.D. diss., Bonn, 1961), stresses the development of the self to individuality in a more negative light, since the self must recognize itself in the objective *Sache* and not opposed to it in a state of supposedly pure individuality (pp. 62–68, 72, 80).

alizing side of Hegel's concept of *Bildung* in order to demonstrate more clearly, sometimes against his explicit pronouncements, how he remains tied to a model of representation taken from the rhetorical model and how he has a more complex solution to representation than mere self-presencing reflection.[51] The solution to the traditional dichotomy within philosophical representation which Hegel develops, namely, his conception of the Spirit's formative development, relies on a dialogue between two disciplines that he had mastered as part of his own traditional rhetorical *Bildung*. This dialogue has long gone silenced and unanalyzed as a result of changes in pedagogy (*Bildung*)—ironically thanks to the reception and rejection of idealism—which have isolated and limited the partners, the spirit from its letter.

51. I thus support Taylor's reading of Hegel as following in the "expressivist" tradition, but find that Taylor, like most other scholars interested in expressivism, limits that tradition to post-Herderian developments. A reading like Taylor's, which wants to go beyond the subjectivist and mimetic theories of reflection and meaning, is supported, I believe, by an analysis of the traditional rhetorical elements in Hegel.

CHAPTER 1

Hegel's Rhetorical *Bildung* in the Stuttgart Gymnasium Illustre

Hegel's most widely quoted statements on the concept of *Bildung* are contained in the speeches he delivered as principal of the Melanchthon Gymnasium in Nuremberg between 1808 and 1815. In those end-of-the-school-year orations, Hegel praises humanistic education, as embodied in the learning of ancient languages, since it leads the students outside of their familiar world so that they might attain the abilities of abstraction and self-reflection.[1] These school speeches are generally considered by their commentators as applications of basic ideas about alienation and knowledge from the *Phenomenology*. And yet they form part of a tradition reaching back far beyond Hegel's efforts in systematic philosophy. Twenty-one years before his first Nuremberg oration, for example, the eighteen-year-old Hegel delivered the valedictory address on the values of education at his own school, the Eberhard-Ludwig Gymnasium (also called Gymnasium Illustre) in Stuttgart, before his fellow students, teachers, and the Duke Karl Eugen of Württemberg. Although his first public declamation in Stuttgart is certainly not as well known and does not contain the extensive philosophical analyses of the later speeches, it does serve to introduce particular features of his education that both implicitly and explicitly influence his philosophical writing and concept of *Bildung*. These features consist of the pedagogical approaches contained in the tradition of *Schul-*

---

1. For a fuller account of these addresses and Hegel's pedagogical theory and practice during his years as principal of the Nuremberg *gymnasium*, see chap. 5, below.

rhetorik as it was handed down through the centuries. This chapter will specify the meaning of both *Bildung* and rhetoric as concrete aspects of the *institutio oratoria* that dominated school instruction.

It is characteristic of the attitude generally shown toward the rhetorical works of the young Hegel that his first biographer, Karl Rosenkranz, saved only the second half of the valedictory speech.[2] From the existing part, however, it is clear that the speech belongs to the genre of laudatory rhetoric, the *genus demonstrativum*, and Rosenkranz remarks on the "ceremonious oratory" with which the pupil praises his school and, by extension, flatters the state and its ruler, who was present in the audience.[3] The first part of the speech has the form of a *refutatio*, for, according to Rosenkranz's summary, it depicted the low state of education under the sultan in Turkey so that on the basis of the negative example of the Turks Hegel can "demonstrate" the close relationship between the state and the quality of education.[4] The young orator closes this standard opening (*exordium* or *prooemium*), which takes on the form of an *enthymeme*, a rhetorical syllogism that draws the audience into the speaker's values, with the pathos-filled conclusion: "So great is the influence of education on the well-being of a state!" (p. 80). The actual *narratio* merely inverts the negative image of life under the Turks with a brief *transitio*—" we, on the contrary . . ."[5] A short *argumentum a maiore ad minus* connects the general principle—"that provi-

2. Karl Rosenkranz, *Hegels Leben* (Berlin, 1844; reprint, Darmstadt: Wissenschaftliche Buchgesellschaft, 1971), pp. 19–21 (with a summary of the first part of the speech). In the following discussion, the speech will be cited from Friedhelm Nicolin, *Der junge Hegel in Stuttgart* (Stuttgart: Kohlhammer, 1976). All page numbers in parentheses in the body of this chapter refer to Nicolin.

3. Rosenkranz, *Hegels Leben*, p. 18. On the *genus demonstrativum*, see Heinrich Lausberg, *Handbuch der literarischen Rhetorik* (Munich: Max Hueber, 1960) pars. 62,3 and 239–54.

4. On *refutatio*, see Lausberg, *Handbuch*, pars. 149 and 902,4.

5. Hegel says: "Looking at this nation we see how striking the dreadful consequences are of having neglected [education]. If we observe the natural abilities of the Turks and then the primitiveness of their character and what they have achieved in the sciences, we will recognize, on the contrary, our great fortune and learn to appreciate it" ("Wie auffallend sehen wir an dieser Nation die schrecklichen Folgen ihrer Vernachlässigung. Betrachten wir die natürlichen Fähigkeiten der Türken und dann die Rohheit ihres Charakters und das, was sie in den Wissenschaften leisten, so werden wir dagegen unser hohes Glück erkennen und würdig schätzen lernen"; Nicolin, *Hegel in Stuttgart*, p. 80). H. S. Harris, *Hegel's Development: Toward the Sunlight, 1770–1801* (Oxford: Clarendon, 1972), considers the possibility that Hegel is speaking ironically here and thereby offering a subtle critique of the duke in the audience (pp. 42ff.). Although that supposition is difficult to demonstrate, it becomes especially interesting when compared to the rhetorical analysis of one of Georg Büchner's school speeches by Gerhard Schaub, *Georg Büchner und die Schulrhetorik* (Bern: Herbert Lang, 1975). Schaub reaches a similar conclusion concerning Büchner's ironic use of school rhetoric against the school.

dence has allowed us to be born in a state whose prince, convinced of the significance of education and of the universal and disseminated use of the sciences, has made both the target of his concern"—to the specific situation: "the most telling demonstration that is so close to us all, the formation of this institution" (p. 80).[6] The closing appeal to the listeners (*peroratio*) rounds out the address with an eightfold variation of gratitude formulas, including a periphrastic *laudatio* of teachers, students, and school, and an edifying look into the future: "and with the gayest serenity may you all face a rewarding and just eternity" (pp. 81–82).[7]

As an isolated document, the Stuttgart valedictory address seems like a mildly amusing but insignificant product of a pedantic schoolboy. The rigid form and bombastic style tend to alienate the modern reader. Considered in the context of Hegel's other writings from the period and of his intellectual surroundings, however, this oration appears as the crowning achievement of an education that had the acquisition and mastery of the rhetorical medium as its main goal. Almost all of Hegel's writings from his years in Stuttgart reveal the young boy's concern with topics and forms from classical and humanistic rhetoric.

Hegel's diary, which he kept during his last years at the *gymnasium* (1785–87), contains a number of rhetorical exercises. The very fact that much of the diary was written in Latin demonstrates the formalistic nature of his composition at this time. The entry from 15 February 1786, for example, demonstrates how such exercises as school orations both motivated and structured his writing. Hegel opens the diary entry by explaining that he wishes to practice writing a Latin speech like the ones delivered every spring at his school (I provide the original for this one entry so that the reader can have a sense of the schoolboy's stylistic endeavor):

> Since it is customary for exercises promoting eloquence to begin in the course of the summer, I shall already prepare myself and sketch out the first [out]lines in this, my diary, so that I shall not be unprepared or have to spend too much time when the time approaches for us to speak and to seek out a topic.

6. The move from general to specific, or vice versa, is just one of the many *loci* that structure arguments parallel to the way tropes structure relations between words and phrases. On *loci argumentorum*, see Lausberg, *Handbuch*, par. 395.

7. The bombastic formulas of gratitude are: *haben zu danken, mit Dankbarkeit zu verehren, unsere Herzen ganz den Gefühlen der Erkenntlichkeit . . . zu überlassen, Dank Ihnen, Dank besonders für . . .* , and *Dank abzustatten*. The art of varying such formulas belongs under the rhetorical categories of *copia et amplificatio verborum*.

Cum soleant per aestatem exercitationes eloquentiae promovendae in-
stitui, ne, si tempus accedat, ut de quo dicamus, aliquid nobis eligamus,
sim imparatus, et ne temporis nimium impendium facere cogar, in hoc
diario me jam praeparem, et primas lineas describam. [p. 51]

It is noteworthy that these yearly exercises in rhetoric promoted eloquence as an end in itself. Hegel wants to prepare himself for the event
by writing out his ideas, even though he does not yet know the topic.
The form of the speech clearly plays a greater role than the content in
this kind of exercise. Such formal training, as he later implies in both
the *Phenomenology* and the Nuremberg speeches, provides him with
mechanistic structures that are perfected in their own right and later
filled with content.

The outline of the practice speech follows closely the rules of traditional *dispositio*, the doctrine of arranging the parts of an address.
Hegel begins with a handbook definition of a prologue: "The prologue
(*prologus*) shall deal (a) with this institution of stylistic exercises (*exercitionum styli*), (b) with material taken quasi from the vicinity of [our]
studies, and which is not too distant from our age and customs; and yet
it should also not be a strictly historical topic, whereby there would be
no place left for one's own reflections" (p. 51).[8] In keeping with the
rules for an *exordium*, Hegel mentions two criteria that determine the
correctness of the opening: The subject matter must be accessible to
the audience and must give the author the opportunity to present his
own position and thoughts. After the introduction and a transition
Hegel arrives at the actual subject, the "matter itself," or in the terms of
his later philosophy, the *Sache selbst*: "Then comes the matter itself (*ipsa
res*), which is to be treated, namely, friendship (*consuetudo*)" (p. 51).
Hegel has chosen an arbitrary theme for his exercise, one that could be
found in Cicero's letters.[9] The *narratio* of this didactic speech begins in
standard fashion with a definition: *sequatur definitio* (p. 51).[10] The middle section consists of the exposition of the central concept using the

8. Hegel's use here of *de instituto hoc exercitionum styli* as an opening recalls the title of
a declamation Hegel wrote in these years: "De utilitate poeseos." Rosenkranz, who still
possessed a copy of the now lost declamation, remarked: "We still have such an essay, *de
utilitate poeseos*, by Hegel, undated and without any remarkable features" (*Hegels Leben*, p.
16). It was common, then, for students to reflect on their own exercises and rhetorical-
poetical activities.

9. *Cassell's Latin-English Dictionary* defines *consuetudo* as "social intercourse, compan-
ionship, familiarity, conversation (freq. and class.; in an honorable sense most freq. in
Cicero)." *Consuetudo* is also a rhetorical category meaning proper (linguistic) usage as
measured by common usage.

10. See Lausberg, *Handbuch*, pars. 89a and 110, on *definitio* as the standard opening
to a factual (legal) speech; and par. 782, on *definitio* as a figure of thought.

traditional means of positive *exempla* ("First I shall speak of the necessity [of *consuetudo*], which has been inserted into us by nature. Then of the advantages, if it is acted upon properly and by the proper persons") and then a *refutatio* of the opposite position through negative examples ("In opposition to this come the harms, if it is not practiced enough or with the proper persons"; p. 52).[11] Since the speech intends to influence the actions of the listeners, there follows a discussion of the tasks and duties of *consuetudo*: "There follow the duties (*officia*) of those who are bound by such friendship" (p. 52).[12] The *narratio* ends with an admonitory call to the audience: "and the little speech (*oratiuncula*) ends with an admonition" (p. 52). Fully aware of the formal and formulaic role dictated by rules of eloquence, Hegel concludes the exercise with a standard epilogue including the commonplaces and topoi of humility, gratitude, flattery, and praise: "The epilogue (*epilogus*) presents (a) a pardon for youth, (b) thanks for this institution made to (1) its creators and (2) those knowledgeable, (c) praise of eloquence (*laus eloquentiae*); and finally the closing formulas (*clausulam*)." Thus, in the diary entry of 15 February 1786, Hegel sketches out his own sample oration and employs a full battery of the *termini technici* of classical rhetoric.

The wider context around this entry reveals that Hegel derived his interest in rhetorical forms from the rhetorical milieu in which he lived and was educated. On 11 February 1786, four days before the sketch of the planned speech, Hegel takes up writing in his diary after a six-week break. He begins by referring to the diary as a "stylistic exercise" and to the fact that it was the duke's birthday: "Let us return to this our institution for the exercise of style (*Redeamus jam ad prisca haec nostra stylo exercendo instituta*), which was interrupted a long time ago, since today was the fifty-ninth birthday of our Most Serene Highness the Duke" (p. 51). The relationship between the renewal of his stylistic exercise and the duke's birthday is not arbitrary. Hegel often mentions in his entries that some social event has motivated him to break a temporary silence. In this case, the celebratory speech that Hegel heard in honor of Duke Karl Eugen's birthday encouraged him to try his hand once again at a rhetorical exercise.[13]

---

11. Here the *exemplum* serves its moral function of a "standard (*Muster*) for ethical conduct." Lausberg, *Handbuch*, pars. 19, 24, 29.

12. The notion of *officia* recalls Cicero as well, for his *De Officia* was one of the most widely read school texts.

13. For some examples of such speeches, see the collection of orations by the *professor eloquentiae* at the Gymnasium Illustre, Balthasar Haug, *Historia Litteraria gymnasii illustris Stuttgardiani*, (Stuttgart, 1786).

Nearly three quarters of the 11 February entry summarizes and analyzes the speech delivered by the director of the *gymnasium*, Professor Schmidlin, in honor of the duke. Hegel isolates the formal components of the address according to standard rhetorical categories: introduction, which states the purpose of the speech as praise of the duke, thereby locating it in the *genus demonstrativum*; exposition, which praises the duke through the various ways he supports the arts and sciences in Württemberg; the closing formulas (*peroratio*), which address the audience (especially the duke and duchess) in more emotional terms (p. 51). Clearly, the rhetorical form of the ceremony impressed Hegel since he ignores the speech's content and concentrates strictly on its compositional subdivision. The formal mechanics of these rhetorical festivities not only attracted Hegel's attention but also stimulated him to imitate, master, and emulate the rhetorical techniques he experienced there. He strove to participate in his oratorical milieu by practicing its forms in his diary.

No critic has dealt extensively with the rhetorical aspect of Hegel's Stuttgart exercises. Karl Rosenkranz mentions its importance only briefly in his general description of the diary: "In any case, however, the diary is proof that Hegel focused mainly on himself. Of course, he did not find anything special in himself and given this lack of experiential material he used the diary for a time in order to perfect his Latin style. Even the description of a fire, which he saw while offering assistance with his father, was utilized as an occasion for a rhetorical showpiece (*zu einem rhetorischen Schaustück*)."[14] However, Rosenkranz does not pursue the young Hegel's rhetorical interests any further. The nineteenth-century and early twentieth-century biographical studies by Haym, Kuno Fischer, and Rosenzweig do little more than cite Rosenkranz on the Stuttgart period.[15] Similarly, Lukács, whose interests in

14. Rosenkranz, *Hegels Leben*, pp. 2–3. This scene of the fire will be dealt with further below.

15. Rudolf Haym, *Hegel und seine Zeit: Vorlesungen über die Entstehung und Entwicklung, Wesen und Werth der Hegel'schen Philosophie* (Berlin, 1857), pp. 24–29. Haym's major contribution to the discussion of Hegel's early period is the treatment of the influences on Hegel's *Bildung* from the two perspectives of *Humanismus* and *Aufklärung*. Hermann Glockner, *Hegels Leben und Werk*, in *Hegels Gesammelte Werke*, vol. 21 (Hamburg: Felix Meiner, 1929), develops the same polarity. See also Franz Rosenzweig, *Hegel und der Staat* (Munich, 1920); Kuno Fischer, *Geschichte der neuen Philosophie*, vol. 8, *Hegels Leben, Werke und Lehre* (Berlin, 1878); Theodor Haering, *Hegel: Sein Wollen und sein Werk—Eine chronologische Entwicklungsgeschichte der Gedanken und Sprache Hegels* (Leipzig: Teubner, 1929–38), esp. pp. 13–32. Haering is most interested in showing how the late Hegel "shines through" in the early works. He is one of the few who deals with Hegel's style, though not in these early years.

the young Hegel lie in the later period of the theological manuscripts, relies on Rosenkranz for the summary of the Stuttgart years.[16] The two most recent and extremely detailed analyses of these earliest writings —Lacorte's *Il primo Hegel* and Harris's *Hegel's Development: Toward the Sunlight*—concentrate exclusively on their content, especially on the emergence of Hegel's views on political philosophy. Harris even explicitly turns his attention away from the rhetorical aspect of the manuscripts with the statement "The *exercitii styli* aspect of the diary is of little interest to us."[17] All studies of Hegel's earliest writing pass over its most striking feature, its concern with issues and forms of classical rhetoric, because modern Hegel scholars fail to place Hegel's oeuvre in Stuttgart within the broader context of *Schulrhetorik* in which it could gain in significance.

Between 1777 and 1786 Hegel attended the Eberhard-Ludwig Gymnasium (Gymnasium Illustre) in Stuttgart, the town of his birth.[18] Like almost every other German *gymnasium*, it began as a Latin school (*Lateinschule,* later called *pädagogium*) associated with the local church. From the founding of the first Stuttgart Latin school in the fourteenth century until the mid-eighteenth the pedagogical goal of the school remained essentially unchanged. That goal was summarized for the

16. Georg Lukács, *Der junge Hegel: Über die Beziehungen von Dialektik und Ökonomie* (Berlin: Leuchterhand, 1948). Lukács deals with Hegel's early interest in and analysis of political economy.

17. Harris, *Hegel's Development*, p. 4. Carmelo Lacorte, *Il Primo Hegel* (Florence: Sansoni, 1959).

18. The following discussion of the Stuttgart *gymnasium* relies heavily on a number of school histories: Gustav Lang, *Geschichte der stuttgarter Gelehrtenschule*, in *Geschichte des humanistischen Schulwesens in Württemberg*, III, II, 1, vol. 3: *Geschichte des altwürttembergischen Gelehrtenschulwesens*, ed. Württembergische Kommission für Landesgeschichte (Stuttgart: Kohlhammer, 1928); Carl Hirzel, *Sammlung der württembergischen Schulgesetze*, pt. 2, containing "Gesetze für die Mittel- und Fachschulen bis zum Jahr 1846," in A. L. Reyscher, *Sammlung der württembergischen Gesetze*, vol. 11, pt. 2 (Tübingen: Fues, 1847); *Herzog Karl Eugen von Württemberg und seine Zeit*, vol. 2, ed. Württembergische Geschichts- und Altertums-Verein (Esslingen: Paul Neff [Max Schreiber], 1909); Reinhold Stahlecker, *Allgemeine Geschichte des Lateinschulwesens und Geschichte der Lateinschulen ob der Steig*, in *Geschichte des altwürttembergischen Gelehrtenschulwesens*, vol. 1, Halbband, *Geschichte der Lateinschulen*, ed. Württembergische Kommission für Landesgeschichte (Stuttgart: Kohlhammer, 1927); *Beiträge zur Geschichte der Erziehung und des Unterrichts in Württemberg*, ed. Gruppe Württemberg der Gesellschaft für deutsche Erziehungs- und Schulgeschichte (Berlin: Hofmann, 1906), esp. F. Raunecker, "Einige Fälle von disziplinuntersuchungen gegen Lehrer an württembergischen Gelehrtenschulen aus dem 18. Jahrhundert"; F. Raunecker, *Beiträge zur Geschichte des Gelehrtenschulwesens in Württemberg im 17. und 18. Jahrhundert*, Prog. des Gymnasiums Ludwigsburg, 1906 and 1907; Paul Würthle, *Zur Geschichte der Gründung des stuttgarter Gymnasiums*, in *Festschrift des Eberhard-Ludwigs-Gymnasiums, 1686–1936* (Stuttgart: Metzler, 1937).

first time in the school ordinance of 1500: "to speak, write, and understand Latin."[19] One slight modification took place under the influence of humanism in the fifteenth and sixteenth centuries. Under the humanists, the emphasis of the pedagogical theory shifted from mere language instruction in the service of the church to the propagation of the Greco-Roman ideal of the *ars bene et sapiente dicendi*. But this modification hardly undermined the basic orientation of the school. On the contrary, the change introduced by humanism provided the late medieval goals of the school with a more solid ideological and philosophical foundation in the older tradition of classical rhetoric.

Certainly the most significant contribution and consequence of the humanist influence was the introduction of Melanchthon's handbooks on grammar, rhetoric, and dialectic, which followed the training of an orator as depicted in Cicero's and Quintilian's writings. In particular, Melanchthon's *Elementorum Rhetorices Libri Duo* structured the curriculum of the *Lateinschule* from the sixteenth century on.[20] This schematic presentation of the classical rhetorical principles embodied the goal of humanist pedagogy, namely mastery of Roman eloquence and style. In the words of the historian of language instruction in Germany, Horst Frank: "The mastery [of Ciceronian Latin] was the sign of all formal education (*gelehrten Bildung*), and thus impeccable eloquence was the highest educational goal (*Bildungsziel*) of the academically oriented

19. The wording of the founding order is: "And so to speak, write, and understand Latin is a keystone, a foundation, and a way, without which students would not prevail and attain competence in other arts. Therefore, the schoolmaster together with his aides should strive actively, with proper and good diligence, to see that each and every student learns to read, write, and understand Latin, and that they, both in the school and in other areas, whenever they are together, converse with one another in Latin, so that each might practice it and attain fluency" ("Unnd so lateinisch reden, schryben unnd versteen ein grundtuestin, fundament unnd wege ist, one den die schuler annder kunsten nit wol erlangen unnd uberkomen mogent, So soll der Schulmaister mitsampt seinen helffern daran unnd darobe sein mit gepurlichem gutem flysse das die Schuler alle unnd jeder besonder, lernet latin reden, schryben unnd versteen, unnd in der schulle unnd an anndern ennde, wa sie byainannder syent in lateinischer sprache mitainannder redent, damit ain jeder des in ubung kom unnd vertig werde"; Lang, *Gelehrtenschute*, p. 7).

The origins of the school go back to the religious Stift and so the very first functions of the school were also musical and liturgical instruction. In the fifteenth century the school separated from the church and came under the official auspices of *vogt und gericht* (Lang, *Gelehrtenschule*, p. 3).

On the *Lateinschule* in Germany, see Horst Joachim Frank, *Dichtung, Sprache, Menschenbildung: Geschichte des Deutschunterrichts von den Anfängen bis 1945* (Munich: DTV, 1976).

20. Philipp Melanchthon, *Elementorum Rhetorices Libri Duo* (1519); this was followed in 1524 by a revised version (*Institutiones Rhetorices*) and at least five other editions of the *Libri Duo* over the next decades. Key elements of this handbook will be discussed below.

schools."[21] Not only did Melanchthon's significant handbook go through numerous editions but it was also radically revised in the sixteenth century by Martin Crusius, who tripled the size of the original text by adding his own explanatory questions and answers to every chapter so that the text could be more readily used in Württemberg schools.[22]

The humanist image of the ideal orator continued to influence the principles of the school in 1686, when the *pädagogium* was extended to a full *gymnasium*.[23] In fact, the new school was based on the model of humanist rhetorician Johannes Sturm's *gymnasium*, founded in Strassburg in 1569. Sturm defined the *gymnasium* as a "middle step, which brings, on the one hand, the study of grammar to completion and prepares, on the other, for study at the university. We have chosen this middle stage, in which we will complete the course of study in part through more precise knowledge of languages and in part through a treatment of the parts of philosophy, namely, rhetoric, dialectic, topic, analytics, mathematics, or geography."[24] In Stuttgart, especially during the age of the baroque, this course of study (*Kursus*) involved mastery of the styles of the ancients in all genres—*stylus philosophicus* (Cicero), *historicus* (Sallust or Justinus), and *poeticus* (Virgil).[25]

---

21. Frank, *Deutschunterricht*, p. 19. Lang summarizes the methods of the school under humanism as follows: "The method is the traditional one: *lectio, repetitio, exercitium*. Exercitium consists in interpretation, declensions, construction (*Konstruieren*), and translation from Latin into German and back again. In the process the main attention [in the lower classes] is directed toward grammar. In dialectics and rhetoric prevails the learning by heart of rules, without applying the rules and working them through. . . . Once a week a difficult German *argumentum* is dictated for translation into Latin" (p. 31).

22. Philipp Melanchthon, *Elementorum Rhetorices Libri Duo*; Martin Crusius, *Questionibus et Scholiis explicati in Academia Tybingensi—Adiectis aliquot epistolis et carminibus, a Rhetorice studio non alienis* (Basel, 1563). I shall quote below from this edition (Melanchthon-Crusius), which exerted a major influence in the Stuttgart *gymnasium*.

23. The founding date of the *gymnasium* is 13 September 1686. The plan to create a full, ten-class school was the idea of Duke Friedrich Karl, the guardian of the heir apparent, Eberhard Ludwig (after whom the school was named). The school also received the name Gymnasium Illustre after the motto above the doors: "Illustre pietatis et liberalium artium gymnasium." The structural shift from *pädagogium* to *gymnasium* affected the school through the eighteenth century. The "lower" *gymnasium* remained quite distinct from the "upper" grades: "The older *pädagogium* was integrated into the new institute as 'lower *gymnasium*,' but it retained for a long time its older name, at least in informal usage. Up to Hegel's time and beyond, a deep-lying, inner structural difference corresponded to the external designations of grade level 'lower' and 'upper' *gymnasium*." Nicolin, *Hegel in Stuttgart*, p. 11.

24. Quoted from Lang, *Gelehrtenschule*, p. 148.

25. The three styles make up the curriculum of the last grades around 1700. The goal of the school remained, according to Lang, "The thorough schooling in the written and oral usage of scholarly Latin" (*Gelehrtenschule*, p. 147).

The conservatism of the school authorities in Württemberg allowed only one pedagogical method in the Stuttgart Eberhard-Ludwig Gymnasium, the rhetorical course of instruction: memorization of formal *praecepta* and *imitatio* of canonical *exempla*. Although in the words of Germanist Wilfried Barner, this "anchoring" (*Verankerung*) of humanist ideas about rhetoric in the education curriculum is common to much of the baroque, since the "main emphasis lay unequivocally on the learning of Latin and the guidance to eloquence," the literal conservatism in Württemberg was even more extreme than elsewhere thanks to the hundred-year domination of one handbook in language instruction, Christoph Kaldenbach's *Compendium Rhetorices*, which replaced Melanchthon's in the mid-seventeenth century.[26] Kaldenbach was one of the most popular and prolific writers of the Swabian baroque and the reign of his textbook, as Barner points out, was both extensive and profitable: "A quarter century after its first appearance, a legal conflict was sparked over a planned reproduction (1707) between the original publisher in Tübingen, Reis, and the Stuttgart bookdealer, Metzler; school books were even back then a particularly profitable business. New editions can be documented for 1709, 1732, and 1765. For 1774, Bök (Professor of Eloquence, Tübingen) confirms . . . that Kaldenbach's textbook, 'with the necessary additions and improvements,' is still used in Württemberg."[27] The *Compendium*, as well as Kaldenbach's numerous collections of speeches and debates (*problemata* and *disputa-*

26. Wilfried Barner, *Barockrhetorik* (Tübingen: Max Niemeyer, 1970), pp. 244, 283. Barner stresses the model provided by Christian Weise's revitalization of Cicero's and Quintilian's ideal public orator. He also indicates why rhetoric was of specific import in the *gymnasium* as a "middle stage" or preparation for the university: "In no area of study is the orientation toward the university as evident as in rhetoric" (p. 263). In other words, the expansion of the Stuttgart school was done in the spirit of rhetorical training. This training meant imitation of the ancients: "Cicero, Horace, Virgil, and Ovid were the models with whose help the progression to one's own *imitatio* was accomplished" (p. 352).

Christophorus Caldenbachius, *Compendium Rhetorices*, Issu Serenissimi Domini Administrationis, etc. Pro Scholis in Ducati Wirtembergio Adoratum, cum grata et privilegio Ducali (Tübingen: 1682).

Actually, between Melanchthon's and Kaldenbach's handbooks, a watered down, erotematic version of Melanchthon was used: Johann Hauber, *Erotemata rhetorices*, Pro Scholis Ducatus Wirtembergici (Stuttgart, 1651).

27. Wilfried Barner, *Christoph Kaldenbach: Auswahl aus seinem Werk*, (Tübingen: Max Niemeyer, 1977), p. li. Kaldenbach was born in Schwiebus in Lower Silesia. In 1656 he was called to the position of *professor eloquentiae, poesos et historiarum* in Tübingen. He delivered a speech, "De Regno Eloquentiae," upon taking the position. Besides teaching, he also delivered and published numerous rhetorical pieces (*orationes, problemata, dispositiones*, and *disputationes*). During the late seventeenth century he exerted a tremendous influence on the school system in Württemberg as pädagogarchia, that is, as director of schools in the region (*ob der Staig*). As Barner comments on Kaldenbach, it made sense to appoint a rhetorician to such a high pedagogical post: "Precisely because instruction at the *gymnasium* culminates in the educational ideal (*Bildungsideal*) of *eloquentia*, it is obvious

tiones), contributed greatly to the tendency in Württemberg to resist the influences of realism (from Locke, Montaigne, Raticius, or Comenius) at this crucial period of the founding of the *gymnasium*.[28]

Through the eighteenth century—until Hegel's graduation—the "conservative" forces in Stuttgart, especially the Protestant school authorities (the *Konsistorium*), struggled against those who attempted to introduce new ideas and methods from the north German Enlightenment, in particular against the initiatives of the Catholic Duke Karl Eugen (1731–94).[29] Under the influence of the Pietist August Hermann Francke from Halle and the "philanthropical" movement,[30] for example, the director Vitus Weihenmajer (1732–46) had proposed more instruction in German and such *Realien* as mathematics and geography. His efforts proved to be in vain, however, since his successor, Georg Adam Göriz (1746–61), turned back the clock concerning pedagogical approaches. The school experienced, in the words of its historian Gustav Lang, "a return to, indeed below, the state of 1686."[31] As a reaction against such archconservatism of the religious authorities

that, above all, the holders of the chairs in humanities must have been brought in to such offices" (p. xlviii).

28. On these more "progressive" pedagogical movements, see Friedrich Paulsen, *Geschichte des gelehrten Unterrichts auf den deutschen Schulen und Universitäten vom Ausgang des Mittelalters bis zur Gegenwart* (Berlin: de Gruyter, 1921); Josef Dolch, *Lehrplan des Abendlandes: Zweieinhalb Jahrtausende seiner Geschichte* (Ratingen: Henn, 1959); Gerhard Reich, *Mutterlicher Grammatikunterricht von der Antike bis um 1600* (Weinheim: Beltz, 1972); and Manfred Heubaum, *Geschichte des deutschen Bildungswesens seit der Mitte des 17. Jahrhunderts*, vol 1: Bis zum Beginn der allgemeinen Bildungsreform unter Friedrich dem Großen, 1763 (Berlin: Weidmann, 1905).

29. This struggle had concrete religious and political causes. The duke, Karl Eugen, was Catholic, and the religious authorities running the school were Protestant. Although Karl Eugen could be considered one of the more progressive leaders in terms of his pedagogical ideas, he was unable to introduce them into the school system: "And yet, precisely under his rule, the higher levels of education sank into complete backwardness and ossification." *Karl Eugen und seine Zeit*, p. 155.

30. Francke served as head of the *pädagogium* in Halle between 1702 and 1720. His pedagogical principles are summarized by Horst Frank in *Deutschunterricht*: "In the Pietist pedagogy of August Hermann Francke the ideal of a piety stamped by the life experiences of the individual is joined with the demand to be at the same time an individual and a useful member of the whole. For the piety of the devout person in the world is seen in his occupying himself for the common good" (p. 78). As Reinhard Breimeyer points out, precisely this emphasis on the public sphere allowed the Pietists to appropriate parts of traditional rhetoric. See "Die Erbauungsstunde als Forum pietistischer Rhetorik," in Helmut Schanze, *Rhetorik: Beiträge zu ihrer Geschichte in Deutschland vom 16.-20. Jahrhundert* (Frankfurt: Athenäum-Fischer, 1974), pp. 87–105.

It is difficult to establish the influence of pietism on the Stuttgart *Gymnasium*. Swabian Pietism was in general very powerful, but the conservative *Konsistorium* attempted to purge it from the schools. See, e.g., the report reprinted by Raunecker on the case raised against the preceptor Spindler because of his Pietist leanings.

31. Lang, *Gelehrtenschule*, p. 230.

running the *gymnasium*, the at least pedagogically (though by no means politically and socially) more liberal-minded Duke Karl Eugen started his own military academy outside of town, the *hohe Karlsschule*. But the duke's decision to found a second school only increased the power of the Protestant *Konsistorium* in the *gymnasium*. As a historian of the reign of Karl Eugen writes, the religious authorities now had a free hand: "Thus, the church authorities, undisturbed from above, could direct the school at its own discretion, and it did this in the strict conservative spirit that was typical of these authorities."[32] Inside the *gymnasium*, "instruction in philosophy was limited predominantly to the mechanical transmission of definitions and rule of dialectics and rhetoric."[33]

The tensions between the conservatives running the *gymnasium* and contemporary, progressive pedagogical movements in other parts of Germany—like north German neohumanism, pietism, and philanthropism—grew under the directorship of Johann Christian Volz (1774–83). During these first years of Hegel's study at the Gymnasium Illustre,[34] criticisms were raised by visiting pedagogues in the name of the "modern taste," the "the spirit (*Genius*) of the present time," and the "edification of the heart [spirit or character, *Bildung des Herzens*]." Furthermore, Karl Eugen's academy moved directly into the city of Stuttgart, thereby increasing the competition between the schools and their methods. New ideas for teaching Latin, German, and the sciences were in the air. And yet: "The *Konsistorium* wanted to have as little to do with the neohumanism of a [Matthias] Gesner as with the pietism of an A. H. Francke. The impulses therefore remained for the meantime without success."[35]

The curriculum in fact remained essentially unchanged for the entire eighteenth century. As in 1724, Latin continued in 1781 to take up eleven and eight of the twenty-five weekly hours in the last two years of

---

32. *Karl Eugen und seine Zeit*, p. 155.

33. Stahlecker, *Geschichte des Lateinschulwesens*, p. 102. As an example of the conservatism, Göriz's curriculum, submitted in 1750, stressed nothing but memorization and repetition in the lower classes. For example, in the fourth grade: "*Sacra*: repetition of the learned material; . . . *vocabularium* repeat [through] six or seven times; . . . of the *Proverbia*, a few sheets are to be learned by heart" (Lang, *Gelehrtenschule*, p. 226–28). One school historian says of Göriz's 1750 curriculum: "One can see that this plan found the approval of the *Konsistorium* for it did not make the least concession to the demands of the time. Religion and Latin are the major subjects, ranked above all others; next to these only Greek, Hebrew, logic, and rhetoric enjoy any attention." *Karl Eugen und seine Zeit*, p. 165.

34. It is still unknown exactly when Hegel started school in Stuttgart, but it was probably in 1776–77. See Nicolin, *Hegel in Stuttgart*, p. 18.

35. *Karl Eugen und seine Zeit*, p. 166.

instruction respectively.[36] The Latin lessons continued to include instruction in rhetoric and letterwriting. The list of classical authors read in the last grade continued to represent the traditional division into philosophical, oratorical, epistolary, historical, and poetical styles: "in [grade] VII *Cic. orationes* 3 [hours], *Cic. epistolae* 1 [hour], *de officiis* 2 [hours], *Sallustius* 1 [hour], *Vergilius* 1 [hour], *Chrestomatia Pliniana* (C. Plini Secundi Historia naturalis in Gesner's selection) 1 [hour]."[37] Significantly, all subjects—ethics, philosophy, natural history—were taught on the basis of classical texts and hence traditional rhetorico-philological methods. This is not to say that there were absolutely no changes in the theory and practice of instruction. For example, in the third quarter of the eighteenth century Kaldenbach's *Compendium* was finally replaced by the work of Göttingen Neohumanist Johann August Ernesti, the *Initia Doctrinae Solidoris* (Elements of Firmer Knowledge), with five parts for instruction in metaphysics, dialectics, ethics, politics, and physics, and an extensive appendix, the *Initia Rhetorica*.[38] A rationally based, modern conception of rhetoric had now found its way into the school. A similar sign of north German influence can be found in Hegel's diary entry of 1 January 1786 (p. 50), in which he mentions receiving a new book, Johann Gerhard Scheller's *Compendium Praeceptorum Styli Bene Latini in primis Ciceroniani, seu Eloquentiae Latine Declarandae* (Compendium of Precepts of Good Latin Style, Foremost Ciceronian, or Explanations of Latin Eloquence).[39] Though this text was not used in classroom instruction, it was, like so many other books, given or at least recommended to Hegel by one of his teachers and it guided him in all his writings.

Moreover, a number of teachers, most noteworthy of whom were Balthasar Haug, F. Lebret, Heinrich Cless, and Johann Löffler, taught in both the *gymnasium* and the duke's military academy and so were aware of the progressives' criticism of older methodologies.[40] Their

36. See Lang, *Gelehrtenschule*, pp. 207–8, for the curriculum (*Vorlesungsplan*) of 1724, and p. 268 for that of 1781.

37. Ibid., p. 268.

38. The full *Initia Doctrinae solidoris* was published in Leipzig in 1750, 1758, 1769, 1776, and 1796. The Appendix, *Initia Rhetorica*, was also published as a separate text after 1784. It is likely that the larger version was used in Stuttgart since both philosophy (dialectic) and rhetoric were taught from Ernesti's handbook. See Haug, *Historia Litteraria gymnasii illustris Stuttgardiani*, p. 112.

39. Immanuel Iohannes Gerhard Scheller, *Compendium Praeceptorum Styli Bene Latini in primis Ciceroniani, seu Eloquentiae Latine declarandae* (Leipzig: 1780, 1785, 1794). I shall quote from the third edition.

40. On Haug, see below. Cless and Löffler both taught religion and philosophy (both of which were also part of instruction in Latin) and had much personal contact with the young Hegel. See Nicolin, *Hegel in Stuttgart*, pp. 18–19, 112.

"reforms" were undoubtedly like those proposed by Frederick the Great to his education minister, Zedlitz, in a letter in 1779:

> Since it has come to my attention that rhetoric and logic are either not taught in schools or are being taught poorly, even though these are excellent and extremely necessary matters that every person of every class must know and that should form the foundation of young people's education, for whoever can reason well will always succeed better than someone who draws false *conséquences*: Thus I wish to make my specific intention known to you: Concerning rhetoric, Quintilian must be translated into German and instructed in all schools; the young pupils must be instructed in providing their own *traductions* and *discourses* according to Quintilian's method, so that they learn how to comprehend things properly. [French in the original][41]

A comment from a report by some outside authorities who visited the Stuttgart *gymnasium* in 1781 gives an example of the kind of "improvements" that had been introduced. The students in the upper classes were to write compositions and speeches as practical training: "Assigning the *auditoribus* of the sixth and seventh classes their own compositions, especially in German, is a praiseworthy innovation; in addition, soon some Latin and some German speeches, letters, and essays will be composed."[42] Of course, this "innovation" was nothing but an implicit *return* to the traditional rhetorical *exercitatio*, as prescribed by Quintilian, and after him the "enlightened" Frederick, for the maturing orator.

Balthasar Haug (1731–92), who taught Ernesti's book to Hegel in courses on Latin, German, style, rhetoric, and philosophy, would have known how to mediate between north German Enlightenment pedagogy and the Swabian oratorical tradition of Melanchthon and Kaldenbach. He held a joint appointment at the duke's *Karlsschule* and the Gymnasium Illustre, delivered his first major public address on a topic uniting south and north ("Melanchthon's Honor in Tübingen and Wittemberg"), and was a dominant figure in Swabian arts and letters

41. Quoted from Paulsen, *Geschichte des gelehrten Unterrichts*, vol. 2, p. 74. Paulsen goes on to make the connection between the enlightened reforms and the classical rhetorical ideal explicit: "His [Frederick's] ideal of *Bildung* for an educated man can be designated with the old word *eloquence*: proper, well-ordered, tasteful speech is the mark of the educated (*gebildeten*) man. Three things are necessary to teach this art, and they are, as they were once designated: *praeceptum, exemplum, imitatio*."

42. Lang, *Gelehrtenschule*, p. 263. Similarly, Lebret wanted to introduce compositions and declamations as an "innovation." The visiting authorities wrote of him in 1781: "He [Lebret] desires that in addition to verbal and practical methods (*Verbal- und Realmethode*) and composition, exposition be practiced as well, and that German as well as Latin, penmanship as well as spelling, be practiced" (Lang, p. 281).

thanks to books like *Der Zustand der schönen Wissenschaften in Schwaben* (The State of Belles Lettres in Swabia; 1762).[43] His basic positions can best be presented in his own words. I shall quote him at length since he, more than any other individual, determined the course and principles of instruction during Hegel's school years in Stuttgart.

Haug formulated his views on the significance of rhetoric in education and public life in a series of theses for a public examination at the Karlsschule in 1779:

xxiv: The language of persuasion [conviction, *die Sprache der Überzeugung*] is stronger than all proofs.

xxvi: Written style belongs to *belles lettres* since it is a branch of rhetoric.

xxvii: Rhetoric is the art of combining beauty and pleasantness with clarity, emphasis, and thoroughness in every oral or written presentation.

xxviii: No course of instruction is as indispensable and beneficial to the public in all aspects of life, in all duties and classes, as that in good written and oral presentation.

xxxi: No science is as completely worked out as the theory of rhetoric or oratory.

xlviii: As much emphasis should be placed on the mechanics of language (*an dem Mechanischen der Sprache*) as on the beauty of presentation.[44]

Concerning the significance of rhetoric in actual classroom instruction, Haug makes abundantly clear that all disciplines should conform to the rhetorical approach of memorization of *praecepta* and *exempla, exercitationes* in the form of *imitatio*, and stylistic independence through *aemulatio*. The result of such instruction is an individual who has mastered public discourse:

The teachers of rhetoric might be at any time great men; but their pupils should also become great. One begins with ethics, the doctrines

43. The address was delivered before the Julius Carls Hohe Schule in Helmstädt on Melanchthon's two hundredth birthday (1760). Haug's *Zustand der schönen Wissenschaften in Schwaben* (Ulm, 1762) presents his perspective of the status and goals of contemporary literary and intellectual culture. The classical and humanist rhetorical ideal remains central. Later he gives a detailed account, including rough statistics, of the state of education and culture: *Versuch einer Berechnung des wissenschaftlichen Zustandes von Württemberg im Verhältniss gegen Teutschland* (Stuttgart, 1774).

44. *Säzze des Professor Haugen über Teutsche Sprache, Schreibart und Geschmack,* zu der in der höchsten Gegenwart seiner Herzoglichen Durchlaucht, den 4. Dezember, darinnen vorzunehmenden öffentlichen Prüfung seiner Zuhörer in der Herzogl. Militair Akademie (Stuttgart, 1779). Schiller was one of the respondents and Hermann Meyer points out the influence of such rhetorical dicta on Schiller in "Schillers philosophische Rhetorik," in *Zarte Empirie* (Stuttgart: Metzler, 1963), pp. 337–89.

of religion, philosophy, histories; then one has one pupil after the other read the proposition of rhetoric; and after he has read one, he speaks extemporaneously, applying it to [the topic of] war, a historical event, or whatever the teacher assigns, first in simple then in complex periods, whereby he attaches two, three, or four examples of disgrace, common good, etc.; the students take turns, continue, speak briskly, even if they make mistakes, and at the end they can be corrected. Would that not make courageous, fluent, and well-spoken people out of them? Such a person can afterward become whatever he wants, but at least he can speak well and the world can use him.[45]

And finally, concerning the process that goes on in the student, what Hegel later calls the *Bildung des Individuums*, Haug adopts the traditional position according to which the pupil not only learns "things" but, more important, internalizes the judgments and structures offered by the teachers of exemplary texts: "The professor of poetry and rhetoric must already be in our head, who then tells us: That is beautiful, that is true, that comparison is appropriate, that conclusion holds, this thought is sublime, that is common."[46]

These passages indicate the principles that guided Hegel's instruction in every discipline. They can be summarized as the memorization and exercise of *praecepta* in order to attain a mastery of stylistic

45. Haug, *Zustand*, pp. 60–61. Haug stresses exercises in reading, comprehension and reformulation of given texts in order to make students "more practiced and astute" (*geübter und scharfsinniger*; p. 46). He goes on to criticize the concrete situation in the classroom for not providing the necessary foundation in rhetorical skills: "The young man begins to write. He writes a poem, he attempts a speech, but he does not allow anyone to see them. He is ashamed, for he still makes mistakes; he is afraid, because either his work is too cheerful, or else his teacher is too gloomy. Finally, he submits his work. It is read. The mistakes are crossed out. It is not made better, he is not told the reason. The beautiful parts are allowed to remain, but are not praised. No discussion of rules is made at all. In the end he is advised not to make too much of these insignificant things." From this description and Haug's reaction to the situation, one can assume that he would have encouraged Hegel's first efforts at *exercitii stili*. In the spirit of classical *exercitationes* (e.g., as described by Quintilian in Book x of the *Institutio Oratoria*) Haug says: "It is practice and not the prescribing (*Vorschrifft*) and explaining of rules that can make one eloquent (*beredt machen*)" (*Zustand*, p. 60).

Moreover, Haug criticizes the public declamations not because they are outmoded, but because they are not held often enough: "The exercises in speaking (*Rede-Übungen*) in the lower and higher schools do not deserve this name. The only times that they are held are either at a ceremony or congratulatory celebration, or when young people are being examined, or when they transfer from one school to another, or when they graduate" (*Zustand*, p. 60). These are precisely the events recorded with such great interest by the young Hegel.

46. Haug, *Zustand*, p. 22. For Haug, the internalization of rhetoric was the main task of the schools: "Whatever background in rhetoric a young man does not bring with him to the university, at least in terms of precepts and terminology, he will not learn there since it is assumed as a prerequisite" (*Zustand*, p. 60).

decorum modeled on past masters so that the student can enter the public sphere.[47] In the eighteenth century, then, Hegel's school resembled its earlier condition under humanism and baroque rhetorical theory rather than a modern Enlightenment institution. Although certain features of neohumanist, Enlightenment (philanthropic), and pietist pedagogy did seep into the Gymnasium Illustre, the school continued to uphold the ideals and methods of its founding periods. Even when the school adopted more modern movements, it abstracted only their conservative, rhetorical core. Thus, although Hegel grew up at a time of conflicting approaches to pedagogy, most of which explicitly criticized the age-old mechanical methods of rhetorical training, his own school rested firmly on its humanist and baroque foundation. Hegel's education, not only in Latin and German but in all the liberal arts, took place in the midst of "flourishing eloquence."[48]

To gain a more precise idea of what was understood under the notion of "rhetorical *Bildung*," that is, under the rhetorical education that Hegel himself received, we can investigate the rhetorical handbooks that influenced the pedagogical program of the Stuttgart *gymnasium*. The basic goals of the rhetorical pedagogical program can be broken down into three aspects: (1) stylistic mastery as dictated in the task or *officium* of *elocutio*; (2) the hermeneutics of tradition building as presented in theories of *imitatio* and *exercitatio*; (3) critical dialectics and argumentative strategy as expounded in the "topics" (*topica*) of *inventio* and in the *ars disputandi*. Since Hegel grew up under the influence of these basic rhetorical pedagogical principles, to become "educated" *gebildet* meant for him, in keeping with the tradition, to master the forms of the written tradition critically and systematically in these three ways.

Stylistic Mastery through Elocutio. The handbooks used for instruction

47. Haug emphasizes the public sphere and connects it explicitly to the classical ideal orator. He decries the banning of rhetoric to schools (Gérard Genette's term is *rhétorique restreinte*) since it makes it more difficult to train little Ciceros: "This art has unfortunately been exiled to the schools. And it appears that our present state of affairs [constitutions, *Verfassungen*] is (are) no longer capable of producing such great men [as a Cicero]" (*Zustand*, p. 28–29). This connection between rhetoric and the ethical-political, already made by Cicero in *De Oratore*, recurs in such works as Adam Müller's 1812 *Zwölf Reden über die Beredsamkeit* (Frankfurt am Main: Suhrkamp, 1967) and Herder's "Haben wir deutsche Ciceronen? und Sollen wir Ciceronen auf der Kanzel haben?" in *Von einigen Nachbildungen der Römer, Sämmtliche Werke*, vol. 1, ed. B. Suphan (Berlin, 1877). This connection explains, I believe, Hegel's emphasis throughout his life on both the ethical and linguistic milieu.

48. In a speech given at the centennial celebration of the *gymnasium*, Haug proudly called attention to the revitalization of the rhetorical tradition in Stuttgart with the phrase *Eloquentiae initia florent* (*Historia Litteraria*, vol. 4, pp. 110–24; also quoted in Lang, *Gelehrtenschule*, p. 271). It is likely that Hegel was present in the audience.

in rhetoric at the Stuttgart Gymnasium Illustre demonstrate a gradual tendency toward what Gérard Genette calls a *rhétorique restreinte* (reduced or restricted rhetoric).[49] That is, the rhetorical systems, which began in the classical Roman spirit of the five equal "tasks"—*inventio, dispositio, elocutio, memoria,* and *pronuntiatio* or *actio*—become increasingly limited to the *officium* of *elocutio.* The handbooks come to focus more and more on the specifically rhetorical aspect of rhetoric, namely, theories of tropes and figurative language for expressing thoughts. This trend is clear even from the basic subdivisions of the textbooks. Melanchthon's 1519 *Elementorum Rhetorices Libri Duo* (Two Books of the Elements of Rhetoric)—as well as the 1563 amended version by Crusius—is divided more or less equally into two parts, the first for the first two tasks, the second for the remaining three. In Kaldenbach's 1682 *Compendium,* however, the tasks of *inventio* and *dispositio* receive brief treatment—in fifteen and ten pages, respectively—whereas *elocutio* (which has subsumed the other tasks) takes up over seventy pages. For Ernesti, the system is even simpler, since it consists of only two parts, *inventio* and *elocutio,* the latter of which is considerably more extensive.

A final, significant development takes place in Scheller's *Compendium Praeceptorum,* in which *elocutio* is replaced by the concept of *stylus.* Before Scheller the word *style* rarely appeared in the other handbooks, and so he must justify his use of the term. Etymologically, he explains, *style* suggests the instrument for writing on wax tablets; by metonymy, the term designates the act of writing itself. The derivation is important for Scheller, since it should be used to refer to the rhetoric of writing, whereas the older term *elocutio* is reserved for oral speech: "Style and *elocutio* are for us today almost the same, and differ only insofar as the former pertains to writing, the latter to speaking, i.e., the former strives to explicate a topic in writing, the latter by speaking."[50] In modern times, then, the traditional study of *elocutio* must be reevaluated, "transferred" (*quodam modo transferri*) in order to do justice to the domination of writing. From this we see that the "restriction" of rhetoric to *elocutio* and then to style brings with it a corresponding increase in the scope and significance of this task.

Despite the shifts in emphasis, *elocutio* contains throughout the rhetorical tradition a constant core of definitions. The task of rhetorical *elocutio* is to "clothe" ideas in language. In Melanchthon's definition,

<hr />

49. Gérard Genette, "La rhétorique restreinte," in *Figures* I (Paris: Editions du Seuil, 1969).
50. Scheller, *Compendium,* pp. 1–2.

elocutio becomes identical with rhetoric itself: "Rhetoric, in truth, adds *elocutio*, like clothing" (*Rhetorica vero addit elocutionem, quasi vestitum*).[51] This image of the "clothing" of thoughts by *elocutio* persists down to Hegel's notions of the Spirit's *Einkleidung* or *Einhüllung* (fitting out or veiling) in various *Gestaltungen* (forms, formations, formulations; *Phenomenology*, p. 32). For Kaldenbach *elocutio* is "the proper accommodation of words and formulations to prediscovered and arranged thoughts" (*elocutio est idoneorum verborum et sententiarum ad res inventas et dispositas accommodatio*).[52] In a German version of his textbook on imitating Ciceronian style, Scheller returns to the humanist topos: "The thought is the body, the expression the clothing" ("Der Gedanke ist der Körper, der Ausdruck das Kleid").[53]

For all these rhetoricians, the "clothing" takes place by means of the four "master" tropes—metaphor, metonymy, synecdoche, and irony. A discussion of these four means of giving expression to thoughts can be found in every rhetorical handbook. Scheller's concise definitions reflect the others: Metaphor is the "translation or transference (*translatio*) of ideas to something similar";[54] metonymy is the "translation or transference of ideas to something connected or bordering";[55] synecdoche is the "translation or transference of ideas to something more narrowly associated with them";[56] and irony is the "alteration or substitution (*commutatio*) of contrary words."[57] These means of "translation" contribute to the larger objective of *elocutio*, the *copia, amplificatio et variatio verborum* (copiousness, ampflication, and variation of words) which can develop a single thought by transforming it from single expressions, through shorter and longer expositions of an idea (*sententiae* and *chriae*), to a rich fullness of extended images. From the point of view of *elocutio*, rhetorical *Bildung* consists in the ability both to produce and to appreciate the richness of expressive forms available to the mind.

Given the emphasis placed on *elocutio* as the specifically rhetorical

51. Melanchthon-Crusius, *Libri Duo*, chap. iii, p. 41.
52. Kaldenbach, *Compendium* (1682), p. 25.
53. Scheller, *Anleitung, die alten lateinischen Schriftsteller philologisch und kritisch zu erklären und den Cicero gehörig nachzuahmen* (Halle, 1783; 1st ed., 1770), p. 340. Consider also the wording of part (*Abschnitt*) vii, chapter 4: "On the Imitation of Cicero in Skillful Treatment and Clothing of Individual as Well as Several Thoughts" ("Von der Nachahmung des Cicero in geschickter Behandlung und Einkleidung sowohl einzelner als mehrere Gedanken").
54. Scheller, *Compendium*, pp. 107ff.
55. Ibid., pp. 114ff.
56. Ibid., pp. 122ff.
57. Ibid., pp. 138ff.

aspect of rhetoric (since it deals with the figurative use of language), these theorists and pedagogues spend considerable effort justifying the function and even necessity of this task. Here we encounter the paradox of the rhetorical concept of representation, a paradox we have already seen as a prestructuring element of Hegel's philosophy: On the one hand, the ideas themselves are the source of truth for the philosophically minded rhetorician; on the other, from the point of view of oratory, the ideas themselves are meaningless, ineffective, in a sense not "real" (*wirklich*) if they are not expressed. Hence, all rhetorical theory must justify the need, *inherent in ideas*, for expression. Again, Melanchthon's formulations become topoi for the later tradition. Since he defines the role of *elocutio* in visual terms—"it expounds ideas (*res*) in distinct and perspicuous speech (*dilucida et perspicua oratione*)"—he can argue that it is necessary for the very intelligibility of thought: "ideas cannot be understood without the light of words" (*res sine lumine verborum intelligi nequent*).[58] Moreover, he defends the learning of rules of *elocutio* (*praecepta*) with a crucial image: "But they are mistaken who think that the focus of speech is ornateness, which is added above and beyond nature. It is the natural form of speech, about which these precepts deal. Those who destroy them create monstrous speech, just as painters create monstrous forms, if they do not imitate nature properly."[59] That is, the precepts of *elocutio* are just as necessary to "paint" an image in language as nature is as a model for the visual artist. Scheller offers a similar defense of *elocutio* by dedicating half his *Compendium* to a theory of *perspicuitas*, which he defines as follows: "it represents a topic distinctly and lucidly and makes each thing properly intelligible."[60] It is required to make thought intelligible, since intelligibility, or our ability to understand, rests on the visual image of "clearly seeing," and sight requires the "light" of rhetoric. As he writes: "that a thing might become as perspicuous as possible: this is why the rhetori-

58. Melanchthon, *Libri Duo*, pt. ii, chap. i, p. 302. Similarly, he defines the task of rhetoric on the whole as that of *elocutio*, namely, "adding the light of words" (*addit lumen verborum*; chap. i, p. 21). Crusius stresses the defensive nature of rhetoricians toward *elocutio* by adding the comment to pt. ii, chap. i of Melanchthon's handbook: "Usefulness and necessity of *elocutio* in the face of those who hold it in contempt" ("Utilitas et necessitas elocutionis contra contemptas").

59. Melanchthon-Crusius, *Libri Duo*, chap. i, p. 305. That this conception of painting as merely imitating nature is actually naive and that painters, like orators, had to follow prescriptive *praecepta*, especially in the ages of humanism and the baroque, is the subject of Marjorie Lee Hendrix, "Joris Hoefnagel and the *Four Elements*: A Study in Sixteenth-Century Nature Painting" (Ph.D. diss., Princeton University, 1984).

60. Scheller, *Compendium*, pp. 514ff.

cians call the figures *lights*" (*ut res quam maxime perspicua fiat: hinc rhetores figuras adpellant* lumina).[61]

Ernesti, in the handbook used by the schoolboy Hegel, offers the most extended arguments to justify the role of rhetoric conceived of as *elocutio*. In particular, he spends much of the "Praefatio" to his larger work, the *Initia Doctrinae Solodoris*, discussing the role of rhetoric in writing philosophy. He criticizes those who would reject the link between the two disciplines, that is, "those who deny this as necessary for a philosopher to think or for teachers of most disciplines altogether, that they unite elegance of speech with subtlety of thought (*ut cum subtilitate cogitandi elegantiam orationis coniungant*)."[62] The antirhetorical philosophers are mistaken, Ernesti claims, because they believe that *one* truth exists independently of its mode of expression: "because in these kinds of teachings, only one truth is seen, and this would be able to be separated from elegance of words (*una veritas spectetur, eaque a verborum elegantia seiuncta esse possit*)."[63] For Ernesti, on the contrary, the success of a philosophy relies on the elegance of its presentation: "For whoever would run through the memory of past ages, thereby reviewing the times of early philosophy: he would discover indeed that elegance of thought arises, thrives, and perishes with elegance in speaking and writing (*elegantiam cognitandi cum elegantia disserendi ac scribendi et exstitesse, et crevisse, et perisse*)."[64]

Not unlike Hegel later in the Preface to the *Phenomenology*, Ernesti criticizes contemporary philosophy largely for "stylistic" reasons, whereby the style and form of philosophical writing belong to the essence of thought. Mathematically oriented philosophers have substituted proofs and formalisms for the exposition of ideas and have thus sacrificed good writing and the appropriate means of expressing philosophical truth: "the fewest are able to write about things pertaining to philosophy and mathematics in a polished manner or are recommended by elegance in presentation (*disserendi elegantia*)."[65] He admits that Christian Wolff still mastered the old style even while combining it with mathematical precision, but his followers have replaced eloquence with dry proofs. Hence, when he claims that he has attached the *Initia*

---

61. Ibid., p. 514. That Scheller is perfectly aware of the quasi-biblical nature of his imagery becomes clear when he chooses the beginning of Genesis ("Et deus dixit: fiat lux") for analysis (p. 517).

62. Ernesti, *Initia Doctrinae*, p. xx.

63. Ibid.

64. Ibid., p. xxvi.

65. Ibid., p. xxiii.

Rhetorica for use in the schools—"in the spirit of accommodating this little book as much as possible to academic teaching"—he is emphasizing the need for rhetorical reflection on the form and formation of philosophical modes of writing.[66] His work links the Ciceronian and humanist ideal with the developments of eighteenth-century philosophy. Philosophical *Bildung* cannot exist without education to *elocutio*.

The Hermeneutics of Tradition Building through Imitatio *and* Exercitatio. In a statement quoted earlier in this chapter, Balthasar Haug, Hegel's teacher and the dominant figure in both the Stuttgart *gymnasium* and Swabian belles lettres, claims that the goal of education is to lodge the instructor of rhetoric and poetry in the mind of the student. This notion of rhetorical education as a process of internalization has parallels, as we saw, in Hegel's description of the *Bildung des Individuums* as an act of digestion and appropriation of past forms. In fact, every rhetorical handbook contains an extended discussion of the techniques by which a student comes to grips with the tradition in order to master its forms and learn to speak or write in an "original" voice.

Given the significance that Melanchthon attributes to the acquisition of rhetorical *praecepta* and the mastery of the forms of *elocutio*—they are to the orator what nature is to the painter—it is understandable that the *Elementorum Rhetorices Libri Duo* conclude with an explicit treatment of pedagogy. The next to last chapter, "De Imitatione," which deals with methods of learning composition, is in fact the longest single chapter in the entire book. The basic principles of Melanchthon's rhetorical pedagogy are memorization of the rules and imitation of classical models: "After the precepts have been learned, imitation is to be practiced."[67] More specifically, in order to cultivate a good style, the student of rhetoric must study the tradition of great orators. The *lectio* of canonical authors, especially Cicero, introduces the student to the tradition. Melanchthon, following the etymological meaning of the term, understands the activity of *lectio* literally: The student "wanders" through the classical works as through a landscape, extracting (*selectio*) the best words, rules, and forms. Reading is followed in the pedagogical program by imitation and *exercitationes* in which the student varies the models by translations of speeches in foreign languages (*alienae orationis tractationes*) and moves toward independent production. Crusius adds a call to teachers: "How much better were the teachers consulted by us if they led the students to read Cicero and taught them not only to excerpt the words from Cicero, but also to imitate the phrasing

66. Ibid., p. xxxvi.
67. Melanchthon-Crusius, *Libri Duo*, chap. XVII, pp. 363–81.

and the total form of the speech, i.e., to copy and represent the order and ornamentation of the sentences."[68] Not just excerpting but the imitation of the "total form" of another's speech contributes to the *Bildung* of one's own mode of representation.

In the 1709 edition of his *Compendium*, Kaldenbach stressed the pedagogical function of *exercitatio* by adding two extensive appendices for school instruction. The first, "De Progymnasmatis" (On Pupil Exercises) outlines the method for building up and practicing speeches by connecting words into periods and periods into short arguments (*chria*). He writes: "Since speech consists furthermore of an ordered series of words, (1) the richness of words (*verborum copia*) must be considered; (2) the structure of sentences must be practiced (*exercenda Periodorum structura*), (3) the modes of composition of *chriae* (*chriarum compositio*) must be treated."[69] Here we see how easily the definitions of *elocutio* could be reformulated to constitute a pattern of rhetorical exercises passing through increasingly complex structures. The second appendix, "De stylo eujusque natura, variis generibus, virtutibus et vitiis" (On Style and Its Nature, Various Genres, Virtues and Vices) expounds a doctrine of reading and writing. First, the student reads the canonical texts in four genres—*poeticum, historicum, philosophicum,* and *oratorium*—in order to strengthen the understanding of grammar, rhetorical precepts, and exemplary style (or, as stated in a subheading: "Regulae Grammaticae, Praecepta Rhetorica, et probatissimorum Auctorum exempla").[70] Only then can the student begin to develop an independent style, that is, the ability to find the mode of expression in writing appropriate for whatever is conceived in the spirit ("Stylus est certa ratio propte decorque scripto consignandi, quicquid animo concipitur").[71] Style is thus the written product of an individual's interaction with the written tradition. Style is the variety of forms of individual expression that results from systematic, imitative interaction with past forms.

Ernesti goes one step farther. Because the means of expression is so central to his concept of philosophy, he sets himself the goal of purifying academic language in order to create a new philosophical *elocutio* and *eloquentia* based on imitation of the ancients: "Next after the carefulness of purity, was—and this was beyond doubt more difficult and serious—[the task] to make the form and appearance of the total

---

68. Ibid., p. 380.
69. Kaldenbach, *Compendium* (1709), p. 250. The specific form and influence of such exercises as *chriae* will be dealt with in the next chapter.
70. Ibid., p. 250.
71. Ibid.

discourse come closest to that which the ancients achieved in their presentation."[72] His task is especially difficult, he claims, since philosophy is written in the *genus subtile*, the "middle style," which, according to Cicero, is the hardest to master and imitate ("Quod genus imitationis hoc difficilius debet existimare, quod ipse Cicero, nullius generis, quam subtilis, difficiliorem imitationem dicit").[73]

Whereas Ernesti writes his own philosophical text in Latin as an example of philosophical elegance, Scheller provides the most extensive systematic treatment of the theory and practice of imitation. He includes lengthy appendices to his works which parallel those of his humanist and baroque models. The addition to his Latin textbook, "Appendix I: On the Aids for Good Latin Style," is divided into two sections: "De Lectione Priscorum" (On Reading the Ancients) and "De Exercitatione in Latine Scribendo, Loquendo, et Meditando Seu Cogitando" (On Exercises in Writing, Speaking, and Thinking or Reasoning in Latin). He closely follows Quintilian's Book x of the *Institutio Oratoria* in arguing that the development of ideas rests on a process of reading and (re)writing.[74] The *res* are not "pure thoughts" but the result of internalization and externalization of traditional forms. This makes it possible to find appropriate forms to express them, since the thoughts and forms of expression are linked from the start of thinking about expression. Similarly, Chapter viii of his German rhetoric, "On the Imitation (*Nachahmung*) of Ciceronian Writing Style (*Schreibart*)," begins with his critique of traditional *exercitii styli* that are mere translations with a dictionary.[75] Like many other "reformers" in eighteenth-century pedagogy, he calls for a genuine *exercitium*, an *elaboratio*, which works out an essay or paragraph in the totality of another's voice, not just using individual words. (Here we can think of Hegel's theory in the Preface to the *Phenomenology* of the Spirit's labor of unfolding itself in a richness of alien forms.) And beyond these individual appendices and chapters, Scheller's work on the whole focuses on the idea of imitation. This emphasis results directly from his concern for writing. His expansion of *elocutio* to a theory of style leads him to stress the reworking of tradition, since tradition, as is clear even in the etymology of the term (of which Scheller was certainly aware) is contained and propagated in

---

72. Ernesti, *Initia Doctrinae*, p. xxxiv.

73. Ibid., p. xxxv.

74. Scheller provides two basic methods: "They are, on the whole, twofold: 1) the reading of the ancient authors and 2) exercises in writing, speaking, and thinking" ("Ea [subsidia] sunt in universum duo: 1) Lectio priscorum, 2) Exercitatio in scribendo, dicendo, cogitando"; *Compendium*, p. 334).

75. Scheller, *Anleitung*, pp. 306–8.

written forms.[76] Thus the textbook that Hegel most likely kept on his desk during his last years at the Stuttgart *gymnasium* informed the activity of his writing as an imitation and emulation of earlier traditions.

Critical Dialectics through Inventio *and in the* Ars Disputandi. The third crucial aspect of *Bildung* as education in and to the individual control of forms of expression can be approached by considering the basic definition of rhetoric found in virtually every handbook from Cicero on, namely the *ars bene dicendi*. The richness of this definition lies hidden in the ambiguity of *bene*. Beyond the obvious understanding of "speaking well" as learning *elocutio* and past masters, there are other connotations. One connotation is clearly ethical: The good orator takes up "good" public causes.[77] Another connotation is often brought out in definitions that add *sapienter* to *bene* in order to imply that speaking well is impossible without knowledge and a sense of the truth. Melanchthon summarizes these two implications when he claims that the rhetorician requires not just natural talent but also "knowledge of many good things" (*multarum bonarum rerum scientiam*).[78] More specifically, the notion of rhetoric as *bene dicere* implies a correspondence between the internally known *res* and the expressing *verba*. We already saw a felt need on the part of theorists to justify *elocutio* as the doctrine of *verba*, here we shall consider the relationship established between dialectics and rhetoric. The paradoxes of representation determine the shifting valorizations of these disciplines.

76. In the *Anleitung* Scheller answers the question "How does one imitate Cicero properly?" ("Wie imitirt man den Cicero recht?") by emphasizing the need to read, understand, and work out in writing the best texts. Such a process will do more to bring about genuine style than mere rules, although both rules and practice are necessary so that "a good mind" (*ein guter Kopf*; pp. 309–13) might develop.

77. The ethical side of *bene* Cicero points out in *De Oratore*: "in the old days at all events the same system of instruction seems to have imparted education both in right conduct and in good speech" (par. 57). This conjunction of the ethical and narrowly rhetorical is crucial for Hegel's later theories of the "objective Spirit." We shall see in chap. 5, below, how this conjunction guides Hegel's neohumanist pedagogical program in Nuremberg.

78. Melanchthon-Crusius, *Libri Duo*, chap. I, p. 1. He defines rhetoric as follows: "the ability to speak wisely and ornately" (*facultas est sapienter et ornate dicendi*). He explains in the Preface (p. 17) that one cannot even speak well without intricate knowledge of "things" (*rerum*): "For perfect understanding of these things, concerning which the art of oratory is taught, is required primarily for speaking well. It is indeed madness, and not eloquence, to speak of things unknown or not understood" ("Nam ad bene dicendum in primus requiritur perfecta earum rerum cognitio, de quibus oratio institutur. Insania est enim, non eloquentia, de rebus ignotis et incompertis dicere"). This notion, together with the stress on the past tradition, leads Melanchthon to extol reading Cicero and Quintilian, for they lead *non solum ad eloquentiam, sed etiam ad sapientiam* (chap. I).

On the one hand, dialectics, which is associated with the *res*, consistently assumes priority over rhetoric, which is associated with *verba*. Melanchthon provides the definition that lays the foundation of the humanist tradition: "Since all speech consists of ideas and words (*rebus et verbis*), the concern for ideas ought to come first, then for words"; this means that dialectic, which presents the "naked idea" (*res nuda*) is distinct from and logically prior to rhetoric's "clothing" or "illumination" of the *res*.[79] Similarly, Ernesti, in a phrase of remarkable significance for Hegel's later philosophy of the *Sache selbst*, identifies dialectics with its concern for the *res ipsa* as opposed to rhetoric's *copia verborum*.[80] On the other hand, however, this sharp distinction between dialectic and rhetoric, a hierarchical distinction that seems to give absolute priority to the former, just as consistently breaks down in the tradition of rhetorical handbooks. As Crusius says of Melanchthon's distinction: "Is this distinction stable? No!" ("Est ne stabile hoc discrimen? Non!")[81] The reasons for the unstable relationship between rhetoric and dialectic lie at the paradoxical heart of this tradition and its concept of representation.

The distinction between dialectic and rhetoric as the distinction between a theory of the *res* and a theory of the *verbum* breaks down, first, because the task of *inventio* within rhetorical practice contains a conception of "discovering" (inventing) and developing thoughts (*res*). In fact, accompanying the growth of *elocutio* in the formation of a *rhétorique restreinte* is an expansion of *inventio*. It, too, begins as one of five *officia* (in Melanchthon's accurate reworking of the classical system), becomes then one of four (in Kaldenbach), opposes *elocutio* (in Ernesti), and finally fuses with *elocutio* (in Scheller's concept of *stylum* as the perspicuous relationship between *res* and *verbum*). With the firm, and ever firmer, location of *inventio* within rhetoric (even within rhetoric narrowly conceived as *elocutio*), the central doctrine of dialectical *inventio*—the discovery of *topica* or the theory of *loci* which structures rational argumentation—also becomes increasingly identified with rhetorical categories. Thus, what began as a discipline separate from rhetoric—Melanchthon, echoing Aristotle, isolates dialectic and *loci* (*dialectica*

79. Melanchthon-Crusius, *Libri Duo*, chap. II, p. 33; chap. I, p. 21; chap. III, p. 41.
80. For example, *Initia Rhetorica*, p. 17: dialectic is the art "that deals with the method of explicating thought itself" (*quae et ipsae rei cuiusque explicandae rationem tradit*). Also pp. 20, 134.
81. Melanchthon-Crusius, *Libri Duo*, p. 19. In the Preface Melanchthon points out that rhetoric and dialectic are intricately bound together, since they are "arts that are so joined together . . . that they are learned more properly together than either of them separately" (*artes, quae ita copulate sunt . . . ut rectius simul ambae percipiantur, quam seorum alterutia (p. 15*).

tradi locos)—becomes one of the tasks of the "well-speaking" orator.[82] In fact, there is even the tendency to identify the *loci*—modes of developing arguments and strategies out of definitions, similarities, cause and effect, contiguity, opposites, and so on—with the fundamental operations of the tropes and figurative speech.[83] Rhetorical *inventio* and *elocutio* incorporate dialectic.

A second reason for the breakdown of the distinctions between the two sisters in the *trivium* is that dialectic is viewed as one form of rhetorical speaking and writing, either in the sense of a genre within rhetoric or as an extension of rhetoric to the dialogue-situation. If dialectics is the site of the *loci argumentorum*, then its goal is to make clear, "matter-of-fact" (*sachlich*, *res*-oriented), and persuasive arguments possible. For this reason, dialectics is identified from Melanchthon through Kaldenbach to Ernesti with the act of teaching (*docere*) and belongs to the didactic genre (*genus didascalicum*). This act and this genre, however, are at the same time treated as subcategories of the rhetorical *genera dicendi*, that is, alongside the acts of moving (*movere*) and entertaining (*delectare*) the audience through the *genus deliberativum* and *genus demonstrativum*. Melanchthon and Crusius even derive it from the other genres: "From where does the didactic genre (*didascalicon*) derive? Thence, from where the demonstrative and deliberative genres arise, to which it is related."[84]

And beyond the question of genre, Ernesti's interest in argumentative strategies in philosophy likewise leads him to cross the unstable border between the disciplines since he stresses the dialogic function of philosophy to inquire into the validity of ideas held by others. For example, he treats the act of disputation in his book on dialectics: "To dispute is to question what is true and false by means of methodological reasoning and arguments carried out to the last detail. Thus, a truth is what has been questioned by disputation (*Una igitur veritas est, quae disputando quaeritur*). . . . But so that a disputation proceeds properly, it is required that the one speak and the other observe, respond, and

---

82. Ibid., p. 15.

83. In his *Topica*, Cicero defines the *loci* as the optimal means of argumentation inherent in every subject, means that must be "discovered" or "invented": "Inherent in the nature of the subject are arguments derived from the whole, from its parts, from its meaning and from the things that are in some way closely connected with the subject that is being investigated." Loeb edition (Cambridge, Mass.: Harvard University Press, 1960), par. 8. Note that these *loci* are closely related to the forms of tropes. This relation will be explored and used in discussing the structuration of *Phenomenology* in chap. 4, below.

84. Chap. IV p. 28. The entire chap. VI ("De Genere Didascalico") deals with the didactic genre and lists different questions for the student to ask of any subject in order to derive the best arguments.

criticize (*ut, quod ait alter ac tuetur reprehendat alter et neget*)."[85] And yet the techniques for developing such arguments can be found in the rhetorical task of *inventio*. At the heart of dialectical truth is a dialogue (often before a third party), thereby shifting the concern with the *res* into the public sphere. For this reason, the acts of disputation or dialectical reasoning and the defense of a "good cause" in an open forum (like the court of law) had always been considered the highest form of academic and public rhetoric.[86] Kaldenbach, for example, published numerous volumes of *problemata* and *disputationes* in which he and students argued the different sides of issues.[87] And from Melanchthon to Ernesti, the models for philosophical argumentation are Plato and, even more emphatically, Cicero because of their ability to unite rhetoric and dialectic in the form of the dialogue. Ernesti writes: "In truth, it was the nature of the Academy's philosophy to dispute all things in greatest detail, because it availed forensic eloquence most sensibly; and it did this not narrowly and dryly, but elegantly, copiously, and ornately, as can be seen in the dialogues of Plato, Xenophon, and Cicero."[88] By praising the ancient philosophers with key terms from both rhetoric and dialectic, Ernesti unites the two in a conception of dialogue located inside the realm of public dispute and forensics.

A last reason for the unstable relation between rhetoric and dialectic raises the issue of judging the relationship between *res* and *verba*. To write and speak "well" (*bene*) means to be able to find the appropriate relationship between thought and expression, that is, to be able to choose among expressions (*copia verborum*). This faculty of judgment is called *iudicium* and it belongs to both disciplines. Melanchthon writes: "The end of dialectics is to make judgments (*iudicare*)." But also: "We would define the ends of rhetoric as passing judgment (*iudicare*) on any extended discourse—which of its parts follow, which are the outstanding, which are ornaments."[89] The dialectical judgment of the *res* seems at first to have priority, but it is in fact superseded by the rhetorical

85. Ernesti, *Initia Doctrinae*, p. 400.

86. A reason for this connection is that classical rhetoric had forensics as its goal: "An ancient rhetoric trained men entirely for speaking, and almost exclusively for speaking in the law court. It is a doctrine of controversy and debate. Furthermore, it is concerned with matter as well as with style. Invention, or the discovery of ideas and subject matter, was the first and perhaps the most important section of any formal treatise on rhetoric." Cicero, *De Inventione*, introduction by H. M. Hubbell (Cambridge, Mass.: Harvard University Press, 1960).

87. Christoph Caldenbachius, ed., *Orationes et Actus oratorii*, in Academia Tubingensi a studiosa juventute, exercendae inprimis Eloquentiae cause publice exhibiti, 1679 (1682). This large collection contains speeches and essays on topics that recall many of the young Hegel's projects: the eloquence of Paul's epistles; the manner of reading ancient poets, art versus nature in the development of eloquence, and more.

88. Ernesti, *Initia Rhetorica*, p. 8.

judgment of the relationship between *res* and *verba* or among *verba*. This faculty of judgment, and its cultivation, are traditionally located within rhetorical *inventio* since even Cicero realized that the "discovery" of "things" or *loci* for an argument always already depends on the *verba* and rhetorical-persuasive purpose to which they will be put. *Iudicium* implies that one can see from the beginning the inherently rhetorical qualities of the "matter." Aristotle's definition of rhetoric as the means of seeing the best way to construct a persuasive argument for a cause stresses its dialectical function and links it, almost against his expressed intention, to the *Topica*. In Ernesti's words: "*Inventio* is the faculty of seeing in any matter whatsoever that which is appropriate for persuasion."[90] This implies further that the "things" invented are themselves part of the rhetorical medium, the rhetorical tradition: "*inventio*, which in . . . totality is derived from inborn talent, documents, reading, and common usage of ideas (*ab ingenio, literis, lectione et usu rerum*)."[91] The end of this line of development within rhetoric is that the critical faculty of *iudicium* becomes more and more related to the tasks of employing rhetorical *verba*.

Scheller, following the other neohumanists like Gesner and Ernesti, fixes on the concept of "critique": "Every person who possesses the skill to judge a matter thoroughly is properly called a critic (*Kritikus, kritikes*, from *krino, iudico*) and every person should be one. However, this name is applied in particular to those who are so experienced in philology that they can pass thorough judgments (*gründlich urtheilen*) on the quality and nature of passages of the ancients."[92] Thus, like the theories of *res* and *loci* and the genre of argumentative and dialogic disputation, the critical faculty of judgment exists within *inventio* at the intersection of rhetoric and dialectic. The task of rhetorical *Bildung* consists, therefore, in educating the pupils not just to the stylistic mastery of *elocutio* and the internalization of traditional forms of writing, but also to the dialectical and philological practices that allow them to participate critically in the public forum of competing discourses.

An analysis of a small selection of Hegel's manuscripts, diary entries, and school essays from the Stuttgart period in terms of what it meant to be rhetorically educated (*gebildet*) and to form a good rhetorical style

89. Melanchthon-Crusius, *Libri Duo*, chap. I, p. 3.
90. Ernesti, *Initia Rhetorica*, p.19.
91. In the Preface to the *Initia Rhetorica* Ernesti criticizes those who would reject handbook forms and schemata (*locos de argumentibus*) as dry and unimportant because they believe (incorrectly) that only the arguments, not the *mode* of argumentation, are important (p. 5). To develop one's critical faculties as a philosopher, then, one must learn *how* to argue by becoming knowledgeable in rhetorical *inventio*.
92. Scheller, *Anleitung*, p. 209.

will confirm the impact of the still powerful rhetorical tradition on the young Hegel. The broader context of *Schulrhetorik* grants the eclectic school writings a formal and functional consistency as exercises in stylistic decorum. Viewed from the perspective of the pedagogical spirit in which they were written, these early texts are nor "mere" exercises or "mere" collections of seeds of ideas germinating in the young Hegel's mind. Rather, as traditional *exercitationes* they fulfill the three functions of a rhetorical education that we have just isolated so that the young writer/orator could internalize the tradition by imitating and transforming it through writing.

One series of texts from Hegel's final years at the Stuttgart *gymnasium*, the so-called "excerpts," testifies both to the young boy's interest in the pedagogical debates in and around his school and to his methodological approach to working through those debates. Rosenkranz was the first to draw attention to the "mass" of excerpts and notes that Hegel made as a schoolboy and carefully preserved his whole long life. Rosenkranz referred to these manuscripts, which Hegel had arranged alphabetically according to general headings, as the "incunabula of Hegel's *Bildung*."[93] In the late nineteenth century, Gustav Thaulow published these excerpts in an attempt to demonstrate Hegel's lifelong interest in a philosophical *Staatspädagogik*.[94] My concern here is less with the "philosophical" content of the excerpts than with the way they document Hegel's awareness of the conflicting pedagogical, and this implies rhetorical, theories of the late eighteenth century. I shall deal with three sample positions, under which most others could be grouped.

In his lengthy excerpt from Johann Georg Heinrich Feder's *Neuer Emil*,[95] Hegel works through a modern pedagogical ideal in the sense of a pragmatic Enlightenment reinterpretation of Quintilian's *Institutio Oratoria*. Though superficially inspired by Rousseau, Feder's text is

---

93. Rosenkranz, *Hegels Leben*, pp. 8–9.

94. Gustav Thaulow, *Hegels Ansichten über Erziehung und Unterricht*, Als Fermente für wissenschaftliche Pädagogik, sowie zur Belehrung und Anregung für gebildete Eltern und Lehrer aller Art, aus Hegels sämtlichen Schriften, gesammelt und systematisch geordnet (Kiel, 1853).

I shall be quoting from Johannes Hoffmeister, ed., *Dokumente zu Hegels Entwicklung* (Stuttgart: Fromann, 1936), since Hoffmeister corrects a number of errors in Thaulow (caused by Thaulow's intent to demonstrate a consistent theory in the precocious schoolboy rather than the internalization of classical and humanist traditions through *exercitationes*).

95. Johann Georg Heinrich Feder, *Der neue Emil oder von der Erziehung nach bewährten Grundsätzen* (Erlangen, 1774–75). Here, as in many other excerpts, Hegel transforms a dialogue into expository prose, as if this were a private *exercitium*.

guided by principles resembling those established in Prussia under Frederick the Great or in the Stuttgart military academy under Karl Eugen. Education begins at the level of "game playing" (*Spiel*) as opposed to the humanist tradition of learning foreign languages through hard work.[96] For Feder, man is defined chiefly as a social being, and so all elements of his education must lead to successful integration into contemporary society. The basic method is derived from the classical tradition: because man's basic instinct (*Grundtrieb*) is to imitate, he learns by repeating positive examples of social behavior.[97] In his excerpts, Hegel isolates and emphasizes the two aspects in Feder that are superficial modifications of basic principles of the classical *ars rhetorica*: *imitatio* and *ethos*. Hegel seems fascinated by Feder's attempt to remold classical pedagogy more than his own school wished to in order to fit the popular philosophy of the Enlightenment.[98]

Hegel's excerpts from Matthias Gesner's introduction to his 1735 edition of Livy offer quite a different viewpoint from Feder's description of the upbringing of an *homme de lettres*. Gesner was the most significant neohumanist of the mid-eighteenth century, and Hegel goes right to the heart of this movement by copying Gesner's reevaluation of the rhetorical principle of *lectio*.[99] In the passage copied by

96. Hoffmeister, *Dokumente*: "Learning must at the beginning be without compulsion, a pastime and amusement" ("Das Lernen muß anfangs ganz ohne Zwang nur Zeitvertreib und Spielwerk sein"; p. 56)

97. See Lausberg, *Handbuch*, pars. 2ff. on *imitatio*. In traditional rhetorical theory as well, *imitatio* connects all aspects of an orator's education, from imitation of the teacher's actions to imitation of the style of the canonical masters.

98. Hegel's excerpt from Johannes Jacob Dusch's *Briefe zur Bildung des Geschmacks an einen jungen Herrn von Stande*, in six parts (Leipzig, 1764–73), is another example of the young boy's interest in Enlightenment reformulations of classical rhetorical *Bildung*. The letter excerpted by Hegel, according to Hoffmeister, "deals with Racine's poem on religion" (p. 86). Hegel copies out the discussion of Socrates' sacrifice of a rooster just before his death. This was a popular topic for school *disputationes* and is used by Dusch and Hegel in a traditional manner to encourage the modern *Ausbildung des Geschmacks* (Dusch, pp. 4–6). See also Hegel's excerpt from Moses Mendelssohn on the relationship between Enlightenment and *Bildung* (Hoffmeister, *Dokumente*, pp. 140–43).

Likewise, Hegel's excerpt from Christian Garve's *Versuch über die Prüfung der Fähigkeiten* (1769) reveals an interest in Enlightenment reformulations of Renaissance rhetoric. Garve's essay is in the tradition of Vives and Juan Huarte and deals with the public *sensus communis* that, according to Gadamer (*Wahrheit und Methode* [Tübingen: Mohr, 1960], pp. 16–27), united rhetoric with other disciplines. What clearly interested the young Hegel were Garve's statements concerning the intricate connection between the development of style and the formation or judgments of thoughts (Hoffmeister, *Dokumente*, 122–25).

99. Gesner had been director of the *Thomasschule* in Leipzig, where he reworked the baroque pedagogical methods in the spirit of a new age. Paulsen summarizes his variation of the traditional as follows: "The aim of the old institution was the attainment of fluency in the imitation of the ancients. The new activity relinquishes this aim, seeing it as

Hegel, Gesner criticizes the traditional method used in schools to attain mastery of a text and style—*repetitionis, imitationis et applicationis ratio*—since by this method a unified work is dismembered into dead parts (*discerpitur*) and the student's desire to read (*legendi cupiditas*) is destroyed.[100] Gesner's "new" form of *lectio* returns, in fact, to the more sophisticated approach offered by the classical rhetoricians: cursory reading to master arguments and style (*lectio cursoria*), then detailed study and memorization of figures and *exempla*, and finally the development of judgment and imagination or wit (*iudicium et ingenium*) for application to all of life ("This one kind of reading is useful for all life; it enriches the spirit designedly, and makes it more appropriate for public and private activities").[101] Not only here as a schoolboy, but years later as director of the Nuremberg *gymnasium* and friend of the Bavarian pedagogue Friedrich Niethammer, Hegel applies this method to his pedagogical theory and practice. Neohumanism confirms as much as it transforms the traditional methods Hegel acquired in school.

A final example of the variety of pedagogical methods that occupied the young Hegel is the excerpt from Joachim Heinrich Campe's *Seelenlehre* (Teachings on the Soul, or Psychology).[102] Campe, one of the major philanthropists—together with Basedow, Trapp, and Rochow—called for pedagogical reforms opposed to those of the neo-humanists: reduced emphasis on foreign, especially classical languages; training of the faculties of understanding and taste; and a pragmatic approach stressing the *Realien* instead of handbooks and catechisms.[103]

---

having been made obsolete by reality. Through the reading of the ancient authors it aims not at an imitation in Greek or Latin, but instead at the development (*bilden*) of judgment and taste, spirit (*Geist*) and insight, and, through these, at the nourishing of the capacity of independent production in one's native language" (*Geschichte des gelehrten Unterrichts*, vol. 2, p. 17). Also Heubaum, *Geschichte des deutschen Bildungswesens*, p. 225, who sees in Gesner the revitalization of Quintilian's ideals. On *lectio* as a rhetorical category, see Lausberg, *Handbuch*, pars. 663–64.

100. Hoffmeister, *Dokumente*, p. 82.

101. Ibid., p. 83. This call for the applicability of rhetorical principles to all aspects of life is made possible by the crucial function of "judgment" (*iudicium*), which, as we saw, related rhetoric to dialectics.

102. Joachim Heinrich Campe, *Kleine Seelenlehre für Kinder* (Hamburg, 1784). See Hoffmeister, *Dokumente*, pp. 101–4. In the following decades, as we shall see in the next chapter, Hegel reflects critically on his own reception of Campe. In particular, Hegel will criticize Campe's popular school text *Theophron, oder der erfahrene Ratgeber für unerfahrene Jugend* (Hamburg, 1783).

103. See Frank, *Deutschunterricht*, pp. 137–50. Philanthropism had a number of basic principles in common with the other movements: The classics were not studied as an end in themselves; the instruction had to be practical; the training of "understanding, heart, and taste" was the goal of education, and hence the individual student received more

He follows the basic dictum of the philanthropic movement as coined by Ratichius: "Things instead of words" (*Sachen statt Worte*).[104] Campe's book on the soul, however, hardly escapes the traditional methods he criticized. It consists of a dry dialogue, broken down into sections that revolve around definitions of concepts that are highlighted in bold print. Hegel's excerpts make the job of mastering the concepts even easier by reducing the dialogue to forty or so definitions of the affects, instincts, and faculties.[105] This is a method that Hegel could have adopted from any number of prescriptions for *exercitationes* or *exercitii styli*. Just as Campe employed the methods he criticized, so too Hegel, in spite of his occasional critiques of Campe—whom he in fact later uses as the most typical example of learning by rote memorization—returns to the same mechanistic approach taken from the rhetorical handbooks.

Thus, Hegel encountered in his autodidactic exercises numerous ideas that in all likelihood did not penetrate deeply into his daily life in school. If one considers the form and function of these excerpts, however, as well as their content, one sees that the basic conservatism of the Stuttgart *gymnasium*, in spite of the exciting debate raging around it, held sway over Hegel's own grappling with ideas. For in these excerpts one sees the most fundamental principles of rhetorical *exercitationes* at work, namely, appropriation through repetition and imitation, and gradual stylistic independence through variation and transformation. The very mode of Hegel's treatment of the "new" methods reveals the lasting predominance of the traditional. Rosenkranz characterizes Hegel's enterprise—and its long-term consequences—as follows:

> By copying out he was able to penetrate the finest fibers of the foreign and he attained the ability to project himself into every, even the most

---

attention; handbooks and catechisms were abolished. The philanthropist critique was more fundamental than that of the Prussian Enlightenment and neohumanism, however, since it went to the heart of language learning. According to the philanthropists, acquiring languages, especially ancient languages, cannot educate human reason since language is an arbitrary system of signs, whereas reason is natural and absolute. Foreign languages were seen as an unnecessary burden on a young child's mind. The philanthropist emphasis on the practical subjects (*Realien*) eventually gave rise to the *Realschule* as an alternative to the *gymnasium* in Germany. We will review the conflict between neohumanism and philanthropism in chap. 5, below, when we see how Hegel sided with his friend Niethammer against philanthropism in Bavaria in the early nineteenth century.

104. See Udo Müllges, "Das Verhältnis von Selbst und Sache in der Erziehung, problematisch aufgewiesen bei Basedow, Humboldt, Herbart und Hegel" (Ph.D diss., Bonn, 1961).

105. The mechanical nature of Hegel's reductive excerpt is clear from the repetition of formulas in definitions like "Our soul is" or "The affect 'x' is."

individualistic, standpoint and to speak in its own terms. He therefore understood in his criticism masterfully how to "place himself into the sphere of the opponent" and to develop that position as if it were his own. This power of *alienation* also resulted in occasional misunderstanding since superficial and cursory readers often confused such objective incarnations of Hegel for Hegel himself and accused him of precisely that which he opposed.[106]

And in the annotations to his edition of *Dokumente zu Hegels Entwicklung* (Documents on Hegel's Development), Hoffmeister expresses the dual purpose behind the very project of the excerpts more succinctly: "1. appropriation (*Aneignung*) of the material, . . . 2. development (*Bildung*) of style."[107] Although neither of these descriptions refers to the rhetorical tradition, they summarize Hegel's *Bildung* in terms that demonstrate the continuing influence of rhetorical ideas and practices on his writing. These excerpts confirm that even when dealing with texts whose pedagogical theories could not have been introduced into the classroom, Hegel's writing practice nonetheless pursued the three goals of a full rhetorical education: mastery of style, internalization of forms, and a critical, dialogic exchange with opposing views.

The diary, which Hegel kept irregularly between 26 June 1785 and 7 January 1787, provides many examples of stylistic imitations, receptions of traditional texts, and playful, argumentative exercises. It consists of twenty-seven entries in German, followed by thirty-three entries in Latin (beginning 29 July 1785); then a longer German essay, "Über das Exzipiren" (On Excerpting) written over two weeks in March 1786, then three more Latin, and eleven German entries. After 22 March 1786 there is a missing section of undetermined length.

It is interesting to trace the reasons Hegel picked up writing, especially after occasional breaks. The first entry is motivated by his listening to a Catholic sermon.[108] A month later, at the end of July, he begins writing again after a two-week silence by stating his specific intention of pursuing *exercendi styli* as a supplement to his schooling (p. 42). In August another Catholic sermon inspires him to return to the diary after a two-week interruption (p. 45). After a long pause between August and December 1785, in part caused by illness, he takes up writing

---

106. Rosenkranz, *Hegels Leben*, p. 8. This conjunction of "alienation," textual praxis, and *Bildung* is crucial for a rhetorical understanding of Hegel.

107. Hoffmeister, *Dokumente*, p. 415.

108. Nicolin, *Hegel in Stuttgart* (pp. 121–22), quotes a passage from the *Wissenschaftliches Magazin für Aufklärung* (1786) which makes clear the reasons Protestants in southern Germany attended Catholic church services: because of the higher quality of the homiletic rhetoric (*Kanzelwohlredenheit, Kanzelvortrag, Kanzelredner*).

again with reference to the "earlier efforts of practicing style" (*pristina studia exercendo stylo*; p. 46). A new start on 1 January 1786 contains nothing but the mention that Hegel had received that day a rhetorical handbook, Immanuel Scheller's *Compendium* (p. 51). And finally, on 11 February 1786, he breaks a six-week silence by describing the ceremonies celebrating the birthday of Duke Karl Eugen and linking them directly to his plan to return "to these our earlier instructive undertakings in practicing style, which have been interrupted by such a long interval of time" (p. 51). Hence, virtually every new period of writing is motivated by some explicitly rhetorical event.

Despite the wide variety of motivations for and topics discussed in these highly pedantic but occasionally touching diary entries, the majority of them can be understood as following the same form and function: the application of rhetorical *praecepta* to concrete *exempla* taken from all disciplines. In the entry from 1 July 1785, for example, Hegel discusses the object of his instruction in history that day. He refers to a definition of a certain narrative form: "A pragmatic history is, I believe, when one narrates not just *facts* [deeds, *Facta*] but also the character of a famous man, of a nation, its morals, customs, religion, etc." (p. 34). By speaking of "*a* pragmatic history" (eine *pragmatische Geschichte*) Hegel indicates that he, like his teacher who is following the curricula outlined above (pp. 63–67), is interested not in the nature of history as a philosophical issue but rather in the *stilus historicus*, one particular mode of writing history. In fact, Scheller deals explicitly with the notion of "pragmatic history writing" (*pragmatische Geschichtsschreibung*) in his German text on imitating Ciceronian style, the *Anleitung*.[109] That Hegel is thinking of his diary in rhetorical terms, even when writing about "history" becomes clear at the end of the month, on 29 July, when he writes his first entry in Latin with an opening line that could stem from Scheller: "For the sake of practicing style and acquiring a firmer, more rigorous style, it does not seem foreign to write down certain notes on [Roman] history" ("Exercendi styli et roboris acquirendi causa non alienum videtur, notam quandam historiam [Romanam] latino idiomate conscribere"; p. 42). The events of Roman history, on which he will only touch lightly (*res Romanas brevi percurrere*) provide him with the apparently foreign material that he will literally merely taste with his lips prior to ingestion (*et primoribus saltim labiliis degustare*) in his stylistic exercises. All of these images of exercises, for-

---

109. Scheller, *Anleitung*, "Fünfter Abschnitt: Regeln für jede Gattung der lateinischen classischen Scribenten insbesondere" ("Section Five: Rules for Every Genre of the Latin Classical Authors in Particular"), p. 237ff.

eignness, rigor, and textual digestion, which since Quintilian were part of rhetorical vocabulary, enter into the metaphorics of Hegel's later concept of *Bildung*.

In addition to the example of the Roman historian à la Scheller, Hegel is also able to follow that of the Ciceronian stoic in the ceremonious and pathos-filled eulogy for his teacher Löffler which he writes in his diary on 7 July 1785. Before beginning the eulogy Hegel lists the books that he had acquired from the library of the deceased professor, almost as if to indicate the models the next entries follow (5 July; p. 35). The exercise in stylistic decorum, finding the appropriate words for the serious occasion, involves the reworking of established texts. Indeed, the entire first half of the eulogy runs through the courses that Hegel took and the books that he translated and memorized under Löffler's guidance. The second half practices the *genus demonstrativum*, the rhetoric of praise: "He was the most upright and impartial man. His main concern was to serve and be of use to his students, himself, and the world" (p. 36). He did not teach merely to earn a living, Hegel adds in the tone of a Mark Antony: "No! that is not what the blessed man thought." This precocious, though in the end somewhat moving, eulogy concludes with exaggerated elegaic formulas: "And now he too has passed away! But I will forever bear his memory unaltered in my heart!" ("Und nun ist auch er entschaffen! Aber ewig werde ich sein Andenken unverrükt in meinem Herzen tragen!") One could well imagine these words in the mouth of the *professor eloquentiae* Balthasar Haug.

One of the most obvious stylizations for its own sake in the diary is the entry from 16 December 1785, in which Hegel converts the commonplace experience of a fire in the town into an emotional Latin description—or as Rosenkranz characterized it, "to a rhetorical showpiece."[110] Hegel sets the quiet mood of the young boy reading (proba-

---

110. Rosenkranz, *Hegels Leben*, p. 17. A word is in order here on Hegel's Latin style. Nicolin characterizes it appropriately: "The passages that Hegel copied down for Latin practice display many errors in choice of vocabulary and in sentence structure, and display a schoolboylike awkwardness despite all the classical turns of phrase interspersed throughout" (p. 90). Hegel seems to be striving on the whole for the complicated construction of the *periodus*, defined by Scheller: "A *periodus* therefore in the proper sense distinguishes a circuit, because the words of a proposition which have been separated by an interjection desire to be together, but are unable to proceed properly, and are compelled [instead] to go around the proposition that has come between them" ("Periodus ergo proprie notat circuitum; quia vocabula enuntiationis per illam interiectionem disiecta colligere vult, non recte progredi potest, sed circum illam interiectam enuntiationem ire cogitur"; *Compendium*, p. 175). This ideal of *latinitas* recurs later in Hegel's characterization of the *spekulativer Satz* in the Preface to the *Phenomenology*.

bly a classical author) at night: "It was night; and I, of a tranquil mind, sat occupied with some little book of mine" ("Nox erat; et tranquilla mente libello cuidam obsidebam"; p. 49, also the following quotations). He is then interrupted by the fire. He interjects his own outcries with strained pathos: "The mind dreads to speak" ("Mens horret dicere") and "Oh! How much dread filled us all!" ("Heu quantus omnes invasit metus!"). He describes the scene with exaggerated and not very successful means of stylization: invented or conventional reversed word order (*donum illam cum* and *Paullo post*); strained metaphors (*senescere jam coepti flamma* and *fumum lati tolli ad astra*); and a weak rhetorical question near the end (*Quid plura?*). Every incident is filtered through the *praecepta stili bene latini*, which explains his pleasure at receiving Scheller's book of the same title. The event (the concrete *res*) has little significance in itself; rather, it provides the opportunity for the exercise of *copia, variatio et amplificatio verborum*.

In keeping with the dictum found in Gesner's preface to Livy and in Haug's theses, Hegel applies the methods acquired in class to all aspects of his life. One of the most typical classroom exercises was the *hebdomadarium*, a translation exercise from Latin into Greek which allows in particular for the argumentative (dialectical) narration of a *sententia* from different points of view.[111] In an early entry (3 July 1785) Hegel describes a playful application of this school technique, namely, how while walking home from school with friends "we, especially I, posed the question: Everything good has its bad side (sometimes more, sometimes less, in proportion to the good). And we applied this sentence with every step" (p. 34). After they have to wait for a friend to catch up, the boys reverse the question and look for the good side in the bad. Having found a solution—"If we had run along, one of us could have fallen or had a bad thought"—Hegel responds with a self-ironic reference to the classical origin of the exercise: "Recht stoisch!" As he says later in the Preface to the *Phenomenology*, the serious accomplishments of the ancients have become the educational games for boys. Similarly, in the *Phenomenology* he will characterize the stoic and skeptical consciousness in terms of playful and contradictory exchanges between schoolboys. In this case, the dialogic strategies that were part of the

111. Nicolin comments: "The weekly homework of translations into Latin or Greek was called the *hebdomadarium* in the school jargon of Württemberg. . . . According to the lesson plan for December 1783 (Lang [*Gelehrtenschule*], p. 267), the first hour of Professor Offterdinger's lecture on Saturday for the sixth class was devoted to the *hebdomadarium*. The diary entry of Hegel's under consideration can be taken as confirmation that this lesson plan was put into practice as intended" (*Hegel in Stuttgart*, p. 112). The *hebdomadarium* was used as well as training in "dialectical" thinking, that is, for disputations.

great *disputationes* from the Romans through Kaldenbach to Haug find their way into the musings of a precocious fifteen-year-old.

It is at times unclear where Hegel's "own" life ends and his rehearsal of acquired forms begins. On 8 August he refers to the diary as a narration of occurrences from his own life: "in this narration of my own deeds" (*in hac factorum meorum narratione*; p. 45). And yet, on that same day, the incident he relates is a description of the life of Livy presented in class by his history and philosophy teacher, Cless. He reports: "[we] began today in the class of the most highly respectworthy Prof. Cless, with God's guidance, [reading] the histories of Livy. The most respectworthy professor just touched lightly on the life of Livy, of which, needless to say, precious little reached us. That which I have learned, I wish to call to mind" (p. 45).[112] Hegel recounts how Professor Cless used a letter of Pliny to praise Livy in class. And yet Pliny's praise of Livy in his *Letters* is itself only an example of Pliny's praise of another orator (Isaeus).[113] Hegel was evidently fascinated by the chain of rhetorical praise which constitutes the *genus demonstrativum*. Each act of praise relies on an expanding tradition of *exempla* from the Greeks and Romans to the present: "The excellence of the historical narratives is demonstrated by means of an example" ("Historiarum praestantia exemplo quodam probatur"; p. 45). In Hegel's narration of "his own deeds" he adopts and varies these *exempla* in order to master and appropriate the forms of discourse that make up the tradition.[114]

As a final example of how Hegel adopted the pedagogical position of his school—namely, stubbornly "enlightened" reevaluation of humanistic rhetoric—we can consider briefly his essay "Über das Exzirpiren" (On Excerpting), which he wrote in his diary during the first two weeks of March 1786. It deals critically with a typical kind of classroom ex-

112. It is interesting to note that Hegel admits, though does not bemoan, that he and his fellow students understood little of the lecture (*de qua quidem pauca ad nos pervenerunt*). This seems to confirm the criticisms made against the conservative pedagogy.

113. See Pliny's *Letters*, bk. II, letter no. 3. The entire letter is a *laudatio* of Livius's rhetorical skills and unfolds in a list of rhetorical *virtutes*.

114. Other examples of how Hegel's narration of scenes from "his own life" actually deal with his encounters with the rhetorical tradition: On 30 July he describes at length how an edition of Cicero's *Officia et Dialogi* from 1582 had recently passed through his hands; he does not reflect on his reading or on the content, but only on the age of the book itself and on the great men who worked on it (appropriately, the humanists Sturm, Melanchthon, and Erasmus). Similarly, in the first days of August, he admits that he lacks a suitable topic to write about (*Deficiente alia quadam materia*) but decides to use the aids from his rhetorical training to write anyway; he reads, selects, and translates some passages from Herodotus. A few days later he is done with the translation and reflects on the difficulty of translating Greek (p. 43). "His own life" is a reflection on his rhetorical *Bildung*.

ercise involving writing a text rapidly in a foreign language. Both the form and content of the essay confirm that he criticizes one form of rhetorical pedagogy while using arguments from the classical tradition. The essay follows the standard pattern of a *refutatio* or polemical argument that lists and then undermines the opposing positions. The *pro-oemium* defines the topic, explains the reason for writing the essay, and offers the ordering principle of the exposition. The involved opening sentence demonstrates that the young Hegel was trying his hand at long periodic sentences, structures for which he will later become infamous:

> Since excerpting, i.e., the rapid composition of a topic in another language from the one in which the topic is written, has, on the one hand, been defended and upheld by many [teachers and others] and yet, on the other, also has been criticized and eliminated by just as many others, if not more, I want to investigate, to the best of my ability, the reasons one seems to raise in its defense.

> Da das sogenannte Exzirpiren, d.i. Niederschreibung eines Themas in einer andern Sprache, als das Thema abgefaßt ist, von vielen theils Lehrern theils andern auf der einen Seite heftig vertheidigt und beibehalten, auf [der] andern Seite aber von eben so vielen oder mehrern verworfen und verbannt wird, so will ich die Gründe, die man zu der Vertheidigung desselben vorzubringen scheint, so weit meine Einsicht reicht, untersuchen. [P. 54]

The *narratio* presents three common arguments in defense of "excerpting" together with Hegel's three counterarguments. They all revolve around the same principle. The defense of excerpting emphasizes that students will avoid bombastic prose (*Schwulst*) if they are forced to compose Latin translations as quickly as possible. Hegel's response sounds at first like a standard critique of rhetoric at the time; in exerpting, he writes, "one merely and strictly concentrates on the words and phrases" (p. 55). And yet in reality Hegel's own defense of slow and methodical translation as opposed to the rapid excerpting of foreign-language texts relies on traditional rhetorical categories.[115] For

---

115. In this, Hegel follows the pattern of many eighteenth-century critics of rhetoric (positions he had excerpted) that reject a specific rhetorical method even while confirming the general rhetorical ideal. Here Hegel's positive judgment of slow writing as opposed to rapid *exzipiren* parallels Quintilian's arguments in *Institutio Oratoria*, X, 3 (5–10): "At first, our pen must be slow yet sure: we must search for what is best and refuse to give a joyful welcome to every thought the moment that it presents itself; we must first criticize the fruits of our imagination, and then, once approved, arrange them with care. For we must select both thoughts and words and weigh them one by one. . . . In order to do this with the utmost care, we must frequently revise what we have just written. For

The Spirit and Its Letter

example, when he says that a student can develop "a complexly and periodically structured Latin" (*ein numeröses und periodisches Latein*; p. 55) only by writing slowly, he repeats one of the common handbook *praecepta* from Quintilian through Scheller. Similarly, as opposed to rapid excerpting he offers a method of "repeated reading of the original sources themselves and slow composition" (p. 57), which recalls the rhetorical methods of *lectio, selectio,* and *translatio.* In fact, Hegel refers explicitly in this regard to Gesner's or Scheller's notion of developing *critica,* the ability "to judge (*beurteilen*) a language" through cursory and then detailed reading. Thus, both the form and reasoning of Hegel's essay situate it among typical arguments in the late eighteenth-century debate of *rhetorica contra rhetoricam.* What seems like a critique of a rhetorical technique of teaching composition actually reconfirms the fundamental values and ideals of classical rhetorical *Bildung.*

The examples of Hegel's exercises in the three basic fields of his rhetorical *Bildung* could be expanded to cover virtually all his writings from the period. His final school declamation (before the valedictory address), for example, is an amplification of the *sententia* that grew out of the *querelle des anciens et des modernes*: "Über einige charakteristische Unterschiede der alten Dichter [von den Neueren]" (On Some Characteristic Differences between the Ancient Poets [and the Modern]; August 1788). The difference he focuses on concerns the kinds of linguistic *elocutio,* the modes of presenting the world—what he calls the "the image of things" (*Bild der Sache*)—in the two cultures (pp. 76–79). He also writes in his diary of his private instruction with Professor Hopf to improve his Latin style: "Latina sumere et in his praesertim elabore" (15 December 1785). When one recalls that *elaboratio* was a standard term in rhetorical handbooks (Scheller's, for example), one is not surprised that the planned exercises involve translations of the classics, among others of Cicero's *Quaestiones* (or *Disputationes*) *Tusculanae.* As if citing Ernesti, Hegel explains that the difficulty in translating Cicero arises not because of the grammar but because of the accomplishment of Cicero's style, namely, the union of rhetoric and philosophy—"be-

---

beside the fact that thus we secure a better connection between what follows and what precedes, the warmth of thought which has cooled down while we were writing is revived anew, and gathers fresh impetus from going over the ground again. . . . The sum of the whole matter is this: write quickly and you will never write well, write well and you will soon write quickly." (sit primo vel tardus dum diligens stilus, quaeramus optima nec protinus offerentibus gaudeamus, adhibeatur iudicium inventis, dispositio probatis: delectus enim rerum verborumque agendus est et pondera singulorum examinanda . . . quae quidam ut diligentius exsequamur, rependa saepius erunt scriptorum proxima. nam praeter id, quod sic melius iunguntur prioribus sequentia, calor quoque ille cogitationis, qui scribendi mora refrixit, recipit ex integro vires et velut repetitio spatio sumit

cause of the philosophy and eloquence, which, as he himself says, are brought to bear here" (*per philosophiam et eloquentiam, quas potissimum, ut ipse ait, hic adhibere visum est*; p. 49).[116]

As final examples, we see diary entries in which the young Hegel never tires of expanding, varying, and debating questions that arose in school or in the verbal play with friends, like the favorite disputation from the tradition of popular philosophy: "Why did Socrates, shortly before his death, have a rooster sacrificed to Aesculapius?" (2 July 1785), or the pedagagical "issue (*quaestio*) discussed by us today" in school whether rapid *repetitio* or slower *praeparatio* is the better aid to translation (12 December 1785), or the playful, argumentative *amplificatio* of the comment "What kinds of different impressions one and the same object can make on different people" (28 June 1785).[117]

What we see in all these examples is that Hegel's education in the Stuttgart Eberhard-Ludwig Gymnasium (Gymnasium Illustre) followed the lines of traditional rhetoric not just in the more general sense that the conservative curriculum hardly wavered from its humanistic and baroque origins, but also in the specific sense that for Hegel *Bildung*, or the goal of being educated (*gebildet*), meant perfecting the basic tasks of rhetoric. These tasks involved (1) mastering the *copia verborum* of *elocutio* so that any idea could be given appropriate (figurative) form; (2) internalizing and emulating the forms from the tradition of classics through a program of *lectio*, *exercitatio*, and *translatio*; and (3) developing critical skills to discover (*invenire*), elaborate, argue, and judge any position in a public forum. These ideals and techniques are self-propagating to the extent that they call for their own internalization and practice. Thus, the fact that Hegel passed through this conservative education—and the Stuttgart *gymnasium* was far more conservative than most—means, on the one hand, that the practice of his

---

impetum . . . summa haec est rei: cito scribendo non fit ut bene scribatur, bene scribendo fit ut cito).

116. It is worth noting that Hegel plans to practice translations with his *physics* teacher—a reminder that all instructors (at least in the Gymnasium Illustre) had Latin eloquence as their goal.

117. Hegel makes explicit the nature of this "dialectical play" with linguistic forms on 2 July 1785, when he says that in school they dealt with the question about Socrates and his rooster. We saw how Hegel had excerpted a passage from Dusch relating to this issue, and here he points out that the goal in class was the "presentation of varying opinions" (*Anführung verschiedener Meinungen*; p. 34). Similarly, on 28 June 1795 Hegel writes a short description of minor incidents from everyday life to practice three techniques he undoubtedly picked up in school: the moral *exemplum* (see Lausberg, *Handbuch*, pars. 19, 24, 29, on the *exemplum* as a *Muster für die ethische Lebensführung*); indirect speech; and the *locus argumentorum a majore ad minus* (see Lausberg, par. 395). The next anecdote in the same entry reverses the argument type (*locus a minore ad maium*) (p. 33).

writing and his concept of *Bildung* become inextricably linked, and, on the other, that both his writing and concept of *Bildung* bear in themselves the traces of his traditional rhetorical education. In the following chapters we explore the developments that combined with this traditional rhetorical background during the following years to grant his writing and philosophy of *Bildung* their unique form.

CHAPTER 2

The Theological Manuscripts: Allegories and Hermeneutics of *Bildung*

> . . . the usefulness of writing will show itself in the slightest essay that one drafts, since by paying attention to the particularities of foreign works one pushes back the obsession with imitation more and more and can gradually develop the particular feature of one's own mode of representation, whereby one's expression receives its form and style develops (*wodurch erst der Ausdruck sein Gepräge erhält, und der Styl sich bildet*).
>
> Karl Philipp Moritz, *Vorlesungen über den Styl oder praktische Anweisung zu einer guten Schreibart* (1793)

The course of instruction that Hegel went through in the Stuttgart Gymnasium Illustre was by no means unique for the late eighteenth century. While the conservative tendencies of the Protestant school authorities led to a maintenance of the status quo for over two centuries, the basic ideas behind the rhetorical model of humanism influenced, as we saw in the examples of north German Enlightenment, philanthropism, and neohumanism, more "modern" pedagogical theories as well. Hence, the fact that the Eberhard-Ludwig Gymnasium insisted to a greater degree than most on the formal training according to the classical and humanist rhetorical program does not yet suffice to differentiate Hegel's own education, and the concept of *Bildung* that he later abstracts out of it, from the formative education and culturation that most poets and philosophers of the period underwent.[1] And yet

---

1. The writers to whose development Hegel's could be best compared are Schelling and Hölderlin, and such a "rhetorical biography" of their writings would illuminate many structures and components of their work. Rhetoric also played a significant role in the development of Fichte's philosophy, but the main difference to Hegel is that Fichte was able to continue his public oratory. See Adelheid Ehrlich, *Fichte als Redner* (Munich: Tuduv-Verlagsgesellschaft, 1977).

perhaps it is precisely the insistence of the Gymnasium Illustre on the rhetorical model of pedagogy that can provide us with the key to how Hegel developed his "own" unique approach to a philosophy of *Bildung*. What we must now consider, then, is how the internalized system of rhetorical instruction—the "professor in the student's head," to paraphrase Balthasar Haug—gave Hegel the tools and structures for him to give his philosophy its initial individual form in the decades following his schooling.

The classical theorists of oratory had already systematically addressed the general question of how an author schooled according to a standardized method could develop an individual "voice," or, as they often reversed the same question, whether such uniqueness was not in fact an innate attribute of the speaker regardless of training. They condensed the issue into the opposition between *ars* and *natura*.[2] Given the systematic form of the classical rhetorics like the *Institutio Oratoria* and their even more systematic followers in the handbooks used in schools, it would seem as if all emphasis was placed on the schematic program at the expense of a writer's individuality. Furthermore, it seems as if one could not use these generalized systems to explain a writer's individual development.

We can, however, overcome this impasse by considering the dynamic nature of traditional rhetorical theory as a model of *Bildung*, and not just as an ahistorical collection of terms and definitions. That is, built into the rhetorical system we find an explanation of how the young orator can develop an individual "voice" by means of a paradoxical confrontation with predecessors in a series of *exercitationes* designed to lead the student from imitation to an independent style. The basic structure, which we encountered in the handbook appendices on further aids to the student, is the same for all would-be writers: *lectio* of the great masters of the past, *selectio* of the best passages on the basis of the faculty of *critica*, *imitatio* of these *exempla*, variation of them through *translatio* and *modi tractandi*, until the pupil's pen (*stylus*) becomes a weapon to defeat his precursor in the struggle of *aemulatio*. When put in this schematic form, the classical program of *aemulatio* through reading and writing exercises might not seem appropriately modern to account for the development of a writer of philosophy in the late-

---

2. Heinrich Lausberg, *Handbuch der literarischen Rhetorik* (Munich: Max Hueber, 1960), considers the conflict between *ars* and *natura* the fundamental opposition behind rhetorical theory (pars. 1–8). It is especially significant for the role rhetoric played in pedagogy since education meant the "art" of leading out or developing the internal natural talents of the pupil.

eighteenth century—especially after the craze of "genius" in the period of *Sturm und Drang* in Germany. And yet, the lasting impact of this traditional program can be seen in the work by pseudo-Longinus, *On the Sublime*, which had been "rediscovered" beginning around the middle of the eighteenth century.[3] Significantly, the young Hegel translated it as part of a rhetorical exercise in his school.[4] Hence a brief discussion of Longinus's treatise can map out the trajectory that from the first century to the eighteenth guided young authors to stylistic and conceptual independence through written reworking of written models.

Longinus deals with a writer's struggle with written tradition in Chapter 13. He begins his favorable account of the powers of written imitation with a reference to Plato, a somewhat ironic remark perhaps given Plato's critique of *mimesis* in the *Republic*. Longinus writes: "Provided that we are ready to give him [Plato] due attention, this author shows us that, in addition to those already mentioned, there is another way that leads to the sublime. And what kind of way is this? it is the *imitation and emulation* of the great historians and poets of the past" (*Sublime*, 13, 2).

Longinus focuses in his account on the power of imitation to invest the poet with his "own" voice rather than on the details of the educative process. He equates imitation with the breath or spirit of divine inspiration:

> For many authors catch fire from the inspiration of others—just as we are told that the Pythian priestess, when she approaches the tripod standing by the cleft in the ground from which, they say, there is breathed out a divine vapour, is impregnated thence with the heavenly power, and by virtue of this afflatus is at once inspired to speak oracles. So too, as though issuing from sacred orifices, certain emanations are conveyed from the genius of men of old into the souls of those who emulate them, and, breathing in these influences, even those who show very few signs of inspiration derive some degree of divine enthusiasm from the grandeur of their predecessors. [*Sublime*, 13, 2]

3. On the reception of *On the Sublime* in Germany, see Karl Vietor, "Die Idee des Erhabenen in der deutschen Literatur," in *Geist und Form* (Bern: Francke, 1952). All citations below are from the Loeb edition trans. W. F. Fyfe (Cambridge, Mass.: Harvard University Press, 1965).

4. Karl Rosenkranz, *Hegels Leben* (Berlin, 1844; reprint, Darmstadt: Wissenchaftliche Buchgesellschaft, 1971), mentions Hegel's complete translation of Longinus (p. 16). Although Hegel himself never mentions it, it was probably a part of the private instruction he received from Professor Hopf (e.g., Hegel does mention translating Cicero with him).

"Inspiration" by the "letter," that is, writings, of past traditions makes it possible even for the otherwise unsuited writer to receive the "spirit."[5] Imitative inspiration affects not only the style of expression but its unique content and direction as well. Longinus finds the process essential to Plato's philosophy, for the struggle with past models helped constitute that philosophy: "I do not think there would have been so fine a bloom on Plato's philosophical doctrines, or that he would have embarked on poetic subject-matter and phraseology, had he not been striving heart and soul with Homer for first place, like a young contestant entering the ring with a long-admired champion" (*Sublime*, 13, 4).[6] For Plato, the harsh struggle with the poet of the past gave his philosophy its drive: "perhaps showing too keen a spirit of emulation in his desire to break a lance with him, so to speak, yet getting some profit from the endeavor" (*Sublime*, 13, 4). For those writers who do not begin their careers with immediately apparent "genius" or "inspiration"— and one can think of Hegel as compared to his younger friend and colleague Schelling—individuation is a long and tedious process in which the course traced out in his imitative readings and writings will determine the direction of his later development.

Hegel's first essay written in Tübingen, where he began studying theology after graduating from the *gymnasium*, clearly continues his rhetorical training from his school years in a Longinian spirit. The essay, "Ueber einige Vorteile, welche uns die Lektüre der alten klassischen griechischen und römischen Schriftsteller gewährt" (On some Advantages, Which the Reading of the Ancient Classical Greek and Roman Writers Grants Us; December 1788), reworks the school exercise "Über einige charakteristische Unterschiede der alten Dichter [von den neuren]" (On Some Characteristic Differences of the Ancient Poets [from the Modern]; August 1788).[7] The new emphasis on

5. This significant reversal of the dichotomy between the spirit and the letter undermines theories of spontaneous genius. Recall that Haug, true to this rhetorical tradition, also thought that great writers could be "made" by imitating and internalizing past models.

Here we also encounter a theory of literary history that leads eventually to something like Harold Bloom's *The Anxiety of Influence* (New York: Oxford University Press, 1973). This chapter can be considered a rhetorical analysis in the field of philosophy of one writer's struggle with the influence of traditions.

6. The wrestling (or general struggle) metaphor is common in treatments of literary or philosophical histories. They most likely can be traced back to Quintilian, *Institutio Oratoria*, in which the young writer must struggle (*contendere*) with the older in matches (*certamen*) (x, 2–3).

7. The Tübingen essay is printed in Johannes Hoffmeister, *Dokumente zu Hegels Entwicklung* (Stuttgart: Fromann, 1936), pp. 169–72. The Stuttgart essay is printed in

"reading" (*Lektüre*), however, reflects Hegel's growing awareness of his role as receiver, transmitter, and reworker of the past tradition.

The Tübingen essay uses arguments that could be found in Quintilian's *Institutio* to justify reading the works of the ancients. Hegel begins by commenting on the tradition formed by their works. The history of their *reception* is now his central interest: "What makes the ancient Greek and Roman writers necessarily noteworthy for us is the respect that they maintained in the same intensity in almost every century, even though they of course were not appreciated at all times for the same reasons."[8] Hegel mentions a key paradox that will occupy him over the next decade; indeed, by quoting Lessing's critique of "bookish learning" (*Buchgelehrsamkeit*),[9] Hegel implicates himself and his own writing within the vagaries of this paradox of modern *Bildung*. That is, as we shall see throughout this chapter, an objectively presented problem of an individual's relationship to tradition applies to his own development. On the one hand, the ancients are not mere "treasure chambers" (*Rüstkammer*) of *exempla*, for their spirit can speak directly to ours. On the other, we learn of their spirit and its concepts only by way of reading their books and reworking (digesting) their content: "they superbly serve the function that one can collect (*sammeln*) out of them the concepts that then become the material that the other faculties of the soul can rework (*der Stoff . . . , den die andern Seelenkräfte bearbeiten*)."[10] Further, since we model the world according to these concepts, the ancients can expand our experience by granting us their spiritual or mental concepts via their language, which is but a form of treasure chest after all: "Moreover, in this regard language is for us a limited collection of determined concepts (*eine begrenzte Sammlung bestimmter Begriffe*) according to which we model (*modeln*) what we see or notice. An essential advantage that the learning of foreign languages can grant

---

Friedhlem Nicolin, *Der junge Hegel in Stuttgart*, (Stuttgart: Kohlhammer, 1976), pp. 76–79. The Stuttgart essay, as mentioned above in chap. 1, praises Greek originality, criticizes modern imitativeness, but then prescribes "the learning of foreign languages" so that our minds will be filled up with words and structures that lead us to original thoughts.

8. Hoffmeister, *Dokumente*, p. 169.

9. In the high school essay he also quoted the lines from Lessing's *Nathan der Weise* which criticize "the cold book-learning that merely imprints onto the brain dead signs" (*die kalte Buchgelehrsamkeit, die sich / mit todten Zeichen in's Gehirn nur drückt*; Nicolin, *Hegel in Stuttgart*, p. 77).

10. Hoffmeister, *Dokumente*, p. 169. Here we have the traces of Quintilian's digestive metaphor for the act of reading (*Institutio Oratoria*, x, 1, 19), a metaphor that accompanies Hegel throughout his philosophical career.

us is certainly that in this way our concepts are enriched, especially if the culture of the peoples who spoke this language is different from our own."[11] Language thus contributes to our formative *Bildung* by giving us the forms by which we then give form to ourselves and our world.

Given the nature of Hegel's training, it is not surprising that he stresses the role of translation as a pedagogical exercise that enriches our understanding as it exploits the role of language as mediator between our thought and the world (of the past): "The attempt to translate such concepts into our language gives us cause to examine the words more closely in terms of their finer distinctions and to use them more correctly. It goes without saying to what extent the concepts themselves gain in precision by the investigation of the differences between the words, and to what extent the faculty of understanding is thereby sharpened and trained."[12] True to the model of classical rhetoric, he then introduces a scheme for exercises in reading and writing based on the age-old subdivision of genres taught in the humanistic *gymnasium*: poetic (*schöne*) works; *die Historie*, that is, *die Geschichtsschreiber*; and philosophy ("what an effective [*zweckmäßige*] preparation for the study of philosophy is the reading [*das Lesen*] of the same").[13] Hegel's graduation from his rhetorically oriented *gymnasium* therefore meant not a break with that tradition but the traditional extension of its didactic program.

We shall consider in the following analysis of Hegel's writings over the next decade—his theological manuscripts from Bern (1793–97) and Frankfurt (1797–1800)—the way he applied his internalized rhetorical *Bildung* to a program of reading, selecting, translating, and writing. Hegel developed and matured intellectually during these years. It is by no means obvious, however, that such development of thought necessarily need occur in writing. And yet Hegel did write during these years—constantly, voluminously—and it is only by tracing the steps of his rhetorico-hermeneutical confrontation with different traditions in writing that we can observe both his further *Bildung* and the development of his concept of *Bildung*. Ever since Dilthey's monograph on

11. Hoffmeister, *Dokumente*, p. 169. This passage also has close parallels in bk. x of the *Institutio Oratoria*, where Quintilian justifies the imitation of past masters.

12. Hoffmeister, *Dokumente*, p. 171. The notion of "sharpening the understanding" is itself a translation of the categories of *ingenium* and *iudicium* (*Scharfsinn*).

13. Ibid. Quintilian also divides the canon of texts which the student must work through into three genres: "Lectio poetarum, historiarum, philosophorum" (*Institutio Oratoria*, x, 1, 31ff.). These genres and their corresponding styles, as we saw, determined the nature of the curriculum of the Stuttgart *gymnasium*.

Hegel's theological manuscripts, Hegel scholarship has recognized the importance of the ideas in these writings for an understanding of his later philosophy.[14] Because the rhetorical context of Hegel's *Bildung* has remained unexplored, however, no study has considered the *function* of the writing itself and the *forms* that these writings possess as significant for his philosophical development.[15] I will show how in these manuscripts Hegel undertook the reworking of traditions—in his case the biblical, Kantian, and humanist-rhetorical—as prescribed by the rhetorical program in order to develop his own sense of identity as a writer. These texts function on two levels of signification and hence might be considered allegories of their own unfolding: They thematize and translate into abstract philosophical vocabulary the process of their own stylistic development. Hegel's analysis of the concept of *Bildung* in particular, which is central to these manuscripts, contains in allegorical form the *Bildung* of the texts themselves as stages on the path to individuality. The paradoxes of that path thus enter into Hegel's earliest representations of his dialectic.

The immediate background of Hegel's rhetorical reworking of various traditions in the theological manuscripts is his study at the "Tü-

---

14. The major intellectual biographies of Hegel during this period are: Wilhelm Dilthey, *Die Jugendgeschichte Hegels*, in *Gesammelte Werke*, vol. 4 (Leipzig: Teubner, 1921; 1st ed. 1905). Dilthey wrote this biography after he issued a call for essays on the young Hegel (dealing with the newly discovered theological manuscripts) but was unsatisfied with the submissions. He is mostly concerned with uncovering "the philosophical predisposition" (*das Philosophische in der Anlage*) of the young Hegel (p. 5). Gunnar Aspelin, *Hegels Tübinger Fragment: Eine psychologisch-ideengeschichtliche Untersuchung*, in *Lunds Universitets-Arsskrift*, N.F. Aud I, vol. 28, no. 27 (Lund: Hakan Ohlsson, 1933). Bernard Dinkel, *Der junge Hegel und die Aufhebung des subjektiven Idealismus*, in *Münchner philosophische Forschungen*, vol. 9 (Bonn: Bouvier, 1974). This is the most detailed treatment of Hegel's philosophical development during these years. Adrien Péperzak, *Le jeune Hegel et la vision morale du monde* (The Hague: Martinus Nijhoff, 1969). Carl-Ludwig Furck, *Der Bildungsbegriff des jungen Hegel* (Weilheim: Julius Beltz, 1953). Furck's work is clearly of great significance for this book. He works through the early works systematically to demonstrate his thesis: "The theological writings of the young Hegel are, seen correctly, pedagogical writings in their substance and origin" (p. 7), the goal of which was the transformation of the world through *Volksreligion*.

15. Two exceptions, radically different from each other, have already been mentioned: Theodor Haering, *Hegel: Sein Wollen und Sein Werk—Eine chronologische Entwicklungsgeschichte der Gedanken und Sprache Hegels* (Leipzig: Teubner, 1929–38); and Werner Hamacher, *pleroma: Zu Genesis und Struktur einer dialektischen Hermeneutik bei Hegel*, introduction to Hegel, *Der Geist des Christentums* (Frankfurt: Ullstein, 1978). Haering's painstaking study is one-sided to the extent that he considers only how Hegel's thoughts influenced the form of his writing, and never how learned formal structures could have influenced Hegel's thoughts. Hamacher, to whom I am indebted, investigates (deconstructs) the digestive metaphors in Hegel's theological manuscripts and thus pursues the influences of Hegel's acts of reading and interpreting on his writing.

binger Stift" (1788–93).[16] His only writings from the period an Tübingen (besides the essay on reading the ancients discussed above) are four homilies delivered during his last years as part of his training toward becoming a preacher. Although the actual homilies are of little interest to us here, the fact that he was trained in the homiletic tradition, which occupies a central position in the development of rhetoric and hermeneutics, can help us better understand the task he faced when he started to write in Bern.[17]

Homiletics underwent numerous shifts in emphasis, function, and context throughout history.[18] Originally, the sermon had the practical function of creating a common forum for the religious community. Later, Augustine's *De Doctrina Christiana* introduced classical rhetoric into the theory and practice of preaching in order to convert. The humanists and reformers stressed understanding the spirit of Scripture over rhetorical *persuasio*, though classical rhetoric still influenced their homiletic practice.[19] In late eighteenth-century Germany the oratory of the pulpit (*Kanzelwohlredenheit*) became one of the last refuges of rhetorical praxis which had no other outlet in the public or political spheres. The underlying feature of all homiletics remained, however, the necessity to "translate," both literally and figuratively, biblical pas-

---

16. See Martin Leube, *Das Tübinger Stift: 1750–1950* (Stuttgart: Kohlhammer, 1954).

17. The Zeugnis that Hegel received upon graduating from the *Stift* indicates the way categories from classical rhetoric were applied to religious training: "an eloquence by no means pleasing, few gestures, good temperament [talent], carefully cultivated discernment, a strong memory, a style of writing which is not difficult to read, an honest character, diligence though sometimes interrupted, sufficient resources. He has not neglected theological studies, has labored, not without zeal, on homiletics. Does not appear to be a great orator in recitation. He is not inexperienced in philosophy, [for] he has expended much exertion on it" ("eloquium haud gratum, gestus pauci, ingenium bonum, iudicium excultum, memoria tenax, scriptio lectu non difficilis, mores recti, industria nonnumquam interrupta, opes sufficientes. Studia theologica non neglexit, orationem sacram non sine studio elaboravit, in recitando non magnus orator visus. Philosophiae non ignarus, philosophiae multam operam impendit"; Hoffmeister, *Dokumente*, pp. 435–36). It is noteworthy that the school authorities see a connection between Hegel's mastery of rhetorical forms but poor *pronuntio*, on the one hand, and the turn to philosophy, on the other. Hegel is a key promoter of this "internalization" of rhetoric.

18. For a general overview on preaching in Germany, see the article "Homiletik" in *Religion in Geschichte und Gegenwart*, ed. Kurt Galling (Tübingen: Mohr, 1957–65). On the role of the homily as a refuge for rhetoric in Germany at the close of the eighteenth century, see Walter Hinderer, "Kurze Geschichte der deutschen Rede," in *Über deutsche Literatur und Rede* (Munich: Fink, 1981). Recall as well Hegel's interest in the homiletic oratory of the Catholic priest in Stuttgart (chap. 1, n. 108).

19. See the essay by Klaus Dockhorn, "Rhetorica movet: Protestantischer Humanismus und karolingische Renaissance," and that by Franz Sieveke, "Eloquentia Sacra: Zur Predigttheorie des Nicolaus Caussinus, S.J.," in Helmut Schanze, ed., *Rhetorik: Beiträge zu ihrer Geschichte in Deutschland* (Frankfurt: Fischer, 1974).

sages for the audience. The homily unites passive reception of Scripture, creative interpretation, and communication of the text's message to the community. Schleiermacher, the father of modern hermeneutics, viewed the sermon as a significant rhetorico-hermeneutical model, characterizing it as a "dialogic process" (*dialogisches Verfahren*), for the preacher conducts a "conversation . . . with his biblical passage . . . and with his community."[20] For Hegel, homiletics introduced a new hermeneutical dimension into his writing. He no longer merely applied memorized *praecepta* and *exempla* to arbitrary incidents from everyday life as in his diaries, but used his rhetorical training to confront a theological tradition in a state of transition.

The problem of "translating" the Bible into "modern" terms took a particular form in Tübingen in the last decades of the eighteenth century. Enlightenment theology had just reached its acme—and faced some of its greatest challenges—in several of Kant's works on religion and ethics (the latter dealing with a nonsupernatural justification of the good and a moralistic foundation for religion): the second *Critique* (1788), *Religion innerhalb der Grenzen der bloßen Vernunft* (Religion within the Limits of Reason Alone; 1793), and *Metaphysik der Sitten* (Metaphysics of Morals; 1797). The father of the Tübingen school of theology, Gottlob Christian Storr, strove to develop a means of exegesis that would combine Kant's critique of reason and doctrine of virtue (*Tugendlehre*) with biblical literalism.[21] Kant even thanks Storr in the second edition of the *Religion within Limits* for his analysis of the work in terms of theological doctrine.[22] Storr and his colleagues in Tübingen attempted to counter both orthodoxy, with its emphasis on symbolic books and convoluted systems of interpretation, and the new philosophical and philological methods of historical criticism. Against the

20. Quoted from *Religion in Geschichte und Gegenwart*, p. 439. Gadamer follows Schleiermacher in his use of the sermon as a key model for hermeneutical understanding (in spite of Gadamer's general critique of Schleiermacher). In *Wahrheit und Methode* (pp. 162ff., and 313ff.) he stresses the tensions inherent in homiletics since, in the end, all that must speak is the prophecy (*Verkündigung*) of the Word itself, although the acts of creative interpretation and rhetorical exposition (*Vollzug* and *Auslegung*) by the exegete and preacher are also necessary.

21. For an account of the Tübinger school of theology, see Hermelink, *Geschichte der evangelischen Kirche in Württemberg von der Reformation bis zur Gegenwart*, esp. "Das Reich Gottes in Wirtemberg" (Stuttgart: Wunderlich, 1949), pp. 301–20; Martin Brecht, and Jörg Sandberger, "Hegels Begegnung mit der Theologie im Tübinger Stift: Eine neue Quelle für die Studienzeit Hegels," in *Hegel-Studien* 5 (1969); and Dieter Henrich, "Historische Voraussetzungen von Hegels System," in *Hegel in Kontext* (Frankfurt am Main: Suhrkamp, 1967).

22. Kant, *Religion innerhalb der Grenzen der bloßen Vernunft*, Akademie Ausgabe, vol. 6 (Berlin, 1907), p.13.

latter they stressed the divine origin of the biblical word (hence this theology was called *Supranaturalismus*), and against the former they stressed, as did Kant, the simple ethical doctrines as stated in Scripture. The resulting method of writing sermons consisted of merely listing and reformulating biblical passages (what Storr called *repetita*) and juxtaposing them with general statements on morality in order to show that the teachings of Christ were in unison with the doctrines of practical reason.[23] His "compromising reconciliation" of these two powerful traditions did little more than allow them to coexist in uneasy contiguity.[24]

But supranaturalism's mere juxtaposition of philosophical and biblical language was soon threatened and replaced by a more powerful rhetorical and hermeneutical effort to interpret the one language or tradition in terms of the other. Hegel apparently refers to this approach when he writes in a letter to Schelling that Fichte was on the verge of "exploding" traditional biblical exegesis from *within*.[25] This attempt to do more than merely juxtapose biblical and Kantian discourse occupied young theologians from the mid-1790s on.[26] In July 1795 the religious authorities in charge of pedagogical issues visited the

---

23. "Supranaturalism . . . is not a science of belief, it must be only exegesis, an exposition of that which has been revealed through the Christ and the biblical authors. The exegesis must not assert anything without being able to support the assertion with a biblical citation. Often, to be sure, the biblical citations become piled up and interrupt the flow of the presentation. Out of this there results a thoroughly atomistic method for the representation of revealed truths. Its usage of the Scripture (*Schriftgebrauch*) consists of the confused placing of citations from all the books of the Bible, one after the other." Hermelink, *Evangelische Kirche*, p. 302. Aspelin implies that though Storr's and Hegel's theological theories did not correspond, the methods of the former were extremely influential: "The work was, from a purely scientific point of view, [full] of exegetical and dogmatic problems of great importance. It was [thus] highly suited to the development of a sense of philological exactness and a logical character" (*Hegels Tübinger Fragment*, p. 20). Precisely this *philological* influence should be kept in mind. Thus, even though Henrich is correct that "in their early writings Schelling and Hegel had set themselves the task of thwarting Storr and the forces allied with him" ("Historische Voraussetzungen," p. 55), the methods had been deeply internalized even in the struggle against the content.

24. The phrase (*kompromißhafte Versöhnung*) is from Dinkel, *Der junge Hegel*, pp. 78–79.

25. See Johannes Hoffmeister, ed., *Briefe von und an Hegel*, (Hamburg: Felix Meiner, 1961) no. 8.

26. For further background on Enlightenment theology in Germany, see Karl Aner, *Die Theologie der Lessingzeit* (Halle/Saale: Niemeyer, 1929); Karl Barth, *Protestant Thought: From Rousseau to Ritchl*, trans. Brian Cozens (New York: Harper, 1959); Hans W. Frei, *The Eclipse of Biblical Narrative. A Study in Eighteenth- and Nineteenth-Century Hermeneutics* (New Haven, Conn.: Yale University Press, 1974); and Emanuel Hirsch, *Geschichte der neuern evangelischen Theologie im Zusammenhang mit den allgemeinen Bewegungen des europäischen Denkens*, 5 vols. (Gutersloh: Mohn, 1948–51). I am grateful to Thomas Saine for his help on these issues.

Stift and voiced their concern over the students' new mode of preaching:

> Ever since Kant, with his highly valued example, led the way, [first], in verifying truths that belong to religion within the bounds of pure reason with scriptural passages . . . containing positive doctrines and, [second], in representing the historical aspects of Christianity merely as a vehicle for pure ideas of reason, ever since then . . . *allegorizing (das Allegorizieren)* about biblical passages . . . has met with widespread applause.[27]

By the time this report was written, Hegel, who abandoned the profession of theology largely out of displeasure with the inadequate solutions offered in Tübingen, had been living in Bern and working as a private tutor for nearly two years.[28] It is not surprising that the frag-

---

27. Dinkel, *Der junge Hegel*, p. 83. Originally cited in Horst Fuhrmans, *F.W.J. Schellings Briefe und Dokumente*, vol. 1 (Bonn: Bouvier, 1962). Hegel's own four sermons (Hoffmeister, *Dokumente*, pp. 175–90) are weak in comparison with this radical imagery. They are all cast in the same rigid structure. The first, on a passage from the Old Testament shows, according to Péperzak, "to what degree the thought of the young theological student is an amalgam of traditional and Kantian elements" (*Le jeune Hegel*, p. 9), whereby the emphasis should be placed on the word *amalgamation*, since he largely relies on a *repetita* of biblical citations and Kantian-sounding formulations. The second sermon, on the Kingdom of God, introduces a favorite topic of Hegel and Hölderlin. Again there is a listing of biblical references (*Dokumente*, pp. 179f.) and reformulations from Kant's *Religion innerhalb der Grenzen der reinen Vernunft*. Only the last sermon goes somewhat farther in the direction of converting the Bible into a catalog of Kantian virtues (*Tugendlehre*). Thus, given the conservatism of the Stift, these "allegories" still consist of a mere juxtaposition of discourses. It takes Hegel years of practice to develop a more integrated means of *translatio*.
An additional point deserves mention here: By considering these early writings as Hegel's rhetorical exercises in Kantian and biblical discourses, one can place the hotly debated question of when Hegel actually studied Kant into a different light. (Dinkel offers an overview of the secondary literature in *Der junge Hegel*, pp. 106ff.). Leutwein, a fellow student of Hegel's, claimed that "Hegel was an eclectic and roamed around cavalierly in the domain of knowledge." Recently, however, Dieter Henrich has placed more emphasis on Hegel's intensive study of Kant in Tübingen. Similarly, Hoffmeister believes that Hegel's Kant studies in Tübingen had the "actual influence" (*eigentlichen Einfluß*) on his theological investigations. From my standpoint, the question of when Hegel grappled on a *theoretical* plane with Kant's ideas is of secondary importance. Hegel, either on his own or through Storr, was concerned with *formal* treatments of Kantian discourse in his homilies. His rhetorical concern came before his philosophical investigations. This progression is in full keeping with Quintilian's statement from bk. x of the *Institutio Oratoria*: "proxima stilo cogitatio est" (6,1).
28. Little is known of Hegel's life in Bern. Dilthey speaks of it as a time of loneliness and despondency (*Die Jugendgeschichte Hegels*, pp. 15f). Lukács stresses the way the idea of the dialectic "grew organically out of the soil of Hegel's thinking about social and histor-

ments he wrote there deal with precisely the concerns voiced in this report: the relationships between traditions—biblical, Kantian, Enlightenment, and classical—and the effects produced by looking at one tradition from the perspective, and in the terms, of another. In a sense, the theological fragments continue the exercises he began in the excerpts as a schoolboy, for here too he strives to appropriate to himself the discourse of given traditions, what he will come to call by a variety of terms "the given" (*das Gegebene, das Vorhandene,* or *das Positive*). The difference between these fragments and his earlier exercises is one of degree: In accordance with the more advanced state of his rhetorical *Bildung* he applies more complex and expansive techniques. As a result, he comments on his own textual enterprise indirectly, that is, not in the obvious rhetorical terminology we found in the diaries but in terms of the traditions he is striving to appropriate and reformulate. In the process of translating traditions, he reflects on his own rhetorical activity in terms of nonrhetorical discourses. Thus, the analysis contained in this chapter is as much interpretive as it is philological since it strives to reveal connections between the level of explicit argumentation of Hegel's texts and an implicit textualizing practice that structures and to some extent even motivates the argumentation.

Let us first consider the form of the fragments from the Bern period. By contextualizing them as *exercitationes* for the attainment of a finer style and ease in writing—what Quintilian calls *firma facilitas* through the copious production of words and ideas (*copia rerum ac verborum*)[29]—we can call upon a historical and systematic rhetorical apparatus to give order to the massive amount of eclectic texts. This apparatus is traditionally employed by the young writer after he has mastered the art of literally translating from one language into the other (as Hegel had done in Stuttgart). It consists of the techniques of *modi tractandi* or *pluribus modis tractare* ("the different compositional modes of dealing with a topic").[30] These *modi* allow Hegel to perform a variety of prescribed textual transformations. In fact, in the theolog-

---

ical questions, out of what the inherent contradiction showed to him" (*Der junge Hegel*, pp. 35–80). Since there is so little information about the Bern period, I shall concentrate on the "biography" of the existing writings in order to see how key ideas and dialectical strategies arose out of the processes of writing and reflecting on writing.

The three groups of texts to be dealt with are: "Fragmente über Volksreligion und Christentum" (1793–94); *Das Leben Jesu* (1794–95), and the "Positivität der christlichen Religion" (1795–96). Page numbers within parentheses refer to the *Theorie-Werkausgabe*, vol. 1, *Frühe Schriften* (Frankfurt am Main: Suhrkamp, 1978). "Das Leben Jesu" is quoted from Hermann Nohl, *Hegels theologische Jugendschriften* (Tübingen: Mohr-Siebeck, 1907).

29. Quintilian, *Institutio Oratoria* x,1,1 and x,1,5.
30. Lausberg, *Handbuch*, pars. 1104–39.

writings and especially in his later work, we find the term *Behandlungs-art*, the literal translation of *modus tractandi*, occurring in significant places.[31] I do not wish to imply in what follows that Hegel sat down and said to himself: Now I'll compose an exercise according to this or that *modus*, or that these fragments are "only" rhetorical exercises. That is, although I place great emphasis on heretofore undiscussed *formal* features of these texts, I do not intend to reduce their philosophical significance. Rather my concern is, first, that Hegel clearly attempted to order and organize his thoughts through writing; second, that such organizational principles already existed in the rhetorical tradition; and hence, third, that his activities in these years involved a gradual formulation of his thought on the basis of "rhetorical" forms.[32]

One of the standard forms of rhetorical periphrasis prescribed by the classical orators in order to cultivate the powers of thought and expression is the rewriting of a poem into prose, that is, the dissolution of verse (*versus solvere*).[33] This gives the young writer the opportunity not only to internalize powerful images but also to sharpen his judgment, as Balthasar Haug taught, on the appropriate use of linguistic forms. We discover such an exercise in a fragment describing the change that has taken place from the religion of the Greeks, in which ceremonies and the gods themselves were fully integrated into all aspects of everyday life, to the modern "enlightened" form of Christianity. It is certainly one of the young Hegel's most powerful descriptions of the richness of Greek antiquity and can be considered a prime example of his vision of a *Volksreligion* as a religion that meets human needs and of its fate under Christianity. No interpretation has yet pointed

---

31. For example, p. 104 in the introduction to the "Positivity" essay, and in the title of Hegel's essay on natural law (see chap. 3, below).

32. Hegel's method of developing his thought and style (*Stilbildung* and *Denkübung*) parallels the insightful argument in Heinrich von Kleist's essay (ca. 1807) on "the gradual completion of thought while speaking" (*Über die allmähliche Verfertigung der Gedanken beim Reden*). Although the content of Kleist's essay focuses on speaking, the form of the essay shows how a written dialogue with traditions accomplishes the same development. The philological method I employ by no means rules out that these texts deal with philosophical issues, but, rather, focuses on the written form of Hegel's working out of the issues. What is at stake in these fragments is, to use the title of a book by Werner Hartknopf, the "breakthrough to the dialectic in Hegel's thought" (*Durchbruch zur Dialektik in Hegels Denken* [Meisenheim am Glan: Anton Hain, 1976]). Hartknopf considers the dialectic a *Sichtweise* by which one views a problem from many sides, each of which reveals a different, even conflicting, aspect of a historical phenomenon. Hartknopf considers these fragments "Hegel's wrestling (*Ringen*) with [the problem of] the representation of a phenomenon that cannot be adequately and completely grasped by the concept of reflection (*Reflexionsdenken*)" (p. 73).

33. Lausberg, *Handbuch*, par. 1100,1.

out, however, the remarkable similarities between this fragment and Schiller's masterful poem "Die Götter Griechenlands," published in 1788 (reworked in 1793 and republished in 1800 in an abridged form removing many of the harshest descriptions of Christianity).[34] Not only are the themes of the two works closely related—this alone, given the fascination with Greece that was sweeping Germany, would not be special—but individual words and images repeat themselves with only minor variation. Both texts contain contrasts between the Bacchanalia and cold reason, and between the concept of "fraternal" Greek festivals and the "sad gaze" accompanying Christian rites; both texts refer to the Greeks as nurtured at the breasts of nature; both use the image of "apron strings."[35]

If these textual echoes lead us—in spite of the lack of extratextual evidence—to pursue what Hegel might be doing with Schiller's text, we can postulate that he is performing a rhetorical transformation from Schiller's poetic apostrophes to the Greek past and extensive use of metonymic description (details and names from Greek mythology) into statements that *summarize* the point of the description in prosaic terms. Let us compare the common treatment of the change of ceremonies introduced by the Christian victory over Greek pantheism.[36] Schiller lists the Greek "crowning festivities" (*kronenreichen Feste*): heroic games, chariot races, dances; Hegel speaks merely of "a public festival" (*von einem öffentlichen Feste*) at which one enjoyed oneself (*sich lustig machte*). Schiller describes the feeling of actually walking into a Christian cathedral: "What am I entering [now]? This mournful silence . . . ominous" ("Wohin trete ich? Diese traurige Stille . . . finster"); Hegel merely mentions the "the too dismal external aspect" (*zu düstere Außenseite*) of Christianity and the sense that one must degrade oneself vis-à-vis the modern church (*in den Tempel schleichen*). Schiller describes in four lines the sacrifices and sacrificial meals that made up the core of Greek ceremonies ("Seiner Güter schenkte man das Beste, / Seiner Lämmer liebstes gab der Hirt . . ."); Hegel merely counterfactually states that one cannot expect men to gladly give up life's pleasures (*die Freuden des Lebens hingeben*) at Christianity's behest (*Forderungen*). Numerous other passages reveal the same process at work: Hegel has internalized the

34. Hegel cites other poems by Schiller on a number of occasions explicitly in the manuscripts (pp. 53, 177, 184).
35. Hegel, p. 41, Schiller, strophe x; Hegel, p. 42, Schiller, strophe xx; Hegel's *inversio* of Schiller's "An der Freude leichtem Gängelband" (strophe 1) into the negative *am Gängelband der Worte* (p. 43); Hegel, p. 44, Schiller, strophe 11.
36. Schiller, strophes 1, xii and Hegel, p. 41.

poem in order to reproduce it "in his own language."[37] Schiller's poetry has given way to the "prose of the world."

The basic form of such a creative textual comparison, which either reworks a text in its entirety or juxtaposes topoi and common images, is provided in Quintilian's rhetorical program by the *modus tractandi* called *comparatio*.[38] It dominates many of the fragments since it offers Hegel the means of bringing together the traditions he has inherited. At this point in his writing, he works exclusively with pairs. Typically, when Hegel writes descriptions, following the related *modus tractandi*, *descriptio*,[39] he selects aspects of the Christian and Greek traditions for comparison. An obvious example is the fragment "On the Difference in the Scene of Death" (pp. 67–69), a favorite comparative description of the eighteenth century.[40] Another of Hegel's favorite comparisons is that between the persons and works of Christ and Socrates. Here Hegel is clearly employing *amplificatio*,[41] the reworking of and expanding upon *exempla* and topoi that he had acquired in school. He returns, for example, to the scene of Socrates' death: "Before his death—he died like a Greek and sacrificed a chicken to Aesculapes . . . —he spoke to his disciples about the immortality of the soul" (p. 53), which he had worked on already as a *hebdomadarium* in school and excerpted from an Enlightenment handbook.

In making these comparisons he even reworks his own images, sometimes reversing their meaning, along the lines outlined by Quintilian: "It is useful not only to translate foreign texts (*aliena transferre*) in this way, but also to treat our own efforts in various ways (*nostra pluribus modis tractare*), such that we take certain of our ideas and transform them, as often as we possibly can, in the manner that out of the same wax different forms (*aliae formae*) can be modeled."[42] One very detailed

37. For example, strophes III and IV of Schiller's poem list the gods and wonders of pantheism, whereas Hegel (p. 41) offers a summarizing assertion: "If religion is to be capable of having an effect on the nation, it must accompany [man] amicably everywhere." It is of particular interest that Hegel crossed out a description in his manuscript that strongly attacks the image of the Christian God (*einen anderen Genius der Nationen hat das Abendland*; p. 44). Schiller removed a number of similar-sounding middle strophes from his revision.

38. Lausberg, *Handbuch*, par. 1130.

39. Ibid., par. 1133.

40. Written descriptions of Greek representations became popular and significant thanks to J. J. Winckelmann, *Gedanken über die Nachahmung der griechischen Werke in der Malerei und Bildhauerkunst* (1755); Lessing turned specifically toward Greek depictions of death in his *Wie die Alten den Tod gebildet*.

41. Lausberg, *Handbuch*, pars. 61,3 and 400–409.

42. Quintilian, *Institutio Oratoria*, x, 5, 9.

example is the way Hegel varies, indeed reverses, a description he has of Socrates when he applies it to Christ. In an early fragment, Hegel writes that Socrates "criticized people in conversation in the most naive way on earth" (*stieg den Leuten so in der Konversation auf die unbefangenste Art in der Welt aufs Dach*; p. 48), whereas later this very description is used when writing critically of Christ as opposed to Socrates: "He [Socrates] left behind no masonic signs, no order to propagate his name, no method of criticizing the soul or pouring morality into it" ("Er [Socrates] hinterließ keine maurerischen Zeichen, keinen Befehl, seinen Namen zu verkündigen, keine Methode, der Seele auf das Dach zu steigen und Moralität in sie zu giessen"; pp. 53–54).

At the end of this transformative process of writing and rewriting, after working a couple of years with these images and opposing descriptions of Socrates to the orthodoxy of the Christian church, Hegel then seems to recognize that such a manipulation of topoi is actually a common practice, a necessary though now tedious exercise of using the ancients as positive *exempla* in relation to Christian pessimism: "One has held up (*entgegengesetzt*) Socrates, [and] so many virtuous pagans, [and] many an innocent race, in opposition to doctrines (*Sätzen*) [of Christianity; for example, that there is no such thing as a 'good man'] to the point of boredom (*bis zum Langweiligwerden*)" (p. 91).[43] The explicit rejection of a commonplace rhetorical structure follows years of its internalizing use.

The other pair of traditions that Hegel formally reworks in his fragments by means of contrastive comparisons is that of Christianity and Kantian ethics. With these Hegel is able to employ a wider variety of rhetorical skills beyond *descriptio*. His first efforts remain within the limits offered him by the homiletics from the Tübinger Stift: mere juxtapositions and crass applications. The so-called "Three Fragments on a Critique of Christianity," for example, extract statements from Kant, which form the "Schema," and then expand them on the basis of examples from Christian doctrine. Hegel's *modus operandi*, one can sur-

43. The other fragments from his first year in Bern deal with similar topoi for comparing the classical and Christian religious traditions. He explores the different modes of representation which they have taken on throughout history. He compares, for example, the *compendia* of Christian orthodoxy to the lyrical language of Matthew's Gospel in terms of their effects on *Bildung* (p. 46). He examines the difference between "oral instruction" (*den mündlichen Unterricht*) of the early Christians and its extension "through writing" (*durch Schriften*) in the modern church (pp. 47–49). He contrasts the lives of Socrates and Christ as moral *exempla* especially in terms of the effects on (the education of) the first apostles or followers (pp. 52–54).

mise from the state of the manuscripts and the textual echoes, seems to have been something like the following: He was working with Kant's *Religion within the Limits of Reason Alone* as a subtext and began by varying and summarizing Kantian arguments into the propositions that formed the schematic outline. For example, under the third section he hopes to discuss human drives and the highest predisposition (*Anlage*) in man, that toward morality and religion; this topic corresponds to Kant's discussion of the "original predisposition (*Anlage*) within human nature toward the Good."[44] Similarly, Hegel's fourth section, which should deal with the "business of the state" to "make objective religion subjective," corresponds with the section of Kant discussing the establishment of an "ethical state" or "community" (*ethischer Staat* or *ethisches gemeines Wesen*).[45] The "first sketch" (*erster Entwurf*) by Hegel then strives to expand on these propositions by investigating concrete aspects of real religions (primarily Christianity).

In the first sketch, however, Hegel seems to encounter difficulty following this procedure since the amplification of the *exempla* gets out of sync with the outline.[46] The technique of summarizing Kant and then expanding on his ideas by using historical examples forces Hegel to revise the outline so much that he finally abandons the effort to connect Kant and Christianity in this way. In the second draft he restarts the effort but because the hermeneutic and rhetorical techniques he is working with at this point are still so simple (based on those of his Tübingen years), he can only yoke the two together and leave them side by side. This is particularly clear at the opening of the second section of the second sketch on "doctrine" (*Lehren*): "Practical reason posits for man as his highest goal, it imposes on him the task: the bringing forth of the highest good [or possession, *des höchsten Guts*] on earth, morality, and the happiness appropriate to it. I believe the general doctrine of Christianity could be assumed to be: Hope in eternal bliss is that which every Christian has as his greatest interest. . . . This idea of bliss corresponds in terms of the content with that which is posited by reason" (p. 90). The appearance of Hegel's "I" at this point—a rarity in Hegelian prose—seems to result from the conflict of these two discourses and from his difficult attempt to represent and synthesize them both. It takes the entry of the writing subject to unite

44. Hegel, p. 70; Kant, *erstes Stück*, I.
45. Hegel, p. 71; Kant, *drittes Stück, erste Abtheilung*, III–v.
46. Nohl comments on the apparent confusion that developed as Hegel tried to carry out his Kantian ideas: "The letters of the scheme are so confused and disordered in Hegel's text that they had to be changed" (*Theologische Jugendschriften*, p. 48).

the conflicting discourses and traditions that would otherwise be merely juxtaposed.[47]

In 1794–95, however, Hegel finally comes up with a form that must have been a breakthrough for him since he writes the only complete manuscript from this period, *Das Leben Jesu* (The Life of Christ).[48] Hegel seizes upon an idea of Kant's to construct a life of Jesus based solely on the principles of practical reason.[49] The text accomplishes what the church authorities criticized in the Tübinger Stift, an "allegorizing" about the Bible in Kantian discourse. It is certainly telling that this manuscript has received the least attention by Hegel scholars; since they have not been concerned with its rhetorical form or function, they have not been able to recognize its significance for the *Bildung* of Hegel's writing despite, or because, of its lack of "originality."[50] It

47. In the second version of the "Kritik des Christentums," Hegel continues the juxtaposition and attempted fusion of discourses. For example, compare Hegel, p. 96 with Kant, *zweites Stück, erster Abschnitt, a)* on the notion of Christ as "personified ideal of goodness"; also Hegel, p. 91, and the *zweites Stück*. But in this version Hegel also introduces a different order into his discourse according to another method (*modus tractandi*) he had acquired: He establishes a literal dialogue and creates an audience in order to place his text into a more general discussion (esp. p. 87). In the excerpts we had seen how Hegel often practiced the reverse (turning dialogue into straight prose).

48. In a letter to Schelling, Hegel hints at a project, probably the *Leben*. Significantly, he implies that it may not be anything "new" (because he lacks books and contacts, he works only with his own internalized ideas), but it nonetheless helps shake dogmatic discourse: "My isolation from many books and the narrow-mindedness of my time do not permit me to carry out the many ideas that I carry around with me. I will at least not do much less than I can. I am convinced that only through a continuous shaking and jostling on all sides is there finally any hope of achieving an effect of any importance, [because] something always sticks. And every contribution of that kind, even if it contains nothing new, has its merit—and shared information (*Mitteilung*) and joint work revives and strengthens" (Hoffmeister, *Briefe*, no. 8). This description recalls the passage by Moritz used as an epigraph for this chapter: every effort, even a partially imitative one, must be considered a step on the path toward individuality.

49. Kant writes: "an interpretation is called for of the revelation that has come into our hands, that is, a thorough interpretation of this in a sense that is congruous with the universal, practical rules of a pure religion of reason (*Vernunftreligion*)" (*Religion innerhalb der Grenzen der bloßen Vernunft*, drittes stück, erste Abteilung, VI). Dilthey was the first to draw attention to this passage as the basis for Hegel's essay and translation (*Die Jugendgeschichte Hegels*, pp. 19, 61–63).

There was much to be gained in these years for a philosopher who could first imitate and then distance himself from Kant. Fichte had very quickly established his position in philosophy by publishing his *Versuch einer Kritik aller Offenbarung* (1792; 2d ed., 1793) anonymously. He so successfully imitated Kantian systematic rhetoric that Kant was assumed to be the author. Similarly, Schelling published his first attempt at a system, *Über die Möglichkeit einer Philosophie überhaupt*, in 1794 and thereby demonstrated his talent in manipulating Kantian and Fichtean discourse.

50. The opinion of the editors of the *Theorie-Werkausgabe*, in which the *Leben*—Hegel's only complete manuscript from the period—is not even reprinted, is characteristic:

consists of an imitative translation—or perhaps mistranslation—of the Bible into Kantian rhetoric. The opening lines—Hegel's interpretive overlaying of the beginning of the Gospel according to John with Kant's theory of pure (practical) reason—set the stage for the work as a retelling. The mode of composition is that of an *interpretatio*, a creative translation of one text in imitation of another:[51]

> Pure reason, incapable of any limitation, is divinity itself. — The very plan of the world is thus arranged according to reason; it is reason that teaches man his destiny and an absolute purpose of his life [also that man is the absolute end of his own life]; reason is often cast in darkness, but never completely extinguished, for even in darkness its shimmer is maintained.

> Die reine aller Schranken unfähige Vernunft ist die Gottheit selbst.— Nach Vernunft ist also der Plan der Welt überhaupt geordnet; Vernunft ist es, die dem Menschen seine Bestimmung, einen unbedingten Zweck seines Lebens kennen lehrt; oft ist sie zwar verfinstert, aber doch nie ganz ausgelöscht worden, selbst in der Finsternis hat sich immer ein schwacher Schimmer derselben erhalten.[52]

In terms of its philosophical *content*, to be sure, Hegel scholars may be correct in dismissing this manuscript as "unoriginal," for it strives for nothing more than to equate the key categories of the Bible (here *logos*, *phos*, and so on) with Kantian concepts (pure reason, destiny, absolute purpose or end). Although it is true that many of these concepts were in general use at the end of the eighteenth century—Kant's vocabulary introduced few *new* words—their condensed occurrence here recalls such passages as the following from an early section of the *Religion within the Limits of Reason Alone* concerning the "absolute, law-giving

---

"This harmony of the gospels (*Evangelienharmonie*), in which Hegel, aided by his own translation, wrote an imitation of the life of Jesus using simple words, indeed, without using any miraculous stories and transfigurations, is the single complete work from Hegel's Bern period which we have received and for this reason is important—yet scarcely for Hegel's philosophical development (*Entwicklung*). The theoretical and exegetical presuppositions of this synopsis are developed in the fragments on 'Volksreligion and Christianity' (1793–94) and in the sketches on 'Positivity of the Christian Religion' (1795–96)" (p. 622). Because they are concerned only with the "philosophical" development, they fail to consider why Hegel might have bothered writing (completing) this manuscript, that is, what role the *writing* played in his development.

51. On *interpretatio*, see Lausberg, *Handbuch*, pars. 751 and 1100,2.

52. Nohl, *Theologische Jugendschriften*, p. 75. Compare Wilhelm A. Schulze, "Das Johannesevangelium im deutschen Idealismus," *Zeitschrift für philosophische Forschung* 18 (1964):106ff. Also Hamacher, *pleroma*, p. 51; he refers to the "paraphrasing, both Kantian (*kantisierende*) and yet also reducing the Kantian, of the initial passages of the Gospel of John."

Reason" (*unbedingt gesetzgebende Vernunft*) within man: "this law [is] the only thing that makes us conscious of the independence of our will from determination by other motives—that is, conscious of our freedom" ("dieses Gesetz [ist] das einzige, was uns der Unabhängigkeit unsrer Willkür von der Bestimmung durch alle andern Triebfedern (unsrer Freiheit) . . . bewußt macht").[53] Hegel's passage also recalls Kant's claim that the *Critique of Pure Reason* "should design (*entwerfen*) the entire plan of a transcendental philosophy."[54] What Hegel seems to be doing is "merely" reworking this dry, philosophical prose into quasi-religious discourse. The very *rhetorical form* of an imitative translation, however, is what makes this text so significant for Hegel's development, since it indicates that he is undertaking an act of "alienation" dictated by rhetorical *Bildung* in order to master styles and traditions. We can consider briefly three formal techniques or *modi tractandi* that Hegel employs in his "translation," techniques that structure the retelling of two stories as one. (The following discussion is, of course, not divorced from the content of the manuscripts but does focus on formal aspects.)

In rhetorical theory, the *narratio* refers both to the specific story or events told and to the more general narrative framework.[55] Hegel plays with modifications of both of these features. At some points he preserves the core of events from the biblical account but alters its context. The very compression of the four gospels into a chronological sequence (*ordo naturalis*), for example, indicates a polemical alteration: The apostles' interpretations should recede behind a "factual" account.[56] Hegel thereby varies the "facts" by merely casting them into the simplified form of the *stilus historicus*.[57] At other points, Hegel changes the events themselves even though they occupy the same position in the structure of Christ's life. By means of mere "stylistic alterations" Hegel casts events into a totally different, more Kantian light.[58]

53. See the note on p. 26 of the *Religion innerhalb der Grenzen*.
54. Kant, *Kritik der reinen Vernunft*, B57.
55. Lausberg, *Handbuch*, pars. 1111ff.
56. This attempt to synthesize and reorder the four gospels into one story belongs to the genre *Evangelienharmonie* or *synoptische Evangelien*. See the articles under these rubrics in *Religion in Geschichte und Gegenwart*. On the *ordo naturalis* as a rhetorical form of history writing, see Lausberg, *Handbuch*, pars. 448–50.
57. The most important "structural" change occurs at the end of the biography, which ends with the death rather than resurrection of Christ. In this way, all attention is focused on the ethical life rather than miraculous return.
58. A further example in which Hegel keeps the basic event in the same relative position, but stylistically varies its tone, function and hence meaning occurs near the beginning: Christ's exchange with rabbis in the temple is presented explicitly as an example of his "not common sense" (*nicht gemeinen Verstand*), his "interest in religious

Like the *narratio*, the principle of the *chria* also guides the unfolding of Christ's life as a whole, as well as in its individual parts. Lausberg defines the *chria* as "an instructive anecdote that demonstrates a *sententia* (*Sentenzwahrheit*) as a reality of practical life."[59] It has the specific function of granting authority both to the historical figure and to the stated truths. Christ himself functions in Hegel's "translation" as a long *chria*. The entire life of Christ serves as a historical example of the Kantian principles that underlie Hegel's reading of the Bible. He personifies a moral ideal and enacts abstract reason in reality. On the one hand this lends greater validity to Christ, who, as a historical figure, nonetheless acts in accordance with modern ethics. Hegel has Christ say at one point, for example, concerning the judgment of his actions: "I subject it to the judgment of universal reason, which everyone can decide to believe or not" ("Ich unterwerfe es der Beurteilung der allgemeinen Vernunft, die jeden bestimmen mag, es zu glauben oder nicht").[60] And on the other hand, Christ's life provides a historical framework within which—not just alongside of which—Kant's doctrines can unfold. Hegel maintains the historical fiction carefully throughout in order to grant greater authority and persuasive power to Kantian ethics.

A final technique, *sermocinatio*, which places a speech in the mouth of an authoritative figure,[61] plays an even greater role in Hegel's reworking of the Bible than the more general form of the *chria*. In *Das Leben Jesu*, Christ literally speaks with Kantian rhetoric. He rejects the devil's temptation in the desert, for example, by a consideration that is a reworked definition of Kantian *Kritik*: "by a consideration of limitations" (*durch die Betrachtung der Schranken*).[62] Moreover, in Hegel's version of the conversation with Nicodemus (John 3), Christ describes man as a divine being in Kantian terms, paraphrased, perhaps, from the section on human predispositions and drives in *Religion within the Limits of Reason Alone*: "Not merely limited to drives for pleasure—

---

subjects," and his "uncommon knowledge and faculty of judgment for his age" (Nohl, *Theologische Jugendschriften*, p. 76). Similarly, the curing of a sick man is shifted from a miracle to an "act of love" (Nohl, p. 88).

59. Lausberg, *Handbuch*, par. 1117. He says further: "The historical personality, who is allowed to speak the truism (*Sentenz*) in the *chria*, or whose conduct is represented as it is reported in the 'sententia,' serves as concrete, authoritative support for the practical validity of the truism, just as, vice versa, the 'sententia' or the conduct appears as the motive of the praise of the historical personality."

60. Nohl, *Theologische Jugendschriften*, p. 89.

61. On *sermocinatio*, see Lausberg, *Handbuch*, par. 1131.

62. Nohl, *Theologischen Jugendschriften*, p. 101. Compare Kant, *Kritik der reinen Vernunft*, B54, 55–56.

there is a spirit in him, even a spark of divine essence, the inheritance of all rational beings has been granted him" ("Nicht bloß auf Triebe nach Vergnügen eingeschränkt—es ist ein Geist in ihm, auch ein Funken des göttlichen Wesens, das Erbteil aller vernünftigen Wesen ist ihm zu teil geworden"); he is born in "the shine of reason" (*dem Glanz der Vernunft*) and recognizes "morals as duty" (*die Sittlichkeit als Pflicht*).[63] The goal of Christianity, as well as of this translation, according to Christ-Hegel, is to "breathe" new life into a dead letter or skeleton (*diesem toten Gerippe Geist einzuhauchen*).[64] Hegel's translation of the Bible into Kantian rhetoric according to the techniques of the classical tradition is an "inspired" completion[65] of traditions in the Longinian sense of inspiration as initially requiring submission to and imitation of the letter of another. Through this imitative exercise Hegel gives over his voice to past traditions so that he might master the skills to enable him to manipulate those very traditions.

We can now turn more specifically to the content of these Bern fragments.[66] Having analyzed their form as *exercitationes* using *modi tractandi* and their function for Hegel as imitations that allow him to appropriate interpenetrating past traditions in order to become independent of them, we now have a different perspective from which to

63. Nohl, *Theologische Jugendschriften*, pp. 79–80; Kant, *Religion innerhalb der Grenzen*, pp. 26–28. Similarly, Christ's descriptions of the Kingdom of God, which Hegel had interpreted in his sermon in Tübingen in a mildly Kantian spirit, now refer more literally to Kant's discussion of founding the Kingdom on earth: "Der Sieg des guten Prinzips über das böse und die Gründung eines Reiches Gottes auf Erden." Compare Nohl, pp. 81, 86, 89, 114, and Kant, pp. 93, 122, 124, 132. Even more striking is Hegel's transformation of the "Our Father" into an "Our Reason": "This spirit of the prayer would, expressed in words, be represented for example so: Father of men, to whom all the heavens are subject, you, the single holy one, be the image (ideal) hovering before us, which we strive to approach; may your kingdom one day come, in which all rational beings make the law alone the standard of their actions—Little by little will all inclinations, even the cry of nature, be subject to this idea" ("Dieser Geist des Gebets würde sich in Worten ausgedrückt etwa so darstellen lassen: Vater der Menschen, dem alle Himmel unterworfen sind, du, der Alleinheilige seiest das Bild [Ideal], das uns vorschwebe, dem wir uns zu nähern trachten, daß dein Reich einst kommen möge, in welchem alle vernünftige Wesen das Gesetz allein zur Regel ihrer Handlungen machen—Dieser Idee werden alle Neigungen, selbst das Schreien der Natur nach und nach unterworfen!"; Nohl, p. 85). The "spirit of the prayer" is an all too literal application of Kant.

64. Nohl, *Theologische Jugendschriften*, p. 83.

65. See Hamacher, *pleroma*, pp. 106–9, for a discussion of the concept of "pleroma" or fulfillment and completion.

66. *Formally*, the longest fragment, the "Positivität der christlichen Religion," does not contain any techniques essentially different from *Das Leben Jesu*. Thus, it will be the focus of the following discussion of *content*. The rhetorical approach has opened up *Das Leben Jesu* as a model for the other fragments, without which they would not be formally possible.

view their arguments. No doubt they are "about" the *development* of and to a true *Volksreligion*; no doubt they are "about" the *formation* of the modern world as it relates to the self-contained totality of classical antiquity, as a result of both the Enlightenment and capitalism. But if they are in general about the *Bildung* of cultural institutions, we must ask what model—or which one possible model—Hegel might have had of *Bildung*. The *form* of the fragments makes clear that he was working with a model of *Bildung* which emphasized that process by which the young writer must paradoxically work his way to independence through imitation, by which he must develop his *natura* through the development of his *ars*. What is unique about Hegel's own course of development (*Bildung*), as well as about his concept of *Bildung* as it developed in these manuscripts, is that at this stage he works through these built in, creative, and productive paradoxes of rhetorical hermeneutics by applying them to and seeing them in the very traditions he is appropriating.

This stage in the education of a writer or orator is considered tension filled even in the classical rhetorical programs—recall that Quintilian called it a "wrestling match" (*certamen*)—since the young writer must engage with his precursors in the attempt to surpass them, must imitate their letter as a means of attaining the spirit-breath of inspiration. This tension between the given and the creative, the dead weight of the past and the liberation of the present-future, occupies Hegel's analysis of Christianity, Greek antiquity, and Kantian ethics in all the Bern manuscripts. Hence, like the Tübingen homilies, these manuscripts allegorize his growth as an individual writer in terms of the way certain traditions oscillate between static and creative forms.

In fact, most of the fragments deal expressly with the very concept of tradition, what it means for cultural and religious achievements of the past to be handed down to later generations, what formal changes they must undergo, and how they affect the present. Understandably given his background, Hegel sees this process as a form of degeneration in time, a hardening of forms as traditions are transmitted through institutional channels, especially through educational practice. Thus, although he rarely uses the term *Bildung* in these discussions, he is dealing with the problem of education as cultural transmission (and vice versa).[67] In this regard, one of the Enlightenment topoi that he repeats

---

67. Hegel is culminating a century-old tendency in Western civilization which sees education, tradition, and self-representation as inextricably linked. Curtius writes: "Education becomes the medium of [the literary] tradition: a fact which is characteristic of Europe, but which is not necessarily so in the nature of things." Quoted from Harold Bloom, *Map of Misreading* (Oxford: Oxford University Press, 1975), p. 34.

and varies gains significance, namely, the analogy between the ages of an individual and the growth of a people.[68] This comparison makes it possible for him to generalize from his childhood experiences to processes of cultivation in general. Children receive the past (religious) tradition in the form of fixed forms, beliefs, practices, ceremonies, rituals: "Already as children we were taught to mumble prayers to the divinity, already our hands were folded in order to raise them to the most sublime being, a collection of at the time still incomprehensible doctrines (*unverständlicher Sätze*) were imposed on our memory for future use and consolation in our lives" (p. 9). The reason for this weight of the past is that "the aging spirit (*der alternde Genius*) of a people" possesses a strong "attachment (*Anhänglichkeit*) to the traditional (*das Hergebrachte*) in every respect" (p. 13). Not only does one teach "our children to say grace and morning and evening prayers," but the entire culture of the Germans (*unser Volk*) suffers from the imposed forms of the foreign: "The memory and fantasy is filled with the prehistory of mankind, with the history of a foreign people, with the deeds and misdeeds of their kings, none of which has anything to do with us" (p. 45).

Hegel argues explicitly that this problematic form of cultural dependence on foreign and externally imposed traditions parallels a form of *Bildung* according to which a child is expected to pursue mere rote memorization of alien structures of expression and religious dicta, that is, a form of *Bildung* remarkably like his own conservative education. That Hegel now views his education in a more critical light does not affect the fact that it nonetheless remains the model of *Bildung* from which he abstracts to discuss developments in his culture in general. Thus, when he describes the fate of an autodidactic boy who withdraws into a world of books and becomes a kind of innocent victim of contemporary *Bildung* he is describing his own experience:

> He decides to educate himself to a virtuous person and yet does not yet have the experience [to recognize] that books cannot make him into that; and so he takes up Campe's *Theophron* in order to make these wise doctrines the guidelines of his life; he reads a section mornings and evenings and thinks the whole day about it — what will be the result? Perhaps genuine perfection? Human understanding? Practical cleverness? These require years of training and experience (*jahrelange Übung und Erfahrung*)—but the meditation about Campe and Campe's yardstick will turn him off in a week. [P. 26][69]

68. One source of this topos was most likely Christian Garve, whose essay in popular philosophy Hegel had excerpted in Stuttgart. See Hoffmeister, *Dokumente*, pp. 115–36.
69. See the similar reference to the methods of teaching Campe's *Theophron* as a *bloße Maschine* (p. 22).

The young Hegel, who had excerpted from and written compositions, even in Latin, on the likes of Campe, was not "turned off in a week," but has now reached the stage where he can have his training and experience. Moreover, is Hegel not summarizing his own education when he writes the following description of those who would impose on pupils dead forms of the Enlightenment?

> They serve [feed, *speisen*] each other plain words and overlook the sacred, tender web of human emotions. Everyone probably has heard such types buzz around; some have probably even experienced this themselves, for this course of *Bildung* is very common in our overwritten times (*denn in unseren vollgeschriebenen Zeiten ist dieser Gang der Bildung sehr häufig*).—If one or the other in fact learns through life itself to understand what used to lie in his soul as dead capital, it nonetheless remains an undigested pile of bookish knowledge in his stomach which, because the stomach has enough to do already, prevents healthier nourishment and doesn't allow nourishing juices to flow into the other parts of the body. [P. 27]

Just as these passages describe (critically) the conservative education he experienced in Stuttgart and Tübingen, which literally stuffed him full of *praecepta* and *exempla*, so too the following passage captures the built-in creative dynamic of that education, for these deadening *ars* can and must be combined with, indeed even contain within themselves, an inner, living *natura*: "Nature has placed in every person a seed of the finer sensibilities that develop out of morality; . . . the task of education (*Erziehung*) and *Bildung* is to make sure that these beautiful seeds do not suffocate, that out of them a genuine receptivity for moral ideas and feelings develop" (pp. 15–16). Even though this passage deals with the development of moral sentiment, it is significant that Hegel generalizes here the "task" of instruction. While these aspects of *Bildung*—suffocating, bookish knowledge and a drive toward creativity—seem contradictory, they are linked paradoxically in the traditional education Hegel experienced, as well as in his own developing concept of *Bildung*. The "seed" and the "undigested material" are both to be internalized and brought to life by potentially deadening acts of reading and imitating. The task and risk of self-formation through self-loss in, and appropriation of, past forms now confront Hegel. He deals with them by projecting the same processes onto the tradition of Christianity as well.

That Hegel works through the concerns of his own *Bildung* in terms of the religious traditions he is grappling with is clear in the short fragment on the modes of instruction used by religions. He differentiates between two means of propagating a tradition: "Besides oral instruction, which always has an effect on a very limited circle and which extends only over those whom nature has linked to us, the only means of affecting a larger circle is [instruction] through writing" (p. 47). One senses the paradox facing the young Hegel: He doubts the validity of the written tradition since it allows for misuse and becomes mere *Exerzitium* (p. 52) as opposed to the living, persuasive oral word, and yet he himself has been trained in *written* rhetoric (*stylus*) and is, as a home tutor in Bern, cut off from direct intellectual contact. He is forced to develop his ideas in the written medium of the tradition and tradition building. Precisely this paradox is projected onto the difference between Socrates and Christ (pp. 50–53): Hegel praises Socrates for his directness, for the persuasiveness of his spirit, for his powerful (oral) language, and yet Hegel himself is manipulating the written tradition in writing this very passage. This tension between the praise of "spirit" in the theological manuscripts and their literalizing form grants to the reworked topoi we saw earlier a greater significance in terms of an overall scheme of the development of traditions.

The generalizing analogy between the individual's (Hegel's own) form of education and the history of religion occupies Hegel in the earlier fragments. For the individual, education is a question of developing the appropriate faculties of the mind: memory, understanding, wit, *critica*, fantasy, feeling, and more. Hegel divides these faculties into two major groups and then associates them in an implicit analogy with two forms of religion: objective and subjective. He defines the former in terms of certain mental tasks called into play by believing in it: "Objective religion is *fides quae creditur*, understanding and memory are the faculties that are at work." (p. 13).[70] "[Subjective] religion, however, is a matter of the heart" (p. 17).[71] Or as he writes programmatically later: "Fantasy, heart, and the senses (*Sinnlichkeit*) must not thereby go empty handed" (p. 33). Seen from the perspective of his own *Bildung*, this crucial opposition between the two forms of religion thematizes the fundamental split within pedagogical camps in the late eighteenth century between rhetorical training through the "artful" exercise of memory and analysis and the development of "natural" faculties of spontaneity.

If the opposition were left in this form, one would see no means of bridging the gap, either for the young writer trying to break free of imitation or for religion attempting to infuse subjective sentiment into

70. See also pp. 17, 21, 25, and 75 for other reworked definitions.

71. Hegel offers an example of such enthusiasm in one of his favorite descriptions, namely, the *Phantasie griechischer Bacchantinnen* (p. 79). Thus, we see how he gradually builds up a repertoire of images that become associated with various ever more complex ideas.

its traditional doctrines. The letter would remain hopelessly opposed to the spirit and the young writer would be, at least in practice, hopelessly dependent on the letter. Hegel's only hope for a solution at this point is that the rhetorical dictum applied to ethics will hold for himself, namely, that good imitation must already have and in turn cultivates some qualities of the original. Thus, Hegel writes in a passage concerning virtue—undoubtedly inspired by Kant and by his imitation of Kant: "However, just as in order to be a good imitator one must also be a bit of an original—just as in other disciplines so even more so in morality, otherwise it is merely something forced, something not quite in its proper place, something that doesn't quite fit and sticks out from the rest—so must especially virtue be something experienced, something practiced by oneself (*etwas selbst Geübtes*)" (p. 83). Although this statement is made explicitly about Christ, it applies concretely to Hegel's own needs and anxieties as a young writer striving to break free of earlier imitations. One appreciates the broader context of this theory of imitation ("as in all other disciplines") when one realizes that Hegel was just about to compose his imitative translation of *Das Leben Jesu*. If he sees Christ as the "model" and "mirror" (*Vorbild* and *Spiegel*; p. 82) of moral action, it is Kant who provides him the model of his own writing. The only means of breaking out of the paradox of imitation and originality is the rhetorical way of working it through, experiencing it in one's own "practice" by imitating in the hope that one's originality will come through in the process.

The experience of the personal and historical transition from imitativeness to originality and vice versa becomes the topic of his longest, though incomplete, fragment from Bern, "Die Positivität der christlichen Religion" (The Positivity of the Christian Religion). Hegel poses half of his topic in the section "Woher das Positive?" (Whence the Positivity?), in which he asks how religious and moral forms can become hardened into authorative canons, that is, "positivistic" givens:[72]

> How could one have anticipated that such a teacher [Christ], who spoke out not against the established religion itself but against the moral superstition that one fulfills the demands of the laws of morality by observing religious customs; who strove for a concept of virtue grounded not on authority but on inner free virtuousness—who could have anticipated that such a teacher would himself have given rise to a

72. Note that I shall use either "positive" or "positivistic" to translate Hegel's *positiv*. It is always meant in the specific way Hegel defines it—namely, as the tendency for given forms to harden over time, to become mere conventions, dogma, objects of belief without feeling.

positivistic religion, i.e., one based on authority and which posits human value either not at all or at least not solely in morality. [P. 108]

That is, part of Hegel's concern in the essay is to document the ironic fact that Christ's moral criticisms against dogma became in turn moralistic dogma. But what is significant for us here is that Hegel's interest in the way positivity (imitation of the letter of the law) develops out of creative moral interpretation (originality) at the same time grounds his hope that *as process* it can be reversed.

My interpretive claim is that in this essay Hegel analyzes in terms of the historical reception of religious traditions the very process he has been undergoing in his own written reception of traditions. This can be observed most clearly in the ambiguity of the term *Bildung*, an ambiguity that will become typical for Hegel's use of this concept. Concretely, he is interested in Christ's individual development and education, that is, how Christ, who attempted "to cultivate (*in sich zu bilden*) a more independent virtue in himself" and who "was preoccupied until manhood with his own formative education (*mit seiner eigenen Bildung beschäftigt*)" (p. 106), could have been reduced to an object of imitation. But the term *Bildung* applies as well in the essay to the development of the form of Christianity, the *Bildung ihrer Form* (p. 110) as a socio-historical phenomenon. The process, or what Hegel later will call "fate" (*Schicksal*) of an individual's development from creative activity to passive receptivity, and vice versa, is applied to the development of cultural institutions. And this use of the term *Bildung* on two levels allows us to relate this entire discussion of the *Bildung* of Christianity to Hegel's own formative education as well. As in the Preface to the *Phenomenology*, *Bildung* makes possible an equivocation between the evolution of cultural forms (the "objective spirit") and the formative education of an individual. The course of the essay, which employs the techniques of *chria* and *narratio* practiced in *Das Leben Jesu*, traces the *Bildung der Form* from Christ's initial liberation of religion from the dogmatic orthodoxy of Judaism (according to Hegel), through the gradual rehardening of Christian doctrines by successive imitations, to a new liberation from the letter.[73]

73. Hegel explains in the opening remarks that he will be following the "method of treating (*Behandlungsart*) Christianity which is in vogue in our times" (p. 104), an indirect reference to Kant, who attempted to write the history of religious representations or historical *Vorstellungen* (drittes Stück, zweite Abteilung, of the *Religion innerhalb der Grenzen der bloßen Vernunft*). The principle of Hegel's *modus tractandi* is the comparison of the "differing formations and modifications" (*verschiedene Gestalten, Modificationen*) with the *Geist* of Christianity (p. 105). Lukács (*Der junge Hegel* [Berlin: Leuchterhand, 1948], pp. 52–135) thus rightly considers the traditional spirit-versus-letter dichotomy central

The power of Hegel's argument demonstrating the historical cor-
ruption of the absolute (moral) Law becomes clear in the final section,
"Notwendigkeit der Entstehung von Sekten" (Necessity of the Birth of
Sects). Hegel draws a parallel between Christ's relationship to the Jews
and Kant's relationship to contemporary theology. Hegel had described in the first section, "Zustand der jüdischen Religion—Jesus"
(State of the Jewish Religion—Jesus), the state of mechanistic imitation
that led to Christ's innovation: "This state of the Jewish nation must
have awakened in men of better heart and mind, who did not give up
or deny their sense of self and who could not bend their will to dead
machines, the need for a freer activity than spending their existence
with the monkish industriousness of a spiritless and empty mechanism
of petty customs and the need for a more noble pleasure than imagin-
ing their greatness in this slavelike handiwork" (p. 106). And now, at
the end of the essay, he reformulates that initial description so that it
can apply to the state of advanced Christianity out of which Kant arose:
"There had to be men from time to time who did not find the demands
of their heart satisfied in this eclesiastic legality or in a character like
that developed by asceticism and who felt themselves capable of giving
themselves a law of morality that sprung forth from the idea of freedom" (p. 187).

What is important here is not the source of his historical information
but the interpretive parallelism he is proposing. That Hegel has Kant
in mind here is first implied by the terms used (freedom, reason, and so
on) and then becomes explicit in the following pages. (For example:
"The healthy separation of spheres of faculties of the human spirit,
which Kant has accomplished for scientific knowledge, this separation
has never been done by the legalistic side of the church"; p. 188.) But
this passage echoes the transition from Judaism to Christianity. Thus,
by working through the tradition of Christianity and its expressions,
Hegel arrives at the identity of Christ and Kant.[74] By means of an essay
consisting of historical analyses in the form of the rhetorical techniques
of *narratio* and *chria*, Hegel is able to ground historically and systematically an abstract identification between Christ's life and Kant's teach-

---

to Hegel's fragment. Hegel offers not a chronological treatment of Christian dogma, but
a series of eighteen sections, vignettes, or *Gestalten*, from the history of Christianity. The
goal of the essay is to demonstrate how and why the *forms* of religion deviate from its
original content as a result of overzealous imitation or application of precepts and principles. This method indicates a use of rhetorical principles against rhetorical forms, as can
be seen in the introductory remarks to the essay (p. 105) which prefigure the opening
paradox of the Preface to the *Phenomenology*.

74. In fact, in this final section, Kant's name is mentioned, one of the first (and only)
times in Hegel's early writings (p. 188).

ings which is different and more powerful than the one he had established in *Das Leben Jesu*, since in the "Positivity" essay his two ideal figures become involved in the same historical interplay of the spirit and the letter. They both attempt to fulfill the letter of the Law and tradition with their new spirits—only to suffer the same fate of literalization, positivity. Christ, arising out of a period of deadening traditionalism (according to Hegel) proposed a new interpretation and his teachings became, during the history of Christianity, the object of too literal an imitation. Similarly, in Hegel's philosophical and rhetorical development, Kant, who arose out of dogmatism and religious sectarianism, became the model for imitation.

At this point, where the fragment breaks off, Hegel must have felt the paradox of his *Bildung* most acutely. For must he not have recognized that Kant, who at first had been the means for him to break free of traditional exegesis, had now taken on for him the function of *das Positive*, the mere given of a literal tradition (see pp. 188–89)? This identity of the history of Christianity and the history of his own *Bildung* must have revealed to Hegel that he too was trapped in a pattern of imitation. The problem now facing Hegel in his writing is how to free himself from the domination of the "positivity" of Kantian forms.

The recognition of a "new" task, that is, the need to free himself from the insufficiency of a self-*Bildung* that still left him in the imitative phase with respect to Kant, coincides with Hegel's move to Frankfurt in 1797, where his friend Friedrich Hölderlin had arranged another position for him as private tutor. Hegel scholars have interpreted the change in his thought that took place after he moved to Frankfurt in various ways. Dilthey sees Hegel as achieving a fuller awareness of the power of religious irrationalism over Kantian reason.[75] Lukács basically agrees with Dilthey, but judges the change in Hegel negatively. For Lukács, the Frankfurt years reflect a turn from Hegel's earlier interest in rational political economy to mysticism.[76] Dieter Henrich has dominated the contemporary discussion by emphasizing Hölderlin's influence as the catalyst to Hegel's sudden and radical break with Kant.[77]

---

75. Dilthey, *Die Jugendgeschichte Hegels*, pp. 40ff. He says, for example: "So there extends also a struggle against Kant through all the works of this period" (p. 60).
See also Ingtraut Görland, *Die Kantkritik des jungen Hegels* (Frankfurt: Klostermann, 1966), *Philosophische Abhandlungen*, vol. 28, for an account of Hegel's philosophical arguments against Kant. Görland emphasizes Hegel's powerfully creative "misreading" of Kant.
76. Lukács, *Der junge Hegel*, esp. pp. 140ff.
77. Henrich, "Hegel und Hölderlin," in *Hegel im Kontext*: "From the time of their meeting in Frankfurt Hegel remained on a continual path of development, which he would not have found without Hölderlin's preceding thinking" (p. 11).

Recently, however, Werner Hamacher, whose lead I will follow, has traced Hegel's initial turn from Kant back into Bern, whereby the Frankfurt writings mainly extend the critical historical arguments of the "Positivity" essay to their logical conclusion.[78] The inherent "logic" at work here, I propose, is that of the rhetorician's shift from *imitatio* to *translatio* and *aemulatio*. My appeal to "rhetorical logic" sheds a different light on the question of when Hegel actually broke with Kant: The break took place for Hegel at the end of the imitative writings in Bern since that is the point at which such a break was dictated by the very process of rhetorical *imitatio* he had to break free of and systematically justified by his reflections on the development of religious models. Through the last imitative fragments in Bern that deal with the problem of imitation (positivity), Hegel had developed the techniques to overcome his imitation.

As in Bern, Hegel first approaches an intellectual problem in Frankfurt—the historicity of his own "positivistic" writings—by writing fragments that deal with a few basic concepts from various perspectives. This approach recalls his school days, in which exercises consisted in "turning a question around." The fragments have been organized around the terms "religion," "faith" (*Glaube*), "love" (*Liebe*), and "life" (*Leben*). The rhetorico-hermeneutical question, to which these fragments can be seen as an answer, has two sides: How is a unification or identification with traditions possible which does not lead to domination by one or the other, the appropriated or appropriating? And how is it possible for Hegel to impose a difference between himself and the Other while still taking his literal debt to the Other into account? His solution to this rhetorico-hermeneutical problem is of central importance to an understanding of Hegel's *Bildung* since it works through religion and idealism to the first formulation of his central dialectic of identity and difference.

Although the first fragment—"Morality, Love, Religion"—seems to make but a slight shift in diction from his Bern manuscripts, it actually opens up new rhetorical possibilities for Hegel's writing. The opening redefines "positivity" in the terminology of idealism:

> A belief is called "positivistic" in which the practical is present in a theoretical form and [in which] the originally subjective is present only as something objective; a [positive] religion holds up ideas of something

---

78. Hamacher, *pleroma*: "Hölderlin's influence on Hegel—as great as it may have been—is so reworked and assimilated in these Frankfurt texts, that it no longer represents the intrusion of an 'entirely different' theoretical orientation, but rather a dialectical rupture of the theorems, which were, to be sure, discussed by him because of this rupture" (p. 58).

objective that can never become subjective as the principle of life and actions. The practical activity acts freely, without the unification of an opposing object, without being determined by such an object— it does not introduce unity into a given manifold but is this very unity that saves itself from the manifold opposing object, which always remains disconnected in relation to the practical faculty; practical unity is established by sublating the opposing object fully.

Positiv wird ein Glaube genannt, in dem das Praktische theoretisch vorhanden ist—das ursprünglich Subjektive nur als ein Objektives; eine Religion, die Vorstellungen von etwas Objektivem, das nicht subjektiv werden kann, als Prinzip des Lebens und der Handlungen aufstellt. Die praktische Tätigkeit handelt frei, ohne Vereinigung eines Entgegengesetzten, ohne durch dieses bestimmt zu werden—sie bringt nicht Einheit in ein gegebenes Mannigfaltiges, sondern ist die Einheit selbst, die sich nur rettet gegen das mannigfaltige Entgegengesetzte, das in Rücksicht auf das praktische Vermögen immer unverbunden bleibt; die praktische Einheit wird dadurch behauptet, daß das Entgegengesetzte ganz aufgehoben wird. [P. 239]

This reformulation does more than affirm Hegel's Kantian foundation. It reveals a recent preoccupation with Fichte. Throughout the fragment Hegel translates oppositions from the "Positivity" essay into Fichtean terms. Whereas he had earlier distinguished between subjective and objective religion, or between belief based on reason and belief based on authority, he now differentiates between "positivistic" and "nonpositivistic" religion in terms from Fichte's *Wissenschaftslehre*: *Einheit-Mannigfaltigkeit* (unity-manifold), *Vereinigung-das Entgegengesetzte* (unification or identification-opposition). He even uses the opposition between the "ego" and "nonego" to differentiate between conceptions of morality.[79] At first sight, then, it seems as if Hegel continues his

79. "What is the concept of morality? The moral concepts do not have objects in the same sense that theoretical concepts do. The object of the former is always the 'I,' the object of the latter, the 'Not-I'" ("Was ist: Begriff von Moralität? Die moralischen Begriffe haben nicht in dem Sinne Objekte, in dem die theoretischen Begriffe Objekte haben. Das Objekt jener ist immer das Ich; das Objekt dieser das Nicht-Ich"; p. 239). These distinctions recall the opening of Fichte's *Wissenschaftslehre* (1797). Hegel uses the terms *Identität* and *Entgegensetzung* in a uniquely self-reflexive manner: They are variations of his precursors' terms, hint at his tense and paradoxical relationship to his precursors, become Hegel's means of developing a discourse of his own, and characterize that new, "metaphorical" discourse, which, according to both Hegel and early romanticism, unites opposites in thought-provoking ways. By viewing Hegel's development in this manner as a self-reflection upon his means of self-representation, one can give meaning to the unexplained observation in Dilthey's *Jugendgeschichte Hegels*: "The new style, peculiar to him, begins to delineate itself toward the end of the period in Bern. It originates in connection with the poetical prose, in which the new view of the world was expressed at that time" (p. 42). Lukács rejects this turn in Hegel's language as "mystical" (*Der junge Hegel*, pp. 145, 161ff.).

imitative translation, with the only difference being that he now relates the Kantian and Christian traditions to the Fichtean metaphysical model.

Hegel's new translation, however, adds a crucial dimension to his thought and rhetoric. He goes beyond his earlier hermeneutical and rhetorical efforts, which strove for either a one-to-one correspondence or a schematic relationship between Christian doctrine and Kantian philosophy. Now he sees the possibility of a more fundamental identity between opposing views. Hegel calls the fundamental unifying force "love" (*Liebe*), a term, as Dieter Henrich argues persuasively, whose source is most likely Hölderlin. Rather than creating parallels between different positions, love makes them identical. Hegel writes: "Love can only take place vis-à-vis the same, the mirror, the echo of our being" ("Liebe kann nur stattfinden gegen das Gleiche, gegen den Spiegel, gegen das Echo unseres Wesens"; p. 243). Suddenly, the Other with whom Hegel had been wrestling, the other voice that he had been following, the model he had been imitating,[80] becomes in this new identification the echo of *his own* voice.

Such a reversal of roles from an identification based on imitative dependence to an identification of equals is the result of a process. Love, which seems to be a simple act, actually contains a life-giving movement which Hegel calls in general "life" and more specifically *Bildung*. Although this movement is couched in largely organic terms, we must also keep in mind the nonorganic, pedagogical meaning of *Bildung* as we read Hegel's description of the development from false unity, to separation, to a higher unification:

life finds itself in it [love] as a doubling and unity of itself; in *Bildung* life has passed through the circle from undeveloped to complete unity; the world and the possibility of separation stood opposed to the un-developed unity; during development, reflection produced more and more oppositions, which are united in the satisfied drive, until it [reflection] opposes the entire human being to itself and then love sublates reflection in a state of total objectlessness, robs the opposed object of its character of foreignness, and finally life finds itself without further lack.

in ihr [Liebe] findet sich das Leben selbst, als eine Verdoppelung seiner selbst, und Einigkeit desselben; das Leben hat, von der unentwickelten Einigkeit aus, *durch die Bildung* den Kreis zu einer vollendeten Einigkeit durchlaufen; der unentwickelten Einigkeit stand die Möglichkeit der Trennung und die Welt gegenüber; in der Entwicklung produzierte die Reflexion immer mehr Entgegengesetztes, das im befriedigten Trie-

---

80. Recall the images of "mirror" (*Spiegel*), "model" (*Vorbild*), and "imitator" (*Nachahmer*; pp. 82–83); see above, p. 123.

be vereinigt wurde, bis sie das Ganze des Menschen selbst ihm entgegengesetzte, bis die Liebe die Reflexion in völliger Objektlosigkeit
aufhebt, dem Entgegengesetzten allen Charakter eines Fremden raubt
und das Leben sich selbst ohne weiteren Mangel findet. [P. 246; my
emphasis]

This abstract and complex passage is important not so much as a description of the natural processes of organic forms but as a reformulation of the development Hegel had postulated for Christianity in the
"Positivity" essay (the *Bildung ihrer Form* through formalized dogmas to
a living unity) and of the *Bildung* he has been undergoing since his
school days. He too has been trapped in an "undeveloped unity" in
which his reflection has created more and more oppositions between
traditions, whereby the ultimate opposition has been between himself
and the "foreign." But now he sees this state of dependence more
clearly as a stage in the development of a neither imitative nor opposing mode of expression.[81] Indeed, the very mixture of abstract and
imagistic language in the passage would imply that Hegel has reached a
stage in his writing where reflection is passing through "objectlessness"
to self-rediscovery. The germ of the dominant dialectic of the *Phenomenology*—*Bildung* as unfolding through reflection and a return to
the self after that alienation—is planted in this fragment on identification.

That Hegel is grappling in particular with problems of representation and expression becomes explicit in the last fragment, "Glaube und
Sein" (Faith and Being; 1798). He begins by defining faith as an activity
that identifies or unites terms falsely posited as opposites. Significantly,
he associates the problematic opposition underlying faith with Kant by
using a central category, "antinomy," which structures the dialectical
argumentation of the second half of the *Critique of Pure Reason*: "Faith
is the way in which a unity that unifies an antinomy is present in our
imagination" ("Glaube ist die Art, wie das Vereinigte, wodurch eine
Antinomie vereinigt ist, in unserer Vorstellung vorhanden ist"; pp.
250–51).[82] Hegel rejects the very possibility of two conflicting sides (*die*

---

81. Hegel couches his discussion in terms of love, property, the recognition of the
proper, and the attraction to the Other's particularity: "The loving thing, which catches
sight of the Other in the possession of a piece of property, must feel the Other's particularity, which it wanted" ("Das Liebende, das das andere im Besitz eines Eigentums
erblickt, muß diese Besonderheit des anderen, die es gewollt hat, fühlen"; p. 250).
Compare this to the epigram from Moritz at the opening of this chapter for the rhetorical or stylistic version of this relation to an Other's particularity.

82. In terms of rhetorical *elocutio*, an antinomy would be the opposite of metaphor, the
maintenance of difference within apparent identity (i.e., antithesis). More generally,
however, antinomy in Greek rhetoric is derived from the forensic sphere and is defined
as the "contradiction or conflict of two laws." Lausberg, *Handbuch*, par. 218.

Glieder der Antinomie als widerstreitende) because even the principle of opposition implies a fundamental comparison.[83] Faith, which yokes together apparent opposites, fails to recognize that the identity already exists in "Being," that is, in the linguistic expression of the copula: "Unification [or identity] and Being are synonymous; in every sentence the copula 'is' expresses the unification of subject and predicate—a being" ("Vereinigung und Sein sind gleichbedeutend; in jedem Satz drückt das Bindewort 'ist' die Vereinigung des Subjekts und Prädikats aus—ein Sein"; p. 251).[84] True identification does not "merely switch one kind of being for another" but recognizes a mutual interdependence of determinations: "In each identification there is a determiner and a determined, which are the same" ("In jeder Vereinigung ist ein Bestimmen und ein Bestimmtwerden, die eins sind"; p. 253).

By considering this concern with the expression of identities and differences as the reformulation of Hegel's identification with and differentiation from the traditions that he is reading and rewriting, we can see new significance in two passages at the end of the fragment. In the first, Hegel claims that precisely the active identification that determines even its own state of being determined has the power to grant *form*: "The determining element is a power, through which the activity receives its direction, its form" ("Das Bestimmende ist eine Macht, durch welche die Tätigkeit ihre Richtung, ihre Form erhält"; p. 254). That is, although he does not mention the term *Bildung* here, we can see that he is again struggling to explain how independent and genuinely unifying form comes about—the problem of his *Bildung*. More concretely, in the second passage, Hegel reformulates aspects of his earlier writings, that is, he redefines "positivity" in terms of identity and difference, and arrives at a remarkable new connection that can liberate him from his dependence on Kant:

> All positive religion has as its point of departure some opposed object, something that we are not and that we ought to become; it posits an ideal before Being; in order to have faith in the ideal, it must be a power. In positive religion Being, identification, is only an idea, a thought—I believe that it is means that I believe in the idea, I believe

83. "But that which is conflicting can only be recognized as conflict by means of that which already has been unified; the unification is the criterion by which the comparison occurs, against which the contrary things, as such, appear as unsatisfying" ("aber das Widerstreitende kann als Widerstreitendes nur dadurch erkannt werden, daß schon vereinigt worden ist; die Vereinigung ist der Maßstab, an welchem die Vergleichung geschieht, an welchem die Entgegengesetzten, als solche, als Unbefriedigte erscheinen"; p. 251).

84. Near the end of *Wahrheit und Methode*, Gadamer refers to this linguistic principle of the identity of the copula as the essential "metaphoricity" of lanugage (*Sprache und Begriffsbildung*, pp. 404–15).

> that I imagine something, I believe in something believed (*Kant, divinity*); *Kantian philosophy—positive religion*.
>
> Alle positive Religion geht von etwas Entgegengestztem, einem, das wir nicht sind, aus, und das wir sein sollen; sie stellt ein Ideal vor seinem Sein auf; um an dasselbe glauben zu können, muß es eine Macht sein. In der positiven Religion ist das Seiende, die Vereinigung, nur eine Vorstellung, ein Gedachtes — ich glaube, daß es ist, heißt, ich glaube an die Vorstellung, ich glaube, daß ich mir etwas vorstelle, ich glaube an etwas Geglaubtes (*Kant, Gottheit*); kant[ische] *Philosophie—positive Religion*. [P. 254; my emphasis]

The cryptic parenthetical appositions have explosive power since they imply that Kantian philosophy both contains positivistic elements and has become like a "positive religion," something believed in and followed to the letter yet without the inner spirit and harmony of the believer. The identification that is the logical conclusion of the "Positivity" essay is here made explicit: just as the Christian religion became the object of mere belief and imitation, so too did Kant become a rhetorical and philosophical ideal that Hegel "ought" to be. In working through these fragments Hegel was able to work through his state of dependency on some "opposed Other" and accept it as a stage in the process of *Bildung* toward a more developed unity and form of expression.

Hegel can now return to the task of the "Positivity" essay and attempt a history of religion that allegorizes his own *Bildung* as a process of internalizing and liberating himself from earlier models. He does so in a series of fragments on the "spirit" of Judaism and Christianity.[85] But this allegory will not end like the earlier one with Kant appearing as a Christlike figure to sweep away the positivistic letter of dogma, since Hegel knows through his own treatment of them how Kant-Christ became an all too literal model of imitation. Rather, in accordance with the stage in which Hegel finds himself, Kant becomes a figure to be emulated, or in the religious terminology of the allegory, a law to be fulfilled by a new, inspired spirit.

In the first part of this history of Western religion, "Geist des Judentums" (Spirit of Judaism; 1798), Hegel writes another critical transla-

---

85. This large complex of manuscripts consists of six short fragments on Judaism, then two versions of the "Geist des Judentums," a *Grundkonzept* with notes and translations for the essay, and two versions of the "Geist des Christentums." Schüler describes the complexity of the various pieces of manuscript in great detail (see *Theorie-Werkausgabe*, p. 631–32). The very form of these manuscripts, the constant writing and rewriting, indicates Hegel's process of gradual clarification of thought through expression.

tion. Literally, he translates the story of the Old Testament, not unlike the way he translated the New Testament in Bern. Significantly, he translates Kantian morality and its insistence on obedience to the law back onto the history of the Jews. If at the end of the "Faith and Being" fragment Hegel postulates a link between Kantian philosophy and positivity since both are merely something thought or believed (*Gedachtes, Geglaubtes*), here he raises this principle to the core of Judaic history. That is, the spirit that motivated Abraham was "the spirit of maintaining strong oppositions to everything [and the spirit that] raised the thought (*das Gedachte*) to the dominant unity against an infinite, hostile nature" (pp. 277–78). Moreover, the Jews were motivated by a principle of legality—an insistence on the absolute Law as the basis of morality—which recalls the foundations of Kant's practical philosophy: "The principle of the entire legality was the spirit inherited from the ancestors—the infinite object, the very concept containing all truth and relations, therefore actually the sole infinite subject" ("Das Prinzip der ganzen Gesetzgebung war der von den Voreltern ererbte Geist—das unendliche Objekt, der Inbegriff aller Wahrheit und aller Beziehungen, also eigentlich das einzige unendliche Subjekt"; p. 203). Jewish law, according to Hegel's implicit argument, parallels Kantian ethics in its imposition of a projected absolute subject onto the will of individuals. This formalized conception of Law, which the Jews inherited from their forefathers, parallels at the same time Hegel's dogmatic inheritance of Kantian rhetoric.

Hegel's association of Kant with the Jews has major consequences for his thought and writing. The rhetorical act of identifying Kant with a past tradition surpasses the imitative translation of *Das Leben Jesu* since Hegel's identification of Kantian and Judaic legality serves not to identify *himself* with those traditions but rather to differentiate himself from the model even in the act of identification. He goes on to criticize the Jews for their historical alienation (*Entgegensetzung*) not so much because he rejects the religion itself as because he is attempting to reject the influence of Kant's rhetoric, which he transposes onto Jewish history.[86] At the end of the "Spirit of Judaism" Hegel relates the "tragedy" of the Jews to that of Macbeth, "who stepped out of the bounds of nature itself and relied on foreign beings" (p. 297). This tragic dependence on the foreign was the same fate that Hegel faced in his imitation of Kant. It is the same fate, as Quintilian and Longinus had pointed

---

86. Hegel breaks off the first version of the "Geist des Judentums" abruptly, as if he had not been able to narrativize this identity. He tries to sketch the lives and effects of Abraham, Noah, and Nimrod, but these figures are all the same and the history never moves forward (pp. 274–77).

out, which every imitator must face and overcome in the course of rhetorical *Bildung*.

Now the history of Christianity can function to reveal a different parallel for Hegel in the extended fragment "Der Geist des Christentums und sein Schicksal" (The Spirit of Christianity and Its Fate). Christ appears as a fulfillment of the Law, as an emulator who simultaneously internalizes and overcomes the Jewish tradition. The conditions under which Christ arose, his search and invention of new forms (*Bildungen*), parallel Hegel's own position as it relates to the tradition of philosophical writing:

> When the spirit has disappeared from a constitution and laws and, by having changed, no longer is in harmony with them, then a search begins for something else, a search in which each finds something different, whereby manifold formations (*Bildungen*), life-styles, claims, and needs arise. When these gradually diverge so far from each other that they can no longer exist side by side, then they bring about an explosion and give existence to a new universal form, a new bond between men. [P. 297]

Christ does not reject the Law but grants it a new spirit, "inspires" it, through an act of internalization. In fact, in keeping with the imagery we have already seen derived from the rhetorico-hermeneutic tradition, Hegel characterizes Christ's achievement as digestion. Precisely in the middle of the essay Hegel analyzes the central event of Christianity, the Last Supper, in terms that make his new rhetorico-hermeneutical position clear. He rewords the problem of the relationship between the Bread-Wine and Body-Blood of Christ in terms of the question of the meaning of the copula when Christ says: This *is* my Body and Blood. Hegel examines a number of rhetorical possibilities, or tropes (*Wendungen*): It is not a metonymy or conventional relation between sign and signified (*nicht ein konventionelles Zeichen*); not a simile with an assumed *tertium comparationis* and suppressed "like" (*Gleich-wie*); not a parable or allegorical figure (pp. 364–66). Rather, Hegel sees the act of transubstantiation in terms that recall the definition of metaphor as an identity that includes and overcomes differences: "For in this identification all difference falls away, hence also the possibility for a mere comparison. The heterogeneous elements are connected in the most essential way . . . the common chalice, the common drinking is the spirit of a new bond that penetrates many; . . . the same feeling is in them all; all are penetrated by the same spirit of love" (pp. 366–67). Christ's words, like Hegel's own writing at this stage, are thus an act of *translatio* which strives to define a new relationship to past traditions.[87] Hence it is no wonder that Hegel continues the discussion of the Last Supper by comparing this crucial metaphor of eating to the act of reading the written word.[88] He says of the act of transubstantiation that it can

> in this regard be compared to a thought that is made into a thing in the written word and that gains its subjectivity again out of a dead object when read. The comparison would be even more accurate if the written word were to be "read up" (off the page) and disappear as thing through the act of understanding.

> etwa in dieser Rücksicht mit dem im geschriebenen Worte zum Dinge gewordenen Gedanken verglichen werden, der aus einem Toten, einem Objekte, im Lesen seine Subjektivität wiedererhält. Die Vergleichung wäre treffender, wenn das geschriebene Wort aufgelesen (würde), durch das Verstehen als Ding verschwände. [P. 367]

As Hegel then quickly points out, however, the metaphor of writing and reading is more appropriate than that of the spoken word after all, for it is an act that can be repeated. The religious act, like the written tradition, can be regenerated by correct rereading and rewriting.[89]

Hegel, who has been "transubstantiating" the Christian tradition, now usurps the role he had formally assigned to Kant as an interpreter

87. *Translatio* here refers less to literal translation than to its use in rhetoric as metaphor. Hegel has moved beyond mere translation to a search and discovery of underlying identities. This corresponds to Aristotle's definitions of metaphor. For example: "The right use of metaphors is a sign of inborn talent and cannot be learned from anyone else; it comes from the ability to observe similarities in things" (*Poetics*, 1458a). Also, metaphor points to a "proportional likeness" in things (*Rhetoric*, 1405a). "We learn above all from metaphors" (*Rhetoric*, 1410b). "As I said before, metaphor must be by transference from things that are related, but not obviously so, as it is a sign of sound intuition in a philosopher to see similarities between things that are far apart" (*Rhetoric*, 1412a). Against this background, and Hegel's description of Christ's love during the Last Supper, and one has a better understanding of the linguistic force behind love. Hegel wrote elsewhere, for example: "Love acquires this richness of life in the exchange of all thoughts, of all diversity of the soul, in that it searches for infinite differences and seeks out unending union, and turns to the whole diversity of nature, in order to drink its life out of each" ("Diesen Reichtum des Lebens erwirbt die Liebe in der Auswechslung aller Gedanken, aller Mannigfaltigkeiten der Seele, indem sie unendliche Unterschiede sucht und unendliche Vereinigungen sich ausfindet, an die ganze Mannigfaltigkeit der Natur sich wendet, um aus jedem ihr Leben zu trinken"; p. 248).

88. Recall the passage quoted above in which Quintilian compares reading and (re)writing to eating. Compare also Hamacher's discussions of eating metaphors in Hegel's theological manuscripts (*pleroma*, pp. 48f., 117ff., 130, 133, 219ff., 256ff.).

89. Hamacher, *pleroma*: "Religion means, according to the etymology of Cicero, which certainly was not unknown to Hegel, the reading through of holy texts once again, and rereading them again and again" (p. 143).

or model of imitation. In the discussion of the Sermon on the Mount, for example, Kant turns out to be a bad reader of Christ's statements, a "Jewish" reader, to use Hegel's peculiar analogy from the "Spirit of Judaism," who would convert the figure (*Wendung*) of Christ's words into a commandment or law as moral duty:

> Even if Jesus did express that which he opposed and placed above the laws as commandments . . . this figure is to be understood in a completely different sense as a command from the "ought" of the commandment of duty. . . . And even if the living appears in the form of a reflected statement said to men, Kant still was very much in error to interpret this mode of expression, which is inappropriate for the living . . . as a commandment that demands respect for the law ordering love.

> Wenn Jesus auch das, was er den Gesetzen entgegen—und über sie setzt, als Gebote ausdrückt . . . so ist diese Wendung in einem ganz anderen Sinne Gebot als das Sollen des Pflichtgebots. . . . Und wenn so das Lebendige in der Form eines Reflektierten, Gesagten gegen Menschen erscheint, so hatte Kant sehr Unrecht, diese zum Lebendigen nicht gehörige Art des Ausdrucks . . . als ein Gebot anzusehen, welches Achtung für ein Gesetz fordert, das Liebe befiehlt. [Pp. 324—25][90]

In this typical misinterpretation, Kant, according to Hegel, is like John the Evangelist, who employed "a series of thetic propositions" (*eine Reihe thetischer Sätze*), "the simplest language of reflection" (*die einfachste Reflexionssprache*)[91] to convey the living spirit (Logos). And why could

90. It is interesting to compare this discussion of the Sermon on the Mount to the parallel discussion in Hegel's fourth homily from Tübingen. Hoffmeister, *Dokumente*, pp. 179–82. Where he had earlier been dominated by the Kantian system, he now identifies with Christ against the Kantian *Herrschaft des Begriffs*.

91. See, e.g., R. Eisler's *Kantlexikon* (Hildesheim: Olms, 1972) for the definitions of the Kantian categories *Reflexionsbegriffe, Schein, Urteil*. The full quote by Hegel makes clear the parallelism established between John and Kant: "The beginning of the Gospel of John contains a series of thetic propositions that are expressed in a more proper [literal] language about God and the divine; it is the simplest reflexive language to say: In the beginning was the Logos, in it was life. But these propositions have only a deceptive appearance of judgments, for the predicates are not concepts, a universal, such as the expression of a reflection in judgments necessarily contains; the predicates themselves are instead again something existing, alive. Even this simple reflection is not capable of expressing the spiritual with spirit" ("Der Anfang des Evangeliums des Johannes enthält eine Reihe thetischer Sätze, die in eigentlicher Sprache über Gott und Göttliches sich ausdrücken; es ist die einfachste Reflexionssprache zu sagen: Im Anfang war der Logos; in ihm war Leben. Aber diese Sätze haben nur den täuschenden Schein von Urteilen, denn die Prädikate sind nicht Begriffe, Allgemeines, wie der Ausdruck einer Reflexion in Urteilen notwendig enthält; sonder die Prädikate sind selbst wieder Seiendes, Lebendiges; auch diese einfache Reflexion ist nicht geschickt, das Geistige mit Geist auszudrücken"; p. 373). Hegel, in other words, is on the way to his "own" form of representation after having worked through Christian discourse and Kant's model of reflection.

John, and by analogy Kant, not capture in their language the inspired nature of the divine? Because of their inadequate *Bildung*, the *so arme jüdische Bildung*, indeed the *höchste Mißbildung des Volks* ("the poor Judaic education, and the highest miseducation of a people"; pp. 372–73).[92] Their interpretation of the Law and of tradition saw it as something to be followed to the letter. Hegel's *Bildung*, on the other hand, posits himself—like Christ—as a fulfiller of the past letter, as an individual who, paradoxically, having passed through the rhetorical and religious exercises of imitation, develops a new, inspired language.[93]

92. See Hamacher, *pleroma*, pp. 131–59, esp. p. 142: "The difficulties of a philosophical diction adequate to its speculative content; and differently, the difficulty of conceiving of pure being in such a manner that the conception of it is one with it; that its language itself is this being in its subjective as well as objective unity—this dilemma of Hegel's ontology and logic in the area of language, which is governed by Kantian dualism, is the dilemma with which the figure of Christ and the language of his evangelists are confronted in the area of Jewish *Bildung*."

93. Hegel, like Christ, is attempting to overcome the past influence, or Law, by "fulfilling" or "complementing" it. Hence the significance of the concept of *pleroma*, which Hegel redefines a number of times. For example: "*plerosai*: to complete, make complete or whole, to fulfill through the way of thought and character, through the addition of the internal to the external" ("πληρωσαι, ergänzen, vollständig machen durch die Gesinnung, durch Hinzufügen des Inneren zum Äußeren"; p. 309). "The harmony of the disposition is the *pleroma* of the law, a being" ("die Übereinstimmung der Neigung ist das πληρωμα des Gesetzes, ein Sein"; p. 326). "Thus is the holiness of love the complement [the *pleroma*] of the law" ("So ist . . . die Heiligkeit der Liebe die Ergänzung [das πληρωμα] des Gesetzes"; p. 329). "The religious is thus the *pleroma* of love (reflection and love united, both thought of as combined)" ("Religiöses ist also das πληρωμα der Liebe [Reflexion und Liebe vereint, beide verbunden gedacht]"; p. 370). All of these passages have a double reference: Christ's love fulfills the Law of the Old Testament the same way that Hegel's metaphorical, speculative language fulfills Kantian *Bildung*. In terms of Harold Bloom's rhetorical "ratios," one could say that Hegel's "fulfillment" of his precursor (at this point, anyway) has the form of a "tessera" relationship (*The Anxiety of Influence*, pp. 49–77).

CHAPTER 3

The Dialectics of *Kritik*
and the *Bildung* of Philosophy
in the Jena Essays

Something new is about to be launched, namely, the first volume
of a critical journal of philosophy, which I am publishing together
with Schelling and which has the goal in part to increase the number of journals and in part to place a limit and end to the un-
philosophical disorder (*dem unphilosophischen Unwesen*). The
weapons of which the journal will avail itself are manifold; people
will call them cudgeling, whipping, and beating (*Knittel, Peitschen
und Pritschen*);—it is all happening for a good cause and for the
greater glory of God; people will probably complain here and
there, but the cauterizing has in fact been necessary.

Hegel to Frau Hufnagel, 1803

149. *Criticism and Pleasure* (*Kritik und Freude*).—Criticism, be it
one-sided and unjust, or understanding, causes so much delight in
the one who practices it that the world owes its gratitude to each
work and every action that calls for criticism: for it is followed by a
shining tail of pleasure, wit, self-bewonderment, pride, instruction,
and intended one-upmanship (*Vorsatz zum Bessermachen*). The god
of pleasure created the bad and the mediocre for the same reason
that he created the good.

Nietzsche, *Human, All Too Human*, vol. 2

Late in 1800 Hegel moved from Frankfurt to Jena, where, thanks to
a modest sum that he had inherited from his father, he could take up
the study of philosophy at the most renowned German university of
the period. Even more than the move from Bern to Frankfurt, this
change in location introduced a major shift in Hegel's own *Bildung* and
in the direction of his writings. First, he undergoes the transformative
process from a writer of theological tracts to a philosopher. Of course,
ever since graduating from the Tübinger Stift, Hegel had abandoned
the idea of actually becoming a practicing minister, but only in these

first years at Jena does he adopt the stance of a "professional" philosopher. This stance involves more than just writing a dissertation in philosophy (the topic of which, the orbit of the planets, would not even be recognized today as fit for the humanities). To become a philosopher is to choose a certain tradition of texts and to insert oneself consciously into that continuing tradition. The names mentioned in the titles of his essays from the Jena period—Kant, Fichte, Schelling, Jacobi, Krug, Schulze, and so on—reveal the shift in textual traditions to which Hegel now refers.[1]

The most important consequence of this shift in tradition for the present study is that Hegel projects the concerns of his *Bildung* no longer onto Christianity but rather onto the development of "philosophy itself." The term *Bildung* becomes associated not with the development of Christ's doctrines from imitation to renewed creativity but with the teachings that make up the discipline or entity of philosophy. The needs of Hegel's *Bildung* become those of *philosophia*, the personification of his chosen field, in whose name Hegel presumes to speak. Furthermore, what we saw earlier as a tension between the rhetorical and the Judeo-Christian traditions—for example, in teaching methods and the propagation of doctrines—becomes now for Hegel a tension between philosophy and rhetoric. Hegel's earlier hermeneutical efforts united his rhetorical education with a religious and homiletic training. In Jena, his polemical efforts will locate his writing at the intersection of philosophy and rhetoric.

The second major shift in Hegel's *Bildung* during these years involves the form and function of his writing, not just the content. The demands of his *Bildung* and the definition of this concept change with the different forum for his writing. Hegel enters the public sphere. Before leaving Frankfurt in November 1800, he writes to Schelling that he wishes to spend a quiet month in Bamberg "before daring to entrust myself to the literary storm (*dem literarischen Saus*) in Jena."[2] As he begins to publish in these years the gradual formation of his thoughts by means of private rhetorico-hermeneutical exercises in writing and rewriting must come to an end since a published piece imposes different rhetorical demands. His *Bildung* shifts from imitations and transla-

1. All page numbers within parentheses in the body of the text of this chapter refer to the *Theorie-Werkausgabe*, vol. 2, *Jenaer Schriften* (Frankfurt: Suhrkamp, 1978).

2. Johannes Hoffmeister, *Briefe von und an Hegel* (Hamburg: Felix Meiner, 1961) no. 29. Actually, by the time Hegel reached Jena, the city had already surpassed its earlier intellectual high point. Fichte had just been involved in the *Atheismusstreit* and was forced to leave Jena for Berlin. The young romantics were beginning to leave as well. Schiller, who had taught history at the university, could not continue due to poor health and was residing exclusively in Weimar.

tions of traditions to an act of taking a position. Taking a position involves simultaneously differentiating oneself from others critically, something Hegel had already begun privately with his critiques of Kant and Judaism, and synthesizing various ideas into one's own stance.[3] Precisely this twofold—dialogic and dialectical—act of formation through differentiation dominates both his own rhetorical development and his concept of *Bildung* in these years. If in Bern and Frankfurt he worked through the age-old rhetorico-hermeneutical paradox of how to attain individuality by means of imitative appropriation of general principles, in Jena he confronts the paradox of how to differentiate himself from others without becoming just one more different position. The term that Hegel will associate with this task is *Kritik,* a term that, as we saw in the rhetorical handbooks of Hegel's schooling, also links him to that traditional point of intersection between rhetoric and philosophy—dialectical *inventio.*

3. For the theoretical framework of my analysis of this broader conception of rhetoric, which is particularly fruitful for philosophy, I am indebted to the work of the Belgians Chaim Perelman and Lucie Olbrecht-Tyteca, and of the Americans Maurice Natanson and Henry Johnstone, Jr. Perelman's and Olbrecht-Tyteca's first collection of essays, *Rhétorique et philosophie: Pour une théorie de l'argumentation en philosophie* (Paris: Presses Universitaires de France, 1952), intends "to show the place that rhetoric, conceived as a theory of argumentation, could be called upon to occupy within thought" (p. viii). Their major work, *The New Rhetoric: Treatise of Argumentation,* trans. John Wilkinson and Purcell Weaver (South Bend, Ind.: University of Notre Dame, 1962), is particularly useful since it relates argumentative and stylistic strategies to the attempt to convince and even construct an audience. Philosophy differs from other disciplines mainly in that it attempts to construct a "universal audience" that, in theory, would provide its rational assent to the philosopher's arguments. They write: "Philosophers always claim to be addressing such an [universal] audience, not because they hope to obtain the effective assent of all men—they know very well that only a small minority will ever read their works—but because they think that all who understand the reasons they give will have to accept their conclusions. The agreement of a universal audience is thus a matter not of fact but of right" (p. 31).

The work of Natanson and Johnstone shifts emphasis from the construction of an audience to the philosopher's construction of a "self" out of his differentiation from other positions. Johnstone's most direct formulation of his approach can be found in his *The Problem of the Self* (University Park, Pa.: Penn State University Press, 1970): "The act in which the self is evoked is essentially an act of philosophical criticism because it is only in responding to such criticism that we are forced to stand outside ourselves. . . . Hence, not only is the self the pivot of philosophical controversy, but also philosophical controversy is the life-sustaining atmosphere of the self" (p. 145). This statement links the notions of criticism and development (*Kritik* and *Bildung*) in precisely the ways pursued in this chapter.

Compare also Johnstone, *Philosophy and Argument* (University Park, Pa.: Penn State University Press, 1959), and *Validity and Rhetoric in Philosophical Argumentation* (University Park, Pa.: Penn State University Press, 1978); and Natanson, "The Claims of Immediacy" and "Rhetorical and Philosophical Argumentation," in *Philosophy, Rhetoric and Argumentation,* ed. Natanson (University Park, Pa.: Penn State University Press, 1965). See also articles in the journal *Philosophy and Rhetoric.*

In 1801 Hegel and Schelling published a statement in a number of philosophical and literary magazines announcing the program of their forthcoming journal, the *Kritisches Journal der Philosophie*. This brief statement announces the program of both Hegel's writing and *Bildung* as a philosopher for the next years.[4] An analysis of its strategies will raise the issues that we will encounter over the course of the Jena essays. The "Announcement" (*Ankündigung*) begins: "Since the large crowd that philosophy has attracted recently against its/her will (*gegen ihren Willen*) as participants or onlookers is gradually beginning to go astray, true scientific knowledge (*die wahre Wissenschaft*) is gaining the time to withdraw back into itself and, forming a living center of the contraction (*einen lebendigen Mittelpunkt der Kontraktion bildend*), to cut itself off forever from nonphilosophy (*Unphilosophie*)" (p. 169). The other philosophers in this struggle for scientific authority are immediately denigrated as the faceless "crowd" that has lost its way. The epithet *Haufen* contains the ad hominem value judgment that not all philosophers are equal in their search for truth, but rather that some belong to the lower class in the empire of thought. Philosophy implies a political structure with a dominant aristocracy. Moreover, philosophy is personified as a being with a will to which Hegel has direct access, for he knows that others follow it/her "against its/her will." The will of philosophy implies further a motivated history that culminates in the present marked by a radical separation from the past (*scheiden*). This critical and decisive divorce is a necessary reaction to the prior self-loss of philosophy and, as we saw in the last chapter, of the philosopher Hegel, in diverse foreign positions. Both philosophy and by implication the philosopher must form (*bilden*) a different, coherent position that escapes this self-loss by being both critical of others and self-contained.

Hegel then expands these opening motifs by relating his own interests to the supposed interests of philosophy "it/herself." He grants that past philosophical movements have accomplished some good both politically and in terms of general intellectual development thanks to their "great cosmopolitan relations, their influence on the education and cultivation of the universal and particular life of man" (*große, weltbürgerliche Beziehung, ihr Einfluß auf die Bildung des allgemeinen und einzelnen Lebens des Menschen*; p. 169). They have contributed, that is, to the formation of a broader and more knowledgeable public sphere. And yet they have not achieved the "genuine effects or accomplishments" (*die echten Wirkungen*) desired by true philosophy. Furthermore,

4. Although many of the essays discussed in this chapter were published under both Hegel's and Schelling's names, I will refer to Hegel as sole author. All the essays discussed are generally attributed to him as major contributor. When the style of the essays was criticized by contemporaries, Schelling quickly distanced himself from the works.

because the history of public philosophy parallels the development of an individual life, it must follow the teleology of natural *Bildung*; that is, health arises from the proper relationship of parts to the whole, whereby the parts are subsumed to, even annihilated (*vernichtet*) by, the whole (pp. 169f.). And so the individual philosophers become mere "particularities" (*Besonderheiten*) of philosophy it/herself. In the name of philosophy they must disappear.

These general comments lead to the specific purpose of the journal: "Above all the representation of the categorical essence of philosophy as opposed to the negative character of nonphilosophy" ("Vor allem Darstellung des kategorischen Wesens der Philosophie im Gegensatz des negativen Charakters der Unphilosophie"; p. 170). Such a statement combines two levels of argumentation. On the one hand, it refers to the concrete task of the journal to criticize specific contemporary philosophers. On the other, it projects differences that exist between philosophers onto a more abstract distinction involving the very nature of philosophy. Hegel's own interests seem to recede behind the purer disinterest of philosophy vis-à-vis its categorical opposite. And yet in spite of the projection onto philosophy, Hegel's specific purpose shines through, for he wishes to use the methods of "philosophy" to win an audience. The purpose of depicting the "essence of philosophy" in this journal is, he continues, to "assure for itself the respect of those interested and to strive to win for itself the inclinations of its contemporaries" ("das angezeigte periodische Werk der Philosophie [wird] sich die Achtung der sich für sie interessierenden Welt versichern und sich die Zuneigung der Zeitgenossen zu erwerben suchen"; p. 170). The development of philosophical ideas takes place not merely between "philosophy" and "nonphilosophy," then, but also, significantly, between philosophers before a public. The argumentation of the journal will simultaneously posit, create, and fulfill the expectations of the public under the guise of "philosophy it/herself."

The announcement ends with an image indicating the role of *Bildung*. Typically, an organic metaphor tends to mask the rhetorical, in this case concretely polemical and public, feature of the concept. Some parts of the contemporary scene, Hegel writes, must

> necessarily dry up and die off as soon as this last aid is cut off. Thereby a path will finally be cleared and the fertile ground of true *philosophy will be able to form itself* by itself and quietly rise up under the hand of *Kritik*.

> unfehlbar verdorren und absterben, sobald diese letzte Hilfe ihnen abgeschnitten ist. Damit wird endlich reine Bahn gemacht sein und *unter der Hand der Kritik* der Grund und Boden der wahren *Philosophie*

sich von selbst bilden können und ruhig emporsteigen. [P. 170; my emphasis]⁵

The function of *Kritik* is to clear a path rhetorically for the new philosophy to which Hegel must give form in his writing. *Kritik* is a rhetorical activity that prepares the way for philosophy. In creating the rhetorical and logical space for a system, preparatory criticism can be said to "invent" the argumentative *loci* for the following philosophy. This announcement leaves us with the following questions: What is the relationship between the "formative self-development" (*sich bilden*) of philosophy and the "hand of *Kritik*"? What is the hand of *Kritik* in both Hegel's own *Bildung* and in that of philosophy?

This advertisement parallels the guidelines that Hegel wrote in 1807 for a journal on German arts and letters, the "Maximen des Journals der deutschen Literatur." Although the maxims, like the later journal, were never published, they point to the link for Hegel between *Kritik*, *Bildung*, and the public sphere. The opening statement of purpose states the connections even more directly than the earlier "Announcement": "The general purpose is the advancement of scientific and aesthetic *Bildung*, in which everyone not belonging to the class of working people (*Gewerbsklasse*) participates by means of the *Kritik* found in the journals on science and art that appear in Germany" (p. 568). *Kritik* provides the access to the *Bildung* of science and art by presenting works in these fields to the public. The public is limited, on the one hand, since class distinctions determine who enters the republic of letters. On the other hand, as Hegel mentions further on, "the *details* of the particular sciences proper . . . have no place in the plan of the journal," since they would limit the audience to the experts. Thus, the encouragement of *Bildung* of—not just in!—science and art depends on the cultivation of the appropriate audience by means of the appropriate form of *Kritik*.

For Hegel, as the planned editor of this new journal, the *form* of criticism is more significant than the content of the work criticized: "Concerning works of general interest, however, whether or not a critique corresponds to the purpose of this institution, and whether or not general intellectual culture and education (*allgemeine geistige Bildung*) and scientific knowledge and taste are thereby increased, depends less on its *content* (*Inhalt*) than on the *kind of the critique* itself (Art dieser

---

5. The word *Kritik* will generally be left in the original throughout this study since the alternatives in English, *critique* and *criticism*, are either too narrow or have inappropriate connotations.

Kritik *selbst*)" (pp. 568f.; Hegel's emphasis). Although Hegel does not speak explicitly of "form," his emphatic opposition of "kind" to "content" implies that at issue in what determines the different *kinds* of criticism is the different forms it can take on. Once again we can ask: How does the form of *Kritik* contribute to "general intellectual *Bildung*"? How can scientific knowledge profit in its development by polemical *Kritik*? What is the relationship between science, art, and the audience addressed and persuaded by *Kritik*?

Since Hegel associates *Bildung* at this stage of his writing with the concept of *Kritik*, we should first consider the historical origins of this concept in order to appreciate the background of his developing understanding of philosophy and its precondition. By briefly examining the history of *Kritik*, we discover rhetorical traces influencing a major stage of Hegel's development, for the activity of *Kritik* calls up a tradition at the intersection of rhetoric and philosophy. One might first be tempted to associate Hegel's quasi-definition of *Kritik* as the hand under which philosophy develops with Kant's philosophical enterprise. After all, Kant coined the famous description of his age as that of a struggle between *Kritik* and all forms of illusory knowledge: "the age of *Kritik*, which does not let itself be held back any longer by illusory knowledge (*Scheinwissen*)."[6] In particular, Kant understood his three *Critiques* as the necessary preparation for the development of any future metaphysics. Although the term is not unambiguous in Kant, the basic notion behind it is the discovery of limitations and the drawing of borders. The originally planned title of the first *Critique*, as Kant wrote in letters to M. Herz (7 June 1771 and 21 February 1772) was: *Grenzen der Sinnlichkeit und der Vernunft* (Borders or Limits of Sensuality and Reason). Kant explicitly differentiates his notion of *Kritik* from the philological use of the term by Matthias Gesner and the neohumanists: "I do not mean here, however, a critique of books and systems, but the critique of the faculty of reason as such, on the one hand from the point of view of all knowledge to which it might strive independently of any experience and on the other with an eye toward the decision of whether metaphysics is possible or impossible and toward the determination of its sources, scope, and limits—all this, however, derived from principles."[7]

6. Kant, *Kritik der reinen Vernunft*, A (1st ed., 1781), p. xi.

7. Ibid. Recall the discussions of these movements in chap. 1, above. This passage indicates a significant point at which Kant begins to distinquish himself from the older rhetorical tradition. It is crucial for Kant to distinguish his enterprise from philology, since the very word *Kritik* was up till then only associated with philology. Kurt Röttgers points out in his outstanding *Begriffsgeschichte, Kritik und Praxis: Zur Geschichte des Kritik-*

As a drawer of borders and limits, the faculty of *Kritik* for Kant culminates an Enlightenment task that sees science as the site of a precise judgment between truth and falsehood before the absolute measure of reason. Vico had been one of the first modern philosophers to formulate this view of criticism, which in the *Scienza Nuova* places all truth on one side, all falsehood, uncertainty, suspected falsehood, opinion, probability, and the like on the other.[8] By placing reason itself under the distinguishing eye of *Kritik*, Kant then went further; he hoped to be assured that any philosophy that developed from the use of reason would be on the right side. And yet it was precisely the connection between the idea of *Kritik* and the idea of a developing philosophy which Kant was unable to clarify; that is, he could not make clear what granted *Kritik* the authority to act as judge *before* philosophy.

Out of Kant's unclarified connection between *Kritik* and philosophy a number of camps developed in Germany. The one group of more or less orthodox Kantians continued Kant's "usurpation" of the term *Kritik*, making it less a universal activity than the flag of their school.[9] For them, *Kritik* was the only way to philosophize, not an activity to be applied by all and to all texts and systems. They reduced philosophy to a the activity of criticism, and this activity to a dogmatic form of Kantian methodology. Other writers, such as Maimon and Herder, resisted the appropriation of the term by a particular school and strove instead for a "metacritique" that would point out the linguistic nature of con-

---

begriffs von Kant bis Marx (Berlin: de Gruyter, 1975): "In Germany the word *Kritik* surfaces in the German language for the first time in 1718 in G. Stolle's *A Short Introduction to the History of Learnedness*: 'Criticism' [*Die Critic*] usually means an art *of understanding the ancient authors* (or making them understandable), of differentiating that which they have written from that which has been attributed to them or has been forged, and of improving that which has become tainted or or replacing it" (pp. 21–22). Röttgers also refers to the definition of *Critic* found in Zedler's *Lexikon* (1733). Hegel's definition of *Bildung* under the hand of *Kritik* clearly sounds more related to this philological sense than to Kant's sense.

8. This notion is undoubtedly related to Pierre Bayle's. Röttgers summarizes his significance: "Pierre Bayle is therefore doubly significant, first, because he is the first great theoretician of *Kritik* (and its first practitioner, that above all!), and, second, because he developed a complete theory of the republic of letters, the impact of which appears to reach to this day and which also exercised a great influence on Kant. Through permanent *Kritik*, raised to a principle, reason is established as the highest court of appeal (*oberste Instanz*)" (*Kritik und Praxis,*, Pp. 20–21).

9. Ibid., pp. 63–73. He deals with a series of post-Kantians and includes among the Kant-*Orthodoxen* who limited the notion of *Kritik*: J.P.L. Snell, J. Schulz, and G.S.A. Mellin. This tendency is already evident in Kant, whose chapters on *Methodenlehre* indicate that *Kritik* follows a specific procedure of establishing antinomies to unmask illusory knowledge. This procedure attempts to set up fixed criteria (Kant calls them *Kanon*) to measure knowledge.

sciousness and make possible a continual critique of modes of expression.[10] They, like Hegel, returned to an older and broader conception of linguistic criticism. Fichte offered another possibility. He believed that Kant did not go far enough, for Kant did not find the unshakable principle (*Grundsatz*) from which one could criticize all other positions. Thus, the opening of his *Wissenschaftslehre* develops out of absolute principles that must be accepted. Finally, the romantics radicalized both Kant and Fichte by stressing the power of absolute criticism and by combining it with a notion of unending irony. They strove not for the fundamental position where all criticism ends but for the constantly shifting criticism of oneself as well as others.

But to better understand what it meant for Hegel to enter the fray at this point and to link *Kritik* with *Bildung*, we must take a brief look at an older tradition back beyond that of Kant and Enlightenment science, for Hegel's notion unites various contradictory strands that had existed for some two thousand years in Western intellectual history. Appropriately, Hegel's synthesis corresponds to the needs of his own *Bildung* at this point, for, having worked through the tradition, he must now constitute his own position out of its conflicting concepts. All of these conceptions from the history of the activity of criticism of which Hegel was aware from his own *Bildung* will reappear at the stage of his development at which he becomes implicated in the dialectics of *Kritik*.

In the classical tradition that connects Plato and Aristotle to Cicero and Quintilian, and beyond them to humanists like Ramus and Sturm, and to Enlightenment figures like Bayle and Vico, *Kritik* and the function of *iudicium* stand at the intersection of four fields or activities: (1) the juridico-political, since, the *kritikes* were the decision makers and to exercise criticism was to take part in the process of public consensus building (forensic and deliberative rhetoric);[11] (2) the philologico-grammatical, since especially after Hellenistic times and the Middle Ages, criticism involved the establishment of the true source texts and proper linguistic usage (*latinitas*); (3) the philosophico-logical, since critique for Plato meant differentiating truth from untruth, and for Aris-

10. Röttgers refers to this group, which also included Bouterweck, Abicht, Beck, and K. L. Reinhold, as the "more independent (*selbständigere*) Kantians." It is certainly significant that many of Hegel's harshest criticisms will be waged against these philosophers, who were involved in the same struggle to use and gain greater independence from Kant's system. Charles Taylor has pursued the connection between Hegel and Herder in greatest detail, but does not point out this historical point of convergence. *Hegel* (Cambridge: Cambridge University Press, 1975), chap. 1.

11. Heinrich Lausberg on *kritikes*, in *Handbuch der literarischen Rhetorik* (Munich: Max Hueber, 1960), pars. 10(3b), 26, 59(1), 426.

totle and the humanists it played a major role in dialectics; (4) the rhetorico-hermeneutical, since critique helps a writer, at all stages in the development of a speech (*inventio, dispositio, elocutio, pronuntio, exercitio*), to work through the interpretations of others (hence reading develops writing skills and vice versa). This intersection leads to a number of paradoxes contained in the history of the concept of criticism. On the one hand, for Aristotle, for example, criticism is exercised by the universally educated mind; on the other, it becomes the task of a select few trained in a given discipline or *technē*. On the one hand, it belongs to rhetoric as consensus formation in the public forum; on the other, to either grammar or logic as rule-giving disciplines to decide objectively between the correct and incorrect usage or even between truth and falsehood.

Moreover, the paradoxical relationships between these disciplines get carried over onto the paradoxes of *Kritik*. A central question that concerned Cicero and Quintilian, for example, revolved around the connection between rhetoric and philosophy. Do *inventio* and *iudicium* both belong under rhetoric, or are they separate activities in separate disciplines—namely rhetoric and dialectic—or are they both parts of dialectic whereby one is subordinated to the other? Cicero stressed the *ars inveniendi* over the *vis iudicii* in an effort to devise a program for training better orators for the public arena. Quintilian, who sees the two as inseparable in the formation of a speech, tries to distinguish between these activities in terms of the audience; for him, *iudicium* exists in both rhetoric and dialectic but has different functions. Rhetorical criticism addresses the judgment of a general audience that "a speech is to be composed in keeping with the judgments of others," whereas dialectical criticism deals with the minute arguments among specialists: "For in them [dialectical disputations], learned men strive for truth among the learned, they research everything into the minutest detail and pursue it to the point of certainty and common acceptance, so that they make use of the parts of invention and judgment that some call topics (*topiken*) and the ancients called *kritikes*."[12] Hence, the history of the very concept of critique has been formed by and continues to bear within itself the debate between rhetoric and philosophy.

What is significant about the history of *Kritik* for Hegel is that he seems to integrate many of these features from the classical, humanist, and Enlightenment traditions. As we know, his schooling trained him

12. Quintilian, *Institutio Oratoria* v, 14, 27–29.

in all three. If at this point in his career, then, Hegel links the development of philosophy to the activity of *Kritik*, he is attempting to come to grips with a paradoxical relationship between modes of rhetorical and philosophical argumentation. The very formation of Hegel's philosophy and the concept of *Bildung* in the Jena essays, because they are linked to the activity of *Kritik*, unfold paradoxically. He must appeal to the universal audience of reason and to the concrete audience he is striving to cultivate. He must differentiate his own views polemically from those of his rivals without becoming a mere polemicist. He must rely on rhetoric to ground a philosophical position. Rhetoric, as the critical activity that prepares ("invents") the ground or place (*loci*) for philosophical argumentation, enters into the representation of truth as a precondition of its discourse.

In the introductory essay to the *Kritisches Journal*—"Einleitung, Über das Wesen der philosophischen Kritik überhaupt und ihr Verhältnis zum gegenwärtigen Zustand der Philosophie insbesondere" (Introduction, On the Essence of Philosophical Criticism in General, and Its Relationship to the Present State of Philosophy in Particular; 1802)— Hegel examines the possibility and forms of critical writing in philosophy. Although the essay has little to say explicitly on the concept of *Bildung*, it deserves detailed analysis since its explication of the principle of philosophical criticism characterizes best what Hegel called philosophy's process of self-formation (*sich bilden*) under the "hand of *Kritik*." In general three arguments can be isolated: (1) *Kritik* and the absolute measure of "philosophy itself"; (2) the forms of *Kritik*; and (3) the function of philosophy in society. And yet in none of these arguments, which will be treated individually below, does Hegel address the essential questions: Why write *Kritik* at all? What does critical rhetoric contribute to a philosopher's or philosophy's *Bildung*? As is typical of the Jena writings as a whole, the arguments of this essay paradoxically employ polemical and critical rhetoric in spite of the explicit insistence on "purely" philosophical terms. By uncovering the rhetorical aspects behind *Kritik* we can better understand how Hegel's conception of the *Bildung* of philosophy under the hand of differentiating *Kritik* contains and relies on the trace of an older rhetorical tradition.

The first argument of the "Essence of *Kritik*" concerns the problem of the measure required in order to practice criticism: "*Kritik*, in whatever aspect of art or scientific knowledge it is practiced, requires a measure (*Maßstab*)" (p. 171). In classical rhetoric, the measure of correctness of an oration or of speech in general was derived from usage. That speech was "correct" or "good" which either succeeded in persuading the public or corresponded to the "canon" (measure) of previously established "good" works.[13] Hegel, however, wishes at least in his explicit pronouncements to escape from such rhetorical criteria and to employ the ideal scientific measure of the Enlightenment. He proposes a "measure that is as independent from the judger as from the object judged and that is derived neither from the particular phenomenon nor from the individuality of the subject, but, rather, from the external and immutable original image (*Urbild*) of the matter itself (*Sache selbst*)" (p. 171). This measure is the *Idee der Philosophie selbst*, which guides all *Kritik* in principle and not merely according to successful usage.

Hegel establishes the validity of one philosophical principle, however, by employing two rhetorical turns, namely *argumentum ad hominem* and *petitio principii*.[14] He rejects the possibility of "essentially different and yet equally true philosophies" (p. 172) with the implicit ad hominem argument that such a possibility might have a certain consolation (*Trost*) for those who believe it, but that it is otherwise unworthy of consideration. That is, he rejects the argument by appealing to the weakness of those who accept it. Then he grounds his belief in *one* philosophy on the fact that "reason itself is singular" (*die Vernunft nur eine ist*; p. 172). But the demonstration relies on a rhetorical circle—*petitio principii*—for the view of *one* reason as the foundation of *one* philosophy already rests on his philosophical standpoint: "reason viewed absolutely . . . or philosophically " (*die Vernunft absolut betrachtet or philosophisch betrachtet*; p. 172). That is, he bases his philosophical starting point, reason, on a "philosophical" way of viewing reason, thereby assuming what he set out to prove. Hence we see in this opening argument that Hegel employs rhetorical forms of argumentation in order to ground an antirhetorical platform for *Kritik*. (It is worth noting here that in taking the polemical stance of a *Maßstab* outside of the subject he is in fact contradicting his earlier critique of Kant and approaching the positivity he spent years rejecting. Later, in the *Phenomenology*, when this polemical rhetoric has been surpassed, that is,

13. See Lausberg, *Handbuch*, pars. 5ff., on the rhetorical concept of *usus*; also on *critica*, par. 10 (3b) and 26. The distinction between praxis- or dialogue-oriented dialectic and a dialectic according to external criteria goes back to the distinction between the Sophists' and Plato's usurpation of dialectic as the sole criterion of philosophy (in the *Sophists* and *Phaedrus*). We shall review that debate in chap. 4, the third section, "Dialectic and Dialogue."

14. Perelman and Olbrechts-Tyteca point out in *The New Rhetoric* that these two techniques are actually related: *petitio principii* "consists of postulating what one wishes to prove. . . . [It] consists of the use of argument ad hominem where it cannot be used because it supposes that the interlocutor has already given his adherence to a proposition which the speaker is in fact endeavoring to make him accept" (p. 112).

internalized in his system, Hegel develops a more tenable intersubjective position: "The measure [*Maßstab*] falls in us.")[15]

The second, more extended argument of the essay deals with the different forms of *Kritik*. It states the rhetorical program of the essays that will follow in the next years in the *Kritisches Journal der Philosophie*. The mixture of rhetorical and philosophical criteria for his writing is already evident in the two general characterizations of *Kritik*. Hegel defines it the "subsuming under the idea" (*Subsumtion unter die Idee*; p. 173), whereby the absolute measure of the "idea" tests unequivocally the validity of propositions. But he also implies that *Kritik* is a kind of "court of law" (*Gerichtshof*; p. 174), a term that recalls the forensic origins of *Kritik* as a debate between parties in which neither the outcome nor the criteria are predetermined.[16]

According to the "philosophical" view—the subsuming of the specific under the general idea—there exists little possibility or reason for dialogue among philosophers. To the extent that a proposed philosophy does not measure up to the idea of "philosophy itself" it becomes simply the object of "derision" (*Verwerfung*; p. 173). Against such misguided efforts in philosophy, *Kritik* takes on the form of the mere depiction of the opponent's worthlessness: "Thus, nothing remains to be done but to narrate how this negative side expresses itself (*wie sich diese negative Seite ausspricht*) and how it reveals its own nothingness, which, insofar as it appears (*Erscheinung hat*) at all, is called its triviality (*Plattheit*)" (p. 174). To the extent, then, that a proposed philosophical system does not measure up to the idea of philosophy it is to be treated with condescension. Basically, though, from the perspective of the *Idee*, *Kritik* has little point: "The business of criticism is lost for those writers and on those works that happen to lack that idea" ("Das Geschäft der Kritik ist für diejenigen und an denjenigen Werken durchaus verloren, welche jener Idee entbehren sollten"; p. 173). Only according to the

15. See below, chap. 4, third section, "Dialectic and Dialogue," for a more extensive discussion of the strategies of the inner and outer measure in the Introduction to the *Phenomenology*.

16. See Röttgers on legalistic images surrounding the concept of *Kritik*: "The self-legitimation of *Kritik* through dialectic: the court of law" (*Kritik und Praxis*, pp. 31–39). This image leads even in Kant to a double role for *Kritik* and *Dialektik*. On the one hand, they are the place of debate between the conflicting parties; on the other, they become the judges who decide finally and absolutely who is right. As Röttgers says: "With this the factual conflict of the contending parties in the republic of letters, the argumentative conflict, is internalized and raised to positions that are logically incontestable, that is, uncorrectable even with traditional means—positions of the one reason that in the antithesis simulates communication" (p. 35). One must recall that this imagery of *Kritik* as relating to a court rests on a tradition of literal judgments and techniques systematized in forensic rhetoric.

second, implicitly *rhetorical* conception of *Kritik* as a struggle for authority at a court of law does criticism seem to have value. The struggle for
authority takes place by criticizing those forms that seem to grant an
opposing system its authority. Hegel describes "yet another manner [of
philosophizing] to which criticism should especially apply itself":

> namely, that mode that pretends to be in possession of philosophy, that
> uses the forms and phrases in which great philosophical systems ex-
> press themselves, that joins in the general discussion, but is fundamen-
> tally an empty cloud of words without inner content. By means of its
> expansiveness and its own pretentiousness, such idle chatter without
> the idea of philosophy acquires for itself a kind of authority partially
> because it seems incredible that there can be so much shell without any
> core, and partially because emptiness has a kind of general comprehen-
> sibility. [P. 176]

Once again, Hegel resorts to essentially rhetorical criteria—formal features and effects of such forms on the public—to justify his critical
activity. Where the philosophical foundation of *Kritik* made its own
exercise seem pointless, rhetorical criteria taken from an older tradition grant it an important function in the struggle for authority and
acceptance.

The third and final argument generalizes the second by raising the
problem of the authority of certain contemporary philosophical forms
to a cultural and social level. At this level the rhetorical component of
Kritik plays an even greater role since philosophy is placed into the
context of the public at large. Hegel relates a number of philosophical
positions to social and cultural practices that he presumes worthy of ad
hominem criticism. For example, against those philosophers who believe in the uniqueness or originality of their position Hegel claims that
they actually remain caught

> within the general mainstream (*Heerstraße*) of culture and cannot even
> boast of having escaped this and found the pure idea of philoso-
> phy. . . .The bit of uniqueness they [have] created within that main-
> stream is a certain form of reflection, picked up from some particular
> and thus subordinate viewpoint, a form that can be got cheaply in an
> age that has so richly developed, formed, educated the faculty of un-
> derstanding (*das den Verstand so vielseitig ausgebildet*) and especially has
> put it to work on philosophy in so many ways. [P. 177]

This biting description, whose basic form we will encounter throughout the Jena essays, contains a number of significant elements: In spite
of its apparently antirhetorical thrust, it recalls Quintilian's argument

that *iudicium* (related to *critica*) is also necessary to "invent" truly original arguments;[17] it recalls the state that Hegel characterized as Jewish
Mißbildung or Kantian *Positivität* since it fixes isolated forms; and it
recalls the role of *Kritik* as the determining factor in an argument's
social authority in the public sphere.

Hegel's goal is to recapture the social and cultural space occupied by
his competitors. This reappropriation will require a rhetorical, quasi-
political struggle that Hegel illuminates with two examples.[18] In the
first, he equates Cartesian philosophy to a revolution that philosophy
must oppose:

> Every aspect of living nature as well as philosophy itself has had to seek
> a cure against both culture at large and Cartesian philosophy in particu-
> lar, which has given expression in philosophical form to the general,
> ever-expanding hegemonic dualism in the culture of the recent history
> of our northwestern world—a dualism of which, as the decline of the
> entire past life, the more peaceful transformation of public life, as well
> as the more clamorous political and religious revolutions in principle,
> are merely the external expressions in a different color.

> Gegen die Cartesische Philosophie nämlich, welche den allgemein um
> sich greifenden Dualismus in der Kultur der neueren Geschichte un-
> serer nordwestlichen Welt—einen Dualismus, von welchem als dem
> Untergange alles alten Lebens die stillere Umänderung des öffent-
> lichen Lebens der Menschen sowie die lauteren politischen und re-
> ligiösen Revolutionen überhaupt nur verschiedenfarbige Außenseiten
> sind—in philosophischer Form ausgesprochen hat, mußte, wie gegen
> die allgemeine Kultur, die sie ausdrückt, jede Seite der lebendigen
> Natur, so auch die Philosophie Rettungsmittel suchen. [P. 184–5]

Philosophy therefore becomes for Hegel a kind of counterrevolutionary force, one that will develop out of the decay of dead *Bildung* (*der*

---

17. *Handbuch für Philosophie*, pp. 1254–55: "In the division of the parts of speech
Quintilian now rejects . . . the separation of *inventio* and *iudicium*, as if the former were
the first and the latter came afterward, because, in his opinion, a person has not yet
found anything if he has not judged it (*ego purro ne invenisse quidem credo eum, qui non
iudicavit* [*Institutio Oratorio*, III, 3, 5])."

18. It should be pointed out here that Hegel was as skilled in political rhetoric as he
was in theological rhetoric. During his years in Bern and Frankfurt he worked through a
tradition of political theory in precisely the same manner as he worked through the
conflation of Kantian and Christian discourses. He began with a literal translation ("Die
Vertraulichen Briefe über das vormalige staatsrechtliche Verhältnis des Wadtlands zur
Stadt Bern" by J. J. Cart [1798]), practiced a series of fragments, and then worked on an
extensive essay on the German constitution. Hence, it should come as no surprise that
Hegel manipulates political rhetoric with the same skill as he employs religious imagery,
especially since *Kritik* has been bound together with the tradition of deliberative oratory.

Geist aus der Verwesung der verstorbenen Bildung). The social and cultural function of philosophical criticism will determine its rhetoric so that a new philosophy can develop out of the *Bildung* of the old.

In the second example connecting criticism to the sociopolitical sphere of discourse, Hegel opposes the tendency—"in these times of liberty and equality, in which such a large public has been formed and educated (*sich gebildet hat*)" (p. 182)—toward popular philosophy. The German is ambiguous in a significant way: The public has developed or the public has educated itself. As in the traditional debate over the role of *Kritik*—for example, in Quintilian and Cicero—the question is whether the writer should appeal to the public at large or to the narrower group of experts. Hegel takes a clear stance for a higher, more noble philosophical style: "Philosophy is by its very nature something esoteric, and is in itself neither made for the masses (*Pöbel*) nor capable of being prepared for mass consumption; it is in fact philosophy only because it is diametrically opposed to understanding and thus even more opposed to common sense, by which is meant the local and temporary limits of a race of men; in relation to common sense, the world of philosophy is in and of itself an inverted world" (p. 182). His social views parallel a conception of stylistic levels. Popular philosophy, like comedy, deals with the "masses" and the "bourgeois life" (p. 183), whereas true philosophy, like tragedy, is "the most sublime and only true earnestness" (p. 184). What is at stake here is the ambiguous function and origin of the critical activity. Hegel seems to be supporting the scientific, logical tradition. However, the form of his arguments, the images of the cultural and social sphere, and the appeals to the audience locate his concept of *Kritik* in the rhetorical-political tradition.

Thus, the essence of *Kritik* for Hegel stands at the intersection of rhetoric and philosophy. Although he explicitly defends *Kritik* with the *Idee der Philosophie selbst,* his argumentation depends implicitly on polemical rhetoric. Only at the conclusion of the essay does this dependence become more explicit:

> If criticism itself strives to maintain a one-sided point of view against other similarly one-sided positions, then it is polemic and an issue of factions; but true philosophy, as well, can resist even less an external polemical appearance vis-à-vis nonphilosophy.

> Wenn die Kritik selbst einen einseitigen Gesichtspunkt gegen andere ebenso einseitige geltend machen will, so ist sie Polemik und Parteisache; aber auch die wahre Philosophie kann sich gegenüber der Unphilosophie des äußeren polemischen Ansehens um so weniger erwehren. [P. 186]

The reason philosophy must enter into polemics does not emerge from "philosophy itself," for as we saw, from the perspective of "the idea of philosophy," *Kritik* is essentially beside the point. Rather, polemic is necessary for the philoso*pher* in *his* rhetorical development:

> If one group wanted to save itself from the danger of the struggle and the manifestations of its own nothingness by declaring the other *only* a faction, then it would have thereby recognized the other as something and would have denied itself universal validity.
>
> Wenn eine Menge sich gegen die Gefahr des Kampfs und der Manifestation ihres inneren Nichts damit retten wollte, daß sie die andere *nur* für eine Partei erklärte, so hätte sie diese eben damit für etwas anerkannt und sich selbst diejenige Allgemeingültigkeit abgesprochen. [Pp. 186f.]

That is, the budding philosopher cannot merely assume the disinterested, condescending position of "philosophy itself," but must enter into a risk-laden struggle (*Gefahr*) to argue his position against the others.[19] He could lose the struggle. But if he succeeds, then the struggle grants him a claim to a position, a "self," and authority. *Kritik* involves a dialectic between philosophy and rhetoric, since both are simultaneously inextricably bound and apparently mutually exclusive. According to this dialectic, rhetoric becomes the precondition for philosophy, even as philosophy claims to reject the role of rhetoric in its own *Bildung*. This dialectic can be traced back through the Western tradition in which *Kritik* is both a weapon of the absolute claims of philosophy against rhetorical opinion and audience consensus and, at the same time, a subcategory within rhetoric. Precisely this dilemma of critical differentiation—the rejection of rhetorical critique even as it is

---

19. Consider the concept of "risk" in Natanson and Johnstone, which makes possible the struggle in an argumentative dialogue that in turn allows one to delineate one's position and thereby a sense of self. Natanson writes: "Risk . . . is the dialectical possibility of argument with the intent to persuade. . . . Risk is established when the affective world of the person is existentially interrupted. . . . The philosophical act which liberates the self is the same act which acknowledges the mystery of dialogue by engaging in the rhetoric of risk. . . . In the act of addressing the Other, I risk the dialectic of not merely his reply through arguments but his insistence that I look beneath and through my arguments to argumentation" ("The Claims of Immediacy," p. 19). He writes in "Rhetorical and Philosophical Argumentation": "Rhetoric . . . is concerned with proto-argumentation and a primordial choice of styles of philosophizing. Its ultimate subject matter is the unique person committed in his uniqueness to a way of seeing and having a world. Perhaps another name for what I have in mind here is *ethos*. If this suggestion is warranted, then it might be said that I have interpreted the philosophical self in rhetorical terms" (p. 156).

a necessary part of argumentation—lies at the center of Hegel's concept of the *Bildung* of philosophy in these years.

By far the most extended formulation of Hegel's concept of the *Bildung* of philosophy appears in his first "original" publication, the "Differenz des Fichteschen und Schellingschen Systems der Philosophie" (Difference between Fichte's and Schelling's Philosophical Systems; 1801).[20] Since it was written shortly before the first issue of the *Kritisches Journal der Philosophie* it does not contain references to the concept of *Kritik*. And yet the opening sections on theory nonetheless locate this essay within the larger framework of the philosopher's and philosophy's struggle with critical differentiation from others. The argument of the essay transfers the need of Hegel the writer onto the development of philosophy. It is significant for this stage of his writing, then, that he stresses the principle of *Differenz* after having immersed himself in foreign traditions for so many years. This essay sets the stage for his other Jena writings since it shows that he must accomplish two things if he is to complete his *Bildung* as a philosopher: He must separate out positions and discourses in order to overcome his earlier hermeneutical *Bildung* and he must project a synthesis beyond the differences if he is to overcome this present polemical stage of *Bildung*. With this essay, then, the paradoxical structure of negativity and differentiation is inscribed into Hegel's dialectic of philosophical representation.

The "Prefatory Reminder" (*Vorerinnerung*) that opens the essay seems to address Hegel's as much as the reader's memory insofar as it recalls components of Hegel's past rhetorical development and transforms them by setting them in a new public and polemical context. True to the function of a traditional *exordium*, the opening gives the "motivation" (*Veranlassung*) (p. 9) of the essay.[21] Hegel writes this essay in response to the "public utterances (*öffentliche Äußerungen*) in which one recognizes a feeling of the difference between Fichte's and Schelling's philosophical systems," but which either avoid (*umgehen*) or cover up (*verbergen*) the difference. In particular, Reinhold's *Beiträge zur leichteren Übersicht des Zustandes der Philosophie beim Anfange des 19. Jahr-*

---

20. The first work Hegel actually published was the translation and annotations of the "Vertraulichen Briefe" (1798).

21. Recall the opening of both the essay "Positivity of the Christian Religion" and the Preface to the *Phenomenology*, in which Hegel discusses the motivations for his writing even as he denies the relevance of such considerations for philosophy. The rhetorical prediscourse that criticizes rhetoric has become a standard topos for Hegel's beginnings, a point not without philosophical significance given his meditations on the problem of a beginning for philosophy.

hunderts (Contributions to a More Convenient Survey of the State of Philosophy at the Beginning of the Nineteenth Century; 1801) provides the "external motivation" (*äußere Veranlassung*; p. 12).[22] Reinhold, Hegel claims, did not "raise that difference to language" (*hat [nicht] jene Verschiedenheit zur Sprache gebracht*; p. 9).[23] This principle of representation, according to which differences between philosophers must be raised to the level of language, will guide Hegel's rhetoric in this essay and beyond.

Hegel discusses this principle here in four ways that place the "Reminder" at a turning point in his rhetorical development. First, the fact that the difference has thus far gone unexpressed allows Hegel to postulate a "need" or "lack of the times" (*Bedürfnis, Zeitbedürfnis*; pp. 12, 13). He posits this lack first in philosophy itself, but then more concretely in the *audience*, thereby preparing it for the reception (*Aufnahme*) of his own work (p. 13).[24] Of course, the fact that this need is the cause of his writing implies that it lies within Hegel himself. Since, as we shall see below, the "need" becomes associated with the *Bildung* of philosophy, we must keep in mind this initial use of the term applied to Hegel and the relation to his audience.

Second, Hegel converts the religious image of the spirit and letter (*Geist* and *Buchstabe*), which permeated his theological manuscripts, into the movement of philosophy through history: "Kantian philosophy had needed (*hatte es bedurft*) to have its spirit separated from the letter and to have the purely speculative principle extracted from the rest" (p. 9).[25] Hegel's bringing to language of the difference between Fichte, Schelling, and Reinhold as followers of Kant thus fulfills the spirit of

22. Reinhold's *Beiträge zur leichteren Übersicht des Zustandes der Philosophie beim Anfange des 19. Jahrhunderts* were published between 1800 and 1802 in three volumes. This was one of the many texts written around the turn of the century which attempted to summarize the developments in philosophy from Leibniz to Kant.

23. I realize that I am stressing a literal meaning of an otherwise common metaphorical expression (*zur Sprache bringen* can mean simply "to discuss, talk about"). But by bringing this "dead" metaphor to life I am not implying one way or the other that Hegel did or did not think of this literal rendering. Rather, this interpretive gesture on my part is a quick way to use Hegel's own words to get to the basic activity of his writing.

24. For example, Hegel says that works like Schleiermacher's *Lectures on Religion* (1799) and their "reception" (*Aufnahme*) point "to the need for a philosophy" (p. 13). The implication is, of course, that Hegel's own yet to be written philosophy will fulfill this need (just as the need will help his philosophy to be written).

25. This statement refers most likely to Fichte's famous claim that he continues the spirit of Kant even though he departs radically from his letter. See Fichte's essay "Vom Geist und Buchstaben der Philosophie" (1794). See also Schiller, "Briefe über die ästhetische Erziehung des Menschen," Letter 17, n. 1. Also Röttgers, *Kritik und Praxis*, on Kant's "usurpation" of the concept of *Kritik*: "As opposed to Fichte, who refered to the spirit of critical philosophy, he [Kant] emphasized 'that *Kritik* of course is to be understood according to the letter'" (p.60).

Kantian philosophy the way the New Testament fulfills the Old. Thus, Hegel places a concept and technique that guided his earlier hermeneutical efforts—namely, "pleroma"—into a new polemical constellation. At this point Hegel brushes over this transformation of the religious into a philosophical image, for here he is essentially extending the hermeneutics that he developed in the theological writings. In a later essay, "Glauben und Wissen" (Faith and Knowledge; 1802), we will see how he comes to grips more fully with this turn.

Third, the overcoming of the "need of the times" is explicitly related as well to the need to surpass Fichte's influence, for he is now Hegel's strongest precursor: "Concerning the need of the times, Fichte's epoch-making philosophy has caused such a sensation that even those who declare themselves against it and strive to launch their own speculative systems merely fall into a murkier and more contaminated form of the principle of Fichte's philosophy, and they cannot even defend themselves against it" (p. 12). Hegel, too, must avoid this danger. More precisely, in developing a position different from Fichte's, he must be sure that it is not "just one more different" position.

Finally, establishing a kind of polemical topos against his own rhetoric, Hegel concludes the "Prefatory Reminder" the way he begins the Preface to the *Phenomenology*: "Concerning the general reflections on need, presuppositions, basic principles of philosophy, etc., which begin this work, they all commit the error of being general reflections. They are all motivated by the fact that by means of such forms as presuppositions, basic principles, etc., the entrance into philosophy is still covered up and concealed, and it is thus to a certain extent necessary to deal with them until, finally, philosophy itself is the sole subject of discussion" (pp. 13f.). Hegel problematizes the rhetorical nature of his own introductory comments. At this stage he accepts his rhetoric as a "mistake" to be made and then overcome.

The first long section of the essay, "Mancherlei Formen, die bei dem jetzigen Philosophieren vorkommen" (Various Forms that Appear in Contemporary Philosophizing), is for our interests of central importance. This section, containing general considerations on the development of philosophical rhetoric, forms less an introduction to the actual essay than a first attempt by Hegel to define his task as a publishing philosopher. In discussing the different modes of writing philosophy, Hegel is implicitly trying to locate himself within the field.[26] What is at

26. The field of idealist philosophers was already well defined. For example, there had been an essay competition on the question "What progress has metaphysics made since the times of Leibniz and Wolff?" Respondents were Johann Christian Schwab, Johann Heinrich Abicht, and Karl Leonhard Reinhold (those Röttgers called the "independent Kantians").

one level an analysis of philosophical systems and their relations among each other is at another level a philosopher's endeavor to see how his development relates to that of his contemporaries. Hence, although this section mentions neither rhetoric nor Hegel's own writing, the concept of *Bildung* as referring to his own formative education in rhetoric can illuminate how notions that are not usually associated with his philosophy left their traces.

The focus of Hegel's interest at this point is the fact that he lives in an age with "such a large number (*Menge*) of philosophical systems" that the very nature of scientific knowledge is changing (p. 15). The individual himself begins to view a system as a dead collection of information (*Kenntnisse*) to be mastered and overcome in a new system. The philosopher's standard trick, given this situation, has been first to give the earlier systems names, thereby marking them as "foreign objects," and second to learn how to juggle the names. Hegel thus seems to be summarizing the conclusion of his theological studies on the "positivity" of traditions when he admits that philosophical systems, as written and read phenomena, cannot avoid this process of literalization: "Just as every living form (*lebendige Gestalt*) also belongs to the realm of appearing phenomena (*Erscheinung*), so too must philosophy, as appearing phenomenon (*Erscheinung*), deliver itself over to that force that can transform it into a dead belief (*tote Meinung*) and, from its first appearance, to a relic of the past" (pp. 15–16). Philosophy is "delivered over" (*überliefert*) to the very power of tradition (*Überlieferung*). Hegel finds in Reinhold's *Beiträge* a typical formulation of the development of philosophical traditions: Past philosophical systems become a "preliminary exercise" (*vorübende[r] Versuch*) and the discipline of philosophy becomes a *technē*, "a kind of handiwork or craft (*Handwerkskunst*)," whereby the later philosopher masters and improves the techniques of his predecessors (p. 16ff.). Each "original" improvement over the "exercises" of the precursors adds to the chain of "peculiar viewpoints" (*eigentümliche Ansichten*), according to Reinhold, and in turn succumbs to the process of tradition building which converts objects of imitation to uniqueness and uniqueness to objects of imitation.

Hegel's response to this conception is similar to the argumentative strategies we encountered in the "Essence of *Kritik*." Namely, his "philosophical" response rests on the belief in "one reason" that remains always the same core in anything we would properly call philosophy (p. 17). But to understand why he might be opening his first published essay with this treatment of Reinhold's conception of philosophical development, we must recognize that the views Hegel criticizes in Reinhold actually predate Reinhold's formulation. They are, in fact, the basic ideas behind the rhetorical concept of tradition building through *exercitatio, imitatio, aemulatio*. In certain formulations, Hegel seems to be playing out the debate that Plato's Socrates had with the Sophists.[27] And Hegel's description of Reinhold's position places the latter closer to a Ciceronian orator trained in the *ars bene et sapiente dicendi*, which can be mastered if combined with a bit of "original talent," than to a post-Fichtean idealist. In other words, what Hegel is criticizing as the "historical view of philosophical systems" is the perspective that he himself had learned and practiced for so many years as part of his own *Bildung*.

It is interesting to note that what Hegel so bitingly criticizes here in his first published text, as if to differentiate himself from both the competition and his former self, will soon become precisely the definition of philosophical *Bildung* in the Preface to the *Phenomenology*, namely, the Spirit's history as a pedagogical progression. One could say paradoxically that at this stage of his formative education Hegel is so involved with the struggle for differentiation that he even tries to differentiate himself from his own *Bildung*. The result is a concept of *Bildung* which is a mixture of adherence to, yet critical transformation of, his rhetorical past. The dialectic that guides Hegel's view of the history of philosophy rests on a conflict between rhetoric and philosophy, on a dispute over the proper manner of "inventing" and "judging" argumentation.

Given this rhetorico-pedagogical background, it comes as no surprise, therefore, when *Bildung* plays a predominant role in the following subsection, "Bedürfnis der Philosophie" (The Need of Philosophy). It opens with a veritable collocation of rhetorical concerns that are overlayed onto the organic imagery of a developing philosophy:

> If we consider more closely the particular form a philosophy has, we see that it springs forth on the one hand from the living originality of the spirit, which, in an act of self-shaping, creates in philosophy its sundered harmony, and on the other, from the particular form that bears the disjunction out of which the system arises. Disjunction is the source of the need of philosophy and, as the *Bildung* of the era, the unfree pregiven of its form. In *Bildung*, that which is the appearance of the

27. For example, when Hegel rejects the approach to philosophy as a kind of "handiwork" (*Handwerkskunst*) which can be acquired through practice and intersubjective interaction, he recalls Plato's rejection of rhetoric as a mere *technē*, to which philosophy should not be reduced. On the whole we have here a (critical) summary of the doctrines of *exercitationes* and *ethos*, which, according to both classical rhetorical theory and contemporary approaches like Natanson's, underlie the controversies and dialogues between philosophers in the struggle for individuality.

absolute has isolated itself from the absolute and fixed itself as an independent entity. At the same time, however, the appearing phenomenon cannot deny its origin and must strive to construct the manifold nature of its limitations as a totality.

> Betrachten wir die besondere Form näher, welche eine Philosophie trägt, so sehen wir sie einerseits aus der lebendigen Originalität des Geistes entspringen, der in ihr die zerrissene Harmonie durch sich hergestellt und selbsttätig gestaltet hat, andererseits aus der besonderen Form, welche die Entzweiung trägt, aus der das System hervorgeht. Entzweiung ist der Quell *des Bedürfnisses der Philosophie* und als Bildung des Zeitalters die unfreie gegebene Seite der Gestalt. In der Bildung hat sich das, was Erscheinung des Absoluten ist, vom Absoluten isoliert und als ein Selbständiges fixiert. Zugleich kann aber die Erscheinung ihren Ursprung nicht verleugnen und muß darauf ausgehen, die Mannigfaltigkeit ihrer Beschränkungen als ein Ganzes zu konstruieren. [P. 20]

In particular, what becomes fixed in the "progression of *Bildung*" (*Fortgang der Bildung*) are oppositions: "*Bildung* has posited such oppositions (*Entgegengesetzte*) in different forms in different ages" (p. 21). Hegel lists a number of them: "spirit-matter" (*Geist-Materie*), "body-soul" (*Leib-Seele*), "reason-sensuality" (*Vernunft-Sinnlichkeit*), "intellect-nature" (*Intellekt-Natur*). *Bildung* is, therefore, that process of the understanding that posits the existence of oppositions, the most fundamental of which is that between subject and object, the mind and preexisting things, the living being undergoing *Bildung* and the "given" content of its transformation. This act of *Bildung* is essentially imitative, albeit a bad imitation of reason by the understanding: "The understanding imitates reason in its absolute positing (*Setzen*) and through the form of its positing gives itself the false appearance (*Schein*) of reason" (p. 21). What kind of *Bildung* is he talking about here if not essentially his own, which consisted in opposing traditions ("the given"), imitating others, and taking on the appearance of the imitated text in order to appropriate the material? The law of the *Bildung* of philosophy dictates that its appearance cannot deny its origin; hence the development of philosophical representation contains the formative education of the philosopher who confronts, loses himself in, and differentiates himself from the given forms of the tradition. The following passage describes the danger he had experienced in his own training as a writer, indeed, according to the rhetoricians from Cicero and Quintilian through Longinus to Melanchthon, the danger all writers must experience:

> The farther *Bildung* thrives and the more manifold becomes the development of life's expressions in which disjunction can become en-

twined [consumed], the greater the power of disjunction becomes, the firmer its climatic environment, the stranger *Bildung* becomes to its totality, and the more meaningless life's efforts become to regenerate a state of harmony. [Pp. 22f.]

Once again, the organic image barely masks the vicissitudes that the continuation of a certain pedagogical and textual *Bildung*, now under the general heading of *Kritik* and *Differenz*, must confront. To save himself from the danger of self-loss in manifold otherness, he must reformulate his theological concept of *Bildung*, which we summarized in terms of originality through imitation, as the need of philosophy to attain future harmony through differentiation: "For the necessary disjunction is *one* factor of life, which develops and gives itself form by generating oppositions (*das ewig entgegensetzend sich bildet*), and the totality is only possible in the highest form of life by reproducing unity out of the highest degree of separation" (pp. 21f.). *Bildung*, first as imitative self-loss and then as oppositional doubling, must contain within itself a movement toward reunification and genuine originality. *Bildung* itself creates the "lack/need of philosophy" (*Bedürfnis der Philosophie*), an ambiguous phrase since lack or need implies here both incompleteness and an inner drive for completeness. That is, in tracing the trajectory of his own development, Hegel sees the direction he must pursue: differentiation from other positions and the creation of his own synthesis, all this in the public eye to gain authority before the audience. Furthermore, this trajectory becomes projected onto the need of philosophy "it/herself" so that Hegel can redefine his task as that of philosophy's development. The development or movement of philosophy consists in the argumentative moves against others and toward one's own developing stance.

The remainder of the essay, in form, function, and content, vacillates between the poles of differentiation and synthesis which characterize this stage of both Hegel's and philosophy's *Bildung* as *Kritik*. Hegel demonstrates his ability to work with the relations that exist between philosophical systems as historical "phenomena"[28] thanks to the rhetorico-hermeneutical skills he developed and mastered in the theologi-

---

28. A contemporary, the Fichte student Johann Wagner, reacted appropriately to the essay; he overcame his confusion by recognizing Hegel's manipulation of forms: "I also did not fully understand Hegel in my first readings in Ulm, but now, since I am reading him again, he is clear to me. He is very skilled in switching around [manipulating] the propositions of transcendentalism (*mit den Sätzen des Transzendentalismus zu schalten*), but his style is not yet cultivated enough; [there is] evidence of a lack of maturity and difficulty for the reader." Günther Nicolin, ed., *Hegel in Berichten seiner Zeitgenossen* (Hamburg: Felix Meiner, 1970), no. 59.

cal manuscripts. They are merely applied, with dexterity, to the new philosophical content. The shift from theology to philosophy has not affected the techniques of representation. The continuity of methods is clear in the titles of two sections: "Darstellung des Fichteschen Systems" (Depiction of Fichte's System) recalls his earlier use of *narratio* and "Vergleichung des Schellingschen Prinzips der Philosophie mit dem Fichteschen" (Comparison of Schelling's Philosophical Principle with Fichte's) recalls his technique of critical *comparatio*. Moreover, Schelling has now replaced Fichte, as Fichte had replaced Kant, in Hegel's line of imitated objects. Only in considering the function of this essay within Hegel's *Bildung* do we see the new dimension added to these techniques. Hegel defines the "need" (*Bedürfnis*) or *Bildung* of philosophy as the fixing of differences. He accomplishes this step in his own formative education (and in that of philosophy) by positing a radical disjunction between Fichte and Schelling. Rather than transferring the one onto the other, as he had done in his earlier hermeneutical exercises with Christianity, Kant, and Fichte, he insists on the untranslatability of the two discourses.[29] Rather than engendering a dialogue, Hegel "needs" to propagate a discursive gap within idealism.[30] But why this need to raise differences in and to language?

The answer lies in the third and final section of the essay, the ad

29. To understand the nature of this critically partial translation, we can compare two passages. The first, taken from the "Darstellung des Fichteschen Systems," criticizes Fichte's fundamental synthesis of the two forms of ego: "However, in this synthesis the *objective I* is not equal to the *subjective I*; the subjective is the I, the objective the I + Not-I. The original identity is not represented in it [in the synthesis]. The pure consciousness I = I and the empirical I = I + Not-I, with all the forms in which this is construed, remain opposed to one another" ("In dieser Synthese aber ist das objektive Ich nicht gleich dem subjektiven; das subjektive ist Ich, das objektive Ich + Nicht-Ich. Es stellt sich in ihr nicht die ursprüngliche Identität dar; das reine Bewußtsein Ich = Ich und das empirische Ich = Ich + Nicht-Ich mit allen Formen, worin sich dieses konstruiert, bleiben sich entgegengesetzt"; p. 58). In the second passage (from the "Vergleichung"), Hegel praises Schelling's solution in the famous formulation: "The absolute itself, however, is therefore the identity of identity and nonidentity; opposition and unity are the same in it [at the same time]" ("Das Absolute selbst aber ist darum die Identität der Identität und der Nichtidentität; Entgegensetzen und Einsein ist zugleich in ihm"; p. 96). Actually, however, both formulations could be translated into each other by substituting *Synthese* from the passage on Fichte for the first *Identität* in the passage on Schelling, *Ich = Ich* for the second *Identität* and *Ich = Ich + Nicht-Ich* for *Nichtidentität*. Then the formulation of Schelling's position would read like good Fichte: "The absolute itself is for this reason the synthesis of I = I and I = I + Not-I; opposition and unity are the same in it at the same time" ("Das Absolute selbst ist darum die Synthese von Ich = Ich und Ich = Ich + Nicht-Ich; Entgegensetzen und Einssein ist zugleich in ihm").

30. In fact, this reading has important consequences for the development of German idealism, as has been pointed out by Helmut Girndt, *Die Differenz des Fichteschen und Hegelschen Systems der Philosophie* (Bonn: Bouvier, 1965). Hegel posits a tripartite schema of "subjective" versus "objective" idealisms, both of which await fulfillment in an "absolute" (or "speculative") philosophy that he is about to formulate.

hominem critique of Reinhold. The section opens: "It still remains to speak in part of Reinhold's view of Fichte's and Schelling's philosophies, in part of his own philosophy" (p. 116). This locates Hegel and Reinhold at the same position in their own developments and in that of philosophy: Both have read Fichte and Schelling and are developing (or about to develop) their own systems; both have written on past forms of philosophy, Reinhold in his *Beiträge* and Hegel in the section "Various Forms that Appear in Contemporary Philosophizing"; both face the same question: where to go from here? Hegel treats Reinhold like a direct rival for philosophical succession. Hegel's goal is literally to write himself into the history of philosophy as the rightful successor to the throne of idealism by bringing the difference between Fichte and Schelling to language, whereas Reinhold falsely equated them. This difference is, for Hegel, not "just" a philosophical issue, but his greatest critical and rhetorical weapon. Because Reinhold has not recognized the difference, Hegel implies, he will not meet the needs of the philosophical public: "Reinhold does not seem to have suspected that for quite a while now a different philosophy other than pure transcendental idealism stands before the public" (pp. 116, 126, 131). Because Reinhold has not recognized the lack in philosophy's *Bildung*, the lack of an expressed difference, he has no claim to power in the republic of letters: "Just as *La révolution est finie* has been decreed numerous times in France, so too Reinhold has already announced many ends to the philosophical revolution" (p. 121). Hegel, however, by bringing the difference between Fichte and Schelling to language, has created the possibility for himself of developing a new, (counter)revolutionary philosophy.

See also Jürgen Werner, *Darstellung als Kritik: Hegels Frage nach dem Anfang der Wissenschaft* (Bonn: Bouvier, 1986), for a philosophical treatment of the relationship between representation and *Kritik*.

We can reformulate Hegel's strategy in terms by Richard Rorty from *Philosophy and the Mirror of Nature* (Princeton, N.J.: Princeton University Press, 1978): namely, Hegel, in shifting from his earlier translations and mediations in Bern and Frankfurt to the differentiations of Jena, is shifting from "hermeneutics" to "epistemology." Rorty distinguishes between two ways of conceiving philosophical exchange: "Hermeneutics sees the relations between various discourses as those of strands in a possible conversation which presupposes no disciplinary matrix which unites the speakers, but where the hope of agreement is never lost so long as the conversation lasts. This hope is not a hope for the discovery of antecedently existing common ground, but *simply* hope for agreement, or at least exciting and fruitful disagreement. Epistemology sees the hope of agreement as a token of the existence of common ground which, perhaps unbeknown to the speakers, unites them in a common rationality. For hermeneutics, to be rational is to be willing to refrain from epistemology—from thinking that there is a special set of terms in which all contributions to the conversation should be put—and to be willing to pick up the jargon of the interlocutor rather than translating it into one's own" (p. 318).

Thus, in his first published essay, Hegel has managed to identify his *Bildung* with that of both "philosophy" and the public by defining them all as the struggle to overcome fixed oppositions. He knows that further development can take place only by introducing *Kritik* into his hermeneutics of imitative translation and by thus polemically calling for a harmonizing position that will answer the need to master the *Bildung* of differences.

If the *Differenzschrift* sets the course of Hegel's further development, and if the "Essence of *Kritik*" introduces a rich, paradoxical philosophical and rhetorical tradition into his strategy, the major essay from the period, "Glauben und Wissen oder Reflexionsphilosophie der Subjektivität in der Vollständigkeit ihrer Formen als Kantische, Jacobische und Fichtesche Philosophie" (Faith and Knowledge, or Reflection-Philosophy of Subjectivity in the Totality of Its Forms as Kantian, Jacobian and Fichtean Philosophy; 1802), accomplishes the task of reworking his former *Bildung* into a new philosophical form. The essay possesses the thoroughly self-reflexive structure we encountered in the "allegories" of the Bern and Frankfurt manuscripts in that it literally enacts in its argumentation the stage of *Bildung* that Hegel is passing through and depicts as a struggle of ideas the rhetorical struggle in which he finds himself. The theory of philosophical representation develops out of his own struggle for representation in the public sphere of philosophers. He is engaged in the transition from private theological to public philosophical writing.[31]

The tension between these two modes of representation becomes reformulated in the essay as the opposition between "faith" (*Glauben*) and "knowledge" (*Wissen*), "Religion" and "reason" (*Vernunft*). Externally, it would seem as if, in both the history of ideas and the development of Hegel's writing, the latter has already proved victorious and moved on to a higher stage of development. And yet using a pregnant image, Hegel doubts the completeness of the apparent victory: "The

31. During these years in Jena, Hegel also wrote a series of biting critiques and reviews of works by numerous minor (or at least long since forgotten) philosophers, among them Jakob Salat, Friedrich Bouterwek, Wilhelm Traugott Krug, J. Friedrich Werneburg, K. Friedrich Gerstaecker, Gottlob Ernst Schulze. These reviews helped Hegel make the transition from the hermeneutical to the polemical, for he was able to develop his arsenal of techniques—some subtler than others—for arguing with contemporaries in public. Although they go beyond the scope of this chapter, a few techniques or polemical "figures" are worth mentioning as part of Hegel's *Bildung* in these writing exercises: a sense of irony, appeals to the audience, revolutionary images (with Hegel often in the role of a counterrevolutionary against the victories of "common" sense), litotic argumentation, and *argumentum ad hominem*. These figures add to the critical thrust of his "translations" and, once internalized, become basic structures of his philosophy (like litotes and the principle of double negation).

question remains, however, if victorious Reason has not met with the same fate as that which the victorious strength of barbarian nations commonly met vis-à-vis the subjugated weakness of *educated* [civilized, *gebildeter*] nations: namely, to maintain the upper hand in terms of external domination, but to become intellectually subjugated to the conquered" (pp. 287–88; my emphasis). From the perspective of the paradoxes of *Kritik* and (self-)differentiation, the ironic, rhetorical question applies to Hegel's development as well: Is not Hegel, like his contemporaries, more educated, civilized, and well formed (*gebildeter*) and yet still caught in oppositions, still struggling with differences, still using the methods of a "mastered" religious and imitative hermeneutic of dependence? The goal for Hegel in this essay, if he is to continue his *Bildung*, is to appropriate and rework his earlier ideas and techniques in a way that makes the new and different stage seem an essential overcoming of the past. Hegel must take his former *Bildung* to the limit of its capabilities and radically break from its form. This experience is played out in this essay as a "placing-in-opposition" (*Gegeneinanderstellung*; p. 301) of philosophical formulations (*Bildungen*).

We can concentrate on the introduction which develops the strategy of the essay implicitly in terms of the concept of *Bildung*. One could consider the introduction an explication of a number of concepts in the full title. (1) "Glauben und Wissen" summarizes the opposition between theology and philosophy with which Hegel has to grapple, an opposition he inherited from his own development. Hence, it is not by chance that the first line also reformulates this opposition in terms of his present and past concerns as a writer as "philosophy and positive religion" (p. 287). This opposition, says Hegel, has been "transposed now into the realm of philosophy itself" (*nun innerhalb der Philosophie selbst verlegt*; p. 287). What for Hegel, the theology student, had been a conflict between two disciplines, two traditional modes of discourse, now becomes for Hegel, the publishing philosopher, a debate carried out within his chosen mode of writing.

(2) By referring to *Reflexionsphilosophie* Hegel does more than pick up a self-characterization from Jacobi and Fichte.[32] We recall the polemical tinge associated with the word in the essay on the "Essence of *Kritik*," in which the "mainstream of our culture of reflection" served as

---

32. Rüdiger Bubner, "Problemgeschichte und systematischer Sinn einer Phänomenologie," in *Hegel-Studien* 5 (1969), pp. 129–54, considers Hegel's grappling with the concept of reflection the core of his Jena experience. Certainly he is correct in pointing out how Hegel introduces a more tenable concept of reflection as a starting point for his philosophy. What Bubner does not reveal is the way this concept according to Hegel contains a principle of differentiation (that is also how it is being used) and hence limits the starting point of Hegel's system. This becomes clear, however, when we consider the rhetorical function of this concept.

an ad hominem critique of the dominant forms of contemporary society. The term *Reflexion*, at least at this point, is associated with the faculty of the understanding, "*common* sense," which is a politically and rhetorically charged category in his critical campaign: "There is, therefore, nothing to see in these philosophies besides the raising of a culture of reflection (*Reflexionskultur*) to a system—i.e., a culture of common sense (*des gemeinen Menschenverstandes*) which raises itself to think about the universal" (p. 298). Hegel's "counterrevolutionary" philosophy will strive to stave off the uprisings of the "common" masses.

(3) The "subjectivization" of these philosophies is one of Hegel's major achievements in the history of philosophy. Although the charge of subjectivity does apply readily to Jacobi, Hegel was the first to develop the opposition of subjective and objective idealism, thereby creating the rhetorical space for his own form of "absolute" idealism. What is presented as the development within philosophy reflects stages of Hegel's own development from Kant, through Fichte, to Schelling, and eventually to his "own" position.

(4) The conflation of a philosopher's subjective development and the objective development of ideas becomes more evident in the explication of the notion of the "totality [perfection or completion] of their forms." Where the question of perfecting form arises, of course, the question of *Bildung* is also present. But these are not imperfect philosophies, like the weaker efforts of minor philosophers which Hegel dismissed in his reviews. Rather, they have already attained a certain perfection of *Bildung*: "The common subjective principle of the above-mentioned philosophies is not, say, a limited form of the spirit of a minor period or of a small group; but, rather, the powerful intellectual form, which makes up their principle, has beyond doubt attained in them absolutely expressed the completeness of its consciousness, its [highest] philosophical knowledge and *Bildung*" (p. 289). The subjective principle, of which these philosophies are the complete formation (*vollständige, vollkommene Bildung*), is that of Protestant and Enlightenment eudaemonism. But Hegel is concerned not just with the principle but also with the form of representation that the Spirit has chosen to express this principle.[33] Where Hegel had earlier traced the *Bildung der*

33. Hegel writes: "But the great form of the World Spirit, which is recognized in those philosophies, is the principle of the North and, seen religiously, of Protestantism—subjectivity, in which beauty and truth are represented in feelings and thinking, in body and understanding" ("Die große Form des Weltgeistes aber, welche sich in jenen Philosophien erkannt hat, ist das Prinzip des Nordens und, es religiös angesehen, des Protestantismus,—die Subjektivität, in welcher Schönheit und Wahrheit in Gefühlen und Gesinnungen, in Liebe und Verstand sich darstellt").

Form of Christianity through the history of its "positivity," here he investigates the *Bildung* of a form of philosophy. The movement is the same: They try to escape eudaemonism but are caught in it, just as the spirit of Christianity tried in vain to escape literalization: "Their conscious attempt is to go directly against the principle of eudaemonism; but precisely because they themselves are this direction, their positive character is precisely that principle; thus, the modification, which these philosophies introduce into eudaemonism, merely perfects its formation (*Bildung*) and is a matter of complete indifference . . . for reason and philosophy" (p. 294).

Bildung here recalls the "poor *Bildung*" and "miseducation" (faulty development, *Mißbildung*) of the Jewish people which Hegel mentioned in the "Spirit of Christianity." In this way, Hegel projects the movement of the history of religion, which he had worked through earlier, with a critical twist onto that of philosophy. All these philosophies, as perfected Protestantism, are in essence perfected "Judaism" and bear the sins or oppositions of their improper *Bildung* within themselves. They have reached the highest level of *Bildung*, but their *Bildung* is one that Hegel does not wish to continue, that is, has reached its own completion.

By defining *Bildung* in this way, Hegel has set himself up in the best position for the polemical struggle with his rivals. He can posit the need for a new form of philosophical representation, a new fulfilment of the Law. "Given the firm principle of this system of representation" (*Nach dem festen Prinzip dieses Systems der Bildung.*; p. 293), Hegel can imply, these three competitors can be presented as bad readers and writers, misinterpreters of the absolute idea, just as the Jews misapplied (literalized) the Law, and the Christian church (and Kant!) misinterpreted Christ's message. Of course, given his own *Bildung* and that of his age, Hegel neither wants nor is able to reject them. Rather, just as Christ fulfilled the completed Law of Judaism, so too must Hegel fulfill their interpretations. Hegel can appear not as a polemicist but as a pleromist. He offers not just a different position but an interpretation that fulfills the message of the Spirit. He has successfully reinterpreted his theological hermeneutic for the task of critical differentiation as a means to a unified system.

His criticisms of these three philosophers revolve therefore around their all too literal adherence to the law of their earlier, concrete, world-oriented *Bildung*. Kant is no longer accused of "Jewish" attachment to law and duty but, for a German philosophical audience at the time just as bad, of Lockean subjective empiricism. A number of pages into the essay, for example, Hegel ironically inverts Kant's position by quoting a long passage in German that captures the supposed shallowness of Kant's "subjectivity or a critique of the faculties of knowledge" (p. 303). At the end of the quote he points out that it actually stems from Locke and adds: "Words that one could find just as well in the introduction to Kantian philosophy, which likewise limits itself to Lockean ends, namely, the considerations of a finite understanding" (p. 304). Hegel has tricked the reader into associating Kant with literal Lockeanism. Similarly, Jacobi is accused of not even getting as far as Kant in his reading of Locke and Hume. Using some playful and caustic puns, he writes of a fundamental proof in which Jacobi distinguishes between the laws of noncontradiction and causality:

> The manner in which he does this . . . is a peculiar piece of Lockean and Humean empiricism, into which a likewise crass piece of German analytical dogmatism à la Mendelssohn is kneaded, whereby the world cannot thank the gods, after Kant, too much for liberation from precisely this.

> Die Art, wie er dies dartut . . . ist ein merkwürdiges Stück des Lockeschen und Humeschen Empirismus, in welchen ein ebenso grelles Stück von deutschem analysierenden Dogmatismus, schlimmer als nach Mendelssohnscher Art, hineingeknettet ist, von welcher befreit worden zu sein die Welt den Göttern, nächst Kant, nicht genug danken kann. [P. 336][34]

Likewise, Jacobi is criticized polemically for being a bad, that is, a polemical, reader of Kant and Spinoza.[35] And Fichte, who was earlier

34. This kind of ad hominem critique, including the images of other philosophers concocting unappetizing dishes out of their ideas, appears even more bitingly in the review of Krug and Salat, in which Hegel uses puns on their names. For example: "Imagine a jug/Krug in which pure Reinhold water, stale Kantian beer, Enlightenment syrup, called Berlinism, and other similar ingredients are by some chance contained as data; the jug/Krug is the synthetic of these = I" ("Man stelle sich einen Krug vor, worin Reinholdisches Wasser, Kantisches abgestandenes Bier, aufklärender Sirup, Berlinismus genannt, und andere dergleichen Ingredienzen durch irgendeinen Zufall als Tatsachen enthalten sind; der Krug ist das Synthetische derselben = Ich"; p. 203). Or the "Salad/Salat . . . without salt and pepper" (*Salat . . . ohne Salz und Pfeffer;* p. 210). It is significant that these techniques do not disappear from Hegel's philosophical writing but become internalized and masked by forms that appear nonpolemical.

35. The actual points of dispute—for example, Spinoza's concept of temporal succession—are of less importance here than the form of Hegel's argument. Hegel is clearly no great defender of Kant or Spinoza. And yet by arguing with the logic of litotes, he need not fully affirm them in order to negate Jacobi's negation of them and to open up new possible avenues for himself. Hegel attacks Jacobi's reading of Spinoza as a projection (*hineintragen;* p. 347), which is the "nature of his polemical activity" (p. 353). He criticizes Jacobi's reading of Kant as "a piece of polemic resting on the same foundation as the one against Spinoza" (p. 361). He lists the different techniques used by Jacobi (pp. 361–364)—false citation, slander and "galimathization"—which he himself has employed. In

rejected for not being translatable into Schelling's terms, is now rejected for being all too easily translatable into Kantian form and Jacobian content.[36] Hegel, the polemical translator, removes his once strongest precursor by making him the perfector of incompleteness.

Hence, Hegel's analysis of the *Bildung* of idealist philosophies allows him to structure the essay according to the religio-hermeneutical principle of pleroma, thereby reworking the earlier stages of his own rhetorical *Bildung* into a philosophical process. The *Bildung* of his age, as differentiation and opposition, is used by Hegel to depict and criticize systems as "perfect" formations of a yet imperfect conception, to propose himself as the fulfiller and true interpreter of philosophical law. The negativity that is thereby inscribed into this notion of *Bildung* implies that his own enterprise will have a polemically negative appearance, "a gruesome surgery that will not leave the person whole, . . . a powerful abstraction . . . [and] a painful amputation" (*ein grausames Sezieren, das den Menschen nicht ganz läßt, ... ein gewaltiges Abstrahieren . . . [und] schmerzerregendes Wegschneiden*; p. 300). After all, *Bildung*, including his own, takes place at this point under the hand of *Kritik*. Its affirmative moment comes only in the form of a double negation: "However, only that which is negation will be negated, thus positing the true affirmation" (p. 301). Because of the needs of Hegel's own development, and out of the development of critical argumentation, negativity, understood as double negation, has entered into his conception of philosophy's *Bildung*.[37]

---

polemicizing against Jacobi's polemical readings, Hegel builds up his philosophical critique on the principle of *rhetorical contra rhetoricam*. Schelling comments on these arguments in a letter to A. W. Schlegel: "only perhaps you find it desirable that the part that concerns him [Jacobi] were itself freer of quarrels and less cloudy, just as the author of Jacobi's polemic finds it desirable. In the same way it could appear to be a real shame concerning the first idea, which is excellent, that it has not been worked out with more clarity and correctness" (*Hegel in Berichten*, no. 62).

36. The content of Hegel's basic arguments against Fichte does not differ from the discussion of him in the essay on "Difference." However, there is a new rhetorical strategy that deserves mention. In the *Differenzschrift*, Hegel was concerned with demonstrating the untranslatability of Fichtean and Schellingean terminology. That is, Fichte's "subjective transcendentalism" merely paralleled Schelling's "objective nature philosophy," and both required completion by "absolute idealism." Here Hegel has provided a negative background for the discussion of Fichte, and the goal is to translate Fichte back into Kantian and Jacobian terms. Fichte "completes" the movement from Kant through Jacobi because he contains elements of both: Kant's "formalism" (pp. 397, 400, 412f.) and Jacobi's subjective content (pp. 393ff.). This strategy of relating one form to an earlier discredited position, a *Bildung* to a *Mißbildung*, connects the earlier theological manuscripts to the later writings on the history of philosophy and religion.

37. For an analysis of the way this principle functions in the *Logic*, see Dieter Henrich, "Formen der Negation in Hegels Logik," in *Seminar: Dialektik in der Philosophie Hegels*, ed. Rolf-Peter Horstmann (Frankfurt am Main: Suhrkamp, 1978), pp. 213–30. He writes,

The Spirit and Its Letter

In order to see the positive side of *Bildung*, the necessary complement to the development of oppositions and differences, we can turn to an argument in the final essay from the Jena period. Here Hegel develops a rhetorical model to justify how his critical position is truly different since it goes beyond mere differentiation. If in "Faith and Knowledge" *Bildung* came to be defined as the process of fixing and establishing oppositions, that is, as the very negative and critical enterprise in which Hegel was engaged as he transferred his arguments from the history of religion to the formation of philosophy, in the essay "Über die wissenschaftlichen Behandlungsarten des Naturrechts, seine Stelle in der praktischen Philosophie und sein Verhältnis zu den positiven Rechtswissenschaften" (On the Scientific Methods of Treating Natural Law, its Position in Practical Philosophy, and its Relationship to Positivistic Theories of Right; 1803) Hegel projects the positive end point of *Bildung*, namely as a *Bild* or "image." The subject allows him to explore the possibilities of writing philosophy which he sees around him as well as to propose his own theory of writing.

Hegel does not have to talk from the start about questions of rhetorical form since natural law itself contains this problematic already. Natural law is that discipline that attempts to demonstrate the existence of an absolute norm, outside of any individual legal activities among people, which can serve as the validation of those activities. The traditional dilemma of natural law and the standard critique of systems of natural law—a dilemma and a critique that date back to the Sophists' arguments justifying any proposition—is that a system merely selects *one* empirical or historical aspect of human society and raises it to the highest principle as if it were beyond its origins. A critical study of systems of natural law would therefore have to compare their respective principles of validation both to each other and to "the" absolute idea. Hegel seems at first to downplay this comparative aspect in one of his more convoluted, hardly translatable sentences:

> It would merely be a curious interest in the historical side of scientific knowledge which could linger (*verweilen*) with them [i.e., false efforts], *either* in order to compare them to the absolute idea so that one could see in its disfiguration the necessity by which the force of the absolute

---

for example: "Hegel's theory comes to its actual theses through the way in which he makes use of the concept of *double* negation" (p. 217). I am attempting to demonstrate one way in which this double negation *enters into* Hegel's philosophy. See Manfred Frank, *Was ist Neostrukturalismus?* (Frankfurt am Main: Suhrkamp, 1984), for a discussion of the untenability of this "autonomous negation" as an absolute starting point for philosophy (esp. lecture 17).

form nonetheless represents itself (*sich darstellen*), albeit distorted, through its particular determination as principle, and dominates these efforts even under the domination of limited principles—*or* in order to see the empirical condition of the world reflected in the ideal mirror of scientific knowledge. [Pp. 437f.]

Hegel is clearly less than honest when he implies mere "historical interest," since he has polemical interests as well in revealing the insufficiencies of his contemporaries. An analysis of this image indicates both the strategy of the essay and the way Hegel has used *Kritik* to bring himself to a new level of rhetorical *Bildung*.

First, the very image of the "mirror" has now been reversed for Hegel. In this essay he deals with philosophers—especially Kant and Fichte—whom he had imitated earlier. In Bern and Frankfurt he became aware of the imitative nature of his own writing and saw them as the original models, himself as the mirror image. Here, however, he holds up the mirror to them; they are the poor copies of his, or philosophy's, absolute idea. Reflection has been transformed from an act of imitation, through an act of criticism, to an apparently self-contained process of philosophical self-representation. Second, the use of the term *Behandlungsarten*—the modes of treating a topic—provides a direct comparison to his earlier writing. There, too, he was working with the *modi tractandi*. But here, under the hand of *Kritik*, the analysis and rewriting of a *modus* attains a subtle polemical power. Hegel rarely mentions philosophers, especially contemporaries, by name. Rather, he treats the struggle of philosophers for authority before an audience as an interplay of systematic discourses which has a necessity beyond authorship.[38] Hegel has practiced and perfected a mode of polemical *Kritik* that replaces ad hominem argumentation with formal criticism. He writes toward the end of the essay about the movement toward "positivity" in terms of a conflict of forms:

> If we consider more closely the reason scientific knowledge becomes positivistic (*positiv*) and the reason in general for false appearance and belief, we see that it is grounded in *form*—i.e,. in isolating or expressing or positing (*setzen*) something as real, as existing in and of itself, which in fact is ideal, oppositional (*Entgegengesetztes*) and one-sided and thus

38. A passage characteristic of this method, a method that will guide most of his philosophical writing in the future, is the discussion of Kant and Fichte which reduces them to *Momente* and refers to them only indirectly (synecdochically) by mentioning individual concepts from their philosophical systems—*Begehrungsvermögen, Selbständigkeit, Entgegensetzung, Neigungen* (p. 458). This method internalizes Hegel's polemical *Bildung* into philosophy's dialectical unfolding.

only has reality insofar as it is in absolute identity with its opposite. [P. 516]

Behind this image lies both his earlier stage of rhetorical *Bildung*, in which he lost himself in acquired forms, and his technique of *Kritik*, for "appearance" (*Schein*) and "opinion" (belief, *Meinen*) belong to the strategy of differentiation through ad hominem argumentation.[39] But now the image implies a new form of rhetoric, one that neither imitates the given nor attacks it in order to differentiate the old from the new. This further development of his rhetoric, which will allow Hegel to judge other systems in formal terms, he calls the *Bild*. With this formal concept, he incorporates his earlier developments into a theory and practice of representation.

Thus, the interest in writing an image, a mirror image, to hold up against the other systems, is not just historical fascination with traditions, nor just polemical, but a necessary step toward developing an independent synthesis. In this essay, Hegel presents an example of such an image in the third section, where he describes the "form[ation] of absolute morality" (*Gestalt der absoluten Sittlichkeit*; p. 480), the *Bild* (p. 491, 495, 496) and "higher *Bildungen*" (p. 502) of classical Greece. The "of" in the formulation "*Bildungen* of Greece" is ambiguous for Hegel, since on the one hand he enumerates and describes cultural forms existing *within* Greek society, and on the other he seems to mean that

---

39. Hegel even makes the polemical nature of his argumentation explicit in a passage that leads directly into the *Phenomenology* as the "science of the experience of consciousness" (*Wissenschaft der Erfahrung des Bewußtseins*): "Philosophy will certainly acknowledge a subjective opinion that would experience something like that, a chance subjective viewpoint. But positive science, if it alleges to find and exhibit in experience its ideas and basic concepts, wants to assert something real, necessary, objective, [and] not a subjective viewpoint. Philosophy alone determines whether something is a subjective viewpoint or an objective idea, an opinion or truth. It can concede ad hominem to positive science its ways, and rather than denying the fact that an idea occurs in experience, it asserts the opposite, that only the idea of philosophy is found in experience" ("Das Meinen, daß so etwas erfahren werde, eine zufällige subjektive Ansicht wird freilich die Philosophie zugeben; aber die positive Wissenschaft, wenn sie in der Erfahrung ihre Vorstellungen und Grundbegriffe zu finden und aufzuzeigen vorgibt, will damit etwas Reales, Notwendiges, Objektives, nicht eine subjektive Ansicht behaupten. Ob etwas eine subjektive Ansicht oder eine objektive Vorstellung, ein Meinen oder Wahrheit sei, kann die Philosophie allein ausmachen. Der positiven Wissenschaft kann sie *ad hominem* ihre Weise heimgeben und außerdem, daß sie ihr das Faktum, daß eine Vorstellung derselben in der Erfahrung vorkomme, leugnet, im Gegenteil behaupten, daß nur die Vorstellung der Philosophie in der Erfahrung zu finden sei"; p. 511). Philosophy thus takes upon itself the function of ad hominem criticism against opinion; the principle of philosophy's dialectical formation is guided by philosophy's ad hominem acceptance and inversion of "opinion."

his own entire description has the form of a self-contained image that he can oppose to the "mere linear narration" (*bloß Erzählung*; p. 440) of other systems of natural law. He summarizes the theory of the *Bild* near the conclusion of the essay in terms that will be crucial for his own developing system:

> Over all the particular stages hovers the idea of totality, which, how-
> ever, reflects back toward itself out of its projected image (*auseinan-
> dergeworfenen Bilde*), where it views and recognizes itself; this totality of
> the extended image (*Totalität des ausgedehnten Bildes*) is the justification
> of the existence of the particular. [P. 523]

The expanded *Bild* is the final stage of a process of *Bildung*. In *Bildung* the forms were first internalized as dead, given, imitated material, and then were isolated, differentiated, criticized. However, were they to stop there, philosophy or the philosopher would remain in a state of polemical *Mißbildung*, epigones that can manipulate the ideas of others but cannot go beyond acquired *ars* to the inspired *natura*. Hegel describes the process in organic terms:

> It is at the same time necessary that individuality progress, metamor-
> phize itself, weaken that which has the power of domination over it, and
> strive so that all stages of necessity appear as mere stages; the positivistic
> exists, however, in the misfortune of the transitional period, when this
> strengthening of the new formation (*Bildung*) has not yet purified itself
> of past forms. And nature, even though she moves on from a particular
> shape (*Gestalt*) with regular, not uniform but uniformly accelerating
> motion, nonetheless takes pleasure in the new shape it has achieved;
> just as she leaps into the new form, so too she lingers (*verweilt*) in it. [P.
> 529]

In apparent contradiction to the opening quotation, the "lingering" with different forms is appropriate when considered as *Bildungen*. This description, in fact, applies to the implanted movement of rhetorical *Bildung* and metamorphosis by which an individual "style" develops only by contact, even confrontation, with other texts. Through such critical confrontations the individual gains strength and an image of self. The *Bild*, as the end point of *Bildung*, is a rhetorical structure that contains within itself both the "given" from the tradition and the expanded differentiations that separate the present point from the past. It is precisely the principle of the *Bild*, as that which contains within itself the past of a rhetorical *Bildung*, which structures the first formulation of Hegel's system, his first "independent" work, the *Phenomenology of Spirit*.

CHAPTER 4

The Representation of *Bildung* and the *Bildung* of Representation in the *Phenomenology of Spirit*

Readers of the *Phenomenology* respond either approvingly or derisively to its claim that in it the Spirit reaches the state of "absolute knowledge," that is, the state of *Wissenschaft* in which truth can be adequately represented. And yet the actual theory and practice of representation in this text have not yet been explored from both historical and systematic perspectives.[1] In the following discussion I shall be analyzing the ways in which different conceptions of self-representation are inscribed into the argumentative movement of the *Phenomenology* by means of the concept of *Bildung*. In the *Phenomenology* Hegel applied, translated, and appropriated the various aspects of his earlier formative education to his narrative of the development of the Spirit. Hegel's legitimation of *Wissenschaft* is effective because it is understood as the representation of *Bildung*, and *Bildung* is the teleological movement toward representation. That teleology—the belief that development involves education and cultivation to form and self-formation—had been inscribed into the *Phenomenology* by the course of Hegel's own *Bildung*, one that had been predefined for centuries by the *institutio*

---

1. Donald Phillip Verene, *Hegel's Recollection: A Study of Images in the Phenomenology of Spirit* (Albany: State University of New York Press, 1985), has provided the most comprehensive "rhetorical" reading of the *Phenomenology* to date. Our independently conceived approaches overlap most in the discussion of figurative language.

All page numbers within parentheses in the body of the text refer to the *Theorie-Werkausgabe*, vol. 3, *Die Phänomenologie des Geistes* (Frankfurt am Main: Suhrkamp, 1970).

oratoria. Hegel's *Wissenschaft*, one of the most powerful philosophical accounts of representation, is thus dependent on rhetorical preconditions for which it has not accounted philosophically. My analysis is therefore neither merely descriptive nor critical. To point out the way rhetorical patterns and categories prestructure the *Phenomenology* is intended neither to satisfy idle philological curiosity nor to deconstruct Hegel's entire project. Rather, the following discussion strives to explain how the *Phenomenology* can make a claim to be *Wissenschaft*, that is, to be the appropriate *representation* of scientific knowledge. The claim of Hegel's philosophy rests on the assumption that it is the representation of an act of becoming, or, more precisely and self-reflexively, the self-representation of an "act-of-becoming-expressed" or an "act-of-taking-on-form." The first major formulation of Hegel's system can be understood, then, as the representation of a process of rhetorical *Bildung* which is itself a development toward (its own) representation. The uncovering of basic rhetorical structures thus both explicates the circular coherency of Hegel's enterprise and reveals its suppressed formative preconditions.

The *Elocutio* of the *Spirit*

Near the end of the *Phenomenology*, Hegel characterizes the development depicted by his work, the history of the Spirit and the story Hegel tells, in terms that subtly relate his philosophical endeavor to more traditional narratological concerns:

> the history is the knowing, self-mediating becoming—the Spirit that alienates and expresses itself in time; but this alienation [expression] is likewise a self-alienation [expression]; the negative is the negative of itself. This becoming depicts a lingering movement and succession of spirits, a gallery of images, each of which, equipped with the complete richness of the Spirit, moves so lingeringly because the self must penetrate and digest this total richness of its substance.

> die *Geschichte* ist das wissende, sich vermittelnde Werden—der an die Zeit entäußerte Geist; aber diese Entäußerung ist ebenso die Entäußerung ihrer selbst; das Negative ist das Negative seiner selbst. Dies Werden stellt eine träge Bewegung und Aufeinanderfolge von Geistern dar, eine Galerie von Bildern, deren jedes, mit dem vollständigen Reichtume des Geistes ausgestattet, eben darum sich so träge bewegt, weil das Selbst diesen ganzen Reichtum seiner Substanz zu durchdringen und zu verdauen hat. [P. 590]

This passage summarizes the richness of rhetorical structures and patterns that form the texture of the *Phenomenology*. Hegel describes his completed work in a remarkable mixture of abstract philosophical and imagistic poetic language. One could, perhaps, consider the literary and figurative quality of this characterization as "merely" rhetorical, a stylistic flair at the end, a transgression not to be taken "philosophically." In my reading, however, this figurative tone is not arbitrary but, rather, appropriate to the rhetorical character of the text it describes. This passages offers a number of directions to follow in order to attain an overview of the rhetorical figuration of the text.

First, we can trace the concept of the "image" (*Bild*) back to the last essay Hegel wrote prior to the *Phenomenology* for the *Kritisches Journal*. There he concluded his study of various forms of natural law by positing an ideal form of philosophical narrative which would unite disparate elements and ideas under a "totality of the extended image" (*Totalität des ausgedehnten Bildes*).[2] He arrived at this ideal form by rejecting both the empiricist method of cataloging facts and the Kantian and Fichtean imposition of subjective forms onto the object. The fact that he contrasted these methods, which he called "modes of representation" or "modes of dealing with a topic" (*Behandlungsarten*; Latin: *modi tractandi*), to the aesthetic model of Greek harmony derived from German classicism and neohumanism indicates that his notion of the *Bild* cannot be reduced to a pictorial image but represents a rhetorical principle for structuring narrative. The image of a "picture gallery" is, then, a metaphor, but not so much for purely conceptual philosophical language as for the rhetorical "painting" of ideas in *elocutio*. In using this metaphor for modes of narration, Hegel recalls the visual terminology traditionally employed in rhetorical theory.

Second, as we saw in both the essay on natural law and the Preface to the *Phenomenology*, the *Bild* in which philosophy is expressed is the product of a process, appropriately called *Bildung*. In the latter, for example, he refers to the entire *Phenomenology* as the "becoming" (*Werden*) of the representation of scientific knowledge (p. 31) and as the "retraced history of the world's *Bildung*" (*nachgezeichnete Geschichte der Bildung der Welt*; p. 32), which repeats the "pedagogical progression" (*pädagogische[s] Fortschreiten*) of the individual and universal Spirit. Thus, when Hegel at the close of the *Phenomenology* refers to this "history" or "story" (*Geschichte*) as "the knowing and self-mediating becoming" (*das wissende, sich vermittelnde Werden*) and as a "gallery of images" (*Galerie von Bildern*) he seems fully to equate the development and

2. *Theorie-Werkausgabe,*. vol. 2, *Jenaer Schriften*, p. 523; above pp. 170–73.

education (*Bildung*) of Spirit with the task of acquiring forms of rhetorical expression. Hegel thereby links the becoming of scientific knowledge with the ability to give external form to that knowledge. As in every rationally grounded rhetorical theory, or rhetorically argued philosophy, from Cicero through the humanist Melanchthon to Ernesti and Haug, Hegel's philosophical conception of the development of knowledge cannot be separated from the development of modes of representation. Both the universal and the individual Spirit attain knowledge only by retracing a history of self-representations. *Wissenschaft* is thereby tied to the key rhetorical principle of *elocutio*.[3]

Third, in order to make more precise the rhetorical characteristics of the images or letters of the Spirit, we can turn to the part of Hegel's lectures on aesthetics, written some twenty years after the *Phenomenology*, in which he analyzes the concept of the *Bild* in the context of artistic symbolism. He locates the section on *Das Bild* between discussions of the two rhetorical figures, metaphor and "simile" (*Das Gleichnis*). The *Bild*, according to Hegel, has the general form of an "extended metaphor" (*ausführliche Metapher*).[4] It is therefore implicitly related to the classical conception of allegory.[5] Hegel defines the *Bild* as follows: "The image (*Das Bild*) can be found especially wherever two phenomena or states (*Erscheinungen oder Zustände*) which are in fact independent, are fused into one so that the one state provides the meaning that is made concretely conceivable (*faßbar*) by the image of the other." In particular, the *Bild* unfolds as an entire story on one level of signification in order to make another present, even if unstated. Hegel continues: "In this connection, the image can have as its meaning an entire course of events, activities, occurrences, modes of existence, etc., and

3. *Elocutio*, as was argued above, in chap. 1, finds its justification in an inherent power of the *res* to become expressed. If the *res* does not "come out of itself," it is neither understood nor effective, and hence hardly to be considered real. The connections between representation, expression, "reality," and alienation will by pursued in the analysis of *Entäußerung* in the second section of this chapter, "Rhetorical Hermeneutics in the World of *Bildung*."

4. *Vorlesungen über die Ästhetik*, in *Theorie-Werkausgabe*, vol. 13 (Frankfurt am Main: Suhrkamp, 1975), pt. 2, chap. 3, B, 3, b, pp. 516–38. This and the following definitions, p. 523.

5. Compare Heinrich Lausberg, *Handbuch der literarischen Rhetorik* (Munich: Max Hueber, 1960), pars. 895–901: "Allegory is for thought what metaphor is for the individual word: The allegory thus stands in a relation of comparison (*Vergleichsverhältnis*) with the intended serious thought (*gemeinten Ernstgedanken*). The relation of allegory to metaphor is quantitative: Allegory is a metaphor carried though an entire sentence (and beyond)." For more general discussions of the role of allegory in late eighteenth- and early nineteenth-century thought, see Hans-Georg Gadamer, "Rehabilitierung der Allegorie," in *Wahrheit und Methode* (Tübingen: Mohr, 1960), pp. 66–77; and Tzvetan Todorov, *Théories du symbole* (Paris: Editions du Seuil, 1977).

can illustrate (*veranschaulichen*) this meaning by means of a similar course from an independent but related area, without bringing the meaning as such to the level of language in the image (*ohne die Bedeutung als solche innerhalb des Bildes selbst zur Sprache zu bringen*)." Hegel gives the example of Goethe's poem "Mahomets Gesang" (Mohammed's Song), in which "only the title indicates . . . that this expansive, shining image of a powerful river in fact depicts Mohammed's bold appearance." The *Bild*, like a metaphor, receives its expressive power by presenting two levels of signification simultaneously and by transferring meaning from one to the other in order to grant the abstract level a "visual" dimension.[6] As such, the *Bild* corresponds to the task Hegel refers to in the Preface as the goal of modern *Bildung*, namely, the labor of "realizing and inspiring (*verwirklichen und begeisten*) the universal by dissolving firm, particular determinations of thought" (p. 37).

By means of these comparisons from diverse works, we thus arrive at an initial conception of the rhetorical *Bildung* of the *Phenomenology*. It presents us with a new form of philosophical *elocutio*, both a theory and practice of figurative expression, which Hegel characterizes, fully in keeping with traditional rhetoric, as *Bild*. The *Bild* is the product of an extensive *Bildung* or formative education, the form of expression which both the individual and universal spirit arrive at only after considerable training. Implicitly, this mode of representation relies on the rhetorical tradition from which it is ultimately derived. This theory and practice of the *Bild* or figuration in the *Phenomenology* differentiates Hegel's from other philosophies just as his use of the *Bild* or *Gestalt* (form, formation) of Greek harmony differentiated his from the disjointed *Bildungen* of contemporary writers on natural law. As the depiction of the history, development, formation, that is, *Bildung* of the Spirit, the *Phenomenology* contains a story of the Spirit in nonliteral language, in the form of extended figurative images.

Hegel's characterization of the *Phenomenology* in terms of the *Bild*, or extended metaphorical figuration, as well as my analysis of these

6. This visual dimension connects rhetoric and philosophy, since Aristotle begins his *Rhetoric* with the definition that rhetoric makes the means of persuasion "present to the mind" and since philosophy has always been associated with *theoria*, which means "a looking at." Both Theodor Adorno ("*Skoteinos*, oder wie zu lesen sei," in *Drei Studien zu Hegel* [Frankfurt am Main: Suhrkamp, 1970]) and Ernst Bloch (*Subjekt-Objekt* [Frankfurt au Main: Suhrkamp, 1971]) emphasize Hegel's ability to make the underlying process of the concept or *Sache selbst* visible, even palpable. Recall that Adorno refers to Hegel's sentences as *Filme des Gedankens* (p. 353), an anachronistic formulation of the rhetorical principle of the *Bild*. (It is also overly simplistic to the extent that it conceives of the expression as strictly secondary to the thought.)

Bildungen, do not refer to what might seem most obvious, namely, individual metaphors or metaphorical turns of phrase. One can, of course, find a great number of them and they often give Hegel's philosophical diction a "poetic" quality that either impresses or disturbs his readers. The Preface, for example, abounds in nature metaphors.[7] Other figurative expressions, like that of the "bacchanalian dance" (*bacchantische Taumel*) as a description of "the true" (*das Wahre*), have entered into the canon of philosophical metaphors. But such images, as interesting and powerful as they sometimes are, do not show the integral role of metaphor in Hegel's philosophical rhetoric of *Bildung*. In fact, as we saw in the Preface, Hegel even criticizes such "poetic" philosophizing for producing "imagistic formations that are neither fish nor flesh, neither poetry nor philosophy" (*Gebilde, die weder Fisch noch Fleisch, weder Poesie noch Philosophie sind*; p. 64), a criticism against romantic philosophers which was, correctly or incorrectly, taken amiss by Schelling. It might then seem like a fundamental contradiction that Hegel nonetheless uses individual metaphors, even here in this criticism of metaphors in philosophy. But Hegel would probably have responded to the charge of contradiction that such images are mere illustrations and have their place in the margins of his argument. Thus, most of these individual metaphorical expressions occur in the Preface, and not in the text "proper."

And yet the paradox extends further into Hegel's philosophy, since he criticizes certain *Gebilde* even as he calls his own work a *Galerie von Bildern*. Like the Jena essays, the *Phenomenology* confronts us with a fundamental issue of philosophical rhetoric: In the former, Hegel had to arrive at a concept of *Bildung* which allowed him to criticize the torn and inadequate *Bildung* of his time; he did so by proposing a theory of

---

7. Perhaps the most famous image is that of philosophy as plant: "The bud disappears in the breaking out of the blossom, and it could be said that the former is contradicted by the latter; in precisely the same way the fruit shows the blossom to be a false mode of existence of the plant and as its truth the former takes the place of the latter" ("Die Knospe verschwindet in dem Hervorbrechen der Blüte, und man könnte sagen, daß jene von dieser widerlegt wird; ebenso wird durch die Frucht die Blüte für ein falsches Dasein der Pflanze erklärt, und als ihre Wahrheit tritt jene an die Stelle von dieser"; p. 12). Hegel's individual images did raise the attention of his contemporaries. In a letter to Seebeck (Weimar, 28 November 1812), Goethe takes offense at this metaphor (probably as it appeared again in the Introduction to the *Logic*). Goethe writes: "To desire to annihilate the sole reality of nature by means of a bad sophistical joke appears to me to be utterly unworthy of a man of reason." He further criticizes Hegel's tendency "to reduce sophistically to a mere joke the process of nature, and to deny and annihilate it by words and phrases artificially negating one another (*sich einander aufhebend*), so that one does not know what to say." See Günther, Nicolin ed., *Hegel in Berichten seiner Zeitgenossen* (Hamburg: Felix Meiner, 1970), no. 159.

the *Bild* that contains disunity within its totality. In the *Phenomenology* he uses this same new conception to criticize contemporary forms of writing philosophy. To see how he can justify the essential significance of *Bilder* for the structuration of his philosophical language in spite of his rejection of metaphoric language, we need a broader theoretical and historical conception of the metaphoric process and figurative representation.

Hegel analyzes the function and effect of metaphor in his lectures on aesthetics. A metaphor, and by extension a *Bild*, uses one mode of expression in order to convey a meaning not contained in its literal or proper (*eigentliche*) level of signification. But why go through this process of double expressions, or, as Hegel asks, "Why this double expression or, what is the same, why the metaphorical, which is this very doubleness?" ("Weshalb dieser gedoppelte Ausdruck oder, was dasselbe ist, weshalb das Metaphorische, das in sich selbst diese Zweiheit ist?")[8] Hegel's answer to this crucial question relates metaphor to a special need and power of the Spirit; many of the terms of his explanation are by now familiar:

> We can consider as the meaning and purpose of metaphorical diction . . . that need and that power of the Spirit and individual mind which are not satisfied with the simple, customary, plain, but which place themselves above and beyond that in order to move on to an Other, to linger with that which is different, and to fuse that which is double.

The notions of "mov[ing] on to an Other," "linger[ing] with that which is different", and "fus[ing] that which is double" recall the description of the *Phenomenology* as a "slow and lingering movement" in which the self must "penetrate and digest this entire richness" (p. 590). Moreover, "that need and that power of the Spirit" not to remain "satisfied with the simple, customary, plain" recalls on the one hand the definitions of *Bildung* in the Preface and in the Jena essay on "Difference," and on the other the justifications of eloquent *copia* in traditional rhetorical theory. The metaphorical or figurative diction of *Bilder* has a privileged status for Hegel and his precursors not because it conveys poetic feeling but because it fulfills a fundamental need of the Spirit or the self to duplicate and experience itself in its expression.

Hegel's defense of metaphor, or more generally figuration (*Bildlichkeit*), emerges from a long history of defenses of rhetorical *elocutio*. Ever since Aristotle, metaphor possessed a privileged episte-

---

8. *Ästhetik*, p. 520; also the following citations.

mological force. For Aristotle, knowledge springs from the juxaposition or posited identity of two seemingly antithetical words (concepts) such that the reader-listener recognizes an underlying similarity. This source of knowledge corresponds to his justification of metaphor. He says in the *Poetics*: "The right use of metaphor is a sign of inborn talent and cannot be learned from anyone else; it comes from the ability to observe similarities in things."[9] And further, Aristotle writes in the *Rhetoric*: "We learn above all from metaphors."[10] In a good metaphor the difference is simultaneously maintained (otherwise it would collapse into a mere tautology) and overcome (granting the moment of insight).[11] Metaphor for Aristotle, therefore, indicates a broader epistemological process that leads to a genuine acquisition of knowledge by presenting an identity in a masked form that allows the reader-listener to repeat the process of discovering that identity.

Through the tradition of handbooks which kept classical rhetoric alive into the nineteenth century, at least in the schools, *elocutio* occupied a significant position in the rhetorical system. Not only was facility in expression the main goal of education (*Bildung*) and the sign of an educated (*gebildeten*) person, but also the theories and philosophical legitimation of figurative expression—in Hegel's terms, the question "Why the metaphorical?"—generally formed the rational core of the *ars rhetorica*. Such was certainly the case in the handbooks that strongly influenced Hegel's own education. It will be recalled from Chapter 1 that Melanchthon, for example, defended *elocutio*, whose tropes add a kind of "garb" to things, against dialectic, which supposedly expounds only the "naked thoughts" (*res nudas*). He argued that the way in which *elocutio* "clothes" one discourse with another is as necessary to understand things as light is to see objects. He compares the orator to the painter, for where the latter requires light and nature for his pictures, the former requires *praecepta rhetorices* and *copia verborum*. Similarly, Ernesti, whose *Initia Rhetorica* was taught in Hegel's *gymnasium* through the late eighteenth century, argues that the precepts of *elocutio* were important for all forms of writing, especially philosophy, if true understanding is to take place. True eloquence of expression, and hence true knowledge, he proposed, follows from the union of two distinct though internally linked levels of signification: the *res* and the rhetorical *verba*. Immanuel Scheller's *Compendium* on Ciceronian Latin, which guided many of Hegel's earliest exercises, ex-

9. Aristotle, *Poetics*, 1459a.
10. Aristotle, *Rhetoric*, 1410b.
11. Ibid., 1410b–12b.

pands the principles of *elocutio* to an entire system of composition. He claims that *elocutio*, for the ancients one of the five "duties" (*officia*) of an orator's *Bildung*, must now form the basis of a modern theory and practice of writing (*stylus*). Finally, for Hegel's own teacher in Latin and rhetoric, Balthasar Haug, *elocutio* was not a superfluous addition to otherwise proper discourse, but the very condition of all proper expression. Hence, he too considered an education in rhetoric and acts of rhetorical or figurative expression as exercises of the spirit's most basic power of reflection through self-representation in a double, other image.

We thus see that Hegel's characterization of the *Phenomenology* as a *Galerie von Bildern*, when placed against the background of his own later statements on figurative language and of the rhetorical tradition of *elocutio*, refers to more than the appearance of individual metaphorical expressions, as mere illustrations, in philosophy. Rather, the metaphoricity, the *Bildlichkeit*, of the *Phenomenology* refers to the rhetorical formation of the text as a whole, to the very mode of presenting the Spirit's development in varying guises and expressions.[12] This presentation is justified by the Spirit's inherent drive to doubling and self-representation. The Spirit expresses itself in a letter, so to speak, that is not properly its own. This double expression (*dieser doppelte Ausdruck*), according to both Hegel and traditional rhetorical theory, functions as the only means for the Spirit and the writer-reader of its history to attain knowledge.

---

12. I am relying in part on Jacques Derrida's treatment of metaphor in philosophy, especially "La mythologie blanche—La métaphore dans le texte philosophique," in *Marges de la philosophie* (Paris: Editions de Minuit, 1967). Derrida complicates the distinction between a literal language and isolated figurative elements within it: "Metaphor *in* the philosophical text. Assured of understanding each word of this *énoncé*, hastening to understand—to inscribe—a figure in a volume capable of philosophy, one would be able to accommodate oneself to consider a particular question: Is there metaphor in a philosophical text? In what form [and] to what degree? Is it essential, accidental, etc.? Assurance is quickly removed: Metaphor appears to engage in its totality the usage of philosophical language, nothing less than the usage of the language that is called natural *in* philosophical discourse, indeed of the natural language *as* philosophical language" (p. 249). Paul Ricoeur, *The Rule of Metaphor* (*La métaphore vive*), trans. Robert Czerny (Toronto: University of Toronto Press, 1977), strives to reestablish the tensions between rhetoric and philosophy that Derrida tries to break down. His own distinctions, however, tend to collapse. On the one hand, he proposes a difference between the "semantic dynamism of metaphorical utterance" and "speculative discourse" (p. 296). The latter puts the "resources of conceptual articulation to work" and thereby builds on and surpasses the "condition of possibility" of metaphor in order to attain a "conceptual gain." On the other hand, he defines the uniqueness of philosophical language as the "intersection of spheres of discourse" (sect. 4, study 8). Precisely this "intersection of spheres" can be considered "metaphorical" in the sense that Hegel gives of a *gedoppelter Ausdruck*.

The image of a *Galerie von Bildern* alone, however, is completely static and therefore not sufficient for the description of the *Phenomenology* as a movement and narration. The *Bilder* must be related by transformative processes, whereby one *Bild* gives way to another. These processes of representation are set into motion textually by Hegel's concept of the *Phenomenology* as the story of the Spirit's *Bildung*—for here it must be remembered that the *-ung* suffix connotes an active, continuing development and transformation of images and forms. In particular, Hegel's description of the *Phenomenology* seems to imply that the forms of textual expression available to the Spirit in its philosophical metamorphoses are limited. Concretely, four possibilities that coresopond to the four major rhetorical figures in the standard systems of *elocutio* can be isolated. These figures relate the Spirit's stages to one another and characterize the Spirit's relation to its world at any given point.

First, Hegel links the *Bilder* in a "consecutive order" (*Aufeinander-folge*), a contiguous chain in which the one follows from the other. By looking at one figure of the Spirit the reader should be able to infer, though not by the logic of the syllogism or proof (which Hegel explicitly rejects), what figures come before and after. We can consider this relationship-by-contiguity of images as structured on the principle of metonymy, the trope based on spatial, temporal, or causal transference.[13] Second, Hegel identifies the individual *Bilder* with the entire work, for "each [image is] equipped with the total richness of the spirit." Each section of the *Phenomenology* stands, then, in a synecdochic relationship, *pars pro toto*, to the whole.[14] Third, each expression of the Spirit is "the negative [image] of itself." The Spirit or self must penetrate these *Bilder* to find their true, positive significance, for they always mean something different from what they say. Thus, each *Bild* is an *inversio*, a litotic and ironic depiction, of the other images and of the Spirit's underlying meaning at a given point.[15] The double negation that characterized so much of Hegel's critical polemics can now be depicted openly as a figure of the Spirit. Fourth, as we have seen, the very term *Bild* relates the expressions of the Spirit to an act of self-doubling which corresponds to the traditional rhetorical theory as well as to Hegel's own later definition of metaphor. Hegel thereby pe-

13. See Roman Jakobson, "Two Aspects of Language: Metaphor and Metonymy," in Vernon Gras, ed., *European Literary Theory and Practice* (New York: Dell, 1973). Also Kenneth Burke, "The Four Master Tropes," in *Grammar of Motives* (Los Angeles: University of California Press, 1974), pp. 503–17.

14. On synecdoche, see Lausberg, *Handbuch*, pars. 572–77 (as figure of speech) and pars. 894, 907–8 (as figure of thought).

15. On irony and *inversio*, see Lausberg, *Handbuch*, pars. 896 and 902–4.

riphrastically characterizes the "history" depicted in the *Phenomenology*, the movement or *Bildung* of the Spirit, as a series of transformations and permutations involving the four "master tropes" of *elocutio*: metaphor, metonymy, synecdoche, and irony. These classical figures make it possible for us to give an initial explanation of the "movement" of *Bildung* in Hegel's text in rhetorical terms—a movement that otherwise would remain vague and mysterious.[16]

Hayden White's theory of historical narrative, which assigns four distinct "modes of emplotment" to the four tropes of classical rhetoric, can help us understand better the at least implicit relationship Hegel establishes between the individual *Bilder* and the "history of *Bildung*."[17] White writes: "Both traditional poetics and modern language theory identify four basic tropes for the analysis of poetic, or figurative language: Metaphor, Metonymy, Synecdoche, and Irony. These tropes permit the characterization of objects in different kinds of indirect, or figurative, discourse. They are especially useful for understanding the operations by which the contents of experience which resist description in unambiguous prose representations can be prefiguratively grasped and prepared for conscious apprehension."[18] For White, the figurative character of narrative in general rests on the "twofold nature of discourse" which is "both interpretive and preinterpretive; it is always as much *about* the nature of interpretation itself as it is *about* the subject matter that is the manifest occasion of its own elaboration."[19] This statement recalls not only Hegel's definition of *Bild* or image in terms of its intrinsic "doubleness" as a "double expression," but also the dual function of *Bildung* as the precondition and expression of *Wissenschaft*.

White attempts in general to attribute one of the four tropological "modes of emplotment" or "modes of historical consciousness" to any given writer. That is, for most writers, he claims, one dominant trope structures their narrative depiction of history. Each individual (spirit), to paraphrase Hegel in the Preface, stands under the sign of one particular determination. However, certain writers like Hegel, Marx, and

16. Such a tropological narrative could perhaps also be uncovered for the *Bildungsroman*. The development of the hero's relationship to himself and his world could be mapped out in terms of these figures. Lacan's interpenetration of psychoanalysis and linguistics/rhetoric would be particularly fruitful for such an interpretation.

17. Hayden White, *Metahistory: The Historical Imagination in Nineteenth-Century Europe* (Baltimore, Md.: Johns Hopkins University Press, 1973). See esp. pages 1–43. The chapter on Hegel deals with his philosophy of history and does not touch on the issues I cover. In fact, White seems to reduce Hegel's rhetorical complexity to one major trope for the sake of his schema. See also White, *Tropics of Discourse: Essays in Cultural Criticism* (Baltimore, Md.: Johns Hopkins University Press, 1978).

18. White, *Metahistory*, pp. 31; also p. 34.

19. White, *Tropics*, p. 4.

Vico also enjoy a privileged status in White's view since their mode of presenting history allows the richness of events to pass through all four tropological transformations. He characterizes Hegel's (Marx's and Vico's) mode of composition as follows: "The archetypal plot of discursive formations appears to require that the narrative 'I' of the discourse move from an original metaphorical characterization of a domain of experience, through metonymic deconstructions of its elements, to synecdochic representations of the relations between its superficial attributes and its presumed essence, to, finally, a representation of whatever contrasts or oppositions can legitimately be discerned in the totalities identified in the third phase of discursive representation."[20] White's description of the "archetypal plot" can be read as a translation of Hegel's own description of the movement of *Bildung* through the *Galerie von Bildern* into explicitly rhetorical terminology.

We can now use White's theory of historical narrative, as well as the classical theories of *elocutio* upon which it rests, to analyze the tropological structure of the *Phenomenology* and the transformations among its "figures."[21] The goal in this analysis of the plot of the *Phenomenology* is to use rhetorical terminology implicit in Hegel's self-characterization of his work so that such concepts as the "movement" and *Geschichte der Bildung* take on precise narratological meaning. This mode of analysis is not just a mere redescription in terms of rhetorical categories. Rather, it has the ability to clarify textual strategies heretofore overlooked in studies of *Phenomenology*. Since scientific knowledge appears, according to Hegel, only in a system, and since a system only appears as a text, the *Bildung* of and to science must make use of textual formations. These formations have been traditionally systematized in the rhetorical task of *elocutio*, and they recur here to structure Hegel's *Wissenschaft*. Moreover, the following rhetorical analysis contributes to recent readings of philosophy as a "kind of writing."[22]

Like these newer critical readings, which follow closely on the heals

20. Ibid., p.5.

21. Although White's tropological scheme for the unfolding of modes of narrative does have a great deal of descriptive power, it can be supplemented by another approach, which strengthens its historical validity. White does not attempt to trace the four master tropes back to the classical rhetorical tradition, emphasizing instead, for example, Vico and Renaissance theories. However, he could also use the tradition to make a link from *elocutio* to dialectics, from the tropes to topoi or *loci argumentorum*. Lausberg defines *loci* as "search rules (*Suchformeln*) and, in their entirety, a reservoir of thoughts out of which the appropriate thoughts can be selected" (*Handbuch*, par. 373). As such, they belong both to the *inventio* (and hence dialectic) and *elocutio* (or rhetoric in the narrower sense). They bridge the gap between *res* and *verba*. In fact, as we saw in the rhetorical handbooks used in Württemberg schools, the tropes and *loci* were inextricably linked.

22. The phrase is taken from Rorty, "Philosophy as a Kind of Writing: An Essay on Jacques Derrida," *New Literary History*, 10, no. 1 (1978), 141–60.

of Nietzsche, Heidegger, and Wittgenstein, my analysis strives to understand the formations of the Spirit as linguistic modes of expression which obey the laws of textual transformations codified in the discipline of rhetoric. Without having to appeal to the ontological status of the Spirit—but also, it must be added, without making a claim to "deconstruct" it—this rhetorical analysis can interpret its movement in narratological terms that underlie our Western tradition of representation. The point here is not to undermine Hegel's equation of logic and ontology but, rather, to show that one can do without it in both explicating Hegel and appropriating his powerful conception of Spirit and its dialectical expression. This manner of reading Hegel thus sees his *Wissenschaft* as the greatest fulfillment of a limited conception of representation since it casts the very development of the World Spirit into patterns of representative rhetorical figures.

Although Hegel never defines explicitly what structural unit of the *Phenomenology*—parts, chapters, or subsections—could correspond to a *Bild*, we do have an idea of its rhetorical characteristics. Each *Bild* is a necessarily indirect, figurative way of expressing the Spirit. Each *Bild* depicts a mode of representing the world, a mode derived from some source of *Bildung*—from everyday discourse to natural science, from artworks to religion, from popular treatises to philosophical texts. Each *Bild* is determined by its own discourse or rhetoric, it "clothes" itself uniquely for internal reasons (in the sense of *elocutio* and figuration). The complexity of the *Bilder* varies with the kind of discourse each one uses to describe the world, or as Hegel said in the *Aesthetics*, with the "course of events" it depicts at another level of signification. The *Bilder* have the form of rhetorical figures since each one represents the world or Spirit in transferred or figurative language, and the "richness" of the text corresponds to a kind of "eloquence" as the Spirit sheds off one figure to try on another. Unlike the strictly linear plot described by White, however, which progresses uniformly from metaphor, through metonymy and synecdoche, to irony, Hegel's history of the Spirit's *Bildung* as "pedagogical progression" constantly repeats and varies the figurative pattern in the way that successive generations rework discursive strategies of the past. The complex and slow "movement" of the *Phenomenology* through the "picture gallery" has a rhetorical structure that reformulates modes of expression according to rules of classical *copia et variatio verborum*.[23]

---

23. For a discussion of *copia* as a central category of humanist philosophy and rhetoric, see Terence Cave, *The Cornucopian Text: Problems of Writing in the French Renaissance* (Oxford: Clarendon, 1979), esp. the Introduction.

Hegel's series of figures begins with the "naive" form of consciousness called "sense certainty" (*sinnliche Gewißheit*). Hegel deals with it as a *Bild*, that is, as a mode of depicting the world. Its discourse tries to deny its own figurative nature and Hegel's argument involves pointing out the rhetorical indirectness or mediation inherent in its discourse. Sense certainty claims to be able to express simple identities, "unmediated or immediate knowledge, knowledge of the unmediated" (*unmittelbares Wissen, Wissen des Unmittelbaren*; p. 82). Its discourse consists of simple terms like "I" (*Ich*), "*this* object" (dieser *Gegenstand*), "tree" (*Baum*), "here" (*hier*), "now" (*jetzt*), which, it believes, can express directly the objects grasped by its senses. Sense certainty identifies what it says with what it subjectively thinks (*meint*). Hegel shows, however, that sense certainty's mode of representation, literally of speaking and writing, indeed, the fact that it speaks and writes down its thoughts (*Meinungen*), forces it to employ the indirectness of rhetoric and a language that does not coincide with its thought-objects (*res*). The reason, Hegel argues, is that "speaking (*Sprechen*) . . . has the divine nature of immediately [unmediatingly, *unmittelbar*] inverting opinion [thought, *Meinung*] and turning it into something else [other, *zu etwas anderem*]" (p. 92). This statement parallels Hegel's later explanation (cited above, p. 180) in the *Aesthetics* of the necessity of metaphor or figurative language (*Bildlichkeit*), namely, "the need and the power of the Spirit and individual mind . . . that are not satisfied by the simple, customary, plain, but which place themselves above and beyond that, and move on to an Other." Hegel thus begins the *Phenomenology* by demonstrating that even the simplest form of consciousness becomes a rhetorical figure of the Spirit when it is viewed from the perspective of how it expresses itself. Appropriately, then, the "movement" of the *Bildung* to scientific knowledge (*Wissenschaft*) starts with an introduction to the inherent *Bildlichkeit—elocutio—*of knowledge. The assumption underlying this chapter and the rest of the *Phenomenology* is that knowledge, even of the apparently unmediated, requires the mediation through universal and systematic forms of representation.

Once sense certainty's discourse has been shown to be ignorant of its own nature since all knowledge is, in principle, indirectly mediated through self-representation, the next form of consciousness, "perception" (*Wahrnehmung*), tries to be more subtle by taking into account the fact of doubling and figuration in its representation of what it "takes to be true" (the literal translation of *wahr-nehmen*). The discourse of perception takes as its point of departure the "double meaning" (*gedoppelte Bedeutung*; p. 94) contained in all verbal expressions about the world.

The uniqueness of perception's discourse derives from its particular "double expression" or figurative quality. Specifically, perception is a mode of expressing the world, a *Bild* or formulation (*Gestalt*), which employs the figure of metonymy in its descriptions. It describes the world in terms of the superficial properties (*Eigenschaften*) of things by making inferences and transferences at the level of contiguous relationships between them. It produces statements like: "This salt is a simple Here and is also complex; it is white and *also* bitter, *also* shaped like a cube, *also* of a certain mass, etc." ("Dies Salz ist einfaches Hier und zugleich vielfach; es ist weiß und *auch* scharf, *auch* kubisch gestaltet, *auch* von bestimmter Schwere usw."; p. 95; also p. 100). The rhetoric, or as Hegel calls it "sophistry (*Sophisterei*) of perception" (p. 105, 106), loosely links varying perspectives, juxtaposes things and their projected essences, and strives "to maintain its truth through the differentiation of *perspectives*, through the *also*'s and *insofar*'s, and to grasp truth through the differentiation of the *inessential* from an opposing *essence*" (*durch die Unterscheidung der* Rücksichten, *durch das* Auch *und* Insofern *festzuhalten sowie endlich durch die Unterscheidung des* Unwesentlichen *und eines ihm entgegengesetzten* Wesens *das Wahre zu ergreifen;* p. 105).[24] The discourse of perception, as a *Bild* or mode of describing the world, decomposes the naive, falsely immediate identities of sense certainty and offers instead metonymical associations of perspectives, which are, alas, also severly limited formulations.

A discourse that would do more than metonymically exchange (*abwechslungsweise*; pp. 101, 105) external characteristics is presented in the chapter on "understanding" (*Verstand*). The understanding is also a *Bild* or way of depicting the world. It relies on the ability to infer the essence of things (*Wesen*) from their appearance (*Erscheinung*) in a more scientific form. In the discourse of the understanding, the essence of things is called their "force" (*Kraft*; pp. 110, 122). The discourse of understanding differs from that of sense certainty and perception in that, for the first time, it makes synecdochic transferences from a particular external event to a general inner principle.[25] It describes the world in terms of absolute laws: "This kingdom (*Reich*) of laws (*Gesetze*) . . . is the truth of the understanding" (p. 120), whereby a law connects not just two external phenomena with the contiguity of perception's

24. Especially in the earlier stages of the *Phenomenology*, Hegel's performs a kind of rhetorico-linguistic analysis on the way the Spirit expresses (misspeaks) itself on its parapraxes. This form of linguistic metacritique of reason through its self-representations reveals Hegel's proximity to critical post-Kantians like Herder and Maimon.

25. Burke, "Four Master Tropes," considers synecdoche the figure of "representation," the guiding rhetorical strategy in natural sciences.

"also" or "and then" but, rather, an external event with a hidden inner principle of which the event is the expression or representation. The rhetoric of the understanding is more complex than the everyday discourse of the first two figures because its synecdochic exposition is embodied most clearly in the rhetoric of natural science.

With the opening of the fourth chapter on "self-consciousness" (*Selbstbewußtsein*), the "movement" of the argumentation takes a sudden turn. It reads: "In the previous modes of certainty (*Weisen der Gewißheit*), truth was perceived by consciousness as something different from itself" (p. 137). Now, however, Hegel will consider the way the self presents itself. The notion of a "mode of certainty" corresponds to the notion of a *Bild*, that is, Hegel is concerned not so much with certainty as such (whatever that may be) as with the mode of expressing a believed certainty. How, then, does the self express *itself* as the object of its own discourse? What image does the self present of itself in its attempt to know not just its Other but also itself?

Hegel offers three images or kinds of discourse which represent forms of self-consiousness, that is, three forms of self-representation of consciousness.[26] The first is that of the stoic, whose rhetoric consists in what Aristotle would call "unhappy expressions," empty metaphors, mere tautologies from which no knowledge can emerge.[27] The stoic speaks in meaningless identities. When asked what is true or good, he answers "reason"; when asked what is reasonable, he responds "the true and the good." Hegel writes: "But this self-identity of thought is again only pure form in which nothing is determined; the general words (*die allgemeinen Worte*) about 'truth' and the 'good,' 'wisdom' and 'virtue,' in which [stoicism] must remain caught, are therefore in general uplifting, but, because they cannot attain any extension of content

---

26. These forms of self-consciousness are prepared for by the famous "master-slave" dialectic. In that dialectic, two "consciousnesses" enter into a struggle against each other in order to maintain their own lives. To prevent mutual annihilation they establish a state of mutual dependence and recognition: The slave (*Knecht*) works for the master (*Herr*), gives him direct recognition and sustenance, and in return is allowed to live and is granted recognition indirectly through the products of his labor. See the analysis by Kojève in his *Introduction à la lecture de Hegel: Leçons sur la Phénoménologie de l'esprit, 1933–39* (Paris: Gallimard, 1947). I am more interested in the outcome, in the forms of self-conscious representation which are made possible by this dialectic. Significantly, the slave comes out ahead (at least in terms of raised consciousness) since he must both engage with the Other as Other and produce something beyond himself (the *doppeltes Tun* of his labor; p. 148). The result is a *Darstellung* of consciousness in the process of *sich bilden* (pp. 152–54).

27. Aristotle, *Rhetoric*, 1410–12b. Aristotle speaks of good metaphors as "happy phrases" that convey knowledge and have an "attractive form" if "there is an antithesis" contained within the identity.

(*Ausbreitung des Inhalts*), they begin to generate boredom" (pp. 158–59). As in the opening chapter on sense certainty, Hegel shows here that the Spirit begins to gain knowledge of a new object (here itself) by adopting a new form of discourse, a simple, almost nonrhetorical language. In the case of stoicism's *Bild* of the nature of its own self-consciousness, the initial mode of expression consists of bad metaphorical rhetoric. The movement of the Spirit from this mode takes place when the naive identities of stoicism are shattered. Hence, the second and third kinds of discourse by which self-consciousness depicts itself to itself are closely related to each other in their rejection of the stoic's simplistic tautologies. The rhetoric of the skeptic, for example, inverts any posited identity and takes on the form of a trivialized polemic:"Its empty discourse (*Gerede*) is in fact a quarreling (*Gezänke*) between two willful boys, whereby one says A when the other says B, and then says B when the other says A; they thereby buy the pleasure of contradicting *each other* at the price of contradicting *themselves*" (pp. 162–63).

Whereas the figure of this skeptical consciousness is that of the ironic dialogue, the "unhappy consciousness" internalizes the double rhetoric of the skeptic and turns it against itself: "the unhappy consciousness is a consciousness of self as a double, contradictory being" (*als des gedoppelten, nur widersprechenden Wesens;* p. 163). Its rhetoric, its mode of speaking (*sprechen*) has the form of a self-contradictory monologue (*sich widersprechen*), for whatever way it characterizes the world or itself it can always justify as well the opposite. In fact, the rhetoric of the unhappy consciousness can be considered a classical variation of irony, namely, *reflectio,* an ironizing dialogue in the form of monologue (as when in a court of law a party takes over and inverts the other party's position).[28] It therefore accomplishes the crucial turn for the Spirit that leads from a discourse about the world, through a discourse with other consciousnesses, to a state of self-reflection. Underlying the attainment of self-conscious reflection is a process of literal self-representation, that is, a self's modes of speaking to and about itself.

The various figures of "reason" (*Vernunft*) begin at the standpoint of self-conscious inner monologue since they all view the world as an extension of the self. They attempt to formalize the relationships between the "self" and nature, which here has the basic form of the "self's other" or "other self," and in so doing the formations of reason repeat the stages of the earlier figures at a higher level of abstraction. Hegel

---

28. Lausberg, *Handbuch*, pars. 663–64. Often used in forensic rhetoric, the figure of *reflectio* allows a speaker to internalize and distort the words of a partner for some persuasive end.

writes of the consciousness of reason that its foundation is a wordplay linking Being to itself: "Although we do see this consciousness, for which *Being* (*das* Sein) has the meaning of *being-its-own* (*des* Seinen), once again enter into the stages of subjective belief (*das Meinen*) and perception, it does not do so as the certainty of a mere *Other* but with the certainly of itself being that Other (*dies Andere selbst zu sein*). Earlier, it only *happened* or *occurred* to consciousness to perceive or *experience* something in a thing; here it performs the observations and produces the experience itself" (p. 185). Because the Spirit has attained enough *Bildung* or formative education to represent itself to itself, reason views the world not just as an object outside itself but as an object of its knowing; hence its figurations consist of different forms of science, for science is a mode of depicting that which is known. The forms of reason vary with the modes of expressing, that is, with the rhetoric of, scientific knowledge of the world and the self. In keeping with the philosophical tradition, although without using these terms explicitly, Hegel divides the scientific disciplines, and thus also the forms of reason, into the theoretical and practical, that is, natural and ethical sciences. The "movement" or *Bildung* from one to the other, however, passes through three stages that correspond to the tropological formations of the first three chapters of the *Phenomenology*: metaphor, metonymy, and synecdoche.

The theoretical sciences of reason (*Beobachtung der Natur*) begin with the naive standpoint we encountered in sense certainty; but reason has formalized its earlier simplistic statements ("Here is a tree" or "Now it is night") by means of the structures of empirical science. The first figure of science thus takes on the form of a metaphorical rhetoric of mere description (*Beschreibung*), as if the description were *like* or identical with the workings of the world. Reason's fundamental identity—the world of reason is the world represented and known by reason—is reduced in empirical description to a tautological assertion without a firm ground. Hegel says of the rhetoric of reason's consciousness: "Its first statement (*Aussprechen*) is only this abstract, empty phrase (*dieses abstrakte leere Wort*) that everything is its own (*sein*)" (p. 184). The pun on *Sein* and *sein*—Being and being-its-own—that underlies reason leads it to propose laws (*Gesetze*) that are often nothing but a "tautological sentence" (*tautologischer Satz*; p. 207).

The next forms of reason's self-expression of its knowledge, the pseudo-sciences of physiognomy and phrenology, displace mere description by trying to define, rather than take for granted, the relationship between the knowing self and its known world. Like the metonymical rhetoric of perception which replaced the naive identities of sense certainty, their rhetoric does nothing but give the external characteristics of things as signs (*Zeichen*) of their inner nature (pp. 251–62).[29] The associative principles of conventional sign systems, which rest on the power of contiguity, determine the kinds of transferences permitted within these pseudo-sciences, for example, from handwriting to deed, from facial features to character, from a skull's shape to the brain's thought.

Reason finally overcomes this mode of arbitrarily connecting man's being and his outer world by postulating a more powerful link, the synecdoche of moral law. That is, reason takes on the rhetoric of Kantian and Fichtean practical philosophy which imposes man's individual inner law of ethics and virtue (*Individualität, Tugend, Gesetz des Herzens*) onto the "course of the world" in general (*der Weltlauf*). In Hegel's words: "The transition [transference] occurs from the form of the *one* to that of the *universal*" ("Der Übergang geschieht aus der Form des *Eins* in die der *Allgemeinheit*"; p. 273).[30] The ethical systems of idealism to which Hegel implicitly refers in this discussion of reason complete the possible figurative relationships between inside and outside in the same way that Kant's notion of the understanding, with its synecdochic relationship between force and event, law and example, concluded the figurative formations of sense certainty and perception.

With the chapter on Spirit (*Geist*) the rhetoric of the *Phenomenology* again changes considerably in tone. The formations of the Spirit in this section repeat once again the basic figurative pattern of the "archetypal plot," but the levels of the discourses portrayed in these images differ from the earlier ones. Whereas the earlier chapters depicted "formations only of a consciousness" (*Gestalten nur eines Bewußtseins*), this chapter contains "formations of a world" (*Gestalten einer Welt*; p. 326). Whereas the earlier images presented modes of expressing a relationship between an individual and itself, or nature, or a self-imposed moral order, these figures of the Spirit paint pictures of the individual

29. The principle of representation at work here is that the external is an "expression" (*Ausdruck* or *Abdruck*) of the internal so that knowledge, according to this form of consciousness, consists in manipulating expressions. "Metonymy" means a change of name or expression.

30. Kant's categorical imperative has the form of a synecdoche since the individual is supposed to consider his actions as if they were extended to the totality of rational creatures. Similarly, Fichte's *Wissenschaftslehre*, at least according to Hegel's interpretation, begins with the limited perspective of the subjective ego and strives to attain a form of totality which is only a "sophistical" (i.e., more precisely synecdochic) generalization. Thus, Hegel's charge against Fichte that he remains caught in "subjective idealism" is inseparable from a charge against synecdochic philosophizing. See Dieter Henrich, "Fichtes 'Ich,'" in *Selbstverhältnisse* (Stuttgart: Reclam, 1982), for an alternative view of Fichte.

within the context of a historical, social world. As representations of the individual's cultivation or acculturation, they thus come closer to the goal of the *Phenomenology* as defined in the Preface as the history of the "*Bildung* of the universal individual" (p. 31, also p. 73). They also recall the ideal *Bildungen* of the public sphere that Hegel posited as necessary depictions for judging other ways of considering natural law. These *Bilder* repeat the stages of Greek, Roman, and modern European culture, which are themselves repeated by all particular individuals in the course of their formative education. The cultural products of past societies—classical tragedy, legal codes, subcultures—are viewed from the modern perspective. As the objects of one's modern study or *Bildung*, they are obviously not experienced directly but, rather, as recorded ways of forming and shaping the world. Hence, each formation (*Gestalt*) corresponds to a mode of rhetorical transformation, for the Spirit experiences them not as realities but as representations.

The starting point, once again, is a state of identification and union, historically the Greek polis. As in the notion of *Bild* from the essay on natural law, Hegel describes here a society where all individuals are united by the underlying principle of "common morality" (*Sittlichkeit*). And yet this entire image of the Spirit's harmony is in fact a metaphorical, even allegorical, reformulation of the brother-sister relationship depicted in Sophocles' *Antigone*. The image of Greece as a harmonious whole has less to do with the actual historical circumstances than with a reception of a classical drama in the spirit of German classicism. In both its content and form, this first "formation of a world" emphasizes the figure of metaphor as a balance of tensions.[31]

But then this "serene balance" (*ruhiges Gleichgewicht*) and "beauty" (*Schönheit*) (pp. 340, 354) is shattered by the individual's conflict with the law. The former identity is revealed to have been incomplete, since it was naive and unaware of the possibility of disjuncture and is transformed into a metonymical state of atomized individuals. The "condition of legality" (*Rechtszustand*) which determines Roman culture—the next stage in "Spirit"—holds these individuals together artificially by the imposition of man-made law. The natural unity of the Greek spirit is torn asunder and replaced by conventionality.

---

31. Hegel's terminology makes clear that he is thinking as much of the ideals of classicism in Germany from Winckelmann to Goethe and Schiller as he is of Greek culture. His understanding of the Greeks is filtered through contemporary interpretations that focus on the harmonization of the symbol, rather than on the arbitrariness of allegory. Prior to Nietzsche, Hölderlin was one of the only Germans to offer an alternative reading of the Greeks based on fundamental, unresolved tensions beneath Greek serenity.

Finally, however, the artificial bond of the legal code can no longer contain "the spirit now split within itself" (*der in sich selbst nunmehr entzweite Geist*; p. 327). Modern society is born out of this division and the result is a state in which the trope of irony prevails as the Spirit's mode of self-presentation. Like the torn consciousness of the skeptic, the individuals and the cultural forms of modernity thrive on their own ironic doubleness. The sections on *Bildung* and *Moralität* depict worlds in which all expression is used to invert the values of society. In fact, the discussion of morality revolves around a critical treatment of Friedrich Schlegel's concept of romantic irony.[32] The "subplot" of figures in this section on Spirit thus repeats the pattern of figuration we saw earlier but now applied to "formations of a world," or forms of modern *Bildung* understood as cultivation.

In "Religion," the last major chapter of the *Phenomenology*, or the last room in the picture gallery of the Spirit's self-portraits, Hegel again unfolds all the possibilities of figurative expression. He treats the different ways in which man gives to the absolute Being "the form and clothing of his imaginative representation" (*die Gestalt und das Kleid seiner Vorstellung*; p. 497). The terms "form" or "formation" and "clothing" indicate that Hegel is concerned less with the absolute per se than with the figurative forms that man has used to represent the inexpressible indirectly. These terms echo traditional definitions of *elocutio* as the "clothing" required to make the *res nudas* present to the mind. Thus, the four modes of imaginative representation (*Vorstellung*) which man employs in religion correspond to the four techniques of giving rhetorical form to ideas.

The series opens with "natural religion," a kind of prestage like that of the natural consciousness of sense certainty, in which man identifies with the divine Being and tries to depict it without mediation as an object. The problem of language and expression is central. Hegel writes:

> The products [of natural religion] are still missing the form and kind of being in which the self exists as a self; — they are still missing the ability to express the inner meaning it contains; it is missing language, the element in which fulfilling meaning is present.

32. These last sections on reason have already been treated as readings or allegories of the romantics (and, I add, their rhetoric). See, e.g., "Die Beisetzung der Romantiker in Hegels *Phänomenologie des Geistes*," in *Materialien zu Hegels Phänomenologie des Geistes*, ed. Fulda (Frankfurt am Main: Suhrkamp, 1973), with the discussion of Novalis as the *schöne Seele*. Also, Ernst Behler's analysis of Hegel's critical treatment of F. Schlegel's concept of irony in the section on *Moralität* and "reconciliation" (*Versöhnung*): "Schlegel und Hegel," *Hegel-Studien* 2, (1963) pp. 203–50.

Noch fehlt dem Werke [der natürlichen Religion] aber die Gestalt und Dasein, worin das Selbst als Selbst existiert; —es fehlt ihm noch dies, an ihm selbst es auszusprechen, daß es eine innere Bedeutung in sich schließt, es fehlt ihm die Sprache, das Element, worin der erfüllende Sinn selbst vorhanden ist. [P. 510]

The works of natural religion are metaphorical identifications between the world and the divine without wanting to be or knowing one is metaphorical. They do not thematize or consciously call attention to the necessary indirectness and mediation of language. They would contain statements like "God is a tree" (parallel to the assertions of sense certainty) and yet not recognize that this identification is already metaphorical. (Or more precisely, since this stage of religious representation lacks figurative language, it just holds up trees and other objects *as* gods.) When man does acquire a more sophisticated understanding of language he first uses it to express the Absolute metonymically, through the arbitrary (*zufällig*; p. 521, 529) sign (*Zeichen*; p. 523), for example, of oracles. The awareness that a thing or word *is* not the divine itself but only a rhetorical relationship to it leads to a mode of conventional representation and interpretation.

Gradually, however, language develops to a stage where it can unite a people. Though only a part of a culture, the new language of the epic poem binds a people into a unified whole: "in this way the particularly beautiful spirits of a people are unified in *one* pantheon, whose element and accommodation is language" ("so vereinigen sich die besonderen schönen Volksgeister in *ein* Pantheon, dessen Element und Behausung die Sprache ist"; p. 529); and further: "The mode of being of this representation, *language*, is the first language, the epic as such, which contains universal content as the *totality* of the world" ("Das Dasein dieser Vorstellung, die *Sprache*, ist die erste Sprache, das *Epos* als solches, das den allgemeinen Inhalt . . . als *Vollständigkeit* der Welt . . . enthält"; p. 531). As in a powerful social synecdoche, the epic singer stands for his entire people (*pars pro toto*) and his song houses (container for the contained) the divine nature of the nation.

In the next form of "religion" other individuals in society also learn to identify like the epic singer with the events that form their collective consciousness. Members of the society perform parts of the epic as tragedies and thereby become one with the figures of their cultural background. Parallel to its function in the formation of Greek morality in the essay on natural law and in the earlier chapter on *Antigone*'s world, tragedy as a religious expression creates a metaphorical identity, more self-conscious than the identification of its precursor forms, by allowing for a transference between actor and role, public and play. All members are in a sense the same as they share in the tragic fates of their heroes. Finally, however, the people learn to raise play acting to a self-reflexive art in which they are aware of their simultaneous positions as "a real, effective self" (*ein wirkliches Selbst*) and an actor with a mask. In performing comedy, the individuals delight in the irony that only a mask separates the actor, the audience, and the gods (p. 542). Comedy, as the last form of religious representation, occupies a higher position than either epic or tragedy and leads to the final state of "absolute knowledge" since its irony both contains and inverts the rhetorical identifications of the earlier stages.

The final chapter seems to jump out of this history of representations, but "absolute knowledge" (*absolutes Wissen*) is *Wissenschaft,* and *Wissenschaft* is nothing but the representation of philosophy as *Bildung,* as the summary of all the past figures. If the course of the *Phenomenology* follows and compares the different expressions of the Spirit, that is, the various and rich ways in which the *res* is clothed in the *verba*, then absolute knowledge would be the identity of form and content. The step from religion to philosophy is one from the mere "content" of the Absolute (images of God) to the raising of objects to pure "form" (p. 575). Once the content is given form, by definition the "series of formations" (*Reihe der Gestaltungen*; p. 579) can come to an end. But how can the content become form, or substance become expression? Because the substance that we have been observing over the course of the Spirit's development "is its *becoming* (Werden) that which it is in itself (*an sich*)" (p. 585). The Spirit, in other words, is not just "becoming" in a haphazard way; rather, it is engaged in a process of *Bildung* which is inherently teleological—with *wissenschaftliche* representation as its goal—since its movement is one of expression (*Entäußerung*; pp. 587f., 589). Since every step along the way is a *Bild* or particular representation, the totality of representations is not something other than rhetoric but its highest moment, representability as such.

*

In summary, then, we can see that Hegel's characterization of the *Phenomenology* as a *Galerie von Bildern* makes possible a rhetorical reading of the work's structures in terms of classical figures of *elocutio*. When Hegel speaks of the "movement" and "history" of the Spirit, he is referring to transformations of the *Bilder*, a process he also calls the *Bildung* of the Spirit. Both his own education in classical *elocutio* and his later theory of the *Bild* in the *Aesthetics* allow us to consider the *Phe-*

nomenology as a series of "double expressions," rhetorical figures along the lines of the standard four master tropes. Through such an analysis we first gain an insight into the relationships between any given chapter of the *Phenomenology* and discourse of which it is the "double expression." The "richness" of the Spirit that Hegel refers to often in the Preface and at the end of the *Phenomenology* corresponds to the *copia verborum*, the variety of expressions to be found in the world of *Bildung*. Second, we gain an overview of the entire structure of the system in terms of its "archetypal plot," which repeats and varies patterns or operations of figurative discourse. The "detailed fullness and necessity" (p. 33) of the development of scientific knowledge follow not the logic of syllogisms but the logic of rhetorical exercises of *variatio*. And third, we gain precision in our understanding of such notions as "movement," *Gestalt*, "story," *Bildung*, with which Hegel characterizes the structure and content of his system. By relating them to rhetorical categories, in this case those of *elocutio*, we give them a concrete significance as modes of textual transformation according to traditional methods. The genius of the formal structure and thematic depictions of the *Phenomenology*, lies, then, not so much in their "organicity" or dialectical necessity as in their application of categories of rhetorical transformation, as acquired by particular individuals in their *Bildung*, to the representation and development (*Bildung*) of the "universal Spirit."

Rhetorical Hermeneutics in the World of *Bildung*

The table of contents of the *Phenomenology* assists the reader in locating a specific treatment of *Bildung*. Section vi b has the heading "The Spirit Alienated from Itself. *Bildung*" ("Der sich entfremdete Geist. Die Bildung"). However, even the subdivisions of the *Phenomenology* illustrate characteristic ambiguities connected to the concept of *Bildung*. The term *Bildung* appears both in the general title of a major stage of the Spirit's development (vi b) and in the subtitle of a smaller unit on a special relationship between man and his produced world: "*Bildung* and Its Realm [Kingdom] of [Effective] Reality" ("Die Bildung und ihr Reich der Wirklichkeit"; vi b i a). *Bildung* both subsumes and parallels the sections on the Enlightenment, faith, and absolute freedom. *Bildung*, one might say after the previous analysis, functions at once as an overarching metaphor, linking the subsumed sections by a hidden identity, and a metonymy, standing in a contiguous or syntagmatic relationship to other segments of the narrative.[33] This kind of ambivalence structures the text and the conception of *Bildung* where it becomes an explicit topic in the *Phenomenology*.

The ambiguity of the subdivisions appears as well in the geographical metaphors that permeate the transitions in this part of the *Phenomenology*. The development of Spirit is presented as a movement between seemingly well-demarcated worlds, lands, empires, kingdoms and realms (*Welt, Land, Reich*). The "World of Common Morality" (*Welt der Sittlichkeit*) gives way to the "Land of *Bildung*," which will in turn be left for the "Land of Moral Consciousness" (p. 362). Within these larger units, the "Realm or Kingdom of the Real World" (*Reich der wirklichen Welt*) passes into (*übergeht in*) "the Realm of Faith and Pure Insight" (*das Reich des Glaubens und der reinen Einsicht*) in the same way as (*wie . . . so*) "absolute freedom," which refers to the revolution in France (*Frank*reich) passes from its "effective reality . . . into a foreign country" (*Wirklichkeit . . . in ein fremdes Land*; p. 441). Moreover, these "realms" and "kingdoms" (*Reiche*), which represent the self's relation to the social world, are subsumed by means of a catachresis or mixed metaphor, namely the notion of "the universal self" (*das allgemeine Selbst*; pp. 361–62). Similarly, the "World of *Bildung*" stands opposed to the "unreal [ineffective] world of pure consciousness or thought" (*unwirkliche Welt des reinen Bewußtseins oder des Denkens*; p. 391). The very attempt to contain *Bildung* spatially leads to a copious display of geopolitical images that transgress their own borders.[34]

Although *Bildung* does not occupy a stable location within the proliferation of topographical images, it nonetheless fits into a temporal or historical scheme of cultural development. As was mentioned above, Hegel begins the history of the objective Spirit's self-representation (culture) with a condition of unity, an idealized image of the ancient Greek world (*Gestalt einer Welt*). He describes the state of harmony

33. Roman Jakobson, "Two Aspects of Language." See also Martin Swales, *The German Bildungsroman from Wieland to Hesse* (Princeton, N.J.: Princeton University Press, 1978). He characterizes the conflict inherent in *Bildung* as one between the *Nebeneinander* and the *Nacheinander* of experience, and he sees the ambiguity in Hegel arising from the attitude toward contemporary reality (p. 21).

34. See Wim van Dooren, "Der Begriff der Bildung in der *Phänomenologie des Geistes*," in *Hegel-Jahrbuch* (1973). He refers in a similar, though far more general, way to this constant confusion: "In the Preface the *Bildung* of the world is discussed, in the Introduction the *Bildung* of consciousness, and in a later chapter (VI B) the world of *Bildung*" (p. 63). *Bildung* could thus be seen as a "symbol" in the sense given the term by Ricoeur (*Freud and Philosophy: An Essay on Interpretation*, trans. Denis Savage [New Haven, Conn.: Yale University Press, 1970]): "The ambiguity of symbolism is not the lack of univocity, it is rather the possibility of carrying and engendering opposed interpretations, each of which is self-consistent."

prior to *Bildung*: "The whole is a calm balance of all parts and each part is an indigenous spirit that does not seek satisfaction beyond the whole but finds it within itself because it thrives on this very balance with the whole.—This balance can come to life, however, only after some inequality arises within the whole and it is brought back to equality by means of *justice*" (p. 340). One invisible principle of balance unites the disparate parts of Greek culture and creates a metaphoric identification. But then a conflict between the family and the state (as depicted in *Antigone*) disrupts the unity and harmony of this image and creates the Roman "Condition of Legality" (*Rechtszustand*) in which artificial, man-made law replaces the organic identifications of the Greek social bond. Society becomes a mere collection of atomized individuals equal but separate under the law: "The universal, which has been split into the atoms of the independently manifold individuals, this dead Spirit is an *equality*, in which *all* have validity only as *each and every one*, that is, as *persons*" (p. 355). The individual, legally defined "person" evolves in a state of opposition to the others. The person lives in a state of alienation. The particular nature of this alienation, and of the individual's attempts to overcome it, occupies Hegel's discussion of *Bildung*. The "world of *Bildung*" thus not only takes up an ambivalent spatial location but also constitutes within the temporal scheme an inherently self-alienated situation of consciousness torn between a lost and a regained harmony.

But what is the temporal structure of *Bildung*? In the last section we considered *Bildung* a relationship of transference between two discourses and analyzed only the "spatial" difference between the literal and figurative levels of signification which make up the different *Bilder* of the *Phenomenology*. Temporality entered our considerations only insofar as these *Bilder* have been strung together by Hegel to form a "story," (*Geschichte*), whose narrative structure follows the "archetypal plot" of tropological transformations. Here, however, we must consider that the two discourses making up any *Bild* also stand in a temporal relationship to each other and that the story of the *Phenomenology* is also a "history of the *Bildung* of the world."[35] Behind the figurative

35. In traditional approaches to rhetoric, figures are understood in strictly spatial terms; a trope is a "turn" to another meaning and a "displacement" from literal to figurative sense (or in French an *écart*). Recently, however, Jacques Derrida has added a radically new dimension to rhetorical theory, the fourth dimension of temporality. Rhetoric (textuality in general) is an example not just of "spatial" difference between meanings, but also of temporal difference. He has thus coined the neologism *différance* to indicate the act of deferring which accompanies the differential relations without which there would be no meaning. He thus points to the paradox: The very conditions for meaning make its presence impossible. Derrida's focus on the temporal aspects of differ-

discourse of each of Hegel's *Bilder* stands a transferred historical discourse. The movement of *Bildung* sketched out in the *Phenomenology* thus traces out, as if between the universal Spirit and its Other, between the Spirit and the letter of its representation, an individual's development in relation to foreign discourse from harmony through alienation to renewed harmony.

The following analysis will develop Hegel's theory of *Bildung* in terms of both hermeneutics and rhetoric. That is, it will demonstrate that for Hegel the hermeneutics of tradition building and the development of individuality within a world of predefined discourse take place through a process of rhetorical *Bildung*. The analysis will first consider the thematic discussion of *Bildung* in section VI B to see how Hegel assigns to this concept the category of "eloquence" or "rhetoric" (*Beredsamkeit*), which, by association, applies to the entire work as well. Then the analysis will pursue formal issues, namely, the basic structure of this chapter as a literal and figurative translation of a masterwork from the Western tradition, *Rameau's Nephew*, by Diderot. In this way we can see the reflexive structure behind the rhetorical hermeneutics of *Bildung* since this section of the *Phenomenology* enacts in its rhetorical form the theory of rhetoric as transmission of tradition which it thematizes. The analysis concludes with a brief discussion of the overall significance of this reflexive form for the *Phenomenology* in order to confirm Gadamer's statement that Hegel worked out the concept of *Bildung* more than any other philosopher, not just in the thematic sense implied by Gadamer but in the rhetoric of Hegel's own system. The "double expressions" that make up the *Bilder* in this gallery contain the hermeneutical temporal structure that allows an individual to appropriate the forms of the past by giving himself over to them in his rhetorical *Bildung*. Individuality becomes inextricably linked to a process of self-representation.

Given the *pars pro toto* synecdoche that characterizes the ambivalent location of *Bildung* in the *Phenomenology*—as a subsection but also as the entire narration of the system—a rhetorical reading of this chapter carries with it consequences for the understanding of the enterprise of Hegelian *Wissenschaft*. For if the entire system is the history of *Bildung*, and if it can be shown that *Bildung* according to section VI B is the temporal "rhetoric of the Spirit," then the *Phenomenology* is not just a

---

ence is related to (in spite of differences) the hermeneutic focus on tradition as a precondition for meaning and interpretation. The following discussion uses rhetoric to work with both the poststructuralist and hermeneutic positions.

series of figurative world pictures but also a series of interpretive translations of traditional discourses. The *Phenomenology* attains the status of *Wissenschaft* since it masters in its own representation the rhetorical forms of earlier self-understandings.

To reach forward to the conclusions of Hegel's analysis of the world of *Bildung*: The state of alienation which is the precondition of *Bildung* in modern society takes on a specific form in the language of that society; the alienated individual attempts to overcome alienation by mastering the linguistic and rhetorical conventions of the surrounding society; at the highest state of *Bildung* the individual becomes a kind of master rhetorician whose "individuality" consists in the ability to adopt any discourse. Hegel writes: "This alienation (*Entfremdung*) . . . occurs only in *language*, which appears here in its proper significance" (p. 376). Hegel calls this state the "language of disunity" (literally, "tornness," *Sprache der Zerrissenheit*; p. 384), for it reflects the disintegrated state of, and the individual's position within, society. The individual must strive through *Bildung* to attain a "self-identity in the absolute disunity" (*Sichselbstgleichheit in der absoluten Zerrissenheit*; pp. 384–85), a personal voice in a preformed world of discourse. The individual with the greatest *Bildung* creates an identity by appropriating the multiple identities available in the realm of social intercourse, that is, by learning to speak the "discourse of this confusion clear to itself, . . . this open and self-conscious rhetoric of the spirit of *Bildung*" (*Rede dieser sich selbst klaren Verwirrung, . . . die offene und ihrer selbst bewußte Beredsamkeit des Geistes der Bildung*; p. 387). Let us work through Hegel's argumentation to see how he arrives at this concept of rhetorical *Bildung* which parallels the traditional pedagogical theories and practices of *imitatio, translatio,* and *aemulatio.*

The process of alienation and reestablishment of a lost identity begins with the state of discrete individuals. Each individual opposes not only the other individuals but also the "world" as such. Hegel describes this alienated state: "that spirit, whose self is absolute discrete, opposes to itself its own content like a hard reality (*Wirklichkeit*), and the world has here the determination of being something external, the negative of self-consciousness" (p. 359–60). But for Hegel the opposition between individual consciousness and its external world is by no means static. He had criticized Fichte in his earlier Jena essays, for example, for positing an unresolvable opposition between the "ego" and "nonego", and so he cannot allow his own dichotomy to stand unmediated. Rather, for Hegel the two sides of the opposition—the individual self-consciousness and "the world" (or effective reality)—actually depend on and influence each other.[36] They are, in a sense, "in motion" since the one helps produce or constitute the other: "But the existence of this world, as well as the reality of self-consciousness, is grounded on the movement according to which self-consciousness alienates and externalizes its personality (*seiner Persönlichkeit sich entäußert*), thereby bringing forth a world that it relates to as a foreign object over which it now must gain control. But the expressed denial of its being-for-itself is already the creation of reality, and through such expressed denial (*Entsagung*) it comes to control reality" (p. 363). This passage, located at the beginning of the section :"*Bildung* and Its Realm of [effective] Reality," offers an overview of Hegel's hermeneutical dialectics, and the interpretation of the major concepts in this description is of great significance for his theory of *Bildung* and the formation of the *Phenomenology*. This self-alienating "movement" between individual and world, in which the former loses him or herself in the latter in order to gain mastery over it, is identified with *Bildung* and hence with the form of Hegel's entire system.

The dominant interpretation of this dialectical process of externalization emphasizes the economic connotations of the term *Entäußerung*": "renunciation, parting with, alienation [of property]."[37] Marx, Lukács, and Adorno, for example, have used this economic sense of alienation to explain *Bildung* in dialectical-materialist terms. For them, *Bildung* is the formation of the external world as the product of the worker's labor, the dispossession from the created object, the education that arises from seeing an objective projection of the self in the produced world, and the final revolution to win back the produced world for the working self.[38] This interpretation of "alienation", and by

---

36. See above, chap. 3, on Hegel's criticisms of Fichte's maintenance of oppositions or *Entgegensetzung* (both in the *Differenzschrift* and "Glauben und Wissen"). Actually, Fichte also sees a dynamic relationship between the *Ich* and the *Nicht-Ich* which he tries to formulate in the third principle of the *Wissenschaftslehre* (*das Prinzip der Teilbarkeit*). Moreover, the concept of the ego's "self-positing" is intended to overcome the dilemmas of reflection philosophy which Hegel points out here. See Henrich, "Fichte's 'Ich'" (*Selbstverhältnisse*). It belongs to Hegel's consistent "misreadings" of Fichte, however, to attribute to him a strict, unresolved opposition (closely paralleling the earlier Kantian or "Jewish" *Mißbildung*). Thus, Hegel's approach in terms of content is quite Fichtean, in spite of the apparently anti-Fichtean rhetoric.

37. *The New Cassell's German Dictionary* (New York: Funk and Wagnalls, 1962): *Entäußerung*.

38. Marx defines *Entäußerung* strictly in terms of the worker's relationship to his product: "The alienation of the worker in his product means not only that his work becomes an object, an external being, but also that it exists outside of him, independent, foreign (*fremd*) to him and becomes an independent power facing him, [and] that the life he had given to the object confronts him hostilely and strangely." *Ökonomisch-phi-

extension *Bildung*, as a phenomenon of political economy can certainly be supported by numerous passages in the *Phenomenology* since Hegel uses many images taken from the realm of work, household, and economics.[39] However, the economic interpretation neglects another, more pervasive linguistic reference in Hegel's argument. That linguistic reference becomes clear if one considers the concept of *Entäußerung* (alienation and externalization) more literally as a kind of *Äußerung* (expression).[40]

In the passage just quoted describing the "existence of this world," Hegel uses words in a powerfully ambiguous manner. On the one hand, the passage seems abstract and it is unclear to what it might refer. On the other, many of the terms are very concrete and can be interpreted literally, even etymologically. For example, the "[effective] reality (*Wirklichkeit*) of self-consciousness" implies the individual's *wirken* and *Werk*, the products and effects of consciousness on objects; and the "personality" (*Persönlichkeit*) echoes the atomized, legally defined "persons" of post-Roman, codified society. Moreover, the two

---

losophische Manuskripte, "Die entfremdete Arbeit," in *Marx-Engels Werke* (Berlin: Dietz, 1968), p. 512. To the extent that Hegel may (does!) differ from this usage, he is then criticized for lack of clarity and mysticism (p. 573).

Lukács repeats and expands Marx's analysis by uncovering three usages of the word *Entäußerung* (which he considers the *Schlüsselbegriff* to the *Phenomenology*): "First, the complicated subject-object relationship that is linked with each kind of work, with every economical and social activity of man. . . . Second, it is a question of the specific capitalistic form, of that which Marx later would call fetishism. . . . Third, there is a broad philosophical generalization of this concept: Alienation then means the same as thingness (*Dingheit*) or objectness (*Gegenständlichkeit*); it is the form in which the history of the coming-into-being of objectness is represented philosophically as a dialectical impulse (*Moment*) on the path of the identical subject-object via 'alienation' [and] back to itself." *Der junge Hegel* (Berlin: Aufbau, 1954), pp. 614ff. Lukács, following Marx, rejects the third meaning as *Mystifizierung*.

39. The introduction to the chapter is permeated with direct references to and metaphors taken from the economic sector: "work" (*Werk*), "power" (*Macht*), "household/economy" (*Haushaltung*), "utensils" (*Gerätschaften*), "property" (*Eigentum*), "business" (*Geschäft*), "the useful" (*das Nützliche*). It is precisely this terminology that impressed Adorno: "The Hegel of the *Phenomenology*, to whom the consciousness of the Spirit as living activity and of its identity with the real social subject was less problematic then it was to the late Hegel, recognized, if not in theory, then surely on the strength of the language, the spontaneous Spirit as work." *Aspekte der Hegelschen Philosophie* (Frankfurt am Main: Suhrkamp, 1957), p. 26.

40. Hegel himself writes: "Speech and work are external expressions in which the individual no longer holds on to himself and owns himself, but rather lets the inner come completely outside of itself and surrenders/reveals the same to the Other" ("Sprache und Arbeit sind Äußerungen, worin das Individuum nicht mehr an ihm selbst sich behält und besitzt, sondern das Innere ganz außer sich kommen läßt und dasselbe Anderem preisgibt"; p. 235).

central concepts—*sich entäußern* and *Entsagung*—imply in this literal interpretation that the world created by individual self-consciousness is one it projects by the ways it expresses itself (*sich äußern*) and by what it says (*sagen*). This prefatory passage thus implies that Hegel is about to describe how the individual confronts a world of foreign forms already created either by the individual or others, and then reappropriates those forms in order to gain power in the world. Most important, those forms are linguistic in nature, they are expressions, modes of speaking, discursive representations of consciousness. *Bildung* is the individual's only means of mastering those forms: "The means, through which the individual here has value and effective reality (*Geltung und Wirklichkeit*), is *Bildung*; . . . [the individual] has as much reality and power as he has *Bildung*" (p. 364). *Bildung* allows the individual to be effective and thus literally real, for reality (*Wirklichkeit*) depends on the individual's effect (*Wirkung*) in the world.

If we recall that rhetoric has traditionally been defined as the art of effective speaking, then we begin to see the connection between the individual's *Bildung* to "effective reality" through alienation and externalization (*Entäußerung*) and an individual's mastery of rhetorical modes of expression through exercises in *imitatio*, *translatio*, and *aemulatio*. In order to clarify this connection, we must make explicit the rhetorical nature of this "world of *Bildung*," that is, we must see how this world consists less of subjects, objects, concepts, and abstract categories than of concrete rhetorical phenomena. We must see how the topic at hand (*Sache*) of the Spirit at this stage is what in the Neohumanist tradition is called a *geistiger Gegenstand* (an ideational or spiritual object), a codified piece of discourse.[41]

In this section Hegel paints the picture of a real social world. When an individual is thrust into that world its forms seem strange at first, even though those forms originally resulted from the work of other individuals: "This [real world], although it has come into being through individuality, is immediately alien to self-consciousness and has for it the form of unshaken reality" (p. 365).[42] The individual enters a world of conventions that no longer seem "merely" conven-

41. See chap. 5, below, for the theory of the *geistiger Gegenstand* (mental, ideational, spiritual object) proposed by Friedrich Niethammer.

42. Werner Becker, *Hegels Phänomenologie des Geistes: Eine Interpretation* (Stuttgart: Kohlhammer, 1971). He points out the mixture of abstract and concrete, literal and etymological, connotations in these passages. For example: "The idealist opposition = objectness (*Gegensätzlichkeit = Gegenständlichkeit*) appears as the 'reality' that has not yet been mastered by the 'individual'" (p. 121).

tional since they have taken on the meaning of an "effective reality" external to consciousness, what Hegel earlier called "the given," or *das Positive*. The individual must learn to master this world through *Bildung* so that he can adopt the forms of the world for his own purposes (p. 365). But what do the forms, the power, and the conventions of this world look like?

Extending the basic ambiguity of his language between descriptions of concrete phenomena and explanations in abstract terminology, Hegel's depiction of the "world of *Bildung*" modulates between historical reality and logical principles. His analysis begins with the individual cast into an abstract opposition to the world. The individual first reacts by calling whatever can overcome this confrontation in the individual's favor "good" (*gut*) and whatever maintains it "bad" (*schlecht*) (p. 366). That is, whatever establishes equality and identity (*Gleichheit*) between individuals and the world is good; whatever increases the tensions and difference (*Ungleichheit*) is bad. These judgments (*Urteile*) seem to be derived logically from a basic principle, for, according to the law of noncontradiction, identity is "right" (or good), and nonidentity is "wrong" (or bad). But actually they refer to something much more concrete. Rather than being derived from logic, they result from an individual's values in eighteenth-century absolutist society. The power that maintains order in society (*Staatsmacht*) is good; that which leads to rivalry and inequality (*Reichtum*) is bad. Society, as a system of oppositions after the Roman *Rechtszustand*, consists of a formal hierarchy in which the individual must find or make for himself an appropriate place. Depending on their basic attitude toward seeking out a place for themselves in society (and thereby creating a sense of social self), individuals, according to Hegel, fall into two categories or "forms of consciousness" (*zwei verschiedene Gestalten des Bewußtseins*; p. 371). The one, "noble-minded consciousness" (*das edelmütige Bewußtsein*), strives to attach itself to the power of the state in order to reduce the inequality and rivalry of individual freedom. The other, "base consciousness" (*das niederträchtige Bewußtsein*), strives to attain the individual, arbitrary, necessarily unequal pleasures of riches. In both cases the individual consciousness faces alienation and tries to come to grips with it by defining his status in relation to the others.

At this point Hegel's argument takes a crucial turn. He defines the alienation these individuals confront as occurring in language: "This alienation (*Entfremdung*) occurs, however, only in *language*, which appears here in its proper significance" (p. 376). Through their "languages," the noble-minded and base individuals establish their positions in society.

They take on different rhetorical postures, different effective modes of speaking in the world (*sich entäußern*) in order to attain an identity within the social hierarchy. The noble-minded individual identifies with the powers of the state by adopting a rhetoric of advice (*Rat*), gratitude (*Dank*), praise (*Preis*), favor (*Wohltat*) or flattery (*Schmeichelei*). By taking such a stance for the state, the noble-minded individual has a share in its power. In fact, the rhetoric of the noble-minded individual virtually creates the power of the monarch, that individual who provides a stable and univeral point of reference in society. Flattery makes the identity of the monarch both very real, since it is effective, and abstract (*geistig*), since it exists in language: "the language of flattery raises power to its purified universality; the instance produced by language, by this existence of purified spirit, is a cleansed self-identity—the *monarch*" (p. 378). The noble-minded individual thereby creates an effective "identity" for himself by employing rhetoric to identify with and create the state's power.

Opposed to this, the base individual does not seek to establish a single position in society as adviser, praiser, or flatterer. Rather, he recognizes the inequality of positions and thrives on their variety by learning to adopt as many of them as possible. He attains the highest form of *Bildung*: the ability to take on any position in effective speech. The base individual finds "self-identity" in the ability so speak a "witty and ingenious language" (*geistreiche Sprache*; p. 390) appropriate for any situation. More significant, the base individual, who is aware that it is impossible to escape this process of identity formation through position taking, penetrates the postures of others and attains in *Bildung* the ability to understand and invert ironically their positions: "[The base individual] knows perfectly how to express each instance in opposition to every other, how to express inversions; he knows better than each instance, what each one is, regardless of the particulars" (p. 390). The base individual exists in society by learning to adopt various modes of speech. Hegel calls this shifting discourse the "language of disunity" (*Sprache der Zerrissenheit*), for it mirrors the alienated, disintegrated, and isolated modern world even as it strives to overcome it in its gesture of individuality. It exists as a true, painful, and highly paradoxical form of self-representation which creates a contradictory, self-alienated individual: "The language of disunity . . . is the perfected language and the true existing Spirit of this entire world of *Bildung*. This self-consciousness . . . is absolute, unmediated self-identity in absolute disunity, the pure mediation of pure self-consciousness with itself" (pp. 384–85).

The process of *Bildung* culminates in a language that comes to grips with the disintegrated world of alienation by reflecting, shaping, and inverting its many forms.[43] Hegel not only calls this language the "rhetoric" or eloquence (*Beredsamkeit*) of the Spirit but also gives it priority over the uniform language of imitative identification which the simple, noble-minded individual speaks: "If we oppose the discourse of this confusion clear only to itself to the discourse of that *simple, unified consciousness* about the true and the good, we see that the latter is monosyllabic compared to the open and self-conscious rhetoric of the Spirit of *Bildung*" (p. 387).

Hegel's discussion of *Bildung* began with a state of society in which the individuals are alienated from each other and from the external world. The individuals attempt to counter this alienation by objectifying themselves, projecting images of themselves onto the world. Although that act, which Hegel calls "alienation" or "externalization" (*Entäußerung*), has been interpreted in economic terms, we have seen that his terminological ambiguity allows for a literal interpretation stressing the linguistic character of the individual's relationship to the social world. In this view *Entäußerung* becomes the individual's means of attaining an identity and power in society by learning to adopt the modes of expression and rhetorical conventions dominating the society. With the highest form of alienation—rhetorical mastery of Otherness, that is, of all modes of expression and the ability to appropriate and invert any rhetorical position—the individual reaches the highest form of *Bildung*. The Spirit arrives at its true form only after its has passed through this process of self-loss (*Zerrissenheit*) in the language of others. Whereas the simplest form is attained by the noble-minded individual's identifications (*imitatio*), genuine mastery (*aemulatio*) can be achieved only through self-conscious interpretation of given forms (*translatio*). The stages of internalization, transformation, and recreation of social conventions and traditional forms lead the individual to a self-identity that contains within itself a temporal, hermeneutical and rhetorical structure of mediation. The Spirit's present form, its identity through self-representation, includes, indeed is constituted by, the reformulations of recorded forms from the past.

Given the self-reflexive nature of Hegel's concept of representation in the *Phenomenology*, it should come as no surprise that Hegel structures his discussion of *Bildung* narratively according to the very princi-

43. It may seem peculiar that Hegel provides such a positive evaluation of a "negative" concept like *Zerrissenheit*. However, in the *Bildung* of consciousness the disruption of normal discourse is a necessary stage. During his years in Jena Hegel wrote the following aphorism: "A mended sock is better than a torn one; not so consciousness" ("Ein geflickter Strumpf ist besser als ein zerrissener; nicht so das Bewußtsein"); "Aphorisms," *Theorie-Werkausgabe*, vol. 3, p. 553.

ples he outlines as the meaning of *Bildung* (or vice versa). That is, his argument about discursive appropriation has the form of a hidden textual dialogue, a translation and interpretation of a text from the past—Diderot's *Rameau's Nephew*—into a different mode of discourse. On the one hand, Hegel employs Diderot's text as a kind of *Bild* to illustrate a stage in the abstract unfolding of the Spirit; on the other, Hegel uses his own philosophical diction to raise Diderot's text to the level of universal abstraction. The techniques he had employed in Bern and Frankfurt have reached their philosophical fruition. In his discussion of *Bildung*, Hegel merges two forms of discourse in order to create a *Bild* that, according to the *Aesthetics*, has the form of a "double expression." In the section of the *Phenomenology* on *Bildung* as the rhetorical mastery of discourses, Hegel himself appropriates a literary text for his own philosophical arguments. The self-reflexive structure of *Bildung*, the agreement between content and form, results, first, from the temporality inherent in the notion of a *Bild*, since its double discourse derives from a process of *Bildung*; and, second, from the nature of Hegel's own *Bildung* since he came to master the Spirit's forms by a process of rhetorical *exercitatio*. The way Hegel hermeneutically and rhetorically appropriates a text from the Western tradition for his discussion of *Bildung* is indeed paradigmatic for the *Bildung* of the entire *Phenomenology*.

Hegel became aware of Diderot's work *Rameau's Nephew* in 1805 when he was well into writing the *Phenomenology*. Goethe introduced the text to Germany that year, appropriately enough by publishing a translation (*Rameaus Neffe*) from a rediscovered manuscript.[44] For Goethe, Diderot's text was significant because of its moral and *rhetorical* intentions. He says explicitly in the notes accompanying his translation: "The rhetorical (*rednerische*) and moral intention [of this masterpiece] is manifold."[45] Goethe believes that Diderot was able to unite these two

44. I shall refer to Goethe's translation: Denis Diderot, *Rameaus Neffe—Ein Dialog*, aus dem Manuskript übersetzt von Johann Wolfgang Goethe (1804–5) (Stuttgart: Reclam, 1967).

45. Ibid., p. 128. Goethe writes in a letter to Joseph Stanislaus Zauper of the importance of translating Diderot (and Cellini) in terms that emphasize the hermeneutic dimension of using translation to bridge the gap between the self (German) and the foreign (French) Other: "Also be thankful because of Cellini and Rameau. I have brought [translated] both these strange characters over here so that one might become aware of the most foreign in German circles. If such representations are read in the original, they appear entirely different and force us into completely foreign circles in order to enjoy and use them to any extent; in translation, however, we are helped as at a business fair, where the merchant from the farthest away brings us his wares. In both cases I have attempted to help according to the need." Quoted from Erika Fischer-Lichte, "Probleme der Rezeption klassischer Werke," in *Deutsche Literatur zur Zeit der Klassik*, ed. K. O.

aspects so masterfully because he captured the social milieu of the modern world as only a Frenchman could. As Goethe says: "The Frenchman is a social (*geselliger*) being, he lives, functions effectively (*wirkt*), stands, and falls in society."[46] Goethe thus traces Diderot's "rhetorical and moral intentions" back to a conception of society as the force motivating the actions of its individual members. Both Goethe and Hegel were fascinated by the way Diderot depicted the rhetoric and morality of an individual in modern society, since in their reception of Diderot the rhetoric and morality of society is the effective reality for the individual.

Diderot's text consists of a dialogue between an "I" (a philosopher) and a "he" (the musician, Rameau's nephew) interpreted with narrative passages describing the partners. The topics the partners discuss cover numerous areas of eighteenth-century French culture: music, politics, the scene of contemporary writers, schemes to earn money, interaction between the sexes, and more. The foremost goal of the dialogue is to depict the character of Rameau's nephew by presenting his rhetorical skills and modes of social discourse in action. Rameau's nephew characterizes himself as a person without a unified character; he inhabits a literally rhetorical world and thrives in it by taking on the appropriate posture for any situation. He says:

> The devil take me, if I really know what I am. On the whole, I have a spirit round as a sphere and a character fresh as a meadow, never false, when it's to my advantage to be true, and never true, if I find it somewhat useful to be false. I call things the way they come into my mouth; all the better if it turns out reasonable; and if it's inappropriate, it usually goes unnoticed. I speak freely and have never worried about thinking neither before, during, nor after my speech. Furthermore, no one seems insulted by this approach.[47]

At one point the nephew implies that all other members of his society act in basically the same way, with the possible exception of the monarch, who, he claims, occupies a stable position and need not take on different poses. But then the nephew is consoled when the philosopher points out that even the monarch must act according to the rules and roles of social rhetoric. For, he argues, "Whosoever needs another has

---

Conrady (Stuttgart: Reclam, 1977), p. 126. It is interesting to note that Goethe uses an *economic* metaphor to discuss a hermeneutical and rhetorical act of translation, not unlike Hegel's discussion of the transfer of "property" in the love metaphor of his Frankfurt manuscripts.

46. Diderot, *Rameaus Neffe*, p. 130.
47. Ibid., p. 49.

a lack and must adopt a position."[48] It is interesting that the otherwise unrhetorical philosopher justifies the universality of rhetorical discourse within the reality of the intersubjectively effective world.

The "rhetorical and moral intention" of Diderot's dialogue consists in portraying the various oratorical stances that the nephew takes on. The nephew delivers lengthy monologues, performs pantomimic theatrics (described by the narrator), and sings musical arias. The nephew adopts every imaginable style required in French society to have an effect on reality, to "be someone." His morality changes with the rhetorical situation, and vice versa. The dialogue reaches a high point when he gives a long series of operatic presentations in which he "mounted together and intermixed thirty arias of the most diverse character, Italian, French, tragic, comic; at first with a deep bass he descended into hell, and then he tightened his throat and tore the airy heights with a falsetto, . . . alternating between madness and calm, domination and derision."[49] His performance is so moving that it attracts a large audience of actors and passersby. His inspired ability to take on these roles is characterized in terms that recall both Longinus's description of imitative creativity and Hegel's definition of alienated or disintegrated language: "[He was] seized by an . . . alienation of the spirit, an enthusiasm bordering on insanity" ("[Er war] ergriffen von einer . . . Entfremdung des Geistes, einem Enthusiasmus . . . nahe an der Tollheit").[50] The nephew, then, is the master of modern styles, of what Hegel calls the "rhetoric (Beredsamkeit) of the Spirit of Bildung."

It is no wonder that Hegel frames his entire depiction of the world of Bildung within two indirect citations from Goethe's translation of Rameau's Nephew. In the first, he refers to a passage in which the nephew criticizes what he calls a social "type" (espèce). Hegel writes of this term that "of all nicknames, it is the most horrible; for it signifies mediocrity and expresses the highest degree of disdain" (pp. 364–65). These "types" are so despicable for both the nephew and Hegel not for the reason one might think—that they are only "types" and not "individuals"—but, rather, because a "type" falsely thinks (meinen) he has an individual personality and thereby fails to recognize that he, like everyone else, must take his personality from the social roles at his disposal. Only an "individual," like the nephew, who lives consciously according to the rhetorical conventions of the society and who thus does not

48. Ibid., p. 92. Recall as well the association in the Jena essays between Bildung and the "need/lack" (Bedürfnis) of a time. Both one's cultivation or education and one's needs in a society or intersubjective medium demand some form of rhetorical skill.
49. Ibid., p. 72. Hegel quotes this passage in modified form, p. 387.
50. Ibid.

worry about a *false* "individuality," can maintain himself, Hegel says, "in this world, in which only the self-alienating and self-expressing and thus universal attains effective reality" (*in dieser Welt, worin nur das Sichselbstentäußerende und darum nur das Allgemeine Wirklichkeit erhält*; p. 364). In the second quotation from Diderot's dialogue, which acts like a closing parenthesis on this discussion of *Bildung*, Hegel uses the high point of the nephew's moving operatic ecstasy to describe the highest form of *Bildung*. Hegel calls the nephew's display of rhetoric "the Spirit's discourse by and about itself, . . . thus the inversion of all concepts and realities" (*die Rede des Geistes von und über sich selbst . . . also die Verkehrung aller Begriffe und Realitäten*; pp. 386–87). Thus, the citations from Diderot's text which frame Hegel's analysis of *Bildung* praise and depict Rameau's nephew's ability to take on external forms in his attempt to attain universal and truly individual expression.[51]

What comes between these quotations in the *Phenomenology*, the *Bild* within the frame, can now be seen not just as Hegel's "philosophical" analysis of the concept of *Bildung* but as his rhetorical reformulation of Diderot's text into philosophical terms. It is itself an act of rhetorical *Bildung* since Hegel employs one of the standard methods of *exercitatio* which he had practiced as part of his own training in school rhetoric: the rewriting of a dialogue into expository prose.[52] As in his theological manuscripts from Bern and Frankfurt, Hegel generates the arguments in this section of the *Phenomenology* by translating a text into another form. Hegel's abstract "forms of consciousness"—the "noble-minded" or "simple" and the "base" individual—generalize the partners in Diderot's dialogue, the "philosopher" and the "nephew." The topics that interest Hegel in his discussion—judgments of good and bad, riches versus political power, the monarch, flatterers, ingratiators—correspond to the topics of interest in Diderot's dialogue. The seemingly atemporal and aspatial "world" and "effective reality" (*Wirklichkeit*) of *Bildung* are abstractions from Diderot's description of mid-eighteenth-

51. Here we see a significant aspect of Hegel's theory of the individual. It is derived from a fundamental adherence to the tradition of rhetorical *Bildung* and hence grapples with the paradox of how individuality *results from* a state of nonindividuality. Although Manfred Frank has explored the various philosophical relations between the universal and the individual (especially playing Schleiermacher against Hegel in *Das individuelle Allgemeine*), he has not, to my knowledge, sought the origins of this position in Hegel's concept of *Bildung*. Such an analysis of the origins of Hegel's position in terms of rhetorical *Bildung* helps explain how Hegel developed a view of the individual as self-representation.

52. A technique we encountered in both the excerpts from the Stuttgart years and the theological manuscripts. See Lausberg, *Handbuch*, pars. 1093–1104 on writing exercises, as well as Quintilian, *Institutio Oratoria*, x.

century Paris and the means of becoming an effective member of French society. The ambiguity of Hegel's discourse, which modulates between pseudo-deductions of logical categories and literal or etymological wordplays, derives from the ambiguity inherent in his method of composition, for like an extended metaphor (*translatio*), Hegel's translation of Diderot's dialogue has the form of a "double expression." The doubleness is the "product of an extensive transformation of manifold forms of *Bildung*" (p. 19), since both the individual and the universal Spirit can attain expression only after encountering other forms and successfully mastering a process of becoming Other (pp. 19, 25). In particular, the reality of the Spirit is only possible if it alienates itself and confronts itself in effective self-representations that it transforms and finally appropriates.

Generalizing from the discussion of figurative transformations in the first section of this chapter ("The *Elocutio* of the *Phenomenology*") and from this discussion of Hegel's translation of Diderot, we can see how *Bildung* not only shapes the structure of the entire *Phenomenology* but also inserts it into a textual tradition. If the system consists of a "gallery of images (*Bildern*)" and if each *Bild* consists of a foreign discourse translated into the philosophical terminology of scientific knowledge, then it should be possible to translate the double images back into their original locutions. In fact, much criticism of the *Phenomenology* has undertaken precisely this philological investigation of source texts. In a great many of cases Hegel makes the philologist's task relatively simple by giving clear indications of the translated texts. (In the terms of *elocutio*, one would say that in a great many of the *Bilder* as acts of metaphorical transference—*translatio*—the connection between "literal" and "figurative" signification is made clear, as in allegories where pointers are required to guide the viewer or reader to the intended level of interpretation.)[53] There are the well-known cases of Hegel's reformulations of the skeptic and stoic philosophers, Kantian and Fichtean ethics, Sophocles' *Antigone*, and more. But there are other cases that had baffled interpreters for longer, like the Schlegel critique in the section on morality, or the reworking of Novalis's (and other romantics') conception of the Middle Ages in the section on the unhappy

53. Recall Hegel's comments in the lectures on aesthetics (*Theorie-Werkausgabe*, vol. 13, p. 523) on Goethe's poem "Mahomets Gesang," in which only the title indicates to the reader that the extended image of a powerful river corresponds allegorically to the rise of a religion. See also Paul de Man, *Allegories of Reading* (New Haven, Conn.: Yale University Press, 1979), in which he refers to painted allegories that require some artificial sign (often a word written onto the scene, like *charitas* or *lectio*) to force the reader or viewer to interpret beyond the literal (p. 77).

consciousness. My interest here, however, goes beyond such citation hunting and source studies. Such studies are based on the strictly spatial notion of intertextual relationships, which Hegel himself undermines when he tries to locate *Bildung*, since their authors believe in a one-to-one correspondence between texts that is merely "displaced" to a different level. Because none of these interpreters concentrates on the crucial sections on *Bildung*, all overlook the act of rhetorical interpretation that must have been accomplished as a precondition for the philosophical appropriation. The section on the concept of *Bildung* thus has a special priority.

Since Hegel himself calls the entire system the "[hi]story of *Bildung*," it would be insufficient to consider the section on this concept limited to an analysis of a particular time or place. That Hegel "translates" a source text from the French Enlightenment, and follows it with scenes from the late eighteenth century and Revolution, is clear from his references to Diderot. But the synecdochic transference to the entire *Phenomenology* shows that Hegel is employing a principle that relates and translates texts interpretively regardless of locations. By extension, then, the same transference allows the interpreter to depart from the specifics of the background texts to more general philosophical ideas. Although one might claim that this transference from particular works in the tradition to universal ideas is obvious (after all, Hegel is a philosopher, not a historian), it is significant to see that the actual mechanics of the transference are worked out in the analysis of the concept of *Bildung*. For this reason the self-reflexivity of the *Phenomenology* becomes particularly evident in the section on *Bildung*. Although each section of the *Phenomenology*, as a *Bild*, engages in the same rhetorical and hermeneutical process of alienation and appropriation (of texts), section VI B is unique in its thematization of its own textual construction. It is no wonder, then, that Hegel himself says that the Spirit arrives at this stage to its most genuine form of expression, its self-consciously ironic rhetoric. Language appears, he says as well, in its "proper form" (*eigentümlicher Gestalt*) in the world of *Bildung*, which would imply that the *Phenomenology*, as the history or story of *Bildung*, is the attempt to appropriate the languages of the past for the most appropriate forms of expression in the present. This rhetorical and hermeneutical reformulation of traditional texts for a present, more universal significance constitutes the driving textual mechanism of Hegel's philosophy of Spirit.

We have already considered the origins of this mechanism in Hegel's own intellectual development as a writer. Precisely because the concept of *Bildung* can be applied to Hegel's own education, it opens up the possibility for a historical understanding at yet another level. The process of self-alienation and identity building through disintegration in and of language, which Hegel describes in the section on *Bildung* and which he enacts there in reworking Diderot's dialogue, corresponds to the training he went through in his early years. His own self-alienation had begun already, as we saw in Chapter 1, with such exercises as keeping a diary in Latin, which turned the events of his own life into nothing but vignettes in imitated styles, and writing and saving his excerpts from the texts he read, which, as Rosenkranz pointed out, taught him to adopt another's position by adopting its language. As Hegel grew older his exercises grew more sophisticated, in part because the content and context became more complex—for example, thanks to his introduction in Tübingen to homiletic theory and practice as well as to the task of uniting Kantian ethics with biblical discourse. Not unlike Rameau's nephew, Hegel experimented with various modes of expression throughout his years in Bern and Frankfurt, always searching for a personal voice by copying, translating, and varying the voice of others. The main difference between the two is that what the nephew accomplished with his speech in society Hegel had to carry out in writing. The process of *Bildung*, however, is the same in both cases.

By viewing Hegel's discussion of *Bildung* in this way we can see how his concept of philosophical representation was fundamentally influenced by crucial rhetorical issues and how his philosophical response to these issues support, rather than reject, rationally grounded rhetoric. The key ideas and basic structure of Hegel's philosphy of *Bildung* can be seen as a continuation of the debates in rhetorical theory and practice concerning the paradoxical techniques of acquiring individuality, that is, concerning the tension between external acquisition of forms (*ars*) and internal inspiration to creation (*natura*).[54] Hegel confronted these issues in theory and in his writing practice during his early years, and these questions found their way into his philosophical formulations. In fact, one might make the radical claim that against his will Hegel was the greatest philosopher of rhetoric since the very concept of a "history of the *Bildung* of the world [Spirit]" transfers onto a metaphysical level the fundamental question of his own writing: how to

---

54. According to Lausberg, this tension is the foundation of rhetorical theory (*Handbuch*, pars. 1–10). The combination of both *ars* and *natura* leads to *scientia* (knowledge, *Wissen*). The goal of rhetorical and poetical theory from Cicero through the humanists to the Enlightenment was to guide the young orator or writer by means of artifice to a state of "natural" productivity. As an educational program, this process deserves the term *Bildung*, the naturalization of a conventional development. See Lawrence Manley, *Convention* (Cambridge, Mass.: Harvard University Press, 1982).

develop an independent voice out of the letters of the tradition. His is perhaps the greatest attempt since Cicero and the humanists to take the history of his own writing and style into account, both thematically and structurally. He offered a solution that rests not on organic develop-ment or genius but, rather, on mechanical appropriation and exercise. Thus, because Hegel requires an Other to attain understanding, he is just as "dialogic" as Diderot and their common model, Socrates; and yet he threatens always to collapse into monological dialectics since that Other becomes appropriated to his own discourse.[55] His relationship to the tradition and Otherness is fundamentally one of developing self-representation.

Dialectic and Dialogue

In the lectures on aesthetics Hegel defines one of the major roles of the orator as persuasion of the audience and differentiates the tech-niques of oratory from those of "science." Hegel writes that the orator must employ techniques that engage all the faculties of the partner in order to persuade him or her better:

> finally, he should not only address our scientific or otherwise rational thought, but should also move us to some conviction (*Überzeugung*) and may, in order to attain this goal, affect the entire person, the feelings, intuitions, etc. His content, namely, is not only the abstract side of the pure [naked, *bloß*] concept of the matter, which he hopes to interest us in, nor the abstract purpose, which he hopes to encourage us to work through, but also in large measure a certain reality and effective situa-tion (*Realität und Wirklichkeit*), so that while the representation (*Darstellung*) of the orator must on the one hand capture the substance of the matter, it must likewise, on the other hand, grasp this universal in the form of appearance (*Erscheinung*) and offer it to our concrete consciousness.[56]

55. See Hans Robert Jauß, "Der dialogische und der dialektische *Neveu de Rameau*—oder: wie Diderot Sokrates und Hegel Diderot rezipierte," in *Ästhetische Erfahrung und Literarische Hermeneutik* (Frankfurt am Main: Suhrkamp, 1982). Jauß emphasizes the difference between Diderot's literal and Hegel's pseudo-dialogue. Although Jauß has brought out numerous significant points in his Diderot interpretation (e.g., his emphasis on the nephew and the Socratic elements of the work), he seems to me not to do full justice to Hegel's reception of Diderot. The dialogic plays more of a role in Hegel's concept of *Bildung* than Jauß is willing to admit, perhaps because he does not want to relate his own notion of "aesthetic experience" to Hegel's concept of "dialectical experi-ence," which is, I would argue, essentially dialogic.

56. *Vorlesungen über die Ästhetik, Theorie-Werkausgabe*, vol. 13, p.262.

This definition is clearly based on the traditional characterization of rhetoric as the *ars persuadandi* whose goal is to move (*movere*) the audience first to accept the speaker-writer's position and so that the audience will act accordingly. Moreover, this definition, in its wording and implicit assumptions, seems to reformulate traditional distinctions between rhetoric and dialectic. In particular, the reference to the "side of the pure [naked, *bloß*] concept of the matter" recalls the classical domain of dialectic, the *res nudas*, as opposed to rhetoric's "clothing and decoration" of thought in language. A closer reading of this passage in terms of the traditions of rhetoric and dialectic shows, however, that the borders between these two disciplines are not as well defined for Hegel as one might think. In tacitly linking the two disciplines, in fact, he is more fully in keeping with the tradition of school rhetoric and dialectic than he himself admits. More precisely, the very ambiguity in the relationship between the two disciplines within Hegel's work demonstrates his reliance on this ambiguous tradition.

The traditional point of intersection between rhetoric and dialectic is the argumentative dialogue or *disputatio*, that is, the art of discovering, composing, and presenting ideas effectively to a partner to gain either the partner's or the audience's (perhaps judge's) approval. This dialogic aspect underlies Hegel's definition of the orator's task at least implicitly in the constant use of the first person plural pronoun (*wir, uns, unser*). Rhetoric is necessarily an intersubjective activity, for the speaker must become engaged with some Other. Neither Hegel's conception nor any rationally based rhetoric views the relationship between speaker and audience as unilateral, for the speaker must always take the other person into account, internalize the other position. A rhetoric that is aware of its dialogic nature borders immediately on any concept of dialectic which is aware of its argumentative character. Rüdiger Bubner comments on the origins of dialectics in Greek thought: "Dialectic comes, as is known, from διαλέγεσθαι and signifies the correct use of speech in dialogues."[57] For the pragmatic Sophists (whom, we shall see in the next chapter, Hegel considered the historical fathers of all philosophical *Bildung*) "correct" usage was determined by the partners while conversing and by the outcome of the dialogue.[58]

---

57. I am indebted in much of what follows to the discussion by Rüdiger Bubner, "Dialog und Dialektik oder Plato und Hegel," in *Zur Sache der Dialektik* (Stuttgart: Reclam, 1980), p. 124.

58. Since the basic tenet of the Sophists was a denial of any reality beyond the phenomenal world, they tended to place conventional laws higher than natural laws. Although this seems to deny any possibility of a search for truth—and the charge of radical relativism and nihilism is the typical one waged against the Sophists from Plato on—

Whoever "won" a debate obviously used the "correct" methods of argumentation as established by the rhetorical principles of persuasion. Plato and Aristotle shifted the site of criteria ever more outside of the dialogue itself to an external location in logic.[59] Cicero, however, who exercised at least as great an influence on the theory and practice of education in European culture, insisted on the relocation of dialectics inside rhetorical exchanges.[60]

The rhetorical handbooks used in Hegel's school responded to the classical tradition by highlighting the uncertain relation between the twin sisters of the *trivium*. Thus, we recall, Crusius's marginal amendation to Melanchthon's discussion of the distinction (*discrimen*) between rhetoric and dialectic: *non est stabile*.[61] The *res nudas* were held to be incomprehensible without the light and clothing of rhetoric, which made them available to a partner. Similarly, in both Ernesti's and Scheller's handbooks, correct usage must always take the particular situation and appropriate means of persuasion into account. This is why they both reject the mathematical method for philosophy. And even Kant unites these various strands in his philosophy by insisting on both a critical logic of "dialectic" to remove all "false appearance" (*falschen Schein*) from the realm of philosophy and on a rhetorico-dialogic meth-

---

intersubjective agreement and consensus do provide criteria for Sophist philosophy. On the concept of *usus*, see Lausberg, *Handbuch* (vol. 2, p. 833). It unites various elements within rhetorical theory: "1) on the general and specific uses of things by men . . . 2) on the practical exercise of art . . . 3) on relationships between men."

59. Plato, though a master of dialogue, was the first to separate dialogue, as a mode of discourse which justifies itself while unfolding, from dialectic. Dialectic for Plato becomes a "science needed as a guide on the voyage of discourse . . . to succeed in pointing out which kinds [of discourse] are consonant, and which are compatible with one another" (*Sophist*, 253c and d). For Plato, the "only person . . . to whom you would allow this master of dialectic" is the philosopher, "the pure and rightful lover of wisdom" (*Sophist*, 253e). Aristotle extended Plato's distinctions even further, first by separating rhetoric from dialectic in terms of nontruth versus truth, and then by even denying epistemological value to dialectic insofar as it dealt with the topoi used for credible and probable arguments for a popular audience (see the opening of the *Rhetoric*). Speech was no longer judged by its power to persuade partners in a dialogue but by the external measure of logic. Gadamer ("Hegel und die antike Dialektik," *Hegel-Studien* 1 [1961]) associates Hegel with pre-Socratic and Platonic dialectics rather than with Aristotle, thus linking Hegel more to the dialogue-oriented tradition (p. 74).

60. See, e.g., the opening paragraphs of *De Inventione* and *Topica*. Cicero sees the "invention" or discovery of persuasive arguments as temporally and logically prior to their "dialectical" judgment; that is, the latter is derived from the former. Since the "invention" of arguments is directly linked to means of persuasion (e.g. the discovery of the controversial aspects of a legal issue), and since *inventio* is one of the five *officia* of rhetoric, the Ciceronian tradition sees dialectics and rhetoric as inextricably linked.

61. Recall the discussion of Melanchthon's *Elementorum Rhetorices Libri Duo* above, chap. 1, pp. 79–83.

The Spirit and Its Letter

od for teaching and communicating the doctrines of reason: "For if someone wants to examine the reason of another, this can only take place dialogically (*dialogisch*), that is, in such a manner that teacher and student ask and answer each other *reciprocally*. The teacher guides the apprentice's line of thought by merely unfolding the disposition to certain concepts in the student by means of presented case studies (the teacher is the midwife of the student's thoughts)."[62] We could say that Hegel strives to make a consistent philosophical principle out of the unification of dialectic and rhetorical dialogism, whereas Kant merely juxtaposes them.[63]

It is significant that Hegel defines rhetoric in extremely broad terms in the *Aesthetics*. The distinction between rhetoric and scientific understanding (the "abstract side of the mere concept") becomes internal to rhetoric itself by Hegel's repetition of the qualifier "not only" (*nicht nur*): The orator *also must* rely on rational, dialectical techniques as part of his dialogic approach. Rhetoric, as in Cicero's conception, becomes a discipline that employs dialectic, specifically the theory of topics, in its search (*inventio*) for the appropriately rational arguments. It consists of the "universal and substantial." But, beyond dialectics, rhetoric links them to a form of appearance. This task of rhetoric relates it to the specific nature of modern *Bildung* according to the Preface of the *Phenomenology*, namely the reassociation of the universal to "the concrete and the manifold in the modes of being" (p. 37). It apparently even has the priority of appealing to the entire human being and not only to a limited number of faculties. Moreover, the notion of rhetoric's "effect" (*einwirken*) on the entire character of the partner relates it to the literal creation of a reality (*Wirklichkeit*) of effective discourse.

In the previous section we saw how the *Phenomenology* represents an individual's passing through rhetorical *Bildung* in order to master the forms of the social world; here we shall consider the precise ways these forms are employed intersubjectively to affect the consciousness of others. What we must investigate is the relationship between philoso-

62. Kant, *Metaphysik der Sitten*, "Methodenlehre," par. 50. The image of the philosopher as midwife, and the philosophical dialogue as an art of midwifery which which helps to bring out an idea indirectly by means of questions and answers dates back to Plato's dialogue, the *Theaetetus* (esp. pp. 149–52 and 210). As was pointed out in chap. 3, above, dialectic for Kant was linked to a method of *Kritik*, which he was striving to differentiate from the earlier rhetorical tradition.

63. Using the theory of Mikhail Bakhtin, which is one of the most recent formulations of this tradition of the dialogue, Hegel does for philosophical discourse what the novel did for literary discourse: He internalizes the dialogic nature of (the search for) knowledge. See Mikhail Bakhtin, *The Dialogic Imagination*, trans. and ed. Michael Holquist (Austin: University of Texas Press, 1972).

phy and dialectic on the one hand and rhetoric and dialogue on the other. Although each side has historically made the problematic, mutually exclusive claim that it contains the other, we shall analyze the dialectical strategies of Hegel's philosophy and traditional notions of a dialogue-based rhetoric as inseparable. As any writer must, he, the defender of the apparently anti-rhetorical *Sache selbst*, also searches for critical arguments with and against partners in a dispute for consensus and a unique, differentiated position. In fact, Hegel's concept of dialectic can be seen as a philosophical reflection on the nature of argumentative dialogue, which is the culmination of traditional rhetorical *Bildung*. In this way we shall see that Hegel's theory of philosophical representation, his "absolute knowledge" and *Wissenschaft der Dialektik*, internalize, recapitulate, and render abstract a paradoxical relationship between two conflicting disciplines.

The Introduction to the *Phenomenology* explains some key concepts that relate to the methods of Hegel's philosophy. It revolves around the definition of "experience" (*Erfahrung*) as a "dialectical movement" (*dialektische Bewegung*; p. 78). The concept of *Erfahrung* is central to the text since its original title, before it was changed on the basis of ideas from the final chapter and Preface, was *Wissenschaft der Erfahrung*. Moreover, the phrase "dialectical movement" (*dialektische Bewegung*), which characterizes experience, recalls the "formative and educating movement" (*bildende Bewegung*; p. 33), which leads to a state of scientific knowledge and which is depicted in the *Phenomenology*. In the Introduction, Hegel reflects on the representation of scientific knowledge as an unfolding dialectic, that is, he reflects on the rhetoric of dialectic. He concludes that the scientific system is a chain of "experiences," each of which makes possible dialectical movement, and all of which together constitute the process or history of *Bildung*. We shall see how the Introduction reformulates the basic rhetorical principle that philosophy consists of polemical dialogues among positions to effect a change of mind. Truly absolute philosophy, Hegel therefore implies, cannot avoid this rhetorical-disputational form; on the contrary, it must internalize and thematize the methods of developing effective argumentation.

The opening paragraphs of the Introduction indicate Hegel's approach of presenting a kind of argumentative dialogue with contemporary views of philosophy. He proposes three "natural representations" (*natürliche Vorstellung[en]*) of knowledge and its philosophical conceptualization: that a philosopher must start by talking about his "knowledge" (*Erkennen*) as a "tool" (*Werkzeug*); that the faculty of knowing is a "medium" through which the truth is seen; and that it may be of concern (*Besorgnis*) that a philosopher could err in the choice of means in the search for the truth (p. 68). By first dealing with other common ways of beginning, Hegel opens his discussion in the traditional form of an *exordium*, a form he later distances himself from when he writes the Preface. He establishes contact with the audience on its ground and grants the apparent reasonableness of its presuppositions (for example, "the concern seems justified"; p. 69). This acceptance of the others' positions is brief, however, for Hegel then rejects the rhetoric of "natural consciousness," that is, its "representations and manners of speaking" (*Vorstellungen und Redensarten*) "straight off" (pp. 70–71). He considers it hardly worth the effort to condemn them (*verwerfen*) and raises the criticism, traditionally used against rhetorical sophistry, that these "manners of speaking" are nothing but "deception" and "empty appearance" (*Betrug* and *leere Erscheinung*; p. 71). After dealing with these common rhetorical appearances of philosophy Hegel seems to want to disregard them totally. The Introduction thus opens at that paradoxical point of intersection between rhetoric and philosophy where critical, polemical arguments are "invented" against other systems even though philosophy can offer no reason for dealing with these systems in its search for the truth.

But Hegel then brings his own argument up short with an "arresting *Aber*."[64] He writes: "But scientific knowledge, because it enters the stage, is itself a phenomenal appearance; its entrance is not yet its existence in the detailed execution and expansion of its truth" ("Aber die Wissenschaft darin, daß sie auftritt, ist sie selbst eine Erscheinung; ihr Auftreten ist noch nicht sie in ihrer Wahrheit ausgeführt und ausgebreitet"; p. 71). Hegel reflects here on the problem with which he opened his discussion—the function of argumentative criticism. Yet whereas at first the one true philosophy could be distinguished from other forms, or "mere appearances," the very appearance of *Wissenschaft*, which, as we know, is a form and result of *Bildung* (pp. 31–33), is

64. The phrase is from Timothy Bahti, "The Indifferent Reader: The Performance of Hegel's Introduction to the Phenomenology," *Diacritics* (Summer 1981):70. Heidegger also sees this *Aber* as the turning point of the Introduction; see "Hegels Begriff der Erfahrung," in *Holzwege* (Frankfurt am Main: Vittorio Klostermann, 1950). Heidegger plays off the possible connotations of the word *Erscheinung* and concludes: "Scientific knowledge is rather in itself already appearance in the sole sense that it, as absolute knowledge, is the beam by which the absolute, the light of truth itself, illuminates us. The appearing out of this shining beam means: presence in the full luster of the representation presenting itself" (p. 159). Heidegger thus casts his discussion of the Introduction in terms of the model of representation and correctly sees Hegel's position within the paradoxes of that model (both presence and representation, thing and appearance). He does not trace these paradoxes back to the paradoxical relationships between rhetoric and philosophy, dialogue and dialectic.

now problematic since it places *Wissenschaft* at the same level as other *Erscheinungen*. *Wissenschaft* must be dealt with as a form of representation of knowledge. On the one hand, "scientific knowledge" lays claim to a position above other appearances of the truth, not to mention all other false appearances. On the other, *Wissenschaft* appears alongside its competitors and must come to grips with them on the same level of argumentative discourse. In the Introduction to the *Phenomenology* Hegel addresses the same problem he confronted in the Introduction to the *Kritisches Journal der Philosophie* on the essence of *Kritik*.[65] Philosophy must appear in a polemical-rhetorical struggle in which other forms of scientific "appearances" (*Erscheinungen*) must be revealed as *mere* appearance (*Schein*). It must enter the dialectic, which characterizes what Hegel calls the highest state of *Bildung* of the time: It must, *like* all other forms, differentiate itself from others without becoming *just like* them in being "just one other different appearance." In Hegel's words, *Wissenschaft* must simultaneously appear and attack its own status as appearance: "Scientific knowledge must free itself from this false appearance (*Schein*), and it can only do so by turning itself against it" (p. 71). Philosophy uses its status as appearance, it uses its rhetoric—for in the *Aesthetics* Hegel associates rhetoric with "form of appearance" (*Form der Erscheinung*)—to attack all other appearances of philosophy. The *Phenomenology* depicts the rise of the form of philosophy against competing forms, the gradual emergence of philosophical representation out of the criticism of others: "For this reason, the representation of knowledge as it appears will be undertaken here" ("Aus diesem Grunde soll hier die Darstellung des erscheinenden Wissens vorgenommen werden"; p. 72). The *Phenomenology* must both thematize its own formal structure, which consists of the means of representing knowledge for an other—that is, such traditional means as *inventio* and *disputatio*—and turn against itself in the spirit of *rhetorica contra rhetoricam*.

Hegel then reformulates this idea of the *Phenomenology* as a critique of other forms of philosophy in terms that might seem to mask the rhetorical or polemical nature of the criticism. The following work, he writes, will present consciousness on a path through a series of forms, formations, formulations (*Gestaltungen*; p. 72). The "movement" of consciousness through its formations and transformations he calls the [hi]story of its *Bildung*: "The series of formations, which consciousness

65. As we saw above in chap. 3, pp. 148–55, the essence of *Kritik* cannot be accounted for without at least implicit appeal to rhetoric. Since Hegel was striving to reject rhetoric explicitly, he was forced to introduce rhetorical argumentation without philosophical grounding to justify his use of criticism.

passes through along this path, is the detailed [hi]story of the *formative education* of consciousness itself to scientific knowledge" ("Die Reihe seiner Gestaltungen, welche das Bewußtsein auf diesem Wege durchläuft, ist vielmehr die ausführliche Geschichte der *Bildung* des Bewußtseins selbst zur Wissenschaft"; p. 73). Hegel's emphasis of the term *Bildung* here leads us back to the use of the term in the Jena essays for the *Kritisches Journal*. There as here, *Bildung* referred to the act of "disjunction" (*Entzweiung*) which characterized his age and the state of philosophical reflection after Kant. To reject that sphere of *Bildung* would be to repeat naively the very act of separation to be avoided. Paradoxically, then, the highest form of philosophy, which corresponds to the highest form of *Bildung*, internalizes the function of negative rhetoric (*Kritik*) in the formation of its argumentation. The *Phenomenology*, as the history of *Bildung*, contains not only the hermeneutical appropriation of past forms but also the critical reevaluation of competing modes of philosophizing.

The polemical nature of the critiques that make up the movement toward knowledge become clear when Hegel mentions the two aspects of a position to be criticized, namely, either the "authority" to which a position lays claim, or the "conviction" and "opinion" (*Überzeugung* and *Meinung*) of the consciousness holding that position (p. 73). By explicitly making these aspects the object of "scientific" critique and of the presentation of *Bildung*, Hegel bases his depiction of philosophical truth on the principles of rhetorical, that is, ad hominem, argumentation. The *Phenomenology* consists of a series of polemical struggles between positions (*Erscheinungen*) in which each must be presented, argued with, and persuaded to give up its conviction and claim to authority. Hegel thus raises the critical writing of the Jena essays to the philosophical principle of scientific representation, *Wissenschaft*. The connection between the two is created by *Bildung*, by his own rhetorical development and his conception of the need for criticism in philosophy's development. Hegel's *Wissenschaft* literally appears in the form of ad hominem dialogues as the Spirit searches for appropriate modes of argumentation.

But how do these dialogues take place? What is the "method of execution" (*Methode der Ausführung*; p. 75)? The "partners" in the dialogue are called "scientific knowledge" and "knowledge as it appears"; for "this depiction" (*diese Darstellung*), Hegel writes, consists of a "Verhalten [relationship] der *Wissenschaft* zu dem *erscheinenden Wissen*" (p. 75). For Hegel, the knowledge that a consciousness has of an object is identical with the way that consciousness represents the object; *Wissen* exists only in its appearance (*erscheinend*). The form and appearance of our knowledge is not something we merely add to it after the fact, nor is the object independent of its presentation "for us" (*für uns*). And yet each consciousness projects its knowledge as if it were not only "for us" but also "of itself" (*an sich*). The individual consciousness forgets, so to speak, that the supposed knowledge *an sich* is only its projection (that is, *für es*). (Needless to say, the qualification "only" in this discussion is actually inappropriate since the expression or appearance is never without the thing represented.) The rhetorical "movement" of the dialogues entails convincing a consciousness to accept another mode of presenting knowledge, different from one it believes or holds to be true (*an sich* or *für wahr halten*). The dialogic exchange reveals to the partner, "quasi behind his back" (*gleichsam hinter seinem Rücken*; p. 80), that its supposed *Ansich* was "only" a way of viewing the world. The dialogue persuades the partner to adopt another way of presenting the world, another "form of appearance" (*Form der Erscheinung*). We thus have a rhetorical phenomenon, a change of form, similar to the ones we analyzed in the first two parts of this chapter, but in this case the persuasive *reasons* for the change of form must be given. This change of form goes beyond *elocutio* since it tries to generate arguments (the task of dialectical *inventio*) to justify one form over another based on the matter at hand (*res*). The intersubjectivity of persuasion complements our earlier discussions of objectified forms and traditions.[66]

When a consciousness adopts a different mode of representing its object, both the consciousness and the object change form. When something new becomes known at different stages of *Bildung*, the entire being of both consciousness and object are transformed. They *appear* differently than they did before. The coming-into-appearance of a new object of knowledge together with a new form of consciousness is called "experience" (*Erfahrung*): "This dialectical movement, which consciousness performs on itself, that is, both on its knowledge and on its object, *insofar as the new, true object arises out of it*, is what is properly called *experience*" (p. 78). Through the dialectical exchange of possible representations of knowledge, consciousness learns different ways to express itself and its world. What was formerly believed to be the case (*das Ansich, die Sache selbst*, the *res*) is revealed by the critical dialogue to be only a way of viewing, presenting, talking about the case—"the being-for-consciousness of the In-itself" (*das Für-es-Sein dieses Ansich*; p. 79). The dialogue results in an "inversion of conscious-

---

66. The richness of Hegel's conception of philosohical form is thus the richness of a rhetorical system freed from the historical restrictions that made it, in Genette's terms, a *rhétorique restreinte*. *Figures* II and III (Paris: Editions du Seuil, 1969, 1972).

ness" (*Umkehrung des Bewußtseins*; p.79) as one partner persuades the other to abandon not just knowledge but an entire mode of depicting and relating to knowledge.[67] As in an ad hominem argument, *Wissenschaft* strives literally to change the mind and form of "knowledge as it appears" (*erscheinendes Wissen*).[68] The modes of argumentation can be called "dialectical" insofar as they (1) involve dialogues, and (2) revolve around the comparison between *res* and *verba* (*Sache* and *Erscheinung*) which constitutes the task of critical *inventio*.

In order to see how this dialogue unfolds, and between which partners, within the strategies of the *Phenomenology*, we can take two quotes from Jean Hyppolite as guides. The first points out the inherent double perspective in dialectic which is caused by the difference between consciousnesses, a difference he considers less in temporal-hermeneutic than in spatial-oppositional terms. Hyppolite writes: "In 'dialectic' there is the *dia*, the *between*, the space where the differential distance (*l'écart*) opens up between natural consciousness of the object and ontological consciousness of the very condition of the object. But this distance is measured in self-consciousness, and self-consciousness is always a reflection in another consciousness."[69] The second quote indicates that some real partners, some plural "we," are involved in the dialectic, thereby constituting a genuine dialogue between individual consciousnesses.

> We believe that the fundamental thesis of Hegel's *Phenomenology* is that this emergence of the philosophical we (*du nous philosophique*) in experience is possible thanks to the *intersubjectivity*, the mutual interrelations between self-consciousnesses, and the confrontation of particular perspectives. It is necessary to add confrontation, since even in Leibniz there were perspectives, but these perspectives never met, are never set into motion. If experience is dialectical, the promotion of experiential truth, it is because this dialectic is a dialogue, a relation of self-consciousnesses. Thus, the pronoun *we*, used by Hegel to designate the perspective of philosophy on experience, and the pronoun used to designate a plurality of particular self-consciousnesses, are the same ("The we that is an I, and the I that is a we").[70]

67. The concept of *Umkehrung* relates as well to the rhetorical figures of *ironia* and *inversio*.

68. Recall the close of the essay on natural law (*Theorie-Werkausgabe*, 3, p. 511) in which philosophy enters into a polemical, ad hominem dialogue with opinion (*Meinen*); see above, pp. 171–72.

69. Jean Hyppolite, "Dialectique et dialogue dans la 'Phénoménologie de l'esprit,'" in *Figures de la pensée philosophique* (Paris: Presses Universitaires de France, 1971), p. 212.

70. Ibid., p. 211.

Hyppolite thus redefines the dialectical experience, which for Hegel seems to take place within an ontological and monological consciousness or Spirit, as the intersubjective confrontation of various individual consciousnesses. In particular, we can also say that an individual "consciousness" in the *Phenomenology* represents not so much a person as a given position or mode of expression. The goal of this exchange between established positions is the emergence of a kind of consensus, a common position or discourse upon which "we"—the "nous *philosophique*"—can agree. The criteria for deciding the truth in this dialogue depend not on the object of knowledge per se but on the way the partners—the "we"—express and argue about their, or our, knowledge. Hegel summarizes this idea in the Introduction: "If we now examine the truth of knowledge, then it appears as if we examine what it is *in itself*. However, in this examination it is *our* object, it is *for us*. . . . The essence or the measure (*das Wesen oder der Maßstab*) would thus fall in us. . . . Consciousness gives itself as a measure, and the examination becomes thereby a comparison of consciousness with itself"(p. 76).[71]

What prevents this from collapsing into subjective idealism is the plurality of consciousnesses, the intersubjectivity implicit in the "we." Not only do "we" engage in a dialectic of experience as in a dialogue with others like ourselves in order to change minds and reach agreements (*Umkehrung des Bewußtseins*), but also we are bound to this dialogue in order to establish the criteria for truth or acceptance of a position. Hegel's discussion of the dialectical comparison between the "In-itself" (*Ansich*) and its conscious representation for others, reformulates the basic task of rhetorical *inventio* to discover the possible relationships between *res* and *verba* so that they can be used in disputations. In neither case is there an appeal to some "thing" outside the dialogue, since the "things" (*Sache, Ansich,* or *res*) only have significance in the "forms of appearance" that "we" give to them in intersubjective dialogue around critical positions.

The pronoun "we" (*wir*), which in fact permeates the text of the *Phenomenology*, is thus not a "mere" rhetorical device that Hegel might have purged from the argumentation. Rather, it makes possible the text's "movement"—as *dialektische* and *bildende Bewegung*—by constructing a series of argumentative "moves" that shift identifications with various positions. The *wir* in the *Phenomenology* is thus rhetorical in

71. Thus we have another rhetorical and intersubjective solution to the problem of the "measure" raised in the "Essence of *Kritik*." It should be noted here that Hegel is speaking of "consciousness," not "self-consciousness," that is, of *inter*subjective not *intra*subjective acts.

the more significant sense that it maintains the fiction of a persuasive dialogue. It literally gives the text its form and formation (*Bildung*) by allowing different partners to compare their proposed verbal representations. In a different sense than that investigated in the previous section, the debates among the "we's" are both a precondition and movement of the *elocutio* of each figure of consciousness: a precondition because the choice of figurative form relies on the "invention" of a convincing mode of argumentation, and a movement because the figures are persuaded to give up their form, or position, for another mode of representation. It is possible to isolate four positions, or partners, identified in the *Phenomenology* as *wir*.

First, the *wir* is associated with the voice of Hegel as the omniscient narrator. That narrator believes to have attained the level of knowledge (*Wissenschaft*) that grants him a position above and beyond that of "knowledge as it appears." From this perspective, the narrator-*wir* merely records the dialogues between other consciousness as he hears them. He is the critic in the original sense of *kritikes*, the decision maker in a dispute who must remain neutral during the debate. He formulates this position in the Introduction: "But an additional act on our part is superfluous not only because the concept and object, the measure and the to-be-tested (*das zu Prüfende*), are both present in consciousness, but also because we are raised beyond the effort of comparing and actually testing them both, so that when consciousness tests itself we merely have to observe from a distance (*das reine Zusehen*)" (p. 77). This dialogue situation could be illustrated by the example of some of the Platonic dialogues in which Socrates, as the narrator-*wir*, knows the answer already and yet allows the others to struggle for adequate expression.[72]

Second, as Hyppolite points out, the *wir*, or higher "philosophical we," is at the same time emerging out of the dialogue. It exists in the beginning only potentially, or transcendentally, as a projected standpoint necessary for the debate to ensue. The consciousness identified as *wir* must pass through this entire dialogue precisely so that it can attain that highest level of abstraction and observation. The *wir* in the dialogue does not impose any privileged position on the dialogue from the outset but, rather, attains that privileged position through arguing.

72. At least this is the tendency of Plato's later dialogues. It gives both Plato and Hegel the image of being more monological than I am presenting them. The "we" can in fact become quite a bully for both these philosophers and I do not wish to deny the element of forceful persuasion involved. However, that does not affect the basic premise of my argument at all, namely, the effect of rhetoric (dia- or monological) on Hegel's argumentation.

In Hegel's words: "by leaving aside [our notions and thoughts (*Ein-fälle*)], we will reach the point where we can observe the matter (*Sache*) as it is in and of itself" (p. 77). The first *wir* is distinct from the second in this sentence, since the first already knows what it is doing, whereas the second must experiment with the different formations given to the *Sache*. As in a sophistic dialogue, in the historical sense, the final outcome of the dialogue, that upon which "we" partners will agree as the best way of expressing the *Sache*, emerges only at the conclusion. The "we" must be open to any possibility of convincing and being convinced.

Third, the fact that different consciousnesses participate in the dialogue and the demand that none imposes a position on the other, both imply that at any given point the partners could be willing to switch positions. The *wir* in the *Phenomenology* therefore attempts constantly to adopt the standpoint of the consciousness which the *wir* is also observing. Only by arguing from the standpoint of the Other can "we" hope to convince the Other, and ourselves, of the validity of our own emerging position.

Fourth, since the emergence of truth depends on the reception of the public, as we saw in the Preface (p. 66), the *wir* that exchanges positions with a position in the text is also associated with the readers of the *Phenomenology*. "We," the readers, must actively participate in the development of the dialogue and are drawn to identify with its positions. Bubner refers to this phenomenon as Hegel's creation of a "literary fiction" that implicates the reader in a persuasive dialogue.[73] Hegel makes it possible for the reader to identify with the position presented in the text by employing the pronoun *wir*. For if a reader reads that pronoun in a text, he or she is forced, at least at some level, to identify with the position represented by the pronoun (as well as with other potential readers). If the *wir* in the text is persuaded to abandon its position, the reader identifying with it will also be persuaded to undergo the same "inversion of consciousness." Hegel traces the act of "inversion" back to the inherent doubleness in representation, the "ambiguity of the true" (*Zweideutigkeit des Wahren*; p. 79), that is, the dialectical and dialogic form of truth.[74]

---

73. Bubner, "Dialog und Dialektik": "The dialogic principle, to expound on philosophical questioning in the give and take of conversation (*in Rede und Gegenrede*), to dig deeper, to enter into an area of expanding horizons or else to remain standing in its puzzling nature, demands the active collaboration of the conscious participant. Literary fiction, as has been observed again and again, aims at the *drawing in of the reader*" (p. 133).

74. As T. Bahti points out ("The Indifferent Reader," p. 75), this ambiguity affects "us" rhetorically: "For as the domain of rhetoric is one of persuasion, and thus of

Dialectic is equated in the *Phenomenology* with rhetorical, persuasive dialogue because of the ambiguous form of the *wir*, which shows, on the one hand, an indifference to the object of observation and, on the other, an interest in persuading and being persuaded. In his lectures on the history of philosophy Hegel characterizes Platonic dialogues as "dialectical" insofar as they demand indifference on the part of the reader: "An indifferent spirit without interest (*ein interessenloser gleichgültiger Geist*) is necessary for the study of Plato's dialogues."[75] To the extent that the *wir* is ambiguous in the text of the *Phenomenology*, however, we, the readers, are not allowed to remain completely indifferent. That is, the "indifferent spirit" is only one of the argumentative positions within the text. Thanks to the plurality of positions, Hegel's structures of dialectical argumentation contain a "movement" of *Bildung* that implicates rhetorical dialogue, that is, persuasive moves, into the attainment and representation of *Wissenschaft*.

The first chapter of the *Phenomenology*, "Sense Certainty or the This and My Opinion [or Subjective, Intended Meaning]" ("Die sinnliche Gewißheit oder das Diese und das Meinen"), exemplifies Hegel's dialectical method. Hegel enacts an ad hominem, rhetorical dialogue that criticizes and changes a proposed relationship between world and expression. Hegel explicitly states at the end of this chapter that it tells the history (or story) of a dialectic and that the dialectic consists of nothing but this very history: "It is clear that the dialectic of sense certainty is nothing other than the simple history of its movement or its experience, and that sense certainty is nothing other than just this history" (p. 90). Insofar as this opening chapter follows the argumentative "movement" of a dialectic of experience, it "can be taken as a model of the figures to follow" in the rest of the *Phenomenology*.[76] We have al-

---

signification of and for an audience, so here is the ambiguity addressed to "us," as it signifies a doubleness or duplicity of signification *and* of interpretation or understanding (*Zweideutigkeit* being from *zwei-deuten*, 'to signify twice' *and* 'to interpret twice')."

75. *Vorlesungen über die Geschichte der Philosophie* 2, in *Theorie-Werkausgabe*, vol. 19 (Frankfurt am Main: Suhrkamp, 1979), pp. 228f. See Bubner, "Dialog und Dialektik," p. 132. This notion of the *interessenloser, gleichgültiger Geist* fits nicely into Bahti's emphasis on the "indifferent reader."

76. Andrzej Warminski, "Reading for Example: 'Sense-Certainty' in Hegel's *Phenomenology of Spirit*," *Diacritics* (Summer 1981):83. Warminski offers a very insightful reading of the function of "example" in the rhetorical structure of the opening dialectic of the *Phenomenology*.

Wieland, "Die Dialektik der sinnlichen Gewißheit," in Fulda, *Materialien*, considers the opening chapter a "Platonic" rather than "sophistic" dialogue, although the terms he uses place the dialectic closer to the historical Sophists than to the later Plato: "It is not a question of being right about a thesis formulated in advance, but rather of coming to an understanding in mutual effort" (p. 77).

ready seen how this chapter depicts a *Bild*, or a mode of expressing consciousness, and must now pursue the argumentative and dialogic techniques that Hegel employs within the figure. *Bildung*, seen as the textual process or "movement" toward knowledge that forces the self by persuasion to abandon a position, which represents the self in the world, for the sake of another mode of representation, is encapsulated in the disputation with and within sense certainty.

The argument begins with a double definition full of wordplay:

> That knowledge, which is our first or immediate object, can be no other than that which is itself unmediated knowledge, *knowledge* of the *immediate* or *being*. We must likewise relate [behave] in a manner of *unmediated reception*, i.e., we must not change anything in our object as it presents itself and must keep conceptualizing out of our act of taking in [understanding]. [P. 82]

Hegel defines here both the object (*res*) under consideration—a type of knowledge—and his, or "our," stance in relationship to that object. The first mention of *wir* in the second sentence of the *Phenomenology* seems to correspond to the position of the disinterested writer and reader observing events at a distance. And yet, at the same time, the "likewise" (*ebenso*) connects the kind of knowledge depicted in the text to our supposedly independent position, for whatever can be said about the one can be transferred to the other. In particular, Hegel implies that he intends to invert that form of knowledge ("sense certainty") which relates passively to its object by showing that it is "in fact the most abstract and poorest truth" rather than the "richest knowledge," as it claims (p. 82). By demonstrating that consciousness must and does participate actively in presenting its knowledge, Hegel by analogy demonstrates that "we" readers likewise (*ebenso*) are not so disinterested. On the contrary, the *wir* very quickly shifts from a disinterested position outside the dialogue into that of one of the partners. The *Bildung* of consciousness from supposedly unmediated to mediated knowledge takes place in a disputation that forces a change of mind.

Hegel conducts a clever polemic against sense certainty by employing two topoi from rhetorical dialectics: the *locus ab exemplo* and *questiones*.[77]

---

77. See Lausberg, *Handbuch*, pars. 410–26, on the use of *exempla* as "Beweisfunction," especially within forensic rhetoric. On *quaestiones*, pars. 66–138. The *quaestiones* are both the internal aspects of any given issue and the actual questions posed (e.g., by a judge or lawyer) during a court case or investigation.

Here we see the way the *loci argumentorum* augment the tropological argument discussed above, in the first section, "The *Elocutio* of the *Phenomenology*," and n. 21.

He allows the most concrete and unmediated form of consciousness to choose an example (*Beispiel*) of a supposedly passive relationship between an object (*res*) and its representation, and then he steps back to a stance from which "we" can "watch" (*zusehen*) what else comes into play (*beiherspielen*; pp. 83–84).[78] To show that something else does indeed play a role in sense certainty's supposedly unmediated representation of "this or that" object, Hegel poses a deceptively naive question to sense certainty: "What is the 'this'?" ("Was ist das Diese?"; p. 84). That is, how would you define your reference to your supposed certainty? Hegel poses the question, apparently, just to hear how sense certainty would characterize the object of its knowledge, not to involve himself, or us, in a debate: "We must, to that end, not reflect about it [the object] and ponder what it might be in truth, but we must *merely observe* (*nur zu betrachten*) the way in which sense certainty deals with it" (p. 84).

And yet the question is by no means so innocent. It is a rhetorical question for which the speaker (*wir*) presumes an answer. In fact, "we," not sense certainty, address the question to ourselves:

> It [sense certainty] must thus itself be asked: *What is the This?* If *we* consider it in the double form of its being, as *Now* and *Here*, then the dialectic inherent in it will take on a form as easy to understand as it is itself. [P. 84]

The form of this dialectic is a rhetorical dialogue in which "we" play the roles of both partners.[79] "We" are not disinterested observers; we pose *and* answer questions. For example: "To the question: *What is Now?*, for example, we give the answer: *Now is night*" ("Auf die Frage: *was ist das Jetzt?* antworten wir also zum Beispiel: *das Jetzt ist die Nacht*"; p. 84). Or further along:

> It is the same case with the other form of the This, namely with the *Here*. The *Here* is, for example, the *tree*. I turn around, however, and this truth has disappeared and turned into its opposite: *Here is not a tree* but, rather, a *house*. [P. 85]

The *wir* that began in a general position of indifferent observation adopts the specific position of its dialogical partner and forces the partner to adopt its position.

---

78. The wordplay—"Beispiel" and "beiherspielen"—is not as innocent as it may seem. See Warminski on the problems of translating the pun ("Reading for Example," p. 92).

79. Wieland, "Hegels Dialektik der sinnlichen Gewißheit": "If it concerns a stylized dialogue situation, it makes little difference whether the dialogue is carried out with a real partner or only with oneself, provided that both levels of consciousness can be distinguished from each other" (pp. 74–75).

By means of these rhetorical questions and topological arguments by example, Hegel has his partner where he wants him (or her)—at the level of rhetoric. On the one hand, sense certainty does not see these as rhetorical questions but attempts to answer them, and in so doing enters into the language, rhetorical strategies, and wordplay of the narrator-*wir*. On the other, the *wir* takes the position of the partner and hardly gives the consciousness of sense certainty a chance to speak at all, for the *wir* (or occasionally a singular *ich*) poses and responds to the questions.[80] Hegel's use here of the "movement of the dialectic" recapitulates that part of his *Bildung* which stressed the "invention" of strategies, "moves," for disputation and ad hominem critique.

Hegel not only employs techniques of ad hominem argumentation and *inventio* against sense certainty, but thematizes them as well. The argumentation of this chapter relies explicitly on a distinction between the beliefs of sense certainty and its means of expressing them. Sense certainty intends or subjectively believes (*meinen*) it refers to an individual, specific object, but whenever it *expresses* its opinion (*Meinung*), either in written or oral language, sense certainty uses general or universal concepts since words, even the most specific, are mere place holders for a variety of phenomena. Every act of expression (*sagen*) undermines the supposed truth of sense certainty. Any expression, whether temporal, spatial, or anything involving "I" (*ich*), ironically says the opposite of what sense certainty means because sense certainty has not reflected on the intricate relationship between *res* and *verba*, whereby insight into the former requires the light of the latter. Hegel writes from the standpoint of an ironized sense certainty:

> I is only a universal, like *Now, Here or This* in general; I most likely mean (*meine*) a *particular I*, but I can no more say what I subjectively mean by I as I can with Now and Here. By saying: *this Here and Now*, or a *particular* thing, I actually say: *All This's, all Here's, Now's, particulars*; likewise, by saying: *I, this particular I*, I say in general: *All I's*; each one is precisely that which I have said: *I, this particular I*. [P. 87]

Sense certainty thinks it can express the concrete objects of its knowledge directly. Yet Hegel demonstrates through questions and examples that "it is impossible to say this" (*aber dies zu sagen ist unmöglich*; p. 87).

Hegel's argument revolves, then, around the demand (*Forderung*; p.

---

80. Warminski sums up the harshness of the one-sided polemic: "Few commentators have failed to note the arbitrariness, unfairness, indeed bullying that victimized sense-certainty undergoes at the hands of the 'we.' . . . This indecorousness . . . is somewhat distressing for anyone expecting the 'earnestness, the pain, the patience and work of the negative'" ("Reading for Example," p. 90).

87) that sense certainty say, express, what it means. He tricks sense certainty into speaking by positing rhetorical questions that ask for examples. He creates a one-sided dialogue by answering the questions himself, by offering his own examples and comparisons. Since sense certainty is implicated in the *wir* who speaks, it is led into a conflict between what it means (its object or *res*) and what it says (*verba*). The criterion for judging the conflict lies in the dialogue itself, in the partners' language or mode of speaking:

> Language, as we see, is the more truthful; in language we even contradict our *subjective opinion* (*Meinung*); and since the universal is the truth of sense certainty and language merely expresses this truth, then it is not possible at all for us ever to be able to express [say] a sensed existence that we *subjectively mean* (*so ist es gar nicht möglich, daß wir ein sinnliches Sein, das wir* meinen, *je sagen können*). [P. 85]

Thus, the ad hominem argument ends with the experience and knowledge (*Erfahrung*) or ironic reversal (*Umkehrung des Bewußtseins*) that sense certainty has not found an appropriate relationship between its object and its mode of expressing that object. Sense certainty is forced to abandon its position, its "invented" image of the world, its unpersuasive rhetoric. As Andrej Warminski says, the argumentation of this chapter is "directed not so much at sense-certainty as at its language, its rhetoric."[81]

Finally, the reader, or the community of "us" readers, has been persuaded by this experience of a figure of consciousness as well, for "we" were also addressed by the ad hominem arguments. The *wir* has shifted positions from the disinterested observer at the beginning, to the poser and answerer of questions and examples within the dialogue, to the status of a stupefied sense certainty itself, and finally to a higher, more knowledgeable (since persuaded) consciousness. Hegel's philosophical dialectic has cleverly employed and masked the techniques of developing a rhetorical dialogue. He allows the readers (a disinterested *wir*) to watch as he persuades a partner to begin talking; then he draws us into the conversation, even allows us to do the persuading; and in the end we see that we have in fact persuaded ourselves. The "movement" that has occurred is that of the formation of a new consensus out of a differentiation of opinions.

The chapters and major subsections of the *Phenomenology* repeat the basic argumentative patterns of the chapter on sense certainty. By developing a fictional dialogue situation, Hegel lets sense certainty "come

81. Ibid., p. 86.

to language" (*zum Worte kommen*; p. 92) and then criticizes its simplistic words, its rhetoric. This recalls the task he set himself in the *Differenz* essay on Fichte and Schelling: the "bringing to language" of differences. Similarly, since each chapter and major subsection of the *Phenomenology* also contains a *Bild* or conscious mode of presenting the world, each also contains an ad hominem argument directed against the given way a consciousness thinks about and expresses its world. Although the dialogic and polemical techniques are generally not as obvious in the rest of the *Phenomenology* as in the first chapter, persuasive rhetoric and shifts in perspective continue to structure the dialectic throughout the text. In keeping with the task of critical *inventio*, Hegel structures his arguments around topoi or *loci*, the means of connecting *res* to *verba*. That is, he develops his arguments no so much by introducing some new proof or fact to a way of thinking about things but, rather, by comparing two ways of relating things (*Sachen*) to their expressions. For this reason he writes in the Preface: "After dialectic has become separated from proof (*Beweis*), in fact the concept of philosophical demonstration (*Beweisens*) has been abandoned" (p. 61).[82] "Proof" has given way to dialogical argumentation. If earlier we viewed the *Phenomenology* as a series of *Bilder* in which the principles of traditional *elocutio* allowed us to analyze the relationship between levels of signification, here we see the *Bildung* of arguments in terms of the topoi and *loci* of *inventio*, which are compared in the dialectic of experience. A few examples should suffice to show how the many "dialectics" unfold in ad hominem disputations that criticize topological modes of thought.

The critique of the "sophistry" of perception in the second chapter employs the same double perspective of the *wir* to generate a dialogue. First, Hegel proposes that "we" merely observe an act of perception: "Let us now observe (*Sehen wir nun zu*) the experience that consciousness has in its real perception" (p. 97). But then he very quickly implicates us in the observed act. *We* have the experience of perception: "it is *for us*" (*sie ist* für uns; p. 97). *We* perceive objects: "The object that I take in" (*Der Gegenstand, den ich aufnehme*); and later: "I perceive further the property" (*Ich nehme nun ferner die Eigenschaft wahr*; p. 97). Thus, when the consciousness of perception expresses its knowledge of an object by means of a series of loosely connected attributes, *we* are the actual

---

82. Hegel speaks here like a good student of Ernesti, who, it will be recalled from chap. 1, spoke in his *Initia doctrinae solodoris* and *Initia rhetorica* of the need for "elegant" philosophy, by which he meant a narrative philosophy that broke away from sterile (mathematical) formalism.

speakers. In particular, we, along with the consciousness of perception, "invent" a means of relating our knowledge of things, of "bringing our thoughts together" (*Gedanken . . . zusammenzubringen*; p. 107) by using the standard *locus a coniunctis* that links particulars and is a weak form of the *argumentum a causa* (which Hegel deals with in the next chapter on understanding).[83] The consciousness of perception is pushed constantly to abandon this simple, monotone mode of determining its object. A gap opens up between perception's initial confidence in its mode of dealing with the world and its insecurity after talking with "us." In Hegel's terms, a "we" that has freed itself from perception's mode of representation reflects on a former inadequacy: "Let us look back (*Sehen wir zurück*) at that which consciousness earlier took upon itself and now takes on itself, [at] that which it earlier attributed (*zuschrieb*) to things and now attributes to them" (p. 101). When "we" look back critically at the consciousness that can only create arguments that attribute or string along characteristics to things, we actually look back at *our own* experience from the perspective of richer argumentation and the recognized need for more sophisticated forms of representation. Hegel's dialectic strives to persuade the readers by identifying them with the persuaded figure in the dialogue.[84]

In the wittiest and most biting section of the *Phenomenology*, "Physiognomy and Phrenology" ("Physiognomik und Schädellehre"; v a c), Hegel employs a battery of techniques of polemical argumentation acquired from rhetorical *inventio*. At first it seems unclear why Hegel spends some thirty pages on these popular sciences of his day. Most commentators do not find much logical necessity in this stage of the Spirit.[85] Considered as a polemical critique of different topoi from

83. Lausberg, *Handbuch*, pars. 377 (3k) and 380.

84. Hegel employs a similar turn of argumentation in the chapter on "Understanding." He says first of the object of the understanding that it is apparently only "in and of itself true (*an sich seiendes Wahres*)" and so we just look on; however, we also take over its place: "It acts this way strictly for itself, so that consciousness does not participate in its realization, but rather only witnesses it and understands it purely. Thus *we* must first of all merely take its place" ("Dieses treibt sein Wesen für sich selbst, so daß das Bewußtsein keinen Anteil an seiner Realisierung hat, sondern ihr nur zusieht und sie rein auffaßt. *Wir* haben hiermit noch fürs erste an seine Stelle zu treten"; p. 108). In taking the place of this form of consciousness, of course, we give it explicit significance "for us."

85. Walter Kaufmann, *Discovering the Mind*, vol. 1, *Kant, Goethe, Hegel* (New York: Macmillan, 1981), par. 42. He has great difficulty seeing the point of this section of the *Phenomenology* and even uses it to argue against the claims to *Ausführlichkeit und Notwendigkeit* which Hegel raises. Hyppolite, *Genèse et structure de la Phénoménologie de l'esprit de Hegel* (Paris: Aubier, 1946), chap. 7, provides a better argument for the significance of this chapter of the *Phenomenology* in terms of a transition from theoretical to practical philosophy, but by no means justifies "logically" Hegel's introduction of these popular and polemical "sciences."

scientific rhetoric, however, this section gains the same significance as the earlier essays for the *Kritisches Journal*. Hegel must attack forms of pseudo-philosophical discourse in order to differentiate and thereby create his own. In particular, physiognomy and phrenology take as a point of departure the same "ambiguity" as Hegel, namely, that the external appearance of the Spirit expresses its being. The point of difference that Hegel must raise to language is: How is this position argued in comparison to "our" way of talking? Once again, Hegel begins by getting us to adopt the standpoint of the forms to be criticized: "Because of this [common] ambiguity we must look around for the core of the issue" ("Um dieser Zweideutigkeit willen müssen wir uns nach dem Innern umsehen"; p. 235).[86] Hegel then allows us to see (hear) the kind of statements that physiognomists and phrenologists make. They employ the *locus a comparatione*, which too readily transfers from the appearance to essence, from a minor to major phenomenon.[87] Hegel interjects a sarcastic dialogue with such speakers (and demonstrates that he has by no means lost his polemical skills!):

> Thus, if someone is told: you (your inner being) is this or that *because* your *skullbone* is so formed, it means as much as: I consider a bone to be *your reality.* . . . at this point the response should actually go so far as to break the skull of the person who judges in this way in order to demonstrate, with a concreteness appropriate to his wisdom, that a bone is not part of a man *in himself*, much less is the being of *his* true reality.

> Wenn also einem Menschen gesagt wird: du [dein Inneres] bist dies, *weil* dein *Knochen* so beschaffen ist, so heißt es nichts anderes als: Ich sehe einen Knochen für *deine Wirklichkeit* an. . . . hier müßte die Erwiderung eigentlich so weit gehen, einem, der so urteilt, den Schädel einzuschlagen, um gerade so greiflich, als seine Weisheit ist, zu erweisen, daß ein Knochen für den Menschen nicht *an sich*, viel weniger *seine* wahre Wirklichkeit ist. [P. 256]

Hegel summarizes the form of statements made by physiognomists and phrenologists in what he calls an "infinite judgment" (*unendliches Urteil*): "It is the *infinite* judgment that the self is a thing" (p. 260).[88] The

86. Also p. 255: "*We* thus receive the possibility" (Wir *erhalten also die Möglichkeit*). Here Hegel implicates the reader in the argumentation.

87. Lausberg, *Handbuch*, points out that "the *locus a comparatione* brings into relation things of unequal rank conceptually" (pars. 395–97). It is also interesting to note that Hegel's distinction between finite and infinite judgments corresponds to the rhetorical difference between *finita* and *infinita quaestiones*.

88. This is a significant formulation because it connects the chapter on phrenology (*Schädellehre*) to the chapter on *Bildung*, where the *Geist der Bildung* also spoke in "infinite judgments" (*unendlichen Urteilen*). Similarly, just as the concept of *Bildung* and its "con-

term "judgment" here shows that Hegel is interested in *inventio*, that area of rhetorical dialectics (or dialectics within rhetoric) concerned with the generation of arguments linking one point to another. Because such a statement could perhaps be mistaken for Hegel's own belief in the reality of the Spirit, he uses a biting comparison to differentiate himself from phrenologists by inverting the opposing rhetoric at the end of the section. He "demonstrates" the inadequacy of such topological transferences by comparing their identity of real and ideal polemically with the unity of functions in the male sexual organ. The *loci*, that is, the argumentative connections and judgments, of the physiognomist and phrenologist capture only the baser side of that identity:

> [It] is the same connection of the high and the low which is expressed naively in living nature by the connection of the organ of its highest perfection, the organ of reproduction, and the organ of pissing.—The infinite judgment as such would be the perfection of self-conscious conceptual life; the consciousness that remains at the level of mere imagination, however, occupies in relation to the infinite the position of pissing.

> [Es] ist dieselbe Verknüpfung des Hohen und Niedrigen, welche an dem Lebendigen der Natur in der Verknüpfung des Organs seiner höchsten Vollendung, des Organs der Zeugung, und des Organs des Pissens naiv ausdrückt.—Das unendliche Urteil als unendliches wäre die Vollendung des sich selbst erfassenden Lebens; das in der Vorstellung bleibende Bewußtsein desselben aber verhält sich als Pissen. [P. 262]

Thus, Hegel employs a harsh ad hominem polemic against those topological forms of philosophical or scientific rhetoric which are related to his own. He engages us in a dialogue with those forms so that we are forced to appropriate, and then differentiate ourselves from, the competing modes of expressing knowledge. The result of this critical *inventio* is that such judgments enter into our argumentative vocabulary but are then transcended for a more sophisticated form.

Finally, the last chapter of the *Phenomenology*, "Absolute Knowledge" ("Absolutes Wissen"), closes the dialogue but does not escape the structuring power of dialogism completely. If throughout the course of argumentation Hegel maintained a genuine dialogue in which "we"

---

fused, self-conscious" rhetoric of *unendliche Urteile* is not restricted to just one chapter but applies to the entire text, so too the notion of the infinite judgments of *Schädellehre* applies to Hegel's own text as a whole, for he refers to his own work in the very last line as the "Galgatha [Place of Skulls] of the Absolute Spirit" (*Schädelstätte des absoluten Geistes*). Hegel thus casts his text as a "phrenology of Spirit."

had to persuade our partner and ourselves, in the last chapter he maintains the principle but simply shifts the position of *wir* temporally. Throughout the text "we" are present in the dialogue and conversed with the various positions in order to see what the outcome would be and in order to test the adequacy of topological forms of argumentation. At the end, however, "we" seem to stand outside since we look back on our development. Almost every verb in the first person plural in the last chapter is in the past tense—for example, "we saw" (*wir sahen*; three times on p. 577). Even the one present tense—"we summarize" (*wir . . . zusammenziehen*; p. 576)—implies an act of reflection. It seems as if a different position, what Hyppolite called the "philosophical we" (*nous philosophique*), has emerged out of the past dialogue, a position from which the dialogue can be observed with disinterest. Hegel calls this final position "absolute knowledge."

And yet "this last formulation of the Spirit" (*diese letzte Gestalt des Geistes*; p. 582) is not independent of the past dialogue or dialogue in general. Rather, it is the entire dialogue itself. Absolute knowledge does not constitute a standpoint "outside" of the other figures, outside of their rhetorical formulations. Rather, it collects all the former topological positions and reformulates them into the philosophical discourse of the "concept": "What we have contributed here is merely the *collection* (*Versammlung*) of the individual moments, each of which represents (*darstellt*) in its principle the life of the entire Spirit, and the recording (*Festhalten*) of the concept in the form of the concept, whose content would have already presented itself in those instances and which would have presented (*sich ergeben*) itself in the form of a *formation of consciousness*" (p. 582). The *wir* that emerges at the end is not essentially different from the rhetorical forms and figures of the dialogue; it merely knows how to summarize and restate them in another form.

The irony of the last figure of the Spirit, which corresponds to the *Phenomenology* itself as *Wissenschaft*, is that it tells us that we will not find "absolute knowledge" beyond the dialogic exchange of positions, for absolute knowledge consists in that very dialogue. The highest formation of consciousness consists in the memory of its own development. Its form contains all the traditional forms—that is, all the means of relating *res* to *verba*, *Sache* to *Erscheinung*—which have been systematically "invented," argued, interpreted, and reformulated over the course of a Spirit's rhetorical *Bildung*. Thus, the *Phenomenology* ends with the paradox of representation: "absolute knowledge" of the Spirit differs from all representations of "appearing knowledge," and yet it is nothing but the history of the Spirit's development and education to the point where it can represent itself. Hegel has formulated a philosophy of scientific knowledge by tacitly assuming a teleology of rhetorical *Bildung* which sees dialogic self-representation as both the means and end of a formative development.

CHAPTER 5

Propedeutics of Philosophy

Hegel's Neohumanist Pedagogy in Nuremberg

One of the most important and certainly most often discussed works by Hegel which directly addresses the topic of *Bildung* is the speech he delivered on 29 September 1809 as rector of the Nuremberg Melanchthon (or Aegidius) Gymnasium at the ceremonies marking the end of the school year.[1] Because the speech was written shortly after publication of the *Phenomenology*, most interpreters consider it an application of Hegel's philosophical ideas concerning the development (*Bildung*) of the Spirit to the field of pedagogical practice.[2] The very context of the end-of-the-year school celebrations indicates, however, that the speech continues in a tradition that can be traced far back beyond Hegel's first philosophical system. Against the background of Hegel's own education, this speech, both in form and content, demonstrates that Hegel,

1. The speech is reprinted in the *Theorie-Werkausgabe*, vol. 4, *Nürnberg und Heidelberger Schriften, 1808–1817* (Frankfurt am Main: Suhrkamp, 1978). All page numbers within parentheses in the body of the first section ("Hegel's Neohumanist Pedagogy in Nuremberg") of this chapter refer to this edition.

2. For a general overview of secondary literature on the Nuremberg period, see Albert Reble, "Hegel und die Pädagogik," *Hegel-Studien* 3, (1965). See also Friedhelm Nicolin, "Hegel im Blickfeld der Pädagogik," in *Geist und Erziehung. Aus dem Gespräch zwischen Philosophie und Pädagogik. Festschrift für Theodor Litt* (Bonn: Bouvier, 1955). For the most extensive philosophical analysis of the Nuremberg writings, see Gerhart Schmidt, *Hegel in Nürnberg. Untersuchungen zum Problem der philosophischen Propädeutik* (Tübingen: Max Niemeyer, 1960).

though never a great orator, continued to be aware of and employ techniques of classical rhetoric, and that those techniques influenced his ideas on *Bildung* more than twenty years after he had graduated as valedictorian from his humanistic *gymnasium* in Stuttgart.

Just as Hegel's own formative education and development into a writer of philosophy stood under the sign of the *ars rhetorica*, so too, we shall see in this chapter, were his ideas about pedagogy and the historical development of philosophy themselves preformed by rhetorical structures. Both the individual student and the universal human mind must, according to Hegel, be discursively preconditioned. The propedeutics and prestructuring of the philosophy of Spirit make its representation possible since they follow principles of rhetorical expression at the same time as they introduce problematic elements foreign to the Spirit's strictly conceptual self-understanding. The analysis of Hegel's pedagogical activities in these years sheds a new light on the rhetorical background of the *Logic*, which was conceived and written while Hegel was in Nuremberg, as well as of the later *History of Philosophy*.

The opening line of the Nuremberg speech captures its pragmatic nature and situates it within the traditional domain of rhetoric by indicating the specific audience, reasons and purpose of the address. The tone is stiffly oratorical: "By the most eminent commands I have been instructed, in a public address on the occasion of the ceremonious presentation of the prizes which the highest government has destined both as a reward and more as encouragement to those students who have excelled in their progress, to present the history of the *gymnasium* over the course of the past year and to touch on that which is significant and purposeful in terms of the public's relationship to the institution" (p. 312). In particular, this speech falls under the category of the *genus demonstrativum*: By praising the accomplishments of the school Hegel praises and thanks the king (who is present in the audience) for his support. The goal, needless to say, is to persuade him to continue his favor. Hence, although the speech clearly employs the "language of *Bildung*" which Hegel described in chapter VI of the *Phenomenology*, it actually returns to older rhetorical forms, like Rector Schmidlin's or the young Hegel's own speeches sketched out in his Stuttgart diaries.[3]

Hegel structures the speech according to the established rules of *dispositio*. After the *exordium* addressed directly to the audience (espe-

---

3. Recall chap. 1, above on Hegel's diary and valedictory address, in which the schoolboy demonstrates his indebtedness to the tradition of *Schulrhetorik* by imitating his principal's speeches.

cially the king), a transitional sentence shifts the topic slightly from the past school year to the purpose of the institution as a whole—"the thought of its whole plan and purpose" (p. 313). The actual treatment of the topic, the *narratio*, unfolds from a definition of a humanistic *gymnasium* as being rooted in the study of classical languages and proceeds according to the standard *locus* or *argumentum a maiore ad minus*.[4] That is, he discusses the positive effects of the ancients on the modern spirit in order of increasing specificity, beginning with the general principle, expressed in organic images, that the ancients form the figural "ground" on which we grow and thrive, through the more particular point of view of classical languages, ending with a concrete example, the discipline of grammar. Having arrived at the most specific level of language instruction, Hegel returns to the actual topic with which he began—the state of the school, the courses offered, and new ordinances. The speech ends with an extended address directly to the audience, that is, a *peroratio*. Thus, the form of the speech reveals Hegel's strict adherence to classical rhetorical patterns.

The content of the speech revolves around the importance of learning foreign languages in the *gymnasium* in accordance with his definition, which recalls Johannes Sturm: "The spirit and purpose of our institution is the preparation for the university study (*die Vorbereitung zum gelehrten Studium*), in particular a preparation built upon the ground of the Greeks and Romans" (p. 314).[5] Hegel justifies this evaluation of foreign languages by proposing a general process or drive (*Trieb*) behind all education: only something foreign to us can be the object of our conscious effort to learn.[6] He says: "It is, in fact, on this centrifugal drive (*Zentrifugaltrieb*) of the soul that the necessity is grounded to proffer the soul the separation that it seeks from its natural essence and state and to inject a distant, foreign world into the young spirit (*eine ferne, fremde Welt in den jungen Geist hineinstellen zu müssen*). The separating wall (*Scheidewand*), through which this differentiation is accomplished for the *Bildung* under discussion here, is the

4. On the *argumentum a maiore ad minus*, see Lausberg, *Handbuch der literarischen Rhetorik* (Munich: Max Hueber, 1960), pars. 377 and 395 (on *loci* in general). In this speech, the *dispositio* follows the *ordo naturalis* (*Handbuch*, pars. 447–48).

5. See above, chap. 1, p. 63, in which Sturm defines the humanist conception of the *gymnasium* as a *Mittelstufe*, especially a training in the linguistic *artes* of grammar, rhetoric, and dialectic. In the fourth school speech by Hegel (2 September 1811), he refers to the *gymnasium* as a *Mittelsphäre* (p. 349).

6. He stresses the importance of this process by calling it a drive: "This demand for separation is, however, so necessary that it expresses itself in us as a general and well-known drive" ("Diese Forderung der Trennung aber ist so notwendig, daß sie sich als ein allgemeiner und bekannter Trieb in uns äußert"; p. 321).

world and language of the ancients (*die Welt und Sprache der Alten*)" (p. 321). More precisely, this law necessitating alienation explains Hegel's positive evaluation of the *mechanical* character of learning classical grammar. The very formal, foreign and mechanistic features, the dead letter of grammar—what Hegel's teacher Balthasar Haug called "the mechanics of language" (*das Mechanische der Sprache*)[7]—leads to spiritual *Bildung*. The terms for this process are familiar from the rhetorico-pedagogical tradition: "For the mechanical is that which is foreign to the spirit, which then has an interest in digesting the undigested material in itself, in comprehending that which is lifeless in itself, and in making it its own property" ("Denn das Mechanische ist das [dem] Geiste Fremde, für den es Interesse hat, das in ihn hineingelegt Unverdaute zu verdauen, das in ihm noch Leblose zu verständigen und zu seinem Eigenthume zu machen"; p. 322).[8] Thus, as director of the *gymnasium* in Nuremberg, Hegel describes *Bildung* as a process of internalizing meaningless forms in order to work on them, appropriate them, and give them new form.[9]

We have, of course, encountered these ideas in philosophical and abstract form in the *Phenomenology*. We have also seen, however, that they can be traced back to Hegel's own self-education to a writer of philosophy and, beyond that, to a centuries-old tradition of rhetorical pedagogy. In the significant 1809 speech, Hegel refers, in fact, to the

7. Haug's thesis XLVIII: "An dem Mechanischen der Sprache ist so viel gelegen als an der Schönheit des Vortrags" (see above, chap. 1, p. 69).

8. Hegel refers to grammatical components of language specifically as "letters": "They are, so to speak, the individual letters, in fact the vowels of the spiritual with which we begin in order to be able to spell and then to read" ("Sie sind gleichsam die einzelnen Buchstaben, und zwar die Vokale des Geistigen, mit denen wir anfangen, [um] es buchstabieren und dann lesen zu können"; p. 322). It should also be pointed out here that grammar is not to be considered distinct from rhetoric, but has traditionally been subsumed under the *ars rhetorica* as *latinitas*.

9. Hegel held, in fact, six such speeches during his years as principal of the Nuremberg *gymnasium*. Schmidt considers the addresses, taken together, as a *systematische Schulpädagogik* (p. 14). Whereas the first is largely a rhetorical *laudatio* for the former school head, Schenk, the others have the same form and similar content as the 1809 address. All the declamations emphasize Hegel's concern with a pedagogy based on the traditional *institutio oratoria*. Moreover, in a gesture that is significant for his ethical theory in these years, a gesture that recalls his earliest diary entries from Stuttgart, Hegel conceives of education as an introduction of the individual into the public sphere. The methods for introducing the students to this sphere are clearly the traditional ones based on a Ciceronian model (see, e.g., pp. 344–45). *Bildung* itself is defined as the propedeutic, the *Vorarbeit* which makes possible future knowledge and self-realization within the public sphere (pp. 352–53). The "new" institution introduced into the *gymnasium*—the major focus on classical languages—makes abundantly clear that Hegel is still in close pedagogical proximity to his own teacher, Haug, and that Hegel considers the *Vorarbeit* for the public sphere a training toward linguistic, rhetorical self-representation.

history of the institution in Nuremberg, thereby consciously inserting himself into a pedagogical continuum: "The *new* institution had, in addition, the advantage of succeeding *older* institutions that have existed for centuries, rather than replacing a *newer* one; thus it could attach itself to the well-established notions of duration, continuation, and the confidence shown to this school was not impaired by the opposite thought that this institution was perhaps only something temporary, experimental" (p. 313). This historical continuity links the concept of *Bildung* outlined here concretely to the humanist and classical origins of *elementa rhetorices* or *institutio oratoria*. For Hegel means here by the "new" and "centuries-old" institutions his in the end successful attempt to revitalize the Melanchthon Gymnasium in Nuremberg. He had been called to Nuremberg from Bamberg, where he had been editing a political journal, in order to reshape and literally to refound the school, which had fallen into academic and even physical disrepair. A brief review of the Melanchthon Gymnasium's history makes clear that the central philosophical and pedagogical concept analyzed by Hegel—*Bildung*—rests on a humanist rhetorical foundation that has left its implicit mark.

As the name of the school implies, the original institution goes back to a *gymnasium*, or more precisely a Latin school (*Lateinschule*), founded by the great humanist rhetorician and dialectian Philipp Melanchthon, whose handbooks guided instruction throughout Germany from the sixteenth through the seventeenth century.[10] Melanchthon had been invited in 1524 from Wittemberg to Nuremberg to establish a school along the guidelines laid out in Luther's open letter "To the councilmen of all cities of the German nation, that they should establish and maintain Christian schools" ("An die Rathsherren aller Städte deutschen Landes, daß sie christliche Schulen aufrichten und halten sollen").[11] After some hesitation, Melanchthon accepted the position and in 1526 he, like Hegel, his successor nearly three hundred years later, held an oration opening the school.[12] The initial curriculum, like

10. The following history rests on Hugo Steiger, *Das Melanchthongymnasium in Nürnberg (1526–1926). Ein Beitrag zur Geschichte des Humanismus* (Munich: Oldenbourg, 1926).

11. On the Luther essay and Protestant humanism, see Horst Frank, *Deutschunterricht* (Munich: Carl Hanser, 1976), pp. 29–38.

12. He explained that "What would be needed, then, is not a man of learning who could deliver lectures of the usual sort, but rather an eloquent man, an orator (*Deklamtor*), who would combine with a knowledge of the subjects to be taught an eloquence on which, in its capacity as a model (*Vorbild*), the young people could develop (sich bilden)" (Steiger, *Melanchthongymnasium*, p. 20). See also Hartfelder, *Philipp Melanchthon als Praeceptor Germaniae*, in *Kehrbachs Monumenta Germaniae Paedagogica* VII, p. 520. Needless to say, this description fits Melanchthon better than almost any other humanist of his day.

that of the original *Lateinschule* in Stuttgart, had one goal, Latin eloquence, and one method, rhetorical *exercitationes*:

> The curriculum [of 1526] emphasizes one thing over and over again, namely, the importance of Latin oratory. To attain *eloquentia*, i.e., Latin oratory, through *imitatio*, through the imitation of classical models, this was valued as the highest goal. To this aim were also subordinated the written exercises that were assigned weekly to the pupils. In this regard, great weight was placed on writing verse, "for (according to the curriculum) the young boy must be schooled in both genres since no one can judge correctly prose expression who is not at least somewhat schooled in writing verse, and for this reason a professor of poetry is to be hired who possesses great virtuosity; the young students should therefore take him as their model."[13]

This ideal and method remained unchallenged for over one hundred years. Although the school underwent various changes—it was moved outside of the city to Altdorf and suffered under the competition with the local, more practical *Trivialschulen*, which attracted the Nuremberg patrician children—rhetoric continued to dominate the curriculum. In 1575, for example, a new rector came from Strassburg, where he had studied under Johannes Sturm. Appropriately, the school order decreed that the rector, in addition to setting down the general guidelines of instruction, was to act as the professor of rhetoric.[14] The justification of the school board reads, in the spirit of Sturm: "For it is certain and true that virtuosity and *eloquentia* are necessary *ad literatam pietatem* and for whoever wishes to attain and acquire it."[15] The method of instruction rested on memorization of *praecepta* and imitation and repetition of *exempla*.

Through the seventeenth and eighteenth centuries, the Melanchthon Gymnasium, also called the Aegidius Gymnasium after the Nuremberg hill of that name to which it was relocated in 1633, experienced the same tension that was encountered in Stuttgart between Enlightenment and philanthropic "reform" on the one hand and humanistic "conservatism" on the other. In 1622, for example, some of the basic ideas of Wolfgang Ratkes (Raticius), one of the first pedagogical reformers to stress subject-oriented instruction in the mother tongue (*deutscher Sachunterricht*), were introduced into the curricu-

13. Steiger, *Melanchthongymnasium*, p. 26.
14. According to the *Schulordnung* of 1575: "The rector was also active as a professor and taught the discipline of rhetoric" (ibid., p. 53).
15. Ibid., p. 58.

lum.[16] Instruction in German was offered for the first time, in part as a response to the competition of the pragmatic *Trivialschulen*, and less emphasis was placed on the catechisms and handbooks of the humanists. Even such changes were dependent on the leanings of the individual rectors, however, and for periods of ten to twenty years some were able to allow Latin eloquence once again to dominate over German, Greek and the more practical subjects (*Realien*).[17]

Undoubtedly the most significant aspect in the historical continuity of this institution is that in spite of changes in the *content* of the curriculum, the *method* remained essentially the same. Through the influence of the realist and Pietist ideas of Comenius and Francke, and through the pragmatic demands of the Nuremberg bourgeoisie, more and more factual knowledge (*Sachkenntnisse*) like geography, history, and mathematics was introduced. Yet a typical method for learning these facts was memorization through rhymes.[18] The method for all readings was derived from Quintilian's guideline for an orator to improve style by reading his forefathers. In the words of one school curriculum, it is necessary "that the pupil excerpt phrases and collect them in a notebook, for he needs them for *imitatio*. . . . Then [after translation exercises], he is required to write a *chria*, a letter (e.g., *epistola ad familiares*), a narrative or a speech."[19] In his *Kurzgefasste Nachricht von dem gegenwärtigen Zustand des Gymnasii Aegidiani in Nürnberg* (Brief Report on the Present Condition of the Aegidius Gymnasium in Nuremberg; 1762), Rector Siegmund Mörl summarizes the dominant pedagogical program in chapter III, "On the Teaching Method which One Is Accustomed to Following at the Gymnasium": grammar, stylistic exercises, and the memorization of *sententia*; at the conclusion of the school years, essays and speeches in Latin; instruction in German follows *expressis verbis* the same course.[20] Hence, as we encountered in the Eberhard-Ludwig Gymnasium in Stuttgart, we see in Nuremberg an institution that managed to continue the old ways of humanist rhetoric in the midst of a pedagogical debate.

By the time Hegel became rector in 1808, the school was on the verge

---

16. On Raticius, see Frank, *Deutschunterricht*, pp. 48–58.

17. Examples of the attitudes toward pedagogical theory and practices that dominated in Nuremberg can be found in the speeches held by the rectors. Steiger, *Melanchthongymnasium*, pp. 81, 91ff.

18. Ibid., pp. 101–6, on the application of older methods (like *Gedächtnisreime*) to "modern" topics of observation and experiential science.

19. Ibid., p. 96f.

20. Ibid., p. 114f.

of collapse. The *Trivialschule* was attracting all the students of the bourgeoisie who felt the need to learn practical disciplines. The Catholic school authorities located in Munich had cut back their support of the Protestant *gymnasium* so much that the physical plant was hardly appropriate for instruction. Radical measures had to be taken to assure the continuation of the humanistic tradition in Nuremberg. These were taken by Friedrich Niethammer (1766–1848), who in 1804 was named to the "district school counsel" (*Kreisschulrat*) in Munich. As practical measures, he disbanded the *Trivialschule*, thereby removing the competition over students, attained permission for a specifically Protestant school, and hired his good friend Hegel, who at the time was working, unhappily, as an editor of a political journal in Bamberg.[21]

To appreciate the pedagogical program under which the newly formed *gymnasium* flourished and to which Hegel's concept of *Bildung* becomes allied, we must briefly discuss Niethammer's major theoretical work, *Der Streit des Philanthropinismus und des Humanismus* (The Contest between Philanthropism and Humanism).[22] By looking at the spirit that motivates this work we can discover the common rhetorical conception of *Bildung* which underlies his and Hegel's efforts in these years. My reading of Niethammer's pedagogical treatises, which sees his ideas beneath Hegel's, or more precisely which sees a common foundation in rhetoric, goes against the grain of the standard interpretation of his relationship to Hegel, according to which Niethammer rests his pedagogy on a weakly founded idealism (especially Fichte) and is therefore drawn to Hegel's philosophical conception of *Bildung*.[23] I shall discuss one key turning point in Niethammer's defense of humanism in order to show how behind the Hegelian-idealist tone lies an older, more traditional argument that informs Hegel's idealism as well.

21. On Hegel in Bamberg, see Wilhelm Beyer, *Zwischen Phänomenologie und Logik: Hegel als Redakteur der Bamberger Zeitung* (Frankfurt am Main: Schulte-Bulmke, 1955). See also the commentary to the letters of this period by Clark Butler in his translation, *Hegel: The Letters* (Bloomington: Indiana University Press, 1984), pp. 125–70.

22. For an excellent discussion of Niethammer, see Werner Hillenbrechts's introduction to the reprint of Niethammer's *Streit des Philanthropinismus und Humanismus* (Weinheim: Julius Beltz, 1968). See also Günther Buck, *Hermeneutik und Bildung* (Munich: Fink, 1981), and *Rückwege aus der Entfremdung: Studien zur Entwicklung der deutschen humanistischen Bildungsphilosophie* (Munich: Fink, 1984). For a systematic discussion of basic concepts of neohumanism, see Udo Müllges, "Das Verhältnis von Selbst und Sache in der Erziehung, problematisch aufgewiesen bei Basedow, Humboldt, Herbart und Hegel" (Ph.D. diss., Bonn, 1961).

23. Especially Nicolin, "Hegel im Blickfeld der Pädagogik," p. 98; Müllges, "Selbst und Sache", p. 53; Schmidt, *Hegel in Nürnberg*, pp. 39, 41, 57.

The innovative response of philanthropism to humanism has its roots in the realism and "natural approach" of Comenius in the sixteenth century, an approach summarized in the slogan "Things instead of words" (*Sachen statt Worte*).[24] And even Niethammer must admit that in some cases humanist schools have been too one-sided in their emphasis on language instruction over factual knowledge (*Sachkenntnisse*). But this is the extent of Niethammer's admission in regard to the philanthropists, his only compromising step in the direction of what he calls the "middle way" between the two camps.[25] The major part of his text, the middle third, responds to the reformers' calls for "things instead of words" by redefining the very terms of the debate. His resolution of the opposition does, in fact, sound very much like the solution offered by Hegel in the almost simultaneously published *Phenomenology*. The alternative *Sache* versus *Worte* is argued to be false since: (1) the goal of instruction is "formative education to reason" or "cultivation of the spirit" (*Bildung zur Vernunft* or *Bildung des Geistes*);[26] (2) reason and Spirit have ideas as their appropriate objects (*Sachen*); and (3) the word is the form in which ideas (mental "things," *Sachen*) present themselves to consciousness.[27] That is, Niethammer's solution to the opposition things (ideas, objects) versus words is to argue for a new kind of object—what he calls a *geistiger Gegenstand* ("ideational, mental, or spiritual object")—which dissolves the opposition by being *in* words while not being "mere" words, since it conveys the spirit, ideas, feelings, of the thing as well. He writes in terms both idealist and traditional:

> for ideas and feelings, comprehended by an eminent spirit and depicted in words, are no less than an actual body a still object for reflection; and it is certainly no more difficult to begin intellectual reflection with these ideational objects than to begin the same operation with material objects.

> denn Ideen und Gefühle, durch einen eminenten Geist gefaßt und in Worten dargestellt, sind nicht weniger als ein Körper ein ruhendes Object für die Betrachtung: und mit diesen geistigen Objecten die geistige Betrachtung beginnen, kann zum mindesten nicht schwerer seyn als dieselbe Operation an materiellen Objecten.[28]

24. Niethammer, *Streit*, p. 163.
25. Ibid., p. 15.
26. Ibid., pp. 93, 119. He identifies humanism with the main purpose (*Hauptzweck*) of all education.
27. Ibid., pp. 102ff., 164ff.
28. Ibid., p. 210.

A new "dialectical" solution to the pedagogical debate of the past to centuries seems to have been found.[29]

Let us look more closely at these "ideational, mental, or spiritual, objects" (*geistigen Gegenstände*), which are the "only proper, overlooked (*das eigentliche, verkannte*) object of instruction,"[30] as they enter into Niethammer's practical considerations of *Bildung*. Concerning the "presentation of ideational objects in word and speech" (*Darstellung der geistigen Gegenstände in Wort und Rede*), he distinguishes between a representation that is an "unmediated expression of ideas, feelings, etc. as communication to others" (*unmittelbares Aussprechen der Ideen, der Gefühle, etc. zur Mitteilung an Andre*) and one that, so to speak at a second order or as a "metalanguage," describes such acts of communication. The first belongs to art, the second to science. Niethammer continues:

> This differentiation is for educational instruction (*Erziehungsunterricht*) all the more significant since its neglect is without doubt the reason the proper object of instruction in *ideational objects* (*geistigen Gegenständen*) has been misrecognized so often, namely, the depictions of such objects *in the art of speech* (*in der Kunst der Rede*). In such depictions, the objects not only seize the soul by moving the innermost depths of the spirit but they also become fixed as objects of reflection in established formations (*festen Gestaltung*). The highest ideas, which lie, of course, in every rational being even if they do not arise as concrete thoughts, thereby become raised in such depictions by inspired men to the property of all, and they especially offer themselves thus as the general object of instruction.[31]

This passage and its explication, occurring precisely at the center of Niethammer's treatise, reveal the rhetorico-hermeneutical core of his neohumanism. A *geistiger Gegenstand*, as synthesis of *Sache* and *Wort,* is a rhetorical opus, an act of speech (*oratio* or *sermo*) as defined by Quintilian.[32] As an object of instruction it fulfills the two dominant functions of rhetorical training: as science it belongs to the *methodice*, the *recte loquendi scientia* or *ratio loquendi*; and as an artistic act of speaking and writing it belongs to the collection of masterpieces known as the *poetarum narratio* or *enarratio auctorum*.[33] Both of these key aspects, the

29. "The mental objects . . . take form in the pattern of speech and appear . . . by being expressed in speech" ("Die geistigen Gegenstände . . . gestalten sich in dem Schema der Sprache, und erscheinen, indem sie . . . sich aussprechen"). Niethammer, *Streit*, p. 172. He casts this solution explicitly into the age-old dichotomies spirit-letter, spirit-flesh (p. 179).
30. Ibid., p. 174.
31. Ibid.
32. Lausberg, *Handbuch*, par. 45.
33. Ibid., pars. 23–30.

methodological and historical position of texts in the training of the young Roman or Greek orator, find their reformulation in Niethammer's theory and praxis of "ideational, intellectual, mental objects." It is no wonder, then, that his methods for the "exercise of the intuition and judgment of ideational objects" are taken directly from the school-rhetorical tradition we traced in the history of both the Stuttgart and Nuremberg *gymnasien*:

> "The initial training of intuition" (*Übung der Anschauung*) means: the pupil should first learn something before he begins reasoning. He should first learn the most necessary, i.e., the ideational objects. *Training of the intuition of ideational objects* in early instruction is nothing else than *memory training* (*Gedächtnisübung*). . . . This training demands, however, that the pupil learn above all to *fix the ideational objects*, i.e., to bring them to a halt (*fixiren, zum Stehen bringen*). For this, it is necessary that they become objective for him. But they can only become objective by their presentation in speeches (*Darstellungen durch die Rede*) and sayings (*Aussprüchen*) in which they receive an objective form from honored and inspired men. . . .
>
> . . . in the *memorizing of such sayings*, therefore, the task of beginning instruction is solved. The more the pupil is held to his kind of learning, the richer is the material he collects for the second main period of instruction, the *training of judgment*; but it is during his occupation with the memorizing of such objects that his spirit gains the most multi-faceted training and education/formation (*die mannichfaltigste Übung und Ausbildung*).[34]

34. Niethammer, *Streit*, p. 306. Earlier Niethammer argued against empirical and metaphysical psychology (pp. 282–90). His "middle way" here consists not of learning through mere content, or of the imposition of form, but of "order[ing] through acquaintance (*Umgang*) with the material in the form of comprehension (*Auffassen*), connecting, etc." What he has in mind here are the figures of thought that are used in *inventio*, *dispositio*, and later *exercitatio* (like *chria*) to give order to material.
In "The General Normative for the Establishment of Public Institutions of Learning" ("Das allgemeine Normativ der Einrichtung der öffentlichen Unterrichtsanstalten"), Niethammer puts this rhetorico-hermeneutical approach to pedagogy into practice. He writes, for example, of his program of instruction for the upper classes of *gymnasium*: "In the aim of the *gymnasium* a.) that classical study should not restrict itself merely to reading and interpretation of the [classical] authors, but indeed should encompass 1. the memorization and recitation of selected passages, 2. imitation of these, 3. translation into the language of the original, 4. one's own compositions, 5. practice of spontaneous oral recitation in speaking, debate, etc." ("In Absicht des Gymnasiums a) daß sich das claßische Studium nicht blos auf Lesen und Erklären der Schriftsteller beschränken solle, sondern vielmehr 1. Memoriren und Recitiren auserwählter Stücke, 2. Nachahmen derselben, 3. Übersetzen in die Sprachen derselben, 4. eigne Compositionen, 5. Üben des freien mündlichen Vortrags im Sprechen, disputiren etc. umfaße"; p. 60).

The concrete problems that confronted both Hegel and Niethammer in their attempt to realize this pedagogical ideal in the *Bildungsprogram* in Nuremberg are documented in the letters they exchanged between 1806 and 1815. This exchange makes up the major section of Hegel's correspondence during these years and testifies to both the friendship and common concerns of the two men. A brief look at their correspondence will show how the constellation in Bavaria around questions of *Bildung* paralleled the situation in the young Hegel's Stuttgart some thirty to forty years earlier, namely, the tension between Protestant humanism and Catholic pragmatism. In Stuttgart, the competition between the "academy" of the Catholic Duke Karl Eugen and the Protestant Gymnasium Illustre had led to the independence and conservative resistance of the latter in the eighteenth century. In the Bavaria of the early nineteenth century, the Protestants could not just withdraw back into their humanist ideals, since they were dependent on the Catholic authorities. Niethammer was only one of four members of the school board in Munich and had to constantly fight off the attempts of his rivals Wismayr, Weiller, and Fraunberg to abolish, or at least make impracticable, his attempts to reform the curriculum as outlined in his 1804 "General Normative for the Establishment of Public Institutions of Learning" ("Das allgemeine Normativ der Einrichtung der öffentlichen Unterrichtsanstalten").[35] The state in which Hegel and his school were kept is reflected in the numerous complaints Hegel writes to Niethammer in Munich concerning the lack of funds for salaries, upkeep of the school, books, and the like.[36] But what was at stake for the two men was a spirit of Protestant and humanist *Bildung*, a spirit that Hegel characterizes in terms of a secularized religion of education. On 3 November 1810, for example, Hegel responds to the report that the Nuremberg *gymnasium* is to be cut back since the need for civil servants had been reduced. Hegel unfolds the ideal of the "classically educated man":

> You yourself know best how highly Protestants estimate their institutions of learning (*Bildungsanstalten*); that these [institutions] are as pre-

---

35. On the situation in Bavaria, see Johannes Hoffmeister, *Briefe von und an Hegel* (Hamburg: Felix Meiner, 1961), no. 88, n. 2. For a general account of the stuggles in the Bavarian school systems at the beginning of the nineteenth century, see Georg Bögl, *Der Wandel der Volksbildungsidee in den Volksschullehrplänen Bayerns* (Munich 1929), pp. 28–29, 37–63, 91–154, Alfons Bock, *Lehrplan für die Volksschulen in Baiern 1804–11* (Munich 1917), Joseph Neukum, *Schule und Politik. Politische Geschichte der bayerischen Volksschule 1818–1848* (Munich 1969), Max Rieder, *Geschichte der politischen Bildung in der Volksschule Bayerns* (Munich 1968). I am grateful to Steven Welch of Columbia University for his research on the Bavarian school system.

36. See Hoffmeister, *Briefe* no. 145, on the condition of the school.

cious to them as the churches, and are certainly worth as much; Protestantism consists not so much in a particular confession as in the spirit of meditation and higher, more rational *Bildung*, not [in the spirit] of training toward the purpose of this or that necessity.—One could not have attacked them [the Protestants] at a more sensitive spot than at their institutions of learning. . . . One needs (or seems to need) fewer civil servants than in former times, but one never has enough classically educated men (*klassisch gebildete Menschen*).[37]

What brings Hegel and Niethammer together is their struggle against the realism and pragmatism of the Catholic authorities. To read their attacks against Wismayr, Weiller, and Fraunberg, one would think that these three were attempting to abolish schools altogether, whereas in reality many of their ideas—emphasis on the mother tongue, natural sciences, and graduated course difficulty—have now become standard pedagogical practice. Hegel and Niethammer are clearly defending a principle that points back beyond idealist philosophy to the ideal of the "classically educated" and eloquent Latin humanist.

It is clear from his letters that Hegel supported his friend's pedagogical programs. Hegel's response in 1807 to Niethammer's forthcoming *Streit* reveals a common belief in the *gymnasium* as the model for *Bildung*. That is, the pedagogical principles are not derived unilaterally from the philosophical concepts since an understanding of the concrete, historical function of the *gymnasium* within German education underlies the more abstract idea of *Bildung*. Hegel writes: "I await your plan for the *gymnasien* with great anticipation; the very fact that you begin with the *gymnasien*, this central point of higher, academic education (*diesem Zentralpunkte der gelehrten Bildung*) is interesting."[38] In response to the treatise, Hegel expresses his agreement with the way Niethammer formulates the opposition between these two major pedagogical camps: "Even more fortunate seems to me the characteriza-

37. Ibid., no. 169. In a similar vein, Hegel writes to Niethammer on 12 July 1816 in response to reports that the Catholic school authorities have finally undermined the Normative. The letter makes clear that whereas Hegel's ideals for *Bildung* rest on philosophical principles, those principles in turn rest on a "religion" of humanism which dates back to the sixteenth century: "The major criticism [against the *gymnasium*] is always that one spends so much time on Latin. Here lies the difference between the Catholic and the Protestant. We have no laymen; Protestantism does not rely on the hierarchical organization of a church but rests solely on universal insight and *Bildung*. . . . Our universities and schools are our church" ("Der Hauptvorwurf [gegen das Gymnasium] ist immer, daß man so viele Zeit aufs Lateinische wende. Hier liegt der Unterschied des Katholischen und Protestantischen. Wir haben keine Laien; der Protestantismus ist nicht der hierarchischen Organisation einer Kirche anvertraut, sondern liegt allein in der allgemeinen Einsicht und Bildung. . . . Unsere Universitäten und Schulen sind unsere Kirche"; *Briefe*, no. 272).
38. Ibid., no. 102.

tion of the older and modern pedagogy as humanism and philanthropism." Given the fact that as a young boy Hegel worked through long
rhetorical exercises in the humanist spirit, in which he excerpted passages from these two camps, it is understandable why he likes Niethammer's terms and the side he chooses. In fact, at one point in 1816 Hegel
even has a dream—to my knowledge the only one he recorded—in
which a debate takes place between a humanist and a philanthropist.[39]

Hegel can support Niethammer's conception of humanism since its
method and *Sache*, its conception of a textually transmitted ideational
object, return to an approach with which he is eminently familiar.
When discussing training in philosophy, Hegel reformulates Niethammer's own thoughts, or, more precisely, he reformulates an approach
to grammar and rhetoric, into terms from the humanist rhetorico-
pedagogical tradition that is common to both men: "Similarly, . . . no
formal exercise can take place without matter and content. One cannot
think without thoughts or conceive without concepts. One learns to
think by receiving thoughts in one's head. Thoughts and concepts must
be *learned*, just as much as one learns that there is a singular and plural,
three persons, this and that parts of speeches—or as much as one
learns the credo and catechism" (*Gedanken und Begriffe müssen so gut
gelernt werden, als es einen singularis und pluralis, 3 Personen, diese und diese
Redeteile gibt,—oder so gut als das Credo und der Katechismus*).[40] Hegel, the
gymnasium director, writing to the neohumanist Niethammer about the
teaching of philosophy, sounds remarkably like the *professor eloquentiae*
Balthasar Haug in Stuttgart speaking to an audience of rhetorically
trained pupils. Hence it comes as no surprise when Hegel writes again
to Niethammer: "*Ciceronian* philosophizing would probably be the ideal
for philosophizing at the *gymnasium*" ("Das *Ciceronianische* Philosophieren wäre wohl das Ideal gymnasiastischen Philosophierens").[41] He
then adds with regret that that would also be against his nature (*wider
meine Natur*)—after all, he was never much of a public speaker himself.
But the basic method involved in the rhetorical pedagogy of a Cicero,
Quintilian, Melanchthon, or Haug—memorizing *praecepta* and applying them to internalized *exempla*, both of which become the *Sache*—has
become a basic aspect of his teaching and philosophy thanks to his own
Bildung.

The most important letter from Hegel to Niethammer dates from 23
October 1812. Here we see clearly that their correspondence deals with

39. Ibid., no. 227.
40. Ibid., no. 200.
41. Ibid., no. 216.

concrete considerations for teaching in Nuremberg. The letter, a public statement on the instruction of philosophical propedeutics in *gymnasien*, was written in response to Niethammer's official request. It is generally referred to by the title "On the Teaching of Philosophy in the *Gymnasium*. Private Report for Immanuel Niethammer" ("Über den Vortrag der Philosophie auf Gymnasien. Privatgutachten für Immanuel Niethammer").[42] As is typical of his writings, Hegel starts with an introduction that was written after completion of the text. It seems to place the entire essay that follows into question and demands a reading of it under a peculiar sign. He writes: "perhaps all philosophical instruction in *gymnasien* could appear superfluous, and . . . the study of the ancients (*Studium der Alten*) would be not only the most appropriate (*das angemessenste*) for the youth in the *gymnasium*, but also, *given its essential substance* (*seiner Substanz nach*), a truer introduction into philosophy" (p. 417). He immediately points out the paradox behind this statement, since he is not only a philosopher but was also called to the directorship of the *gymnasium* in order to execute the order in the *General Normative* which called for philosophy to be introduced at the school level. But more significant, we can see in this statement the paradox that runs through Hegel's entire work concerning *Bildung* to and of philosophy: Philosophy is to exist in and of itself, and yet it requires a *Bildung*—both its own and that of the persons who practice it—whereby that *Bildung* is not already, in and of itself, philosophy. On the contrary, that *Bildung*, as he says in the first speech, must involve "that which is alien to the spirit" (*das [dem] Geiste Fremde*). In fact, he concludes the short introduction to the letter by implying that the only real contribution he sees which philosophy could make in the *gymnasium* would be to enliven the dry methods of philology which still dominate the pedagogical scene (p. 417). Hence, we see a repetition in different terms (philosophy versus pedagogy) of the conflict of rhetoric against itself which cast its shadow over the entire eighteenth century. That is, the kind of philosophy that Hegel thinks can be taught at the *gymnasium* as propedeutic bears within itself traces of rational rhetorical pedagogy. Only from this point of view can we understand why Hegel would otherwise be willing to replace philosophy with the study of the ancients.

Hegel begins the philosophical curriculum outlined in the letter with a class on "Religion and Teachings on Rights and Duties" ("Religion, Rechts- und Pflichtlehre"). He points out that at one time he tried to begin with logic, but has returned to and stayed with a start in ethics.

42. In the *Theorie-Werkausgabe*, vol. 4, pp. 403–17.

His justification seems paradoxical until one introduces a wider context for his approach:

> The logical categories (*Bestimmungen*) of the universal and particular, etc., are, for the mind (*dem Geiste*) that is not yet at home in thought, mere shadows when compared to the effectively real (*das Wirkliche*), to which it takes recourse before it is trained in holding fast and observing the former independently from the latter. . . . But in the concepts of freedom, the *existing* and *unmediated* are present, which, at the same time, are also already *thought* without prior anatomy, analysis, abstraction, etc.—Thus, these teachings do in fact begin with that which is sought: the true, the ideational [spiritual, mental, *dem Geistigen*], the effectively real. [P. 405]

It seems paradoxical that the ethical is considered both "reality" (*Wirklichkeit*)—as opposed to abstract logical categories—and also "already thought" (*schon Gedanke*). But this is, first, a way of looking at acts of will (in which the act is the thought and the thought is the act) and, second, a crucial doctrine of Hegel's philosophy (the reality of the rational). In this context, however, the statement has yet a different background, one that predates and preforms Hegel's philosophical concepts, namely, the notion of *ethos* which underlay the public nature of an orator's task and education.[43] Hegel's decision to begin teaching with these subjects recalls the dominance of Cicero in the traditional curriculum, the fusion in him of public orator, philosopher, and moralist. This is, for example, the function Hegel assigns to Cicero in the history of philosophy, where Cicero's philosophical stoicism is criticized even as his contribution, as rhetorician, to the *Bildung* to philosophy is highlighted.[44] Moreover, if we think of Cicero or a figure like him when we read Hegel's letter, then a number of things come together, among them Hegel's emphasis on the "the study of the ancients," ethics, and the union of Spirit (*Geist*) and object (*Gegenstand*)—since the works of the ancients, viewed from the modern perspective, are *geistige Gegenstände*. It is on this foundation, an implicit principle uniting *res* and *verba*, that he can build a study of logic, in which the categories

43. See Klaus Dockhorn's ground-breaking studies on the influence of rhetoric, especially the doctrine of ethos, in late eighteenth-century German and English culture, *Macht und Wirkung der Rhetorik* (Bad Homburg: Gehlen, 1968), esp. "Die Rhetorik als Quelle des vorromantischen Irrationalismus in der Literatur- und Geistesgeschichte," pp. 46–95.

44. *Geschichte der Philosophie*, in *Theorie-Werkausgabe*, vol. 19 (Frankfurt am Main: Suhrkamp, 1978), p. 16.

have objective status, and a study of Spirit, in which self-representation is central.[45]

Concerning Hegel's discussion of methodology, we can start from his conclusion of the 1812 letter to Niethammer on the three stages of philosophy and then see how they rest on three features of rhetorical training. He writes:

> The philosophical content, according to its *nature (Seele)* and *method*, has three forms: it is 1. *abstract,* 2. *dialectical,* 3. *speculative. Abstract,* insofar as it is in the element of thought at all; but insofar as it is the so-called *reasonable understanding (das sogenannte Verständige)*, which knows and holds fast onto categories *(Bestimmtheiten)* in their differences, it is merely *abstract* vis-à-vis the dialectical and speculative. The *dialectical* is the movement and confusion of those firmly determined particular categories, or *negative* reason. The *speculative* is the positively rational *(das positive Vernünftige)*, the *mental* [ideational, spiritual, *das Geistige*], that which can be properly called the philosophical. [Pp. 412–13]

As in Johannes Sturm's definition of the humanist program, the first two are the main points emphasized in the *gymnasium* and the third is the product; that is, the pupil is prepared for philosophizing at the university. Significantly, these three stages correspond to concrete pedagogical movements. The first is worded in direct terms: "philosophy contains the highest *rational thoughts about the essential objects,* contains their *universality* and *truth*; it is of great importance that the students become familiar with this content and *have these thoughts placed into their heads*" (diese *Gedanken in den Kopf zu bekommen*; p. 410). That is, philosophy must be taught and learned, which means that preexisting ideas have to be presented to the pupils as fixed categories. This notion recalls the standard approach to rhetorical pedagogy of memorization of precepts and their application to *exempla.* The second refers to the fact that a particular view develops only out of a critical internalization of others: "Once the head is full of thoughts, then only does the student possess the possibility of himself advancing scientific knowledge and attaining a truly unique and particular position *(eine wahrhafte Eigentümlichkeit)* within it" (p. 412). This can be started in the *gymnasium* but will take longer since it requires years of hermeneutical practice

45. It is interesting that just below this quotation Hegel (p. 403) refers to Joachim Heinrich Campe's *Kleine Seelenlehre für Kinder* (Small Psychology, or Teachings on the Soul, for Children; 1780) which had accompanied him throughout his youthful exercises in writing (see chaps. 1 and 2, above). The pejorative tone is not as relevant here as is the close association to textbooks from Hegel's own education.

and the public forum for argumentation. The goal, as the third stage, is that internalized doubleness—"the knowledge of the opposed in its unity" (*die Erkenntnis des Entgegengesetzten in seiner Einheit*; p. 415)—which makes up the *Bild* or appearance of philosophy. Hence, these three crucial stages and concepts (the movement from abstract, through dialectical, to speculative thought) correspond to stages in the individual's *Bildung* (internalization, argumentative reworking, representation) which Hegel himself went through and which he identifies with the proper curriculum in Nuremberg.

The courses that Hegel taught according to the program outlined in the letter from 23 October 1812 fall under the general heading *philosophische Propädeutik*. The form of these texts for school instruction is of particular significance since it becomes the model for all Hegel's future works. Although the *Phenomenology* has a basically narrative structure in which the chapters and subsections provide thematic elaborations, tropological variations, or argumentative turns, the *Propedeutic* begins a trend in Hegel's philosophical rhetoric toward a more schematically structured handbook. The basic form of the three courses "Teachings on Right, Duties, and Religion" ("Rechts-, Pflichten-, und Religionslehre"), "Philosophy of Spirit or Science of Consciousness and Logic" ("Philosophie des Geistes oder Wissenschaft des Bewußtseins und Logik"), "Doctrine of the Concept and Encyclopedia" ("Begriffslehre und Enzyklopädie") is so similar that one could begin to understand how the charge of formalism, which Hegel made against nature philosophy in the *Phenomenology*, could then be raised against his own late works. Each begins with an introduction, which becomes increasingly brief as the courses progress, undoubtedly because of the familiarity that the students gradually gained with their teacher and his methodological concepts. In almost every case the course is divided into three parts: right, duty, religion; consciousness, self-consciousness, reason (with consciousness divided in turn into sense-consciousness, perception, understanding); Being, essence, concept; doctrine of the concept, realization of the concept, doctrine of ideas; logic, science of nature, science of spirit. Where bipartite divisions occur, they result most likely from the fact that the courses stretched over two years of instruction.

This schematization extends down to the smallest subdivisions of the courses. The handbooks are broken down into many numbered paragraphs, anywhere from ten to eighty per larger chapter or unit. The paragraphs tend to consist of definitions of one or more concept. One or two passages, selected at random, indicate the straightforward, though dry and abstract manner of presenting definitions. From the teachings on duties, for example, there is a definition of improper dealings with fellow citizens; the *definiendum* is highlighted by Hegel (not unlike the presentations of definitions in the books he used and excerpted from as a schoolboy): *"Defamation of character is related to slander, which is a real lie.* Defamation is the telling of such things that are injurious to the honor of a third party and that are not known in and of themselves to the teller" (pp. 268–69). The definition of logical conclusions is given in a form that makes clear Hegel's statement in a letter to Niethammer that his philosophical propedeutic will combine the older presentations in handbooks of school logic with a more sophisticated depiction:[46] "The [syllogistic] conclusion is the complete representation of the concept. It contains *the judgment with its ground.* Two determined categories are joined together in it by a third, which is their unity. A concept is present in its unity, in the middle proposition of the conclusion, and in its disjunction, the extremes" (p. 149). In many cases, especially in the course on ethics, Hegel includes more expository "explanations" (*Erläuterungen*), a practice that continues throughout his later published university lectures. The structure of these courses repeats a basic pattern that informed pedagogical style from antiquity onward: the presentation of definitions and precepts for memorization by the students so that they can later apply the acquired information to examples taken from every sphere of life.

After transforming key principles of the rhetorical tradition into the quasi-historical narrative of the theological manuscripts and the *Phenomenology*, each of which tells the very story of their own formal development and Hegel's formative education, Hegel now returns to the fundamental structures of the rhetorical pedagogical tradition and employs them directly. The return is understandable in this case since he is in fact engaged in school instruction, and so, although his methods are certainly a distillation of ideas out of the *Phenomenology*, those ideas had their origins in the older pedagogical methods that are being reapplied. Just as in the *Phenomenology* Hegel argues for the "detailed fullness and necessity" of his presentation, so here too he at least implicitly raises a claim to the systematic nature of the courses since the definitions are not merely juxtaposed but allowed to develop out of each other formalistically. This claim, however, does not affect the reliance of the system on an earlier methodology. In fact, to the extent that the claim itself does not take its foundations into account, the recognition

---

46. Hoffmeister, *Briefe*, no. 122. The number of these kinds of definitions could be increased at will. The rigidity of structure is perhaps the most striking feature of Hegel's courses at the *gymnasium*.

that rhetorical *Bildung* structures the pre-science of philosophy places limits on the claim to total systematization.

The principle of formal development and formative education not only structures but also occupies a crucial position within the system Hegel was developing during these years. The concepts of *Bild* and *Bildung* do not take up much room in the system of the philosophical propedeutic, but their significance lies in their ability to bring his earlier views and experiences into focus and to thematize the development of his own ideas. By examining Hegel's analysis of these concepts we see how the development of modes of representation in language lies at the heart of his philosophical enterprise. Hegel taught his students the same message explicitly, philosophically, that they were picking up from their experience of the age-old method of instruction: The formation of the faculties of expression leads the individual out of himself toward a knowledge mediated through foreign forms of representation.

The paragraphs on *Bildung* in the "Teachings on Duties," for example, are located in the section entitled "Duties toward the Self" ("Pflichten gegen sich"). The discussion opens with a definition of human beings which, in general terms, makes the duty of self-*Bildung* the very condition of humanity: "Man, as individual, relates to himself. He has the double side (*die doppelte Seite*) of his *particularity* and his *universal* nature. His duty toward himself exists partially in his *physical maintenance*, and partially in raising his particular nature to the universal, i.e., self-formation [education, *sich zu bilden*]" (par. 41, p. 258). *Bildung* makes man man, makes him what he should be. At the heart of this definition lies the inherent doubleness of the human spirit, a doubleness that, as we saw, was fundamental to the rhetoric of the *Phenomenology*. The goal of *Bildung* is to unite these two sides, the particular and the universal, the self and its alienated self-representation. As Hegel writes: "Man must bring his double-sidedness (*gedoppelte Seite*) into harmony." *Bildung* is inherently dialectical. Or, to reverse the priorities, out of Hegel's experience of what it means to become *gebildet* he develops a philosophy of dialectical process. Indeed, if *Bildung* here, which links the individual to the universal by means of the self's drive toward self-expression, is based on the model of an individual's development and formative education, then we can better understand how the *Phenomenology* was able to present the *Bildung* of the World Spirit as "science." *Wissenschaft* possesses a self-reflexive structure since its universality derives from its claim to depict the Spirit's *Bildung*, which in turn is the process of the individual's development toward universalization and self-representing knowledge.

Furthermore, the concept of *Bildung* in the *Propedeutic* both introduces traditional philosophical structures into Hegel's philosophy and interrelates those structures among one another. In particular, Hegel refers to two kinds of *Bildung* which rely on the standard division of philosophical systems into the theoretical and the practical. The former refers to the development of a sense for the independence of objects under observation: "The sense (*Sinn*) for objects in their free independence, without a subjective interest" (par. 42, p. 259). It thus entails more than mere knowledge and information since it concentrates on the intersubjective medium that relates objects to subjects so that an individual subject, in comparing such relations, can gain distance from his or her own self. Through theoretical *Bildung* the individual comes to possess "universally interesting objects" (*allgemein interessanter Gegenstände*) which recall the *geistigen Gegenstände* that Niethammer sees as the products of tradition. Hence, theoretical *Bildung* requires a faculty of judgment ("An inherent part of *Bildung* is judgment about relationships and objects in reality") whereby, as we have seen in the rhetorical tradition, the connection is not just among objects as it is between them and their modes of effective presentation (*Wirklichkeit*).[47] When Hegel then teaches his pupils that "an educated person (*ein gebildeter Mensch*) knows at the same time the limits of his faculty of judgment," he unites under the goal of *Bildung*, as he had done in the Jena essays, the Kantian notion of *Kritik* with the more traditional view that arises from the "study of sciences, and especially the arts, . . . for their own sake."

The relationship between theoretical and practical *Bildung* is on the surface straightforward. The ethical side of *Bildung* also entails self-control, in this case so that the individual can fulfill the needs of his or her natural drives without becoming subordinated to their force, that is, without having individual will annihilated: "It is a part of practical *Bildung* that a person demonstrate that thoughtfulness and restraint in satisfying his natural needs and drives which lie within the borders of their necessity, namely self-preservation" (par. 43, p. 260). Through the appropriate self-control, the individual's physical needs do not disappear completely but, rather, become unnoticeable since the body works like a smoothly running machine.

Hegel's concept of an occupation (*Beruf*) is explained at first by a similar line of reasoning: Whereas one's occupation could seem imposed on one's will (as is one's body and physical drives), one must learn to impose *self*-restraint in pursuing one's occupation, thereby

---

47. Recall that "judgment" (*critica, iudicium*) is a central category of rational rhetoric since it makes possible the fitting appropriation of *res* to *verba*.

removing external coercion and freely integrating oneself into a larger social totality. In Hegel's words, such practical *Bildung* allows man literally to "be someone": "The occupation is on the one hand a particular limited sphere, but it does, on the other, constitute a necessary part of the totality and is also *in itself a totality*. If a person *is to become something, he must know how to limit himself*" (par. 45, p. 263). However, individuals must also *actively* select and practice an occupation; they must view it as equivalent to their "fate," from which they "free" themselves only by seizing it aggressively; they must exercise a certain degree of control over their own destiny: "It [fate and also occupation] is to be seized, borne, and carried out freely" (par. 44, p. 262). One must behave in such a manner toward external circumstance and fate "that [one] makes fate his own, that he takes away from fate the form of external existence." One's job, according to Hegel, is like "a kind of matter (*Stoff*) or material that one must work through in all aspects so that it no longer has anything foreign, recalcitrant, opposing." An apparent contradiction has entered into Hegel's discussion of *Bildung*: It seems as if practical *Bildung* has now completely reversed the ideal of its theoretical counterpart. Where the former calls for the "independence of the object," the latter calls for the individual subject's seizure of it; where the latter calls for self-restraint in relation to the object, the latter calls for self-control to dominate it.

The link between the two forms of *Bildung* cannot lie in the human attitude toward drives and self-preservation, that is, strictly *within* the subject, or in the relationship between humans and the dead material of an objective world. Rather, the theoretical and practical aspects of human development and formation can be brought together only if they are understood as referring to the process of developing and maintaining some form of individuality in a *culturally preformed world*. *Bildung*, both theoretical and practical, is thus understood as modeled on the entrance of the human being into the linguistic world of *geistige Gegenstände* that are both independent and a human product. The distance called for in theoretical *Bildung* and the control called for in practical *Bildung* are not mutually exclusive since they repeat the steps in a process of dependence on and gradual independence from forms of tradition. From this perspective we see how *Bildung* is the precondition for public human interaction: "Through intellectual and moral *Bildung*, man receives the capability to fulfill duties toward others" (par. 46, p. 263). Through *Bildung* one becomes a public, political being by confronting, internalizing, and representing one's surrounding, pregiven cultural reality (destiny).

This interpretation of *Bildung* as an individual's development through and to the universal forms of representation, the traditional realm of the *institutio oratoria,* can be supported by Hegel's discussions of the related concepts of *Bild* and *Einbildungskraft* (imagination). In the notes clarifying the introduction to the course on ethics ("Rechts-, Pflichten-, und Religionslehre") he speaks of the link between the theoretical and practical, this time in terms of consciousness. The theoretical consciousness allows itself to be determined by the objects, which become its rules and precepts, whereas the practical consciousness learns to determine objects according to its image or will. In both cases, the faculty that is doing the linking is the imagination. Imagination has the ability to substitute and connect one image with another: "that it calls up for us, when we are viewing an object, the image (*Bild*) of another object that is or was connected in some way to the first one" (par. 5, p. 213). It is, we can say based on the discussions of *elocutio* in the rhetorical handbooks, *the* rhetorical faculty since its task is that of figuration. Hegel's introduction tries to separate out this mode of representation from the "thought" (*Gedanke*), which focuses solely on the "matter" (*Sache*). However, the *Einbildungskraft* cannot be so easily contained since its greatest product is language itself: "The most extensive work of the imagination is *language*" (par. 5, p. 213). At the core of thought is language and at the core of language is a rhetorical process of image making and substitution.

In the *Wissenschaft des Geistes* for the final year of the *gymnasium* (also called the *philosophische Enzyklopädie für die Oberklasse*) Hegel seems to offer the possible union of the process of *Bildung* with the faculty of *Einbildungskraft* and its product, language or interconnected *Bilder*. Here we see how the images develop and take form (*Bilder sich bilden*). The process begins with the very development of subjectivity by means of the internalization of an image: "Intuition [visualization, *Anschauung*], however, is an object at the same time *for the subject.* The latter, being in and for itself, withdraws from its state of being outside itself, reflects upon itself, and divorces itself from objectivity by making intuition (*Anschauung*) subjective in an *image*" (para. 139, p. 45). By comparing this image not just with an external object but, more important, with other internalized images, the notion of an internalized ego develops.[48] The fundamental concept of reflection rests on, indeed is a product of, a prior act of self-representation and representation of the Other as image. The faculty that can manipulate these images is the "imagination" (*Einbildungskraft*). It works according to rhetorical prin-

---

48. See Hegel's fascination with the reflexive form *ich erinnere mich* in par. 144. Memory is a process of internalizing the self by comparing inner representations.

ciples of figuration, which Hegel calls "very figuratively laws of ideational association" (*sehr uneigentlich Gesetze der Ideenassoziation*), which we
saw as the core of *elocutio*. Hegel summarizes them in abstract
terminology:

> The determination of the connection can be a more or less superficial
> or fundamental context: mere *simultaneity or spatial congruence* of two
> ideas [representations]; or some *similarity*, also their *contrast*; a relation-
> ship of *part* to *whole*, *cause* and *effect*, *reason* and *consequence*, etc., indeed
> any kind of sensual or ideational relation whatsoever.

> Die Bestimmung der Verknüpfung kann ein mehr oder weniger
> oberflächlicher oder gründlicher Zusammenhang sein: blosse
> *Gleichzeitigkeit oder gleicher Ort* zweier Vorstellungen; oder irgend eine
> *Ähnlichkeit*, auch *Kontrast* derselben; Verhältnis als *Ganzes* und *Teile*,
> *Ursach* und *Wirkung*, *Grund* und *Folge* u.s.w., überhaupt jede Art sinn-
> licher oder geistiger Beziehung. [Par. 149, p. 47].

The figurative relationships between the World Spirit's formations,
which we saw in the narrative *Bildung* of the *Phenomenology*, are derived
from a conception of the individual's internal rhetoric of imagistic
association.[49] In general terms, the productive imagination has the
ability to "symbolize," that is, it can substitute one expression for another: "The *symbolization* of imagination consists in the way it ascribes to
sensual phenomena or images representations or thoughts that are of *a
different nature* from what the former express and yet which stand in
some analogous relationship to them such that the images depict their
expression" (par. 154, p. 50). Thus, the *Bildung* of the individual begins
with the formation and substitution of various modes of representation
according to the basic forms of tropological transformation.

For Hegel, however, *Bildung* must go beyond this concreteness of the
Bild and develop universal forms. The faculty that makes this further
transition possible is the "memory" (*Gedächtnis*),[50] which purifies the
image of its concrete and sensual nature: "In the connection made by
the productive memory, the sensual mode of existence has no value in

49. This discussion can be traced back prior to the *Phenomenology* to Hegel's Jena
lectures on *Geist*; see Hegel's *Gesammelte Werke*, "Kritische Ausgabe," vol. 6 (ed. Klaus
Düsing, and Heinz Kimmerle, *Jenaer Systementwürfe*), pp. 273–96 and vol. 8 (ed. Rolf-
Peter Horstmann, and Johann Trede, *Jenaer Systementwürfe 3*), pp. 185–201. The verbal
echoes in the discussions of language, consciousness, and images are remarkable, a sign
that the concern with rhetorical figuration at the heart of Spirit has been with Hegel
from his earliest philosophizing.

50. The difference between *Gedächtnis* and *Erinnerung* has been investigated most
recently by Jacques Derrida in his lectures on Paul de Man, *Mémoires*, (New York: Columbia University Press, 1984).

and for itself, but only the value that the spirit gives to it" (par. 156, p. 51). The apparently inherent relationship between an object and its image becomes replaced by the arbitrary relationship between a meaning and a sign: "The highest achievement (*Werk*) of the productive memory is *language*" (par. 158, p. 52). Whereas earlier we saw language defined as the product of the imagination, here we see a more abstract conception. But neither is language divorced from the process of *Bildung* nor the "spiritualizing" *Bildung* divorced from figuration. *Bildung* takes place as the *Bild* gives way to written or spoken signs: "The concrete mental representation becomes by means of the *word-sign* something *imageless*, which is identified with the sign" ("Die konkrete Vorstellung wird überhaupt durch das *Wortzeichen* zu etwas *Bildlosem* gemacht, das sich mit dem Zeichen identifiziert"; par. 159, p. 52). Echoing the biblical language of the spirit and the letter, Hegel implies that the image is destroyed by the logos in a paradoxical process of literal and spiritual substitution: "The image is killed and the word represents the image. This is a lion; the name *takes the value of the thing itself. Logos; God spoke*, etc." ("Das Bild wird ertötet und das Wort vertritt das Bild. Dies ist ein Löwe; der Name *gilt für die Sache.*—Logos; Gott sprach u.s.f."; par. 159, p. 52). Ironically, and significant for Hegel's semiotics, however, it is precisely the figurative substitution of letter or sign for image that leads to higher stages and life of *Bildung*.[51]

The highest stage of *Bildung* is attained when the individual internalizes the *Bild* in language and imposes the arbitrary and universal rules of association onto the medium of representation: "For the signification of abstract relations and categories (*Bestimmungen*), *symbolization* enters, and so the further development (*Fortbildung*) of language is a part of the force of the universal, the faculty of understanding" (par. 160, p. 53). That is, the individual returns to the rhetorical form of symbolization but now with a systematic understanding of how it functions.[52] *Bildung* links the individual to the universal because it can develop a language that contains an inherently figurative structure, a structure that is created and passed on by a method of externalization, internalization, and critical judgment. Hegel seems to be saying to his pupils at the Melanchthon Gymnasium that the methods they are em-

51. Paul de Man deals with such biblical phrases (especially *fiat lux*) as examples of one form of the sublime in Hegel's *Aesthetics*. See de Man, "Hegel on the Sublime," in *Displacements: Derrida and After*, ed. Mark Krupniak (Bloomington: Indiana University Press, 1986), pp. 146–47.

52. See Kant on *schema* and *Bild* (*Einbildungskraft*), *Kritik der reinen Vernunft*, B 176–87. De Man relates Kant's discussion to a theory of tropes in the "Epistemology of Metaphor," *Critical Inquiry* (Autumn 1978), 13–30.

ploying in the classroom can be generalized to a concept of *Bildung* as the development of the Spirit to a language with a double structure of the individual and the universal. The form of the *Propedeutic*, which can be traced back to a pedagogical method that Hegel learned and taught by, finds its theoretical justification in a theory of *Bildung* that systematizes the process of education to linguistic and discursive forms.

The *Propedeutic* is a significant contribution to the development of Hegel's philosophy since it links his early work to both the *Logic* (1812–15) and the first formulations of the *Philosophical Encyclopedia* (1815–16). Although a detailed analysis of Hegel's *Logic* is not within the scope of the present study—especially since it contains little within its argumentation on the concept of *Bildung*—a brief discussion is necessary to indicate how the form and content of the *Propedeutic*, which were developed out of a concrete pedagogical context and a wider neohumanist tradition, enter into Hegel's abstract dialectical logic as its preformed *Bildung*.[53]

The *Logic* is certainly Hegel's most nonrhetorical work. Indeed, it contains his most antirhetorical, or "antirepresentational," statements concerning philosophical representation since, he claims, the *Logic* can offer "the truth as it is in and of itself, without covering, . . . *the representation of God in his eternal essence prior to the creation of nature and a finite spirit*" ("*die Wahrheit wie sie ohne Hülle, an und für sich ist,* . . . die Darstellung Gottes, wie er in seinem ewigen Wesen vor der Erschaffung der Natur und eines endlichen Geistes"; p. 44, Hegel's emphasis). To appreciate the rhetorical traces covered up by this anti-rhetoric, one must understand the role of a pedagogical *Bildung* of representation which underlies and precedes the *Logic*. The claim to the absolute priority can be questioned by considering the possibility that the form of this "realm of truth" might have its own propedeutic or prehistory. Although a full-scale reading of the rhetorical argumentation of the *Logic* remains to be accomplished, its propedeutic can be examined in the way the concept of *Bildung* is subtly interwoven into the web of prefaces and introductions in advance of the work itself. Hegel dismisses them as being of mere "historical" interest (pp. 50, 65), but the two prefaces and the two-part introduction cannot be considered "merely" prior or outside (*hors d'oeuvre*) since they reveal that Hegel's absolute logic rests on a beginning prior to his dismissal of representation. The further introductory chapter, "At What Point Can the Beginning of Scientific Knowledge Be Made?" ("Womit muß der Anfang der

---

53. All page references in the body of the following discussion refer to *Wissenschaft der Logik*, in *Theorie Werkausgabe*, vol. 5 (Frankfurt am Main: Suhrkamp, 1979).

Wissenschaft gemacht werden?"; pp. 65–79), demonstrates the significance of this issue of the propedeutics of representation.

Thus, although the concept of *Bildung* does not play a role in the argumentation of the *Logic*, it does figure into its motivation and preformation. In this regard, the opening essays of the *Logic* are reminiscent of the Preface and Introduction to the *Phenomenology*, even though the body of the former does not thematize the topics of its introductions as does the latter. It is perhaps this lack of *thematizing* the topics of the introductions in the *Logic* that has led scholars generally to take Hegel at his word and dismiss them as marginal. The introductions gain in significance, however, even in Hegel's own terms, if they are viewed as statements of the necessity of the prior *Bildung* of philosophy's representation.

Hegel opens the Preface to the first edition of the *Logic* (1812) with some ironical polemics recalling his Jena critiques. Kant's critical philosophy, he argues, has led people to criticize the very enterprise of speculative thought. Given Hegel's pedagogical concerns at the time, we can understand why he adds that this misreading of Kant against philosophy corresponds to "the cry of modern pedagogy" (*dem Geschrei der modernen Pädagogik*; pp. 13–4) to focus on experience and practical training (also pp. 46f.). What has developed in Germany, he writes pointedly, is "the bizarre drama, *an educated people without metaphysics*" (*das sonderbare Schauspiel,. . .* ein gebildetes Volk ohne Metaphysik; p. 14, Hegel's emphasis). Hegel's proposed "formation" and "transformation" (*Ausbildung* and *Umbildung*; pp. 15, 16) of a logic/metaphysics is thus offered as a kind of supplement to a lack in education or cultivation. His statement that this period of culture is experiencing "the need or lack of reformulation" (*das Bedürfnis einer Umgestaltung*) of philosophical forms (p. 46) further recalls the Jena essays and the role of *Bildung* as fulfilling a need in representation. He writes: "The demand (*Anforderung*) for a reworking and extensive formulation (*Ausbildung*) of this material is all the more pressing now. There is one period in the development (*Bildung*) of an epoch, as well as in the development or education (*Bildung*) of the individual, when it is primarily a question of the acquisition and statement of principles in their undeveloped intensity. But the higher demand aims at making it into scientific knowledge" (pp. 15–16).

The *Logic*, as a form of *Bildung*, occupies this crucial point of transition between the first sphere of (rhetorical) pedagogy and practice on the one hand, and an antirhetorical, pure conceptuality on the other. As Hegel says in the Introduction, the *Logic* demands both a formal *Bildung*—which means a training in self-representation—and a denial of traditional categories of representation; he expresses this dual and paradoxical goal of the *Logic* in a powerful rhetorical image that then denies imagination:

> The study of this science, the sojourn and labor in this shadow realm, is the absolute cultivation and discipline of consciousness. Therein it pursues its activity far from sensual intuitions and purposes, from feelings, from a merely intended world of representation.
>
> Das Studium dieser Wissenschaft, der Aufenthalt und die Arbeit in diesem Schattenreich ist die absolute Bildung und Zucht des Bewußtseins. Es treibt darin ein von sinnlichen Anschauungen und Zwecken, von Gefühlen, von der bloß gemeinten Vorstellungswelt fernes Geschäft. [P. 55]

The *Logic*, then, like Hegel's neohumanist pedagogy, only in a masked and antirhetorical form, stresses three features of rhetorical *Bildung*: a particular method of developing thought through internalization of prior abstractions, a paradoxical relation to its object or thought (*Sache, res*) and its expression, and a conception of the inherent need for formulation of ideas in language.

Concerning the method of the science of logic, Hegel emphasizes the point made in the *Phenomenology* (in part against formalistic idealisms) that philosophy may not borrow its method from other sciences, for example, mathematics. Instead, philosophy qua science must develop its method out of its proper subject: reflection. That is, the science of logic captures the "self-movement of thoughts" (pp. 17, 49). And yet this representation would not be possible unless the self-movement had some inherent development toward self-representation, for otherwise the self-movement of thought would possibly escape attempts at expression. Though not as explicit as the *Phenomenology*, the *Logic* does indicate such an inherent movement toward representation.

In order to recognize what such a "self-movement of thought" could be without falling into either panlogism or mysticism, one must consider the pedagogical model that Hegel had been developing out of neohumanism. He writes that his logical method consists of the famous three steps that are connected to three faculties: The understanding fixes the categories of thought, negative reason dialectically dissolves them, and a higher speculative reason fuses the particular and universal in a hermeneutical act.[54] These three steps, of course, are the same

---

54. He writes: "*The understanding determines* and holds fast to the determinations; *reason* is negative and *dialectical* because it breaks up the determinations of reason into nothing;

as those outlined above (p. 255) as Hegel's variation of Niethammer's pedagogical program in Bavaria. As in the *Phenomenology*, the method of *Bildung* in the *Logic* does not accept the familiar as the known (*das Bekannte* as *das Erkannte*) but instead resists the familiar by imposing alienation through abstract knowledge from the start (p. 22). This notion of beginning with hardened, foreign categories also recalls Hegel's letter to Niethammer on the teaching of philosophy in the *gymnasium* in which he says that he felt better starting with the logic since the students did not get confused with the plurality of interpretations of the concepts. This pedagogical practice of beginning with abstract definitions and precepts, which in this case are not "filled" with content but which become the very object of reflection, becomes in the *Logic* Hegel's paradoxical theory of beginning with "the simple" (*das Einfache*). Although one might think that Hegel's abstract categories are anything but simple, as he emphasized in his *gymnasium*, the neo-humanist sees "the simple" not as concrete *Realien,* which demand subjective interpretation by students, but as forms already abstracted and thus "simplified." Hence, the simple with which one begins is precepts and definitions that must be dialectically and dialogically dissolved in order to be given fulfilled meaning. This age-old pedagogical method now has a new "logical" legitimation.[55]

Pursuing these arguments on method further, a second way in which the *Logic* is prestructured by the concept of rhetorical *Bildung* that underlay the pedagogical program of the Nuremberg *gymnasium* becomes clear in Hegel's discussion of the relation of this *Wissenschaft* to its represented object or *Sache*. Recalling the arguments above from the *Propedeutic* on "theoretical and practical *Bildung*" (pp. 258–61), one sees that the *Logic* follows explicitly Hegel's paradoxical ideas about what kind of training young people should go through. In the *Propedeutic* he argued for a theoretical *Bildung* in which students deal disinterestedly with the object of their study so that they can then turn to a practical *Bildung* in the social world of occupations. Likewise, in the Introduction to the second edition of the *Logic*, Hegel says: "This logic tends to be located first of all in the studies of young people, who have

---

it is *positive* because it produces the *universal* and comprehends the particular within it" (pp. 16–17). See also Manfred Frank, *Das individuelle Allgemeine* (Frankfurt am Main: Suhrkamp, 1977), for a fuller understanding of the creative hermeneutical and rhetorical act involved (especially for Schleiermacher) in any fusion of the particular and universal.

55. Hegel provides as well a new validation of dialectic which combines abstract logical arguments with the concrete aspect of dialectic as the playing out of positions in dialogue (*Logik,* pp. 51–53).

not yet entered into the interests of concrete life, who live in leisure relative to those interests, and who are concerned with the acquisition of the means and possibility of later dealing with the objects of those interests only theoretically and for their subjective purposes" (p. 23). In contradistinction to Aristotle, Hegel sees *Logic* as one such means of introducing young people to a world of "interests" through a disinterested study (pp. 23–24). That is, if the study of logic is an objectified and disinterested activity, a "place" (*Ort*) of freedom and abstraction (p. 25), Hegel understands this explicitly as a "school" (*Schule*; p. 24). Thus, the *Logic*, though it does not thematize *Bildung*, is itself an enactment of the very process of "educating and disciplining thought" (*Bildung und Zucht des Denkens*; p. 33) which made his philosophical propedeutic a "middle stage" in an educational program.

Finally, if the *Logic* is itself a movement of *Bildung*, and if *Bildung* is the movement toward self-representation, then we would expect to encounter a discussion of the language of the *Logic* in terms of *Bildung*. What Hegel is horrified at in the idea of "an educated (*gebildetes*) people without metaphysics" is a people incapable of expressing itself in a manner appropriate to thought. What Hegel hopes to undertake in the *Logic* is not the gradual development of consciousness *to* such an appropriate self-representation—that had been the task of the *Phenomenology*—but, rather, the actual depiction of the language in which such an advanced consciousness would speak and think. The concern of the Preface to the second edition, written near the end of Hegel's life (November 1831), focuses both on the difficulty of the topic and its representation (*Darstellung*, p. 19). Whereas other sciences undergo a process of progressive *Bildung*, whereby their vocabulary becomes more developed and rarefied (p. 21), the *Logic* must work with ordinary language. As he writes: "The forms of thought (*Denkformen*) have been set forth and fixed first and foremost in human *language*" (p. 20). The *Bildung* that one must go through to and in the *Logic* is made possible only by the recognition of the thought categories represented in language and hence the linguistically mediated nature of thought, since language and thought are inseparable: "Into everything that is made internal or an idea (*Vorstellung*) of man, into everything that he makes properly his own (*zu dem Seinigen*), language has penetrated, and whatever he makes into and expresses (*äußert*) in language contains more or less covered up [clothed, *eingehüllter*], impurely, or worked out a category" (p. 20)

Hegel's *Logic* is an extension of the *Phenomenology* and his earlier work since it relies on the language that has resulted from the progression of his own *Bildung*, a language conceived of as a double entity, a fusion of the individual and universal. Thus, in some of the most significant passages by Hegel on the language of his philosophy, he praises German for its "extended formation" (*Ausbildung*), its linguistic richness, and its myriad possibilities of expression (p. 20). The rhetoric of his logic derives not from a "particular terminology," but from its ability to work with ideas preformed in language (p. 21). As in Niethammer's neohumanist argument, the *Logic* lays claim to the "truth without cover" (*Wahrheit ohne Hülle*) because, ironically, that truth is already the product of rhetorical *Bildung* and of a language that contains it more or less covered up (*eingehüllt*). This *Bildung* has led to a new kind of *Sache*, like an "ideational object" (*geistigen Gegenstand*), which unites us, thoughts, and things in a unique way. According to Hegel, it is not as if thoughts lie between us and things but, rather, the three come together in their inherent movement toward representation (pp. 25–26). The notion of "coming-to-form," the paradigm of which is rhetorical *Bildung*, allows Hegel to conceive of a union between ontology and logic.

Hegel states in his own neohumanist spirit that a representation that captures the movement of the "speculative spirit of language" (*spekulativen Geist der Sprache*)—which is like a *geistiger Gegenstand*—is particularly difficult in modern times, since we lack the strict training and a sense of the power of language that could make an appropriately "supple presentation" (*plastischer Vortrag*) (pp. 30–31), like Plato's, possible. It comes as no surprise, then, that in Hegel's consideration of the question of "education (*Bildung*) and the relationship of the individual to logic" (p. 53), he argues that the best training for his *Logic* would be a thorough, traditional study of language, more specifically grammar in the widest sense of the term, which would include the entire pedagogical program of neohumanism (from precepts and categories to fulfilled meanings). Such a traditional training in language prepares the individual for logic since logic is based on an abstraction of what it means to be so trained in modes of representing thought. The *Logic* is thus not a break from the hermeneutical-rhetorical tradition of *Bildung*, but its culmination as a self-reflexive mode of representation. When Hegel writes to Voß concerning his *Wissenschaft*, saying that it would have the status of Luther's Bible translation insofar as it would make philosophy speak German, he does this in the spirit of humanist rhetoric.[56] According to Hegel, after him there could really be no *gebildetes Volk*

56. Hoffmeister, *Briefe*, no. 55.

without metaphysics since he made his metaphysical language the goal of *Bildung* and *Bildung* the movement toward dialectical rhetoric.

*

Thus, the method of instruction in Nuremberg and Hegel's statements on the *Bildung* of scientific knowledge through the study of language correspond to the theoretical background mapped out by Hegel in his speeches on the state of pedagogy in the Melanchthon Gymnasium. A mastery of traditional linguistic forms by means of a mechanical hermeneutics of exercises and repetition in order to participate in the public forum of ethical and cultural consensus building—these ideas belong to Hegel's basic concept of *Bildung* as he wrote about and practiced it in the years between 1808 and 1815.

Moreover, Hegel knew that philosophy could not be taught (at the *gymnasium*) without an appropriate introduction. The best introduction would be a thorough training in the works and methods of the ancients. Although on the surface (and given his nature) Hegel's own philosophy does not seem to conform to such classical forms, in fact the structure and arguments for a philosophical propedeutic demonstrate that he relied on the doctrines of rhetorical pedagogy. The stages of the *institutio oratoria*, as steps on the way to knowledge through representation, thus became inscribed into the formative development even of dialectical logic. Hegel's claim that the *Logic* represents the truth (*Sache*) relies on a conception of both the true (*Sache*) and language that sees them as fused within the same broader process of *Bildung*.

Sophistry and the Prehistory of Philosophy

Given the powerful equivocation in the concept of *Bildung* which we have seen throughout this study—namely, that for Hegel the education of an individual to philosophy corresponds to the formation of the Spirit and of philosophy itself—one would expect to find that philosophy experienced through its *history* a rhetorically oriented propedeutic that corresponds to the pedagogical program Hegel learned in Stuttgart and applied in Nuremberg. Significantly, Hegel's last major statement on *Bildung* appears in his lectures on the *History of Philosophy* (1816–31).[57] Here we find the fusion of the individual and universal

57. All page numbers in the body of the text of the second section of this chap. ("Sophistry and the Prehistory of Philosophy") refer to the lectures on the *Geschichte der Philosophie, Theorie-Werkausgabe*, vol. 18 (Frankfurt am Main: Suhrkamp, 1978).

character in a process of formative education to rhetorical expression. In particular, Hegel's concept of a philosophy of *Bildung*, that is, of philosophy's own *Bildung*, universalizes his experience of an education that led him from rhetoric to a philosophy of representation. A detailed reading of his opening lectures on pre-Socratic philosophy shows how Hegel applied ideas of classical and neohumanist rhetorical training not just to the propedeutics of the individual but also to the historical preparation needed for the very appearance of true philosophy. In these lectures on philosophy Hegel summarizes in generalized historical form his own rhetorical *Bildung* and his ideas of philosophical pre-science. Inscribed into philosophy's history is a teleological movement toward *Wissenschaft* as self-representation, since philosophy's precondition is constituted by self-conscious rhetorical expression.

Hegel's history of philosophy consists of a series of cycles. In each cycle, thought proceeds through a movement from a vague subjectivism, through an application of subjective categories onto objective reality, to a union of the two in the belief that being is thought. The Sophists make up the middle transition in the first cycle, which passes from Anaxagoras and Heraclitus to Socrates, Plato, and Aristotle. What is of interest to us here is not just the position of the Sophists in the dialectical scheme but the background and characterization of their position. The very terms that Hegel uses to define the Sophist position are crucial since they point to a scheme beyond that contained within the dialectical system. Hegel calls the Sophists, namely, the "teachers" of the Greeks, the introducers of *Bildung* to the ancient world: "The Sophists are the teachers (*Lehrer*) of Greece, through whom formative education (*Bildung*) came into existence in Greece" (pp. 409f.). This characterization clearly gives the Sophists a privileged position, since through their act of *Bildung* the entire process of philosophical history and the development of thought in the Western world could begin. For Hegel, *Bildung* has always had associated with it general activities of the individual spirit, for example, the link between subject and object in the sense of an individual's entrance into an effective reality with practical (that is, ethical) implications. Here, this concept summarizes the first major step of philosophy out of its pre-Socratic subjectivity. It is certainly not mere chance that these teachers of philosophical propedeutics for the Greeks were also teachers of rhetoric: "The Sophists were, in particular, teachers of rhetoric (*Beredsamkeit*). That is the aspect of culture in which the individual could both assert himself before his people and execute what was the best for his people; and for this, rhetoric was one of the major requisites" (p. 412). The reader or listener of these lectures can then draw the conclusion that rhetoric is the best, highest form of *Bildung* since it allows the isolated individual to have an impact beyond the particular individuality on the universality of the social order. Rhetorical *Bildung*, especially as practiced by the Sophists, is the precondition of Western philosophy.[58]

What is this *Bildung* and the form of this formative rhetoric? On the one hand, Hegel seems to leave the notion in the vaguest of terms: "*Bildung* is undetermined (*unbestimmt*)" (p. 410). On the other, this whole discussion seems to aim at a redefinition of Hegel's precise concept of *Bildung* in different terms. He begins by defining *Bildung* in the general, apparently antirhetorical terms of the "power of the concept." The Sophists have the ability to take their particular (subjective) position seriously and to apply it to everything: "It is the Sophists who now applied the simple, unified concept, as thought . . . to worldly objects, and by means of the concept penetrated all human relations. The concept becomes conscious of its own power, conscious of itself as the absolute and sole essence — jealous toward any Other that would place value on a particular, which does not belong to the realm of thought — and exercises its power and domination over any Other" (p. 409). The concept undergoes a process of *Bildung* since it now gains a content that it did not have earlier. Hegel redefines his initially vague notion of *Bildung*: "For we give the name *Bildung* to the concept that is applied to effective reality (*Wirklichkeit*)" (p. 409). The notion of reality here, as we have seen elsewhere—for example, in the Preface to the *Phenomenology*—is not an existence in principle different or opposed to the subject that is undergoing the process of *Bildung* but, rather, the effective application of the subject's will, the subject's own externalization. In fact, at this stage the great advance made for thought is that the subject realizes its ability to transform "reality" by means of thinking and expressing it differently. "That which is hard and fast (*das Feste*) . . . begins to vacillate and lose its hold" (p. 406).[59] The art of the Sophist is to invert and disturb the accepted order of firm truths so that they can be rearranged to suit a different goal. The Sophist introduces the fundamental truth that nothing is as it seems to be in the fixed order of opinion, for everything can be explained differently, indeed becomes something different when expressed from a different perspective. Needless to say, such literally willful treatment of established beliefs

58. Rhetorical *Bildung* is even equated parenthetically with philosophy in a number of passages (pp. 6, 8, 11, 27).

59. Recall the definition of the "speculative sentence" from the Preface to the *Phenomenology* in which effective language according to Hegel has precisely this result on the listener-reader (see above, pp. 11–13).

brings about a harsh reaction on the part of common sense, which wants to hold onto its simple truths. Hegel, however, wants to consider the positive aspects of this rhetorical skill (p. 409), for without this rhetorical *Bildung* there could be no philosophy that rests likewise on the power of the concept and its expression to invert and set in motion fixed categories.

If we look more precisely at the way Hegel defines what it means in sophistic philosophy to be *gebildet*, we see that it consists of the three basic aspects of rhetorical pedagogy: the skill of employing the richness of expressive forms of speech; the immersion in an intersubjective medium of traditional forms; and the invention of dialectical arguments for critical argumentation. By tracing out these arguments in detail we can see how, in the historical depiction from Hegel's mature philosophy, his own pedagogical experience and the resulting theoretical conception of *Bildung* are projected back onto the beginnings of Western philosophy.

Hegel defines the art of the Sophists, that which they desire to teach, in traditional terms by rewording Plato's formulation: "This is what strikes one first about an educated person—the art of speaking well" (p. 413).[60] Education involves rhetoric in the sense of mastering the forms of oral and written expression. Such mastery means the ability to reproduce the *copia rerum et verborum* that one has internalized: "For this, the *Bildung* is necessary that can make manifold points of view present to the spirit, that can make them immediately accessible to it, and that gives it a rich fullness (*Reichtum*) of categories for considering any matter" (p. 413). Put in its crassest and most direct form: "An educated person knows how to say something about every matter" (p. 411). All of these definitions make clear that in Hegel's view of the Sophists, and hence in his view of the very beginnings of philosophical knowledge, *Bildung* takes the form of mastery of *elocutio*. The good speaker and budding philosopher—for here they are the same—must be able to give every idea a mode of representation which attains a desired effect. This involves, as every rhetorician from Aristotle and Quintilian to Haug teaches, learning expressions and traditional forms so that they will be handy for application at the appropriate moment. The goal and effect of sophistic speech, in general, was to move the audience: "They taught how these powerful forces [anger, passion of the audience] could be aroused." (p. 425). Hegel seems to be tracing his

---

60. *Bildung* in pre-Socratic philosophy is thus associated directly with the commonplace definition of rhetoric as *ars bene dicendi*.

own education in eloquence and *elocutio*, with its doctrines of *suavitas* and *perspicuitas*, back to its origins in classical rhetorical theory and practice.

Implicit in the role Hegel assigns to the Sophists is their emphasis of the cultural and social nature of their enterprise. They make clear for the first time in Western thought that people are beings in an intersubjective and historical medium. Although Hegel implies that the Sophists try to undermine two kinds of firm truths—"a firmness (*Festigkeit*) of Being, or a firmness of particularly determined concepts, principles, customs, laws" (p. 406)—he clearly sees their contribution in terms of their treatment of the latter. The *Sache* with which they work is not that of "objective" things but of the public sphere, opinion, shared beliefs. Indeed, the Sophists break down the false distinction between subject and object by stressing that the objects only exist within our internalized images of them; which is not to say that everything is "only" subjective (for that would be "bad idealism"), but, rather, that all reality is effective reality (*Wirklichkeit*), is the result of an interaction between subject and object. The forms they work with are cultural institutions (especially the state) which have taken on the status of fixed and unalterable truths. Hegel attributes to the Sophists a number of objects as *Geistesbildung* in general: "common ethics, presence of mind, sense of order, capability of spirit" (*Sittlichkeit, Geistesgegenwart, Sinn der Ordnung, Anstelligkeit des Geistes*; p. 415), that is, those things that the Spirit produces in its self-representation in the world of society. Hegel continues: "The manner of this *Bildung* was, by imaginative representations (*Vorstellungen*) and examples, to focus attention on what people take to be right according to their experience, feelings, etc." (p. 420). The Sophists show that what people take for granted as experience is, to use the terms from Hegel's theological manuscripts, *das Positive*. That is, the Sophists make people realize that their ideas are the products of successive unconscious imitation and can—should—be overcome by working through the forms of the tradition. Their critical hermeneutic rejects the idea of passive adoption of the past.

The result of the sophistic struggle with accustomed experience is the power of the individual to recognize the power to determine the forms that had been determining him: "the individual is his own final form of satisfaction. By coming to know power I know how to determine others according to my purpose" (p. 426). Seen from this perspective, *Bildung* for Hegel could be dangerous since it grants the individual so much power vis-à-vis the established forms of normal consciousness: "Thus, [because of this confusion in common consciousness] the Sophists have been accused of promoting the passions and private interests, etc. This follows directly from the nature of *Bildung*. It makes accessible the different points of view, and which one is the decisive factor is left up to the whim of the subject, if the latter does not rely on firm principles. Herein lies the danger" (pp. 426f.). But it also cannot be overlooked that the accomplishment of *Bildung* to bring the individual the power over the dominating forms of the past, precisely by having him or her work with and through them, is the necessary condition of philosophical development. As prefigurations of Rameau's nephew, the Sophists show that human self-representation in terms of existing discourse constitutes human reality, and that human individuality results from the self's position within the discursive nexus.

Finally, Hegel points out in the discussion of the Sophists that the rhetorical *Bildung* that initiates the history of philosophy entails, beyond the overcoming of the past forms, also a struggle with the present structures in a public forum. The acts of the Sophists' *Bildung* arise, in fact, out of a need or lack (*Bedürfnis*; pp. 404, 410) in their own time. This need consists in the connection, missing in the earlier pre-Socratics, between general principles and conrete content. The Sophists fulfill this need by developing a conception of judgment that allows them to criticize, analyze, and compare the existing state of things: "Thought seeks universal principles in order to judge anything of value to us; and nothing is of value which is not in accordance with these principles. Thought thus has the task of comparing its positivistic content to itself. It must select that which was previously concrete belief and on the one hand analyze [split up] the content and on the other isolate and reflect on these particulars, specific points of view and aspects" (p. 410). The model for such an act of critical judgment is, for Hegel, the court of law (p. 411). Thus, what he seems to have in mind with this aspect of prephilosophical *Bildung* is the development and cultivation of forensic rhetoric.

Hegel follows Plato (and implicitly Cicero and all other rhetoricians) in locating the realm of critical discourse in the public sphere (p. 417f.) since it is in the judgment of human action—the expressions of the Spirit—that the individual (Sophist) can introduce various perspectives and motivations. This ability to judge a case from as many angles as possible is, for Hegel, both a main component of rhetoric and, significantly, a sign of *Bildung*: "In particular, rhetoric (*Beredsamkeit*) includes the following: the ability to isolate and emphasize the various points of view on a particular issue, and to assert those that are related to whatever seems to me to be useful and purposeful. Such concrete cases have many sides: It takes an educated person (*ein gebildeter Mann*), however, to grasp these differentiated points of view; and it is precisely rhetoric that emphasizes these relevant points of view, while placing the others into the shadows" (p. 412). The particular aspect of the rhetorical system that he is referring to here becomes explicit in the next line, when he mentions the field of "topics" (*topous*), that is, the "dialectical" aspect of *inventio* according to whose principles the speaker can "discover" the possible arguments for a critical dialogue. That this aspect of rhetoric and the *Bildung* of the individual to mastery of the *ars disputandi* contributes to the history of philosophy signifies quite clearly that philosophical dialectics develops out of rhetorical, forensic, or polemical dialogue. Thus, although Hegel sees this feature as well as a potential danger (p. 421) since any point can be made against any other, the ability to engage in critical exchanges is a necessary prestage for the *Bildung* to and of dialectical philosophy.

Although Hegel locates these three features of rhetorical *Bildung*—mastery of form, individual power against the tradition, and polemical dialectics—in the historical moment of the Sophists, he also makes numerous comparisons and parallels that problematize this relationship between past and present. He seems to want to differentiate strictly between the Sophists and modern *Bildung* since the latter is characterized by the spiritual principle of Christianity: "It is different in our European world, however, in which *Bildung* was introduced, so to speak, under the protection and precondition of a spiritual religion" (p. 421). Hegel clearly strives to separate the origins of Greek philosophy in the letter of sophistic rhetoric from the completely spiritual origins of Christian modernity. But we know from the history of pedagogy, as well as from Hegel's letters to Niethammer, that the modern spirit of humanist and neohumanist *Bildung* arose under the sign of the classical rhetorical ideal. Hence there are many places in Hegel's discussion of the Sophists where the distinction between an earlier rhetorical and a modern religious *Bildung*, between the discursive letter and the purely intellectual spirit, breaks down. He associates the sophistic movement, for example, with a modern development, "the so-called Enlightenment of modern times" (p. 410). Indeed, given the discursive principles of the Sophists, which we all must apply constantly in our lives, Hegel can generalize: "Sophistry is not so far removed from us as one might think" (p. 423). In fact, Hegel even goes so far as to imply that to the extent that the principles of sophistic rhetoric-philosophy are not present in modern "learnedness" (*Gelehrsamkeit*), the latter is insufficient (p. 406). Although claiming a radical divorce between the rhetorical *Bildung* of the Sophists and the needs of contemporary education, Hegel nonetheless must introduce critical rhetoric as a propedeutic to philosophical and self-conscious representation.

The ambivalent location of rhetorical *Bildung* in the history of philosophy summarizes the function of rhetorical *Bildung* in the development of Hegel into a writer of philosophy. The section on the Sophists,
like so many other sections of Hegel's philosophy of *Bildung*, appears to
be an extended metaphor, an allegory of his own formative education
and ideas on development to form. The Sophists, as teachers of the
Greeks, employed the same methods and cultivated the same ethical
ideas as did Hegel's own teachers, with their emphatic Ciceronianism in
the Stuttgart Gymnasium Illustre. In both cases the goal was that of the
ars bene dicendi et scribendi. The working through of various perspectives, by which means the Sophists were able to shake the foundations
of past forms and locate the power of thought in the individual, recalls
the long process of *exercitationes*, the long struggle with "positivity"
which Hegel himself had to pass through before he could attain his
own individual voice. In fact, just as the *Phenomenology* recapitulates
that act of rhetorical *Bildung* in the translation of and reflection on the
French society of Diderot's *Rameau's Nephew*, so the Sophists are related
to "French *Bildung*" (p. 413). And finally, the Sophists introduce that
aspect of rhetoric which comes to play the greatest role in Hegel's
struggle with his contemporaries and in the form and content of his
philosophy, namely, a polemical dialogue and the dialectics of polemical discourse. Hegel's years in Jena, including the writing of the *Phenomenology*, were occupied with the dialectic of the particular perspective and the overarching perspective of philosophy itself, that is, with
the *inventio* of a new mode of philosophical argumentation.

In all these cases we see not only the way Hegel applies certain
philosophical ideas to different aspects of intellectual history but also,
more important, that his fundamental ideas of the *Bildung* and *Vor-
bildung* of philosophy derive from his own schooling in and critical
internalization of rhetorical propedeutics. Philosophy can come to represent truth since it has itself been trained in and has internalized all
the rhetorical means that allow an individual to gain knowledge
through self-representation. Ironically, thanks to their rhetorical
Bildung, both the individual and philosophy, regardless of their antirhetorical stance, have no other truth than the effective reality of their
rhetorical self-representation.

Index of Latin
Rhetorical Terms

Index

lectio, 20; in schooling, 76–95; and *selectio*, 98
loci argumentorum, 57n, 80–81, 143, 148, 185n, 229–30, 233, 241, 276

modi tractandi, 98, 108–18, 171, 176

narratio, 116, 124, 162, 241

officia, 3, 42

petitio principii, 149
peroratio, 57, 60, 241
perspicuitas, 8, 13, 44, 74
praecepta, 20, 42, 52; Hegel's pedagogy, 255; method of instruction in Nuremberg, 244; in schooling, 64, 69, 70, 74, 89, 91, 94

prooemium. See *exordium*
res: and alienation, 177n; and debate, 22–23, 27–28; and dialectic in *Phenomenology*, 223–32; doubling in *Phenomenology*, 187, 196; and *elocutio*, 13, 20; in handbooks, 74–81; in Latin diary, 58; versus *verba*, 4, 43–44
res nuda, 80, 181, 216–17
rhetorica contra rhetoricam, 5, 27, 94, 169n, 221

sermocinatio, 117–18

translatio: in Frankfurt manuscripts, 127–35; in *Phenomenology*, 201–12; technique, 98

280

General Index

Adorno, Theodor, 37–38, 178n, 202–3
alienation (*Entfremdung, Entäußerung*), 199–208, 211–15
allegory, 103, 132, 164, 177–78, 277
Announcement (Ankündigung) to the Kritisches Journal, 141–43
Antigone, 193, 199
Aristotle: on critique, 146–47; on dialectic and rhetoric, 178n, 217; on metaphor, 12, 135n, 180–81, 189n
Augustine, *De doctrina christiana*, 104

Barner, Wilfried, 40, 64
Bild (*Gebilde*, image), 13; in essay on Natural Law, 172–73; in *Philosophical Propedeutic*, 258–64; structuring principle in *Phenomenology*, 176–97
Bildung, 45–54
Bildungsroman, 5, 6, 47, 49–50, 184n
Bloch, Ernst, 34–35, 178n
Bloom, Harold, 100n, 137n

Campe, Joachim Heinrich, 86–87, 120, 255n
Cicero: "Ciceronian philosophizing," 252; critique, *inventio, iudicium*, 146–47; dialectic, 217; and ethos, 254; Hegel translated in school, 94–95; on *loci*, 81n; on philosophy and rhetoric, 38

clothing (of ideas by words), 9, 73, 80, 181, 186, 194, 216
concept (*Begriff*), 14–15, 18, 25, 28, 32. *See also Sache* and *res* (in index of Latin rhetorical terms)
consensus: in *Phenomenology*, 21–28, 225
critique, 83, 94, 98, 149n. *See also Kritik*, history of the term, and *iudicium* (in index of Latin rhetorical terms)

Derrida, Jacques, 30, 36, 40–41; on metaphor in philosophy, 182n; temporality and rhetoric, 199n
dialectics, 79–83, 147–48, 215–38, 276
diary (Hegel's *Tagebuch*), 57–61, 88–95
Diderot, *Rameau's Nephew*, 200, 208–12, 277
Differenz des Fichteschen und Schellingschen Systems der Philosophie, 155–64, 233
digestion (as metaphor for reading), 16, 18, 20, 52, 76, 89–90, 101, 121, 134–35, 175, 180, 242
Dilthey, Wilhelm, 102–3, 126, 128n
Dusch, Johann Joachim, 85n

Ernesti, Johann August: handbooks, 75–83; precepts, 181; in Stuttgart curriculum, 67
Essence of Kritik (Das Wesen der Kritik), 148–55

281

Index

Library of Congress Cataloging-in-Publication Data
Smith, John H., 1954–
    The spirit and its letter.

    Includes index.
    1. Hegel, Georg Wilhelm Friedrich, 1770–1831.
I. Title.   II. Title: Rhetoric in Hegel's philosophy of
Bildung.   III. Title: Bildung.
B2948.S6   1988   193   87-47960
ISBN 0-8014-2048-2 (alk. paper)